ON YOUR MARK, GET SET, GROW

DION PARKER

Distributed by English Woods Publishing

For ordering information or special discounts for bulk purchases, please contact:
English Woods Publishing
26246 Wesley Chapel Blvd #153
Wesley Chapel, FL 33559

Cover and interior formatting by KUHN Design Group | kuhndesigngroup.com

Published by English Woods Publishing
www.englishwoodspublishing.com

ISBNs:
Hardcover: 979-8999145406
Paperback: 979-8999145420
E-book: 979-8999145413

Scripture quotations are from the King James Version of the Bible.

Library of Congress Control Number: 2025915970

Printed in the United States of America

TO THE TWO PEOPLE WHO MADE THIS BOOK POSSIBLE—
ONE WHO GAVE ME LIFE, AND ONE WHO HELPED ME REBUILD IT.

To Jennifer Parker, my mommy.
*I was only able to write this book because you never wrote
me off. When the world tried to erase me, your love was
like permanent ink. You stuck with me through the rough
chapters, and your love helped me turn the page. Your love
became the inspiration that turned my scars into sentences
and my pain into paragraphs. You are the reason this
book will help others rewrite their own stories. I love you.*

To Tayoun, my wife.
*You opened your door to me when I was at my lowest. You're
the reason I'm pushing hope into people's brains and not dope
into my veins. You believed in me when all I had were warrants,
withdrawals, and a reputation I couldn't outrun. You didn't
just love me—you launched me. This book exists because you
helped me rebuild when I didn't think I could. I love you.*

CONTENTS

WHY YOU SHOULD READ THIS BOOK

You've read plenty of books that tried to motivate you with polished quotes and watered-down stories. That's not this. What you're holding isn't here to coddle—it's here to confront.

If you're looking for comfort, close it now. But if you're ready to be challenged, checked, and changed, read on. Every story is designed to strip excuses, rip off blindfolds, and remind you that growth don't happen in safe zones—it happens when you face yourself head-on.

And that's the whole point—you don't grow by being rocked to sleep with lies, you grow by being rattled awake with truth. These words ain't entertainment; they're eviction notices to the parts of you that have been squatting in your spirit for too long. If you can stomach the raw, the real, and the ruthless, then you can finally step into the version of yourself that fear and failure tried to bury.

This was written for the bruised, the bitter, and the barely holding on. The ones who smile in public but suffocate in silence. The ones who feel too broken for church and too bruised for therapy. The ones who were told they'd never bounce back. The ones who've been pacified with pretty lies when they needed to be spoon-fed the ugly truth.

This ain't no chicken soup for the soul. This is chicken soup laced with cyanide—made to heal you by killing off the old version of you that's been dragging you through hell. If you're looking for a feel-good escape, close this now and go feed your ego with empty inspiration. This ain't that.

This book doesn't care about your degrees, your status, or your image. It cares if you're ready to stop pretending. Because this ain't about change—it's about evolution. And to see the difference, I broke it down for you. Change is deciding to put on some clothes. You look in the mirror and don't like the outfit, so you change into something else. But that don't feel right either. So, you go back and throw on that first outfit you started with. That's change—going back and forth, trying on who you want to be, then running back to who you used to be.

But evolution? It means outgrowing what used to fit. A toddler can't fit back into infant clothes. A teenager can no longer fit into the toddler outfits they once did. That's evolution. And once you evolve, going back ain't even on the menu.

Most people don't really want to grow—they just want to feel better. They want a pat on the back, not a push in the back. They don't want to be healed—they want to be held. If you've had enough of bleeding from the same place, trapped in the same cycle, losing to the same lies, this book is your turning point.

It exposes. It convicts. And if you let it, it evolves you. You don't read this to feel better—you read it to *get* better. You read it to become something you've never been by facing everything you've tried to avoid.

If you're not ready to be confronted, convicted, or completely undone… if you're content being misused, abused, and devalued… then keep wearing that pitiful life like it still fits you. This wasn't written for cowards like you anyway.

But if you're fed up with that busted-ass life and ready to get real—read on.

PREFACE

This book didn't start at a desk—it started in a court-ordered rehab facility with bars. I was locked up when I realized I had a gift I never knew how to use: Words. Not just words to argue or defend myself—but words that could reach, restore, and rebuild. In prison, I started learning five new words a week. Not to sound smart, but because I hated sounding stupid. I was tired of leaning on fillers: "You feel me?" "You know…" "Yah mean…" "Like…" and cuss words that filled in for thoughts I didn't know how to express.

So, I made a choice. I sharpened my vocabulary, not realizing that one day I'd have to speak for more than just myself.

That challenge caught fire. Other men joined in. What began as building vocabulary later turned into the building of a vision. We weren't just growing our minds—we were rebuilding our manhood. And that's when I started writing letters for other inmates. Love letters to women they'd lost. Letters to judges before sentencing. Letters to children they hadn't seen in years. Some of those words won back the hearts of women. Some softened hard verdicts—reducing sentences for certain inmates. Some gave men the chance to hug their children in visiting rooms. That's when I discovered the power of words. The words I put together were powerful enough to put broken families back together. But I never thought I'd write a book.

It took other people believing in me before I believed in myself. Every time someone said, "You need to put that in a book," it planted a seed. And every time I saw someone drowning in the same mindset that once tried to drown me, that seed grew a little more.

In that jail-based rehab, in 2021, I began scribbling the scraps of my life on scrap paper—just trying to make sense of everything I had survived. I didn't write this book because I wanted to be an author. I wrote it because I didn't want to waste the pain. I wrote it because I knew there were people out there just like me—lost, confused, and fed up with fake hope.

This ain't a product—it's a process. It's not meant to impress—it's meant to impact.

Before you flip another page, just know: These words weren't written in comfort. They were born in chaos. And if even one line pulls you up from where you've been stuck, then it was worth the five years it took to write.

INTRODUCTION

This book ain't here to impress the scholars—it's here to impact the strugglers. It wasn't made for the folks who already got it together. It's for the ones still bleeding in silence, battling doubt, and trying to figure out how to crawl out of the hell they've been stuck in. It's not meant to inspire—it's meant to interrupt. If you're fed up with surface-level stories and fluffy inspiration, you're in the right place. This book ain't therapy—it's a tool for transformation. Each story starts with a thought-provoking line: *ReTHINK this cliché… THINK about this story… Take this day to THINK about…* That's not decoration—it's your challenge. That was by design. If you breeze through it, your bruises may not heal. You don't just read this book. You wrestle with it. It's meant to be read like a daily devotional—but not the kind that makes you feel cozy or sits on a coffee table. This one pokes, presses, and confronts. One page, one story, one thought per day. That's all it takes. For the ones who've never finished a book before, this one was written with you in mind.

This whole book is built around one command: *On your mark, get set, GROW.* And no—that ain't just a catchy title. It's a mindset. Your *mark* is wherever life has you right now—whether that's rock bottom, rehab, heartbreak, depression, prison, or toxicity. You don't have to wait for peace to begin. You don't need perfect conditions to evolve. You just need to show up where you are. The *set* is the preparation—getting your mind right, your heart open, and your surroundings ready for what's next. And then comes the *growth*—the decision to move forward. Don't wait for steady ground— lace up your pain and run with it. Taking off. And if you stumble along the way? Get back up, dust yourself off, slap a Band-Aid on the scrapes, and continue the race. Because this ain't about running flawlessly—it's about running faithfully. Flip through it front to back. Or don't. If you're hurting from betrayal, skip straight to that. If you're tired of your own lies, find a story that calls that out. There's no rule here except this: Let it work. Let it hit. Let it sit with you long enough to stir something up. Some pages will feel like a mirror. Some will feel like a punch. And some might be both. Don't finish this book proud you read it—finish it pissed you waited.

But here's the deal—reading it ain't enough. Information supplied ain't information applied. A toy without batteries don't work, no matter how many times you read the instructions. You've got to insert the power if you want it to come alive. Same with this. You can highlight every page and still stay stuck if you don't apply what you read. Don't read this just to say you read it. That's not growth—that's performance. Sit with the discomfort. Argue with it if you must. But don't walk away from it unchanged. I don't want you to finish this book and say, "That was a good book." I want you to say, "That book did a good thing in me." This book wasn't built to be devoured in one sitting. It was built to be digested over time. Let one story punch you in the chest. Let another one whisper to the part of you that still believes evolution is possible. And when you need it again? Come back—as many times as you need to. These pages ain't coupons—they don't have an expiration date.

CHAPTER 1

YOU KEEP BELIEVIN' IT— THAT'S WHY YOU KEEP BLEEDIN' FROM IT

*"The reason you think life is sweet is because
you keep believing these sugarcoated lies."*

DION PARKER

BEFORE YOU READ THIS CHAPTER

Some lies sound good enough to live in. They're easy to repeat and easy to hide behind. But lies don't just keep you stuck—they keep you bleeding. Quietly. Repeatedly. You've been taught things that felt safe but weren't true—and that's why you're bleeding in places you never got cut. This chapter was built to pull the mask off the mantras, to unlearn what's been poisoning your progress.

These ain't just myths—they're mind traps. And once they get in your head, they play on loop until you break the cycle. So don't just read this to feel convicted. Read it to finally see the chains you wore like a necklace—not knowing they were shackles.

And be warned—some of these clichés you've been clutching like comfort blankets since you knew how to talk are really barbed wire. They don't cover you—they cut you. If you keep believing this bullshit, don't be surprised when life keeps bleeding you dry. This chapter ain't here to pat you on the back. It's here to slap the lies out your mouth and dare you to live without 'em.

ReTHINK this cliché: "*All men are dogs*" gets tossed around like an old chew toy—usually by someone fed up with chasing the same untrained, territorial, and commitment-phobic types. But let's keep it a hundred—this ain't a universal truth. It's just a reflection of the breeds you've been entertaining. Not all men are strays or hounds. Some are loyal, protective, and build homes—they don't just mark territory. If all you attract are hound dogs, it might be time to check the scent you're putting out. Vulnerability? Desperation? Insecurity? Men can smell that shit from a mile away. You don't attract what exists—you attract what you allow. If you keep walking through the same dog park, don't cry when you keep stepping in the same dogshit. Stop gettin' mad when you keep picking pups and getting your ass chewed up. You the one out here running a pet store. If your thirsty, desperate ass quit falling in puppy love with men who lick your wounds one day and chase tail the next, you wouldn't keep having this problem. If all you're entertaining are mutts with no manners, then don't be shocked when your relationships stay "ruff."

In my younger years, I was a bloodhound—able to smell vulnerability from afar. Barking at anything that moved, sniffing around for females in heat, leaving scent marks everywhere I went. Loyalty? Commitment? That wasn't in my nature—I was just out to hump and roll over after, which is why I have three different baby mommas—that I know of. No cuddle, no callback, just on to the next fire hydrant. The energy and expectations you set determine the kind of men who pursue you. It's like shopping on Temu and expecting Tiffany's—if you buy cheap, expect fragile. You can't expect a man with pedigree if you keep hanging out where the strays roam. You get what you tolerate—and if what you tolerate is lazy, jobless, unmotivated dudes who just want a place to hump and nap, then you're not looking for an in-house partner—you're looking for an in-house pet. One you gotta feed, clean up after, and keep alive like a damn stray you brought in off the street. All this is your fault—'cause you keep opening the door and turning your home into a kennel for strays. Not all men are dogs—some just never got trained on how to treat a woman.

If you want someone who respects you, it starts with respecting yourself enough to stop entertaining mutts who don't deserve to sleep in the master bedroom. It ain't about a man's bark—it's about what he builds. Any dog can bark loudly, but when it's time to protect, most ain't shit. If he's not bringing peace, provision, or protection—leave his ass outside. No plan? No papers? No place. Here's the truth: The loudest women crying, *all men are dogs*, are usually the same ones who give up the "kitty cat" too easily. You can't be a lady and a tramp, investing too soon and ignoring the signs. If your tail is always waggin' for attention, don't be taken aback when the only men who chase you are the ones looking for heat—not heart. Before you bring a man home, make sure he has his papers—bank statements, life insurance, written goals, and a damn résumé. Make sure he has his shots—a shot at working a job, a shot at being a loving husband, and a shot at being a devoted father. Don't adopt a man who ain't been trained in emotional maturity, stability, and accountability—or he'll piss and shit all over you. If you're tired of being dogged by men, then stop postin' up doggystyle on the first day and fetchin' after men who drop every ball life throws at them. If he can't carry his own weight, then, damn it, don't your ass dare carry his last name.

Growth Affirmation: I will **GROW** out of the mindset that, "All men are dogs." Before I curl up with a man, I will check to see if he has fleas and, more importantly, a future.

ReTHINK this cliché: "*Change people, places, and things*" is often said as the ultimate solution to turning a life around. On the surface, it makes sense—if toxic people, bad environments, or unhealthy habits got you into trouble, cutting them off should be the answer, right? Wrong. You can relocate, but you can't outrun your own mind. You can change your address, but if you don't address your mindset, that same mess will greet you at the door—with a fake smile and a "Welcome to the neighborhood" gift. Changing locations without changing your mindset is like switching seats on the *Titanic*—your delusional ass still gon' drown. If your thinking stays the same, your problems just pack up and move with you. People, places, and things might influence behavior, but your mindset controls it. You don't need a new scene; you need a new script. Your past ain't just tied to where you've been—it's tied to how you think. Pouring spoiled milk into a brand-new glass don't make the milk good. The packaging never purifies the content. You can surround yourself with positivity, but if your thoughts stay toxic, you'll poison every room you walk into.

When I first moved to Florida, I really thought I had outrun pills. I got to Florida and sang out, "Na na na na na, y'all can't get me." Landed a solid job, clean urine, clean slate. I was shaking hands with the boss like I was finally somebody. But addiction don't care about new zip codes. One day in the breakroom, I overheard a dude asking his boy, "You ain't got no more Percocets?" That one word made my ears perk up harder than my paycheck ever could. I played dumb at first, acting like I ain't really catch it. But three days later, I doubled back with a fake limp and a fake story about my back—lying through my teeth just to get a pill. From that moment on, I was on a silent scavenger hunt, sniffing around the job site like a hound for a high. I went from standout employee to standing outside unemployed. Turns out, it wasn't the people or the place—it was the pain I never faced. I brought the same addict with me, just dressed him up in a uniform and clocked him in. I thought a new zip code would fix me, but changing zip codes won't change what's coded in your mind. Once my mindset changed, nothing no longer controlled me.

It's not people poisoning you—it's you. It's not a place—it's your misplaced thoughts. It's not something external; it's that internal thing between your ears—your mind. Transformation starts within, not around. Without renewing your mind, your toxicity is going to spill over to the new people and places around you. Take responsibility for your mindset. Stop thinking a fresh start means a new location. If you want better, stop making the same choices in different places. People, places, and things can be factors, but only you determine if they become excuses. It's not about escaping; it's about evolving. You can cut off people, places, and things, but until you unfollow your old mindset, you're still subscribed to failure. Should you be cautious about who you're around, where you go, and what you do? Absolutely. But don't put yourself in a trick bag by thinking a new environment is enough. Evolution is internal. Change what's inside, and the outside will adjust. If your mindset doesn't change, your circumstances never will. Same mindset, same mess—no matter how new the address. You can't outdrive your demons in a U-Haul when they're riding shotgun in your head.

Growth Affirmation: I will **GROW** out of saying, "Change people, places, and things." I can't outrun what I refuse to outgrow. Before I change my address, I will be sure to address my mindset.

ReTHINK this cliché: "*You made your bed, now lie in it*" is usually thrown around when someone is facing the consequences of their choices. It's less about accountability and more about writing people off. Listen here—you who've fucked it up and think that's the finale. Whatever you've done, whatever bed you made—you don't have to snuggle in it just because you messed up. And for the ones pointing fingers, let's talk. This ain't about skipping accountability—it's about rejecting the lie that your worst mistake is your final identity. Who are you to condemn somebody for the bed they made when you ain't even seen the full room? You weren't there when they cried themselves to sleep. You ain't felt the fear in their chest or the hell they had to survive just to stay sane. But you quick to throw that lame-ass cliché like it's scripture— "You made your bed, now lie in it." No. Beds were made to be laid in and made up. That's like telling someone, "You peed in the bed, now lay in it." Or like telling a toddler or a senior, "You messed your diaper, now sit in it." That ain't correction—that's cruelty. Life for them never became a comforter. You just want them to suffer, not heal—because if they heal, you'd have to face the fact of sitting in your own mess.

Back when I was on my Billy the Kid days, I got caught carrying a pistol and started calling around for bail, thinking someone might come through. Instead, the only thing they offered was judgment— "You made your bed, now lie in it." And yeah, I did some dirt. I ain't running from that. I caused pain. I broke trust. But I also came from broken examples. I laid down in lies that were passed down like heirlooms. My decisions were mine—but they were made inside a world that never gave me real options. And when I started evolving, trying to clean up what I wrecked, you know what I kept hearing? "Nah, you made your bed. Stay in it." Like redemption wasn't on the menu. Like growth had an expiration date. That's when I realized most people don't want to see you rise—they want to keep you where they left you.

Because your evolution reminds them of their stagnation. But I ain't staying down to make nobody comfortable. I flipped that bed. Burned the frame. I refuse to listen to people who haven't made their own. And I'm sleeping just fine now—in peace, not in punishment.

Some people never had the chance to fix their bed because life kept blanketing them in bullshit and covering them in chaos. You would really say to a girl who was molested by her uncle and got pregnant, "You made your bed, now lie in it?" She didn't make her bed—a monster threw her in one. That's not consequence—that's evil. Or even a woman who caught AIDS from a cheating husband—whom she trusted. You think she chose that? She didn't make that bed—she just laid in it with a man who was busy dirtying the sheets behind her back. That cliché don't offer accountability—it hands out a lifetime of punishment for pain that wasn't even self-inflicted. If you've outgrown your mistakes, stop tucking yourself into shame and covering yourself in guilt. You're not a prisoner—you're a producer. And to those who are perfect, stop judging people for trying to stand up in a room you've never stepped foot in. If you ain't passing someone a damn pillow to ease their nightmare, shut the fuck up about their bed.

Growth Affirmation: I will **GROW** out of the mindset of, "You made your bed, now lie in it." A bed can always be remade. So can my character.

ReTHINK this cliché: "*Blood is thicker than water*" emphasizes the idea that family bonds are the strongest and most unbreakable. It's used to guilt people into tolerating toxic relatives simply because they share the same DNA. But if that were true, why do some family members treat you worse than strangers? Blood may be thicker than water, but some family members dilute the bond—acting as blood thinners by wearing your patience thin. They don't pay back borrowed money, they sleep around with your partner, or they make you take on their responsibilities. Cut off family members who disrupt your peace—ain't a damn thing wrong with that. Family members are people— like everyone else—and that qualifies you to remove yourself from them just like you would any outsider who attempts to affect your sanity. A last name is just a label—real family is proven through action, not ancestry. Not all apples from the same tree are sweet; some turn out rotten. Family ties don't guarantee loyalty, just as origins don't guarantee quality.

At the start of my involvement in the drug game, I reached out to a cousin who promised to help me get started—for a price. He said he could set me up, but the cost would be the Oldsmobile 98 I had at the time. Eager to make quick money, I agreed. Things seemed to be going well until word got around that the transactions I was making were bad. The people I sold to came back furious, saying what they had snorted wasn't cocaine at all—it was washing powder. To keep from being killed, I added humor and said, "Well, that's one way of keeping your nose clean." But the joke didn't save me from the reality of betrayal. I washed my hands of him. Family members said, "That's your cousin, y'all shouldn't fall out." Bullshit! I could've been killed. They weren't going to guilt-trip me. Trick no good. Blood may be thicker than water, but so is syrup—it can get messy too. Blood made us family, but betrayal made him history.

If blood makes you family, why do some relatives bleed you dry? If blood makes you family, why don't their organs match? Just 'cause we're kin don't mean we're compatible. Biology may make you family, but behavior determines if you stay one. Being related don't make you reliable—some kin will let you down quicker than a stranger in the street. Some family ties need mending—others need cutting. Don't be afraid to distance yourself from family members who don't measure up. Bloodlines need boundary lines. If not, family will make you feel guilty for choosing yourself. Don't be afraid to treat someone inside the family as an outsider. If a family member is disloyal, I know you must keep the blood—but don't forget to keep your boundaries. Blood may be thicker than water, but not at the cost of your mental health. Blood ain't a license to drive you fucken crazy.

Growth Affirmation: I will **GROW** out of the mindset that, "Blood is thicker than water." Just because they inside my family don't mean I won't treat 'em like an outsider.

ReTHINK this cliché: *"Everything happens for a reason"* suggests every experience—good or bad—serves a greater purpose or is part of a grand plan. While comforting to some, it oversimplifies life's complexities and can distort how we understand tragic or senseless events. Imagine telling a woman who was raped that her violation had a purpose—that somehow her hell was a goddamn homework assignment to make her stronger. This implies her trauma was necessary for growth, which is not only insensitive but also deeply misguided. Or consider children who were abused. Are we to tell them that their suffering was part of a divine design to make them better adults? This mindset trivializes pain and undermines the healing that's truly needed. Looking at real-world tragedies, this cliché falls apart. What was the reason behind 9/11? Was it meant to unite America? Clearly, that hasn't happened. Divisions still run deep. What about school shootings? Are we supposed to believe these acts were meant to promote better school safety? That hasn't happened either. Schools remain vulnerable, and countless children are left traumatized. Telling grieving families that their loved ones' deaths served a higher purpose is far from comforting; it's dismissive and cruel.

Getting shot, getting high, and getting locked up—none of that happened to me for a reason. They weren't some divine plans to make me stronger. They were the direct results of my choices and the environments I placed myself in. My addiction wasn't part of a bigger purpose—it was me chasing euphoria at the cost of my soul. Prison didn't happen for a reason; it happened 'cause I kept choosing the same dumb-ass path repeatedly. The reasons a lot of things kept happening to me were because of the poor choices I was making. The pain I endured didn't make me stronger—it left scars. Growth didn't come until I decided to take responsibility for my life. Not all messes have meaning. If everything happened for a reason, I wouldn't have spent half my life giving myself reasons to fail.

Everything don't happen for a reason—some shit just happens. Period. No divine setup. No deep-ass moral. Just dumb decisions, bad timing, or reckless people with too much power and not enough conscience. Some stuff happens 'cause folks are selfish. Some 'cause you were evil. Some 'cause life don't give warnings—it just swings. Are we really gon' pretend like fate don't exist? Life has a way of throwing random punches with no prophecy behind 'em. Quit trying to spiritualize every fuck-up or disguise chaos as some kind of cosmic assignment. Not every storm is sent. Some just hit. And you ain't gotta decode it—you just gotta respond like it ain't about to keep you stuck. Everything ain't meant—but you still get to decide what it means moving forward. If it broke your plan, make a better one. If it shattered your comfort, build a new standard. Stop wasting your energy trying to make trash smell like a lesson—just take it to the curb and don't let it rot in your spirit. Some shit just is. Not every mess has a meaning—but you can still find meaning in every mess.

Growth Affirmation: I will **GROW** out of the mindset that, "Everything happens for a reason." The reason isn't in what happened—it's in how I respond.

ReTHINK this cliché: *"Don't judge a book by its cover"* is widely thrown around by simple-ass people who want to act like discernment is disrespect. Like observation is judgment. As if noticing bad behavior makes *you* the problem. But let's be real—if the cover is dirty, torn, and smells like chaos, maybe the content is nasty as hell. People love to shame you for setting standards while they make excuses for staying in chaos. But calling out a pattern isn't evil—it's evidence. If he cheats, believe it. If she lies, believe it. If they keep showing you their mess, stop hoping for a complete rewrite. Not everyone deserves a deep nosedive when they can't even keep their nose clean. Some books belong closed. And, no, that doesn't make you coldhearted—it makes you cautious. You don't need to study a fire to see that it'll burn you. Calling out bad character don't make you judgmental; it makes you a filter, not a damn fool. You're done with making excuses for people who ain't evolving. Stop letting guilt keep you loyal to what's already proven itself dangerous as hell. Not every cover hides a hidden gem. Some covers *are* the warning label.

There was a day I walked into a job interview with hope in my head and hell in my system. I'd been job hunting for a few months and finally got a call back from an employer I'd applied to twice. Right before stepping in, I wrestled with temptation—but the pill won. I thought I had it together. Hair brushed, shirt tucked, smile staged. But you can't spray cologne over collapse. The manager didn't even blink. After the interview, he called me over quietly. "Can I talk to you, man?" he said. "I could hear it in your voice… slurred, slow. Your eyes ain't lying either. You look like you need an intervention more than you needed an interview." That man didn't know me. But he saw through me. And he was right. I didn't need sympathy—I needed sobriety. He judged the cover. And because he did, he spoke to the sickness I was still trying to ignore. Had he not, I would've gone in there and created a shitstorm like I've done before.

Let them talk. Let them say you're judgmental. Let them roll their eyes when you keep your distance. You weren't built to pamper brokenness. You were built to break cycles. You don't owe anyone an explanation why you don't want to fuck with somebody. In time, they'll see what you had the wisdom to see beforehand. It's okay to look at someone and say, "Nah—I'm good. I don't even want to fool with you." That's not arrogance—it's awareness. You ain't cruel for guarding your energy. You ain't wrong for choosing calm over chaos. And let's be real—the people who throw that tired-ass, "Don't judge a book by its cover," phrase around the most? They're usually trying to hide the mess they know is inside them. People will guilt-trip you for walking away like you didn't give them a chance—but the truth is, you saw what you needed to and bowed the hell out before it blew up in your face. Stop letting people put you in a trick bag and make you think being wise means being foolish. Not every book deserves to be cracked open. Some of them deserve to stay their ass right on that shelf—collecting dust.

Growth Affirmation: I will **GROW** out of the mindset of "Don't judge a book by its cover." When actions scream, "Beware," I won't silence the whisper saying, "Be careful."

ReTHINK this cliché: People often say, "*The grass is greener on the other side,*" when they leave a situation or relationship, thinking there's something better waiting for them elsewhere. Although few people will openly admit to this mindset, it's a common trap many fall into when they believe external circumstances are the key to happiness or success. But the truth is, the grass isn't necessarily greener on the other side—it's greener where you water it. People often look at others' lives, careers, or relationships and assume they have it better. What they fail to see are the struggles and sacrifices behind the scenes. The illusion of greener grass is often fueled by comparison and dissatisfaction. Instead of cultivating what they already have, they jump from one situation to the next, thinking they'll find something better—but rarely do they find lasting satisfaction. Fresh grass won't help if you keep dragging old mud with you. The problem ain't the grass—it's the gardener.

You couldn't tell me I didn't just hit the lottery. I had a good woman, but I got distracted. My girl was plain, but she held me down. Then along came a woman who looked like she stepped straight out of a music video—curvy body, flawless nails, lashes long enough to fan herself, and slick baby hair. She made my girl look homely, so I dipped. But what I thought was the winning lottery ticket turned out to be a worthless scratch-off. I hadn't upgraded—I had just traded stability for special effects. She started farting without shame, like a grown man after a big bowl of chili with beans. At bedtime, she sat her wig on the dresser like a helmet after a yearlong war in Ukraine. She snored. And those long lashes? Found a few stuck to my pillow like spider legs. I had been scammed by a prettier brochure. She wasn't fine—she was filtered. Fake as fuck. She dangled the bait, set the hook, and reeled me in—but in the end, I had caught a catfish. Be careful of that line; there are plenty fish in the sea, 'cause you might just catch one too when you decide to throw yours back in the ocean—making her or him a good catch for someone else. Maybe even your friend who's been wanting her all along.

Stop job-hoppin', bed-hoppin', church-hoppin', thinkin' greener grass would solve your problems. It ain't the lawn—it's your triflin' ass that won't grow. All you do is drag weeds from place to place. Wherever you go, your mindset follows—happiness isn't found only in new places; it's found in renewed perspectives. The best opportunities aren't always elsewhere; they're often hidden in what you failed to nurture. You can keep hopping fences looking for better grass, or you can stay put and finally learn how to grow your own. The secret to greener grass isn't moving—it's mastering the art of cultivation. Think about how lawns are maintained. The healthiest, greenest grass isn't that way by chance—it's regularly treated, cared for, and nourished. You don't need a new yard—you need better maintenance. Before you assume someone else's grass is greener, remember—sometimes it's just a better filter. You still need to remove the seeds of doubt, laziness, and comparison and water your own situation with effort, patience, and care. That grass you're jealous of? Watered with consistency. Yours? Dried up from neglect. If you never water your own grass, of course every lawn will look greener than yours. By hopping fences, all you're doing is getting more mud on your shoes and tracking it into the next job or relationship. The grass isn't always greener on the other side—sometimes, it's just artificial turf with better lighting.

Growth Affirmation: I will **GROW** out of the mindset
that "The grass is greener on the other side." My peace
won't come from running—it'll come from rooting.

ReTHINK this cliché: "*What doesn't kill you makes you stronger*" gets thrown around like trauma is some kind of personal trainer. But does pain automatically build muscle? Hell no. If a man loses his legs in a car crash, is he stronger—or just forced to survive in a different way? If someone loses a parent, does that mean they're stronger to handle the loss of a child? Survival alone ain't strength. It just means the hit didn't finish you. Real strength isn't what happened to you—it's what you *did* after it. Strength isn't built by trauma— it's built in therapy, in self-work, in rebuilding the pieces. Believing this cliché is like thinking a drowning man becomes a world-class Olympic swimmer just because he didn't die. Or that drinking spoiled milk makes your stomach stronger. No—it just makes you sick. Pain doesn't hand out power; it tests whether you'll pull it out of yourself. Some people come out of hell more hardened, not more healed. Some come out colder, not stronger. Not everything that doesn't kill you lifts you. Sometimes it just leaves you limping until you decide to get physical therapy.

Pills didn't kill me, but they damn sure didn't build me. They wrecked me. The strength came when I crawled through detox, sat in therapy, owned my mess, and rebuilt brick by brick. Prison didn't kill me either—but it broke my pride, shattered my ego, and exposed my weakness. What made me stronger wasn't the cell—it was what I did with my sentence. Studying, exercising, programming. Getting shot didn't give me courage—it gave me trauma. The strength came from showing up to physical therapy when my body wanted to quit. Don't twist the story—pain didn't make me powerful. It gave me two options: I could break down or break through. If pain built power, every addict would be a leader. Every abuse survivor would be unstoppable. But some people stay stuck, broken, angry, and bitter because they never do the work. The pain didn't make me powerful—it gave me a choice. I made myself stronger with the help of God.

Pain is a test—not a teacher. You don't get stronger by suffering. You get stronger by fighting through what tried to kill you. Stop romanticizing survival like it's a win. Just because you made it through doesn't mean you grew. Plenty of people survive hell and still walk around broken, angry, or emotionally paralyzed. Strength don't show up from what hurt you—it comes from how you flipped it. That's the truth this cliché tries to avoid. Strength ain't automatic—it's intentional. You build it through healing, accountability, and effort. You don't earn power just by not dying—you earn it by refusing to stay dead inside. Don't confuse "still here" with "leveled up." One means you endured it. The other means you evolved from it. And the difference? That's the work you do *after* the bleeding stops. What didn't kill you didn't make you stronger. What made you stronger was the fight you chose from what tried to take yo ass out.

Growth Affirmation: I will **GROW** out of the mindset that "What doesn't kill you makes you stronger." Survival is step one—strength is built in every step I build after.

ReTHINK this cliché: *"Sticks and stones may break my bones, but names will never hurt me"* is often used as a defense mechanism, suggesting that physical harm is worse than verbal abuse. But let's be real. Sticks break bodies. Words break identities. Physical wounds heal—bruises fade, bones mend, and scars eventually disappear. But the wounds inflicted by words can linger for years, sometimes even a lifetime. You can set a broken bone, but you can't set a broken spirit. Those emotional wounds require a different kind of healing—one that involves untangling the invisible knots that hurtful words leave behind. If words didn't hurt, half the damn therapy industry wouldn't even exist. A broken bone gets a cast, but what does a broken spirit get? The wounds from words may not bleed, but they cut just as deep. Words won't break bones— but they'll crush the belief in oneself.

In prison, one of my cellies had a story that sounded straight off *20/20*— the kind of crime you wouldn't believe unless you heard it from the source. He said his girl got real sick and nobody could figure out why. By the time they did, her organs were shutting down. Eventually, they found out—he had been slipping antifreeze into her drinks, little by little, killing her slowly. Here's what I think of when I think back to his story: Poison doesn't just come in a bottle. It comes in words, in the kind of pain you don't taste until it's already inside you. People think pain is about what you can see, but the real killers don't leave bruises. They just sink in, eat you alive, and by the time you realize what's happening, the damage is already done. Words are like anti- freeze—odorless (unless somebody's breath stinks while they talk), tasteless, and deadly as hell when swallowed. You don't always notice the damage right away, but by the time you do, it's already poisoning you from the inside out.

Sticks and stones may break bones, but words become whispers that won't shut the fuck up. They play on repeat—especially when they come from people you trusted. Physical wounds leave scars you can point to. Verbal wounds leave ones you can't even name—but they burn every time someone touches that part of your soul. Some folks walk around bleeding from things nobody ever sees, because the damage wasn't on their skin—it was in their spirit. You think words don't break people? Ask the little girl whose uncle said, "Don't tell nobody—it's just between us." Ask the child who still hears their mother say, "I wish you were never born." Ask the woman who stayed with her abuser because he convinced her no one else would want her—that she was fat or just butt-ugly. Words don't fade—they fester. Words won't put you in a hospital, but they'll keep you in therapy. A shattered bone heals. A shattered spirit might never. And the more you pretend they didn't hurt, the deeper they dig in. Bruised bones don't make you question your worth—bruised hearts do. That's the real damage. That's why the most dangerous weapon ain't in the hand—it's in the mouth. Because sometimes the thing that hurts the most… never even laid a finger on you.

Growth Affirmation: I will **GROW** out of the mindset that "Sticks and stones may break my bones, but names will never hurt me." I will respect the power of my words—because what I say can hurt or heal.

ReTHINK this cliché: *"Let go and let God"* is widely used in the Christian community, implying that surrendering control to God will resolve all issues. It sounds spiritual, but most people use it as a permission slip to sit down when they should be standing up. It's marketed like some magic trick—just hand your problems over to God, kick your feet up, and watch everything fall into place. But that's not surrender—that's laziness in holy packaging. Faith doesn't mean stepping back, it means stepping *with* Him. God never asked you to quit—He asked you to cooperate. You can't just pray for a breakthrough and then fall asleep at the wheel. If success and peace were as easy as "letting go," then every lazy ass sitting on a couch would be a millionaire and stress-free. The truth is, God guides, but you still have to grind. It's not about handing off responsibility—it's about working in partnership. A fisherman doesn't just cast his line and walk away. He waits, watches, and stays engaged, knowing that just because he cast his line doesn't mean his job is done. He knows that when a fish bites, he has to be the one to reel it in. Faith is the rod, but it's our actions that pull the line and bring the results to shore.

I bought into that lie when I was fighting a court case. I was sitting in jail with charges hanging over my head, just walking around like everything was handled. "Let go and let God," I kept saying—like that slogan was gon' swing the gavel in my favor. I threw all my hope into the lawyer's hands and clocked out mentally, thinking I didn't need to do anything else. I wasn't asking questions. I wasn't going to the law library. I wasn't filing motions—I was just going through the motions, floating around the pod like I was on vacation, not on trial. I confused surrender with silence. And because I stayed passive, the system played me. The courts railroaded me. Not because God ain't good, but because I didn't do my part. I had faith, but no fight. I prayed, but I didn't prepare. And God don't bless closed eyes and crossed arms—He blesses movement. I had to grind while trusting God to guide. There's nothing wrong with putting it in God's hands, but don't forget to use the ones He gave you in the process.

God's favor ain't a handout—you still have to have a hand in it. Surrender don't mean stepping back; it means keeping your hands on the steering wheel while God rides shotgun. God can open doors, but you still have to walk through them—unless you're waiting for Him to carry you too. Even Jesus had to carry the cross before He conquered the grave. He didn't just "let go and let God"—He got up and got bloody. And it ain't like He didn't want out—He cried, "My God, my God, why have You forsaken Me?" That ain't weakness; that's honesty. But even in the pain, He kept dragging His burden until purpose showed up. So don't just give it to God and walk away—give it to God, get to work, and keep grinding your ass off until it shows up. Pray like it depends on Him, but grind like it depends on you. God provides the blueprint, but we have to pick up the hammer. God ain't your trampoline. You don't get to *spring* your prayers on God, *bounce* your concerns off Him, and *fall* back. It's your responsibility to *jump* to your feet and *leap* into action. When petitioning God, you still have to be on the front lines, not the sidelines. So if you're handing God your court case, your custody battle, your business, your healing, your kids, your marriage, your goals—don't get mad when He hands you back instructions. Trusting God means casting your cares, but it also means staying ready to reel in the catch. When you want something from God, you can't just roll up on Him and not roll up your sleeves. Letting go don't mean letting up. It means pray about it but grind for it. Stop wanting God to step in and step up, while you step off and step away. That ain't faith—that's freeloading.

Growth Affirmation: I will **GROW** out of the mindset of "Let go and let God." I will give it to God, but remember to get to work. Heaven helps those who help themselves.

ReTHINK this cliché: "*Go with your first instinct*" is often said to encourage people to trust their gut and act without hesitation. Like your gut is some kind of flawless compass. But instincts aren't always rooted in truth—they're often born from trauma, fear, ego, or emotion. Your gut might be reacting to your past, not your potential. You can't call it "intuition" if it's really just insecurity in disguise. You know how many times you've been wrong by going with your first instinct? Going with your first instinct is like buying a car because the paint job's clean—but refusing to check under the hood. Just because it looks right don't mean it won't leave you stranded. Sometimes your first instinct ain't direction—it's a defense mechanism. Your instincts deserve a voice, but your wisdom deserves the final say. First instincts can feel right but be completely wrong. What feels natural isn't always what's necessary. Smart choices come from reflection, not just reaction. Get in the habit of slowing down with your instincts rather than speeding up.

It seemed like a day didn't go by without heartburn—I was popping Tums like M&M's, brushing it off as nothing serious. One doctor told me it was GERD, and it sounded legit since it came from a respectable gastroenterologist. But for some reason my gut wasn't convinced. I got a second opinion, and thank God I did. That heartburn? It wasn't acid. It was a blocked artery. If I'd waited, I'd be six feet deep—maybe eight, the way I was living. If I had blindly trusted my first instinct, my daughters would've been grieving instead of hugging me. Gut feelings aren't always gospel. Sometimes they're guesses—and guessing wrong can cost you everything. Don't let your first thought be your last act.

When it comes to real-life choices, your first instinct is usually the loudest—but that doesn't make it the wisest. Your first instinct might be to cuss his ass out, quit your job, slide back into a toxic situation, or swing first instead of thinking shit through. But impulse has a price—and you usually pay in consequences. Every decision made in haste carries the weight of consequences you can't rewind. Just because it feels right doesn't mean it is. Just like a second medical opinion can save your life, a second thought can save your job, your relationship, your freedom—your ass. You don't tame your instincts—you test them. You don't silence them—you slow them down and put them on trial. Slowing down ain't weakness—it's wisdom. Taking time to pause, reflect, and evaluate doesn't mean you're abandoning your instincts— it means you're using them in a safer, smarter way. It's not about doubting yourself—it's about giving yourself the space to make the best possible decision. Discipline isn't the absence of impulse—it's the ability to pause when everything inside you wants to act. Think twice before acting once. Every first instinct deserves a trial before it becomes your verdict. You don't grow by trusting your first reaction—you grow by learning to question what fashioned it. Because what shaped it could be a whole lot of shit you still ain't healed from.

Growth Affirmation: I will **GROW** out of the mindset that says to "Trust your first instincts." I will think twice before acting once. It's wise to second-guess my first instincts. 'Cause my hurt, habits, and history may be playing a part.

ReTHINK this cliché: *"You can be whatever you set your mind to"* sounds like motivational gold, but it's often just shit dipped in sugar. It sets people up for heartbreak by pretending hard work can override hard facts. Your mind might be powerful, but it doesn't rewrite physics, genetics, or reality. A blind man ain't flying no damn plane. A 4'11" dude ain't dunking on LeBron. That's not hating—it's just the truth with the sugar scraped off. You can work your butt off, but if your dream is built on fantasy, all that effort becomes a treadmill—burning energy, but getting you nowhere. The truth? You can't be *whatever* you want. You can only be what you have the physical, mental, and practical capacity to be. However, you *can* be something powerful when your ambition aligns with your assignment. Stop trying to fit into dreams that weren't designed for your reality. Some dreams ain't in your DNA—meaning Do Not Attempt.

Growing up, I swore I was the next Kareem Abdul-Jabbar. And when I told others, they spat out, "You can be what you put your mind to." Never mind the fact that I was 5'6"—on a good day—with Reebok Pumps and two pairs of socks on. I had heart, hustle, and hoop dreams. I practiced like my life depended on it, convinced that if I wanted it bad enough, it would happen. Then came reality—a dude built like Ray Lewis bulldozed my ass and smacked me into next week. I hit the floor, and in that moment, not only was I knocked down—but the lie was knocked out of me. I didn't just lose the ball—I lost the lie. No matter how much I set my mind to it, I was never gon' dominate the paint like a 7-footer. You can grind all day, but you can't outwork biology. Hustle don't change height. Dreams need alignment—not just desire. That day, I learned something important: You can chase what's not for you, or you can pivot toward what actually fits you. I stopped chasing fantasy and started building around reality. That's when things started working for me instead of against me.

Believing you can be whatever you set your mind to is like trying to start a Chevy with a Ford key—if it wasn't built for it, it ain't gonna work." Instead of chasing an impossible dream, put your dedication toward something where you actually have a shot at winning. We got a habit of holding on to shit that ain't good for us—whether it's a relationship that should've been over, or a dream that was never meant to be ours. Your potential is real, but so are your limits. You weren't built to be excellent at everything—you were built to be excellent at something. Greatness isn't about chasing pipe dreams—it's about finding the lane where your gifts can go full throttle. Effort can't erase limits, but it can stretch potential. Don't confuse passion for permission. Your dream needs a foundation, not just a wish. Purpose isn't just about dreaming big—it's about dreaming smart. Some people waste their whole lives grinding for a stage that was never theirs—when they could've been owning the one built for them. The secret isn't in forcing a dream—it's in recognizing where your talents, opportunities, and reality intersect and making the most of that. Because when you find what fits, success isn't forced—it's inevitable.

Growth Affirmation: I will **GROW** out of the mindset that "You can be whatever you set your mind to." I can only be whatever my physical, mental, and practical capacity will allow me to be.

ReTHINK this cliché: "*It takes 21 days to form or break a habit*" has misled many into thinking change is just a matter of time. But time alone doesn't break cycles—discipline, pain, and raw commitment do. Saying it takes 21 days is like expecting your jacked-up ass credit score to bounce back after three weeks of good financial behavior. Habits don't fear calendars—they fear confrontation. Addiction doesn't bow on the 21st day—it laughs at it. If breaking a habit was just about clocking three weeks, relapse wouldn't be a revolving door. Habits aren't undone by countdowns—they're broken by consistent choices, repeated in silence, especially when nobody's watching. You can keep waiting if you want to, but don't be surprised when the habit outlasts your hope. Evolution doesn't happen because time passes. It happens because you were ready. Habits don't care about dates—they care about a decision. They don't break when time's up—they break when you get fed up.

Percocet didn't take 21 days to grab me—it took 21 seconds. One swallow, and I was hooked. Habits happen fast. But breaking them? That's a brutal battle. I'll never forget when the judge gave me 90 days in rehab. I was looking at my lawyer and I'm like, "You just gon' sit there?" I then yelled out, "Hell, Judge, it only takes 21 days to break a habit!" Truth is, no calendar can cure this. I went through rehab—twice. Did jail time longer than 21 days. Still wasn't free. The habit had its claws so far up my ass, not even time could yank it out. No calendar cured me. The turning point wasn't a program—it was a decision. A moment where I looked my demon in the face and said, "No more." Rehab couldn't break me free. Jail couldn't scare me straight. The only thing that worked was when I wanted my freedom more than I wanted my fix. Most people don't relapse because they forgot the rules—they relapse because they never established a strong enough "why" to quit.

Habits don't give a fuck about 21 days. They don't break with time—they break when the pain of staying the same outweighs the fear of change. Sure, external help matters—rehab, therapy, support groups—but they don't work until you do. We all wish time could cure us, but if that were true, addiction wouldn't bury people daily. Time doesn't bring healing—action does. For some, that shift happens fast. For others, it drags through decades of damage. You can't wait your way out of a war—you have to fight. Time don't heal what discipline refuses to confront. The 12 Steps won't save you if you ain't ready to walk them. Telling people it takes 21 days sounds cute as hell—but it's an ugly ass lie. Breaking a habit isn't about counting days. It's about making the days count. You don't beat demons by outwaiting them—you beat them by outlasting, outworking, and outgrowing them. Until you decide to kill a habit at the root, 21 days, 21 weeks, or 21 years won't break a damn thing.

> **Growth Affirmation:** I will **GROW** out of the mindset
> that "It takes 21 days to break a habit." A timeline
> don't get rid of a habit. A turning point does.

ReTHINK this cliché: "*Just be yourself*" is often thrown around as feel-good advice, encouraging confidence and authenticity. It's meant to reassure people that they don't have to wear masks to fit in or pretend to be something they're not. But what happens when "being yourself" is harming yourself? When who you are in this moment is holding you back instead of moving you forward? Telling someone destructive to just be themselves is like telling a thief to keep stealing or an addict to keep using—because hey, "That's just who they are." Would you really hand car keys to a drunk and say, "Just drive home how you always do?" Without correction, they're bound to crash—taking others down with them. If a person's "self" is impulsive, reckless, or toxic, reinforcing that identity only validates evilness. Comfort doesn't equal strength, and self-acceptance without self-improvement is just a convenient excuse to avoid growth. Self-awareness isn't just about knowing who you are—it's about recognizing who you need to become. Growth don't come from clinging to your comfort zone—it comes from cutting off the parts of you that keep cutting into your future. Growth means knowing when to be yourself and when to outgrow yourself.

Sitting in rehab during a class, another recovering addict asked me, "Don't you wish you were your old self again?" Without hesitation, I said, "Hell no." Being myself is what got me here. I wasn't battling the world—I was battling the enemy within. People romanticize their past like it was some golden era, but my old life was dysfunctional, not a home I wanted to return to. I didn't want my old self back; I wanted to evolve. Like a caterpillar tired of crawling, I was ready to break free and fly. The version of me that once existed rebelled against hope, rejected healing, and clung to destruction. I had been weak, pitiful, and powerless, caught in a cycle that was slowly killing me. Growth didn't mean going back; it meant breaking through. I had to stop saying, "That's just who I am." Who I was was holding back the person I needed to become.

You can't cling to a version of yourself that's dragging you down. Neither who I was nor who I used to be could take me further. "Being myself" was just an excuse to stay the same.

Caterpillars don't become butterflies by staying comfortable in cocoons. Be yourself, but don't be afraid to upgrade. Self-acceptance is important, but self-improvement is essential. Imagine a so-called friend sneakin' in your house, slippin' in your bed with your spouse—and shrugging it off by sayin', "That's just who I am—*physical touch* is my love language." If it was your spouse, I bet your ass won't be sayin', "Just be yourself," then. In this case, "being yourself" is less about authenticity and more about a refusal to take responsibility. The best version of you doesn't emerge by standing still—it's born through pressure, pruning, and progress. Growth requires you to outgrow the parts of yourself that no longer serve you. Authenticity without accountability is just arrogance dressed up as self-love. Don't just be yourself—be your evolving self. True authenticity isn't about hugging every flaw; it's about healing them. Who you were yesterday shouldn't be who you are today—and who you are today shouldn't be enough for who you're becoming tomorrow. Stop worshiping your weaknesses like they're your identity—call them out, cut them out, and grow the hell up. Stop tellin' people to "just be themselves" when it's themselves that's the damn problem.

Growth Affirmation: I will **GROW** out of the mindset of "Just be yourself." Be yourself—but only if your self is not your own worst enemy.

ReTHINK this cliché: "*I know you like the back of my hand*" is a big lie that people love to believe. Parents swear, "I know my child!"—until they shoot up the school. People swear they know their partner—until they sleep with their best friend. The moment you think you know someone inside and out is the moment you stop paying attention. We don't meet people—we meet their presentations. You never know someone—you only know what they allow you to know. People don't show their flaws upfront; they show what's safe, what's acceptable, what keeps them in your good graces. People hide their whole hand, afraid that if you see the real them, you'll wash yours of them. Some people don't even know who they are until pressure introduces them to themselves. Never say you know someone until you've seen them lose everything. You can share a bed, a bank account, and a bloodline—and still not know the beast buried inside someone. Thinking you fully know someone is like assuming you know how the movie will end just from watching the trailer—what you see is only a preview, not the whole story.

A girl I met thought she had found "the one." But the truth? I was a pill head. She thought she knew me like the back of her hand—until she discovered that my hand was stealing her pills from her medicine cabinet. After seeing behind the mask and meeting a version of me who I never introduced, she treated me like COVID and stayed six feet away. Masks don't fall off— they get ripped off by life. You don't really know someone until your presence no longer benefits them. Some people only love you as long as they can lie to you. If you think you've seen every side of a person, congratulate them on their Oscar-worthy performance for best actor.

Do you really think that woman who married her high-school sweetheart thought he'd end up being the star of a *Dateline* episode—or that man who said, "I do," ever imagined his bride would land them both on an episode of *Snapped?* Wisdom isn't in believing you know someone—it's in understanding that people are never fully known. People wear different faces depending on what serves them. Some hide their true selves for fear of rejection, others to maintain control. The ones you trust most often carry secrets that would shatter the image you built of them. When you stop being naïve and stop setting expectations, you lessen the blow of the hurt they cause—because you weren't dumb enough to think you truly knew them. That's why you never let your guard down based on familiarity alone—because time doesn't reveal character, circumstances do. Years don't reveal people—pressure does. You've just met the versions they wanted you to see. The moment life applies pressure, the mask slips, and you're either looking at someone you never truly knew or a version of them you were never meant to meet. Never become too arrogant to think you know someone fully. Everyone has multiple personalities—you just haven't met them all yet. You think you know them like the back of your hand—until their hand stabs you in the back or smacks the shit out of you.

Growth Affirmation: I will **GROW** out of the mindset of thinking that "I know you like the back of my hand." I will wait for trying times to meet the real them.

ReTHINK this cliché: "*Work smarter, not harder*" is often used as an excuse to avoid putting in real effort. The idea sounds good—why struggle when you can strategize? But here's the problem: Smart work without hard work is just a plan without execution. Smarts will get you started; effort will get you finished. You're not being smart if you're only working smart. True power comes when you put both to work—when you think critically and move relentlessly. The ones who win aren't just the smartest or the strongest—they're the ones who know when to strategize and sweat. The brain writes the recipe, but the grind does the cooking. If life was just about thinking your way to the top, the laziest genius would be the richest person in the world. But that's not how it works. Sure, it's smarter to use a chainsaw instead of an ax to cut a tree— but you still gotta hold on to it to bring it down. Both are needed. Intelligence without discipline is wasted potential, and effort without direction is wasted energy. You can't outthink what you refuse to outwork.

In prison, I ran one of the biggest stores—if you needed something, I had it. But to keep myself from being the go-to guy for every single trade, I got smart. Instead of having people come straight to me for their 2-for-1s, I rented out other inmates' lockers. They held my inventory, handled the transactions, and kept the system moving. This kept me out of the way. Lowkey. It was the perfect setup—until it wasn't. I rarely did inventory, too confident in my own system to check the details. One of the guys I trusted was skimming off the top, stealing from me little by little. By the time I caught on, I had already lost more shit than I could count. I thought I was being smart by delegating the grunt work, but I got lazy, mistaking a good strategy for good execution. The hustle wasn't just about playing chess—it was about putting in the work to protect the board.

Convenience without commitment is just laziness dressed up in logic. Efficiency won't save you if you're avoiding effort. The people who succeed aren't just the ones who think big; they're the ones who act boldly. If you're planning a road trip, it may be smarter to let a GPS bark out directions instead of fumbling with a paper map, but the car ain't moving until you press the gas. Knowledge without effort is just potential sitting on a damn shelf, collecting dust. A plan without action is just a dream waiting to be forgotten. If working smarter was enough, how do you explain that there are Harvard graduates who work for others and dropouts who run their own companies? Intelligence opens doors; effort walks you through them. Those who win aren't just the smartest—they're the ones who know that success isn't about choosing between two extremes—smarts and hard work. It's about balance. Brains and brawn aren't enemies—they're business partners.

Growth Affirmation: I will **GROW** out of the "Work smarter, not harder" mindset. I will work smart, but I won't be so dumb to think that I don't have to work hard.

ReTHINK this cliché: *"If it ain't broke, don't fix it"* suggests that if something seems to be working fine, there's no need to change or improve it. While that might hold true for a toaster that still makes perfect toast, it completely misses the mark when we're talking about human growth, success, and development. Life doesn't demand that you wait for a breakdown before you build better— growth should be constant. The quickest way to stay low is to stop reaching high. Life don't give warnings—it gives wake-up calls, and most show up after you've been snoozing through the signs. It's a sad-ass truth that you'll upgrade your phone, but you won't upgrade your dull life. You'll upgrade your wardrobe, but you won't upgrade your wisdom. You'll trade in your car when it starts to break down, but you won't trade in bad habits when they start to break you down. Are you sayin' that your phone, your clothes are more important than your future? People put a lot of energy into upgrading external things, but never stop to upgrade what matters most—themselves.

When I got clean, I thought being sober was enough. I stopped using, got out of the program, and told myself I didn't need meetings or anything else. I got comfortable, and comfort is where destruction waits. I wasn't checking in with myself, wasn't doing the work, and eventually those old habits came back swinging. I learned the hard way—just because something looks good on the outside doesn't mean it's solid on the inside. Growth and recovery don't stop when things start going right. You either maintain what you've built, or you watch it crumble. The work never stops. To understand this, I looked no further than my phone. Even when it's working flawlessly, I still receive regular prompts to update it—to fix bugs and introduce new features to enhance optimal performance. Neglecting those updates can cause the device to start running slower or malfunction. Maintenance is what keeps you from breaking all over again. You don't climb out of hell to sit at the edge—you keep climbing, because falling back is always one step away.

Look at it this way: You wouldn't wait for your teeth to rot before you brush them. You wouldn't wait for your phone to die before you charge it. You wouldn't wait for an engine to blow to get an oil change. So why wait until your life is falling apart before you start fixing it? If it ain't broke, upgrade it anyway—'cause the moment you don't stay on top of things, life will drag your ass straight to the bottom. Growth is a muscle—if you don't keep working it, it shrinks. Staying great means staying hungry for growth, even when life feels good. Growth is about maintaining what works and improving what can be better—before it breaks. Just because it ain't broke doesn't mean it can't be better. You don't have to hit rock bottom to get better. Growth is maintenance, not damage control. Growth ain't what you do when life falls apart—it's what you do to keep your life from falling apart.

Growth Affirmation: I will **GROW** out of the mindset of "If it ain't broke, don't fix it." Growth ain't reserved for emergencies. I will do regular checkups to help keep things in check.

ReTHINK this cliché: "*Practice makes perfect*" is widely thrown around in classrooms, locker rooms, and workplaces like gospel truth. This cliché tricks people into believing that if they practice hard enough, they'll reach some mythical level where mistakes disappear. That's a lie straight from hell. Perfection is a fantasy. The idea that relentless repetition somehow leads to flawless execution is nothing but a setup for disappointment. Because people are told they can be perfect and they fail, they start to turn on themselves and quit. Saying that "practice makes perfect" don't motivate people—it manipulates them. No matter how much you grind, no matter how many hours you put in, perfection is an illusion. Even legends aren't perfect. Jordan missed thousands of shots, but he never stopped shooting. Serena double-faulted a bunch of serves, but she never stopped serving. Tiger missed many putts, but he never stopped putting. They didn't reach perfection—they reached precision through repetition. Practice didn't make them perfect. It made them powerful. What separates the greats from the rest isn't flawlessness—it's fearlessness. Constant practice gave them consistent preparation, nothing more. Perfection ain't the point—preparation is.

When I first worked on sobriety, people kept feeding me that lie, "The more you practice, the easier it gets." That was a damn lie. So when I relapsed, I said, "Fuck it, I may as well go all in." I thought I had to be perfect, and the second I wasn't, I threw my hands up like it was over. In time, I learned that practice ain't about being perfect; it's about not going backward. I don't wake up chasing perfection. I chase another clean day. Some days I'm strong, others I'm shaking, but I still show up. I've stumbled sober more times than I ever did high, but I kept showing up. Perfection never kept me clean— progress did. Practice gave me tools for sobriety—not immunity from it. I've had close calls, moments where the craving hit like a freight train. But practice taught me how to brace for impact without folding. People love quoting clichés, but they don't know the fight behind staying consistent. It's not pretty. You train to survive the storm, not avoid the rain. I didn't practice to be perfect—I practiced so relapse couldn't catch me off guard.

Practice doesn't make perfect. It makes consistency. Stop lying to people. They don't need perfection—they need endurance. The grind doesn't promise greatness, it just makes quitting harder. The ones obsessed with being perfect get paralyzed. They freeze, hesitate, stall out, overthink. Meanwhile, the ones who embrace the grind keep leveling up because they ain't scared to fall. Greatness is a club, and its membership comes with the unlimited use of mistakes. Perfect is for posers. Practice is for people preparing for war—'cause life don't give a damn about flawlessness, only fearlessness. The truth is, you don't practice to become perfect—you practice so you don't panic when it counts. The goal of practice isn't to become flawless; it's to become relentless. You ain't practicing to be perfect—you're practicing to keep from getting punked by pressure. Practice builds muscle memory, not mistake immunity.

Growth Affirmation: I will **GROW** out of the
mindset of saying, "Practice makes perfect." Practice
doesn't make perfect. It makes consistency.

ReTHINK this cliché: "*You can't teach an old dog new tricks*" is thrown around to write people off—as if age means you're unteachable, incapable of learning or evolving. But let's be real—what people are really saying is, "Stay in your lane. Stay limited." They use that cliché to keep you boxed in, like your best days are behind you. But just because you've been through known hell doesn't mean it's too late to reach unknown heavens. Growth doesn't come with an expiration date. It comes with a decision. You don't stop growing because you get old—you get old because you stop growing. People think experience makes you tired—but experience can make you wise enough to move smarter. If trees don't stop growing new branches, why should we stop growing new dreams? Their "too late" ain't your deadline—it might be your liftoff.

After wasting so many years of my life to the streets, with drugs, and in prison, I thought it was over. I thought I missed my shot. And people around me made sure to remind me of that. "Just get a warehouse job and be thankful," they'd say—not because warehouse work ain't honorable, but because they thought that was all I'd ever be worth. In their story, they counted my wasted years—but in mine, I was too busy counting the lives I'd impact with what I went through and with what I had left. At 47, while people commanded me to "sit" as if I were a dog, I became a certified personal trainer. Then at 54, I became an author. Both achievements are now helping to improve the lives of others. My late start was nothing but a legendary comeback. If you can't teach an old dog new tricks, then I must be a damn good magician. I'll be damned if I'm going to let anybody tell me that it's too late for me to do anything. Who are they? Being "an old dog" didn't stop me from learning new tricks—it made me not just wanna roll over and fetch my dream even harder. I'm not late to the race. I'm just lacing up.

Believing people can't learn with age is like assuming a classic car with a lot of mileage can't travel new roads. Don't tell me a man can't evolve—folks who grew up dialing rotary phones now FaceTime grandkids across the country. It ain't the age that matters, it's the attitude. It's not that old dogs can't learn new tricks; it's that too many people let their excuses tell them to "sit." Age is just a number—fear is the real leash. If they expect you to roll over because of your age, show 'em you can still roll up your sleeves. You're never too seasoned to spice up your life and give it flavor. You can either let people keep you chained, or you can break out and run free. Being too scared to grow is worse than being too old to grow. You ain't too old to evolve—you're just too loyal to the same rusty ass cage. The key is to never stop being curious, never stop being courageous, and never let fear of failure outweigh the excitement of new possibilities. They might call you ancient, but age don't cancel out ambition. Stay trainable. Curiosity and courage don't retire. And when they call you history—don't argue. Just let 'em watch you make it.

Growth Affirmation: I will **GROW** out of the mindset that "You can't teach an old dog new tricks." My age won't be the reason I don't make it; my excuses will.

ReTHINK this cliché: "*God works in mysterious ways*" is often thrown around when people don't know how to explain what's happening—like God is some ghost in the shadows—spooky but beatable, like you could call the Ghostbusters or run Him off with some candles and a chant. But let's be real—there is nothing mysterious about God. His Word spells everything out for anyone willing to open the book. Amos 3:7 says, "*Surely the Sovereign Lord does nothing without revealing His plan to His servants the prophets.*" Calling God mysterious is like ignoring the directions, getting lost, and blaming the GPS. He gave us the blueprint—we just don't follow it. The only mystery is why people keep calling God mysterious when He's been clear from day one. God is not a God of confusion; He's a God of instruction. His wisdom is deliberate, never disguised. His Word is a manual, not a maze. It's not that God hides His plans—it's that most people don't seek them. Don't call it divine mystery when it's really human ignorance. The closer you get to God, the clearer His direction becomes.

There was a time when my life was a full-blown dumpster fire—I was addicted, reckless, and rotating between the streets and a cell like it was a time-share. Every time I survived close calls, people would say, "God works in mysterious ways," like I was some spiritual riddle. But there was nothing mysterious about the mess I made. God wasn't hiding—*I was hiding from Him.* His Word straight-up says, "The wages of sin is death," and I was collecting like it was a good ass paycheck. My downfall wasn't part of a divine mystery; it was the byproduct of disobedience. The warnings were loud as hell—I just kept hitting mute. It wasn't that I couldn't hear God—it's that I didn't like what He said. We treat God's Word like confusion so we don't have to feel convicted. When I opened up the Bible in the prison hole and actually started listening, I realized that God had been speaking the whole time. That wasn't mystery—that was mercy. God's message is clear. His Word is not cryptic; we just don't open the damn book.

God is not puzzling. We're just puzzled by His infinite wisdom. We love to give an excuse for what we don't understand. Truth is, when people say, "God works in mysterious ways," what they really mean is, "I don't understand what's going on." But God is not the Author of confusion—He's the Author of clarity. He already laid out how this life works: Blessings for obedience, consequences for rebellion. Simple. It's not mystery—it's math. Don't confuse mystery with selective understanding—it ain't hard, you're just dodging the truth that makes you uncomfortable. You don't need to decode the Bible—you just need to live by its code. Stop acting like God is hiding His moves. He's been clear. He's been consistent. And He's been waiting. It ain't that His Word is too deep—it's that your sinful ass refuses to dive deep into it. Again, God is not some mystery. The only mystery is how long we will keep ignoring His Word. God's instructions for our lives can't be any clearer. His words are written in red, yet yo ass act like it's invisible ink.

Growth Affirmation: I will **GROW** out of the mindset that "God works in mysterious ways." God isn't confusing; He's convicting. He's not mysterious—He's methodical.

ReTHINK this cliché: "*God won't put more on you than you can bear*" is misquoted scripture—it's a survival slogan we slap on suffering to keep from falling apart. People cling to it like a spiritual painkiller, hoping it numbs the pressure. But the truth? The Bible doesn't say that. What it actually says—in 1 Corinthians 10:13—is that God won't allow you to be *tempted* beyond what you can bear. Not burdened. Not broken. Not overwhelmed. Tempted. There's a difference between pressure and seduction. Struggles hit harder than temptation ever will. Pain doesn't come with a back door—but temptation does. Think about it like this: Temptation is when you're in your car outside that married person's house, knowing damn well what you came there for, and something in you says, "Turn your ass around." That's the kind of moment God promised you'd never face without a way out. Pain, on the other hand, is burying your mother, watching your child suffer, or doing time in a cell when you're already losing your mind. That ain't temptation—that's pressure. And God never said pressure wouldn't crush you. He said sin wouldn't own you if you took the escape.

There were days I didn't feel pressure—I felt punishment. If God never puts more on you than you can bear, then why the hell was I buried under so much shit I couldn't even breathe? The kind of pain that would've left most people with PTSD—or locked away in an insane asylum. Shot seven times. Stabbed. Locked in cells like a caged animal. High out my mind. Losing a grandson. Losing hope. Two times divorced. They aired my mug on the news like I was a villain, not a man trying to escape his own past. My daddy bounced early, and I still followed his shadow into addiction and prison. I've overdosed and remember thinking—*so this is how it ends?* Ain't no scripture feel-good enough when you're face-down in trauma that don't let up. Don't tell me God won't give you more than you can bear—I had more than I could carry every day. But He didn't let it kill me. That's the part people miss. He didn't keep the weight off—He gave me stronger legs under it. What crushed me also changed me. I wasn't tempted—I was torn apart. And somehow, through all that pressure, He showed up in pieces and still carried what I couldn't. Not because I was strong—but because He never left.

It's the burden, the breakdown that builds you. Just like a muscle—growth doesn't happen without tearing. The fibers have to tear so they can rebuild stronger. It's the same with you. A breakdown is how you rebuild stronger. Pain might not be optional, but participation in your downfall is. You can't pray away pressure and then ignore the path out of temptation. Just because you're overwhelmed doesn't mean you're being tempted—sometimes you're just facing life at full volume. Stop quoting scriptures you never studied and blaming a God you never gave a damn about consulting. He will let life bend you—but He won't let sin own you. Just ask Job. And for those unfamiliar with God's Word, Job isn't a workplace—it's a man in the Bible whom God put through hell, and he came out stronger. He's proof that God will put more on you than you can bear. Stop confusing suffering with seduction— one breaks your heart, the other breaks your soul. And the only way you'll know the difference is if you stop letting comfort clichés replace raw truth. Let's stop pretending God only gives light loads. He gives people purpose, and sometimes that purpose is birthed through pressure. Don't confuse being overwhelmed with being overlooked. God isn't trying to see if you're strong— He's showing you that He is.

Growth Affirmation: I will **GROW** out of the mindset that "God won't put more on me than I can bear." I won't confuse pain with temptation or lean on misquoted comfort.

ReTHINK this cliché: "*Old habits die hard*" is something weak-ass people say when they don't want to do the work to change—so they just bow to their bondage and call it human nature. But that ain't truth—that's a cop-out. It's laziness dressed up like reality. It's a slogan for people who want to keep doing the same shit without feeling bad about it. Breaking a bad habit is hard—but so is leveling up. So is staying broken. So is waking up every day with regret and resentment because you didn't have the guts to change. You don't get to avoid the pain—you just get to choose which kind. You either suffer through the discipline of growth or the destruction of staying the same. Either way, you're gon' bleed. It boils down to which one you want to focus on: The habit or the healing. Don't quote the saying, "Old habits die hard," like it's a law—quote it like it's a challenge. Because anything you keep feeding ain't dying. It grows stronger while you grow weaker.

When I was a kid, I had a habit of peeing in the bed. I tried everything— no water before bed and alarm clocks. My mom would lift me up in the middle of the night, like maybe if she helped enough, the habit would break itself. But every morning, same stain—just in a different spot on the mattress. You would've thought I slept in a waterbed. That pattern followed me into adulthood. But it wasn't pee this time—it was pills. All I thought about was how I was going to get more. I was afraid to even wake up the next day, scared as hell I wouldn't come up with any. They became my personality, my pulse, my peace. Come nightfall, when the weight hit and the world got quiet, I'd reach for what numbed me. I'd wake up in the aftermath, wondering why I was still stuck. Just like that bed, I kept washing the sheets of my life instead of changing the behavior that kept soiling them. I didn't need a clean blanket—I needed to break the pattern. My mom couldn't carry me out of this. I had to stand in my own soaked shame and say, "This shit ends with me."

It's not that old habits die hard—it's that old excuses live too easy. You ain't special 'cause you're stuck. You just don't want to sweat. You want pity, not pressure. But change don't happen by hoping the urge leaves. It comes by killing the trigger, choking the comfort, and daring to sit in the fire until discipline takes the wheel. You wanna stop blowing money you don't have? Retrain your discipline. You wanna stop living like a slave to your urges? Retrain your will. You can't conquer what you keep coddling. You can't heal from what you keep hugging. Ain't nobody coming to clean it up for you. This ain't about willpower—it's about war. You're either the killer of your cycles or the corpse in your comfort. So rip the sheets off your shame. Burn the blanket of denial. Grab the damn shovel and bury what's been burying you. Because whatever you don't kill, you feed. And whatever you feed, eventually feeds off you.

Growth Affirmation: I will **GROW** out of the mindset that "Old habits die hard." I refuse to give CPR to the very thing that's been suffocating me.

ReTHINK this cliché: "*Fake it till you make it*" sounds like ambition, but it's really just staged confidence. It trains you to front while you fight. It teaches you to act confident or successful—even when you're not—until you eventually become that way. It's a costume party for people who fear being seen for where they're really at. But the problem is, when you fake it too long, you start forgetting who you actually are. You end up chasing image over identity. And eventually you'll either run out of lies—or run into someone who's been through real shit and can see straight through your fake ass. Faking it don't make you—it masks you. That phrase is nothing but a bandage over broken dreams and bruised self-worth. You don't need to pretend to be successful to become successful. You don't have to look like you got it before you actually do. You ain't gotta dress like a boss while you're still learning how to show up on time. And if your confidence is built on camouflage, don't be shocked when you get exposed in the spotlight.

Back in high school, I was deep in that illusion. I sewed designer labels onto off-brand clothes like I worked in a knockoff sweatshop overseas. I stacked singles thick and sat three twenties on top to make it look like money overflowed. I wrapped gold cigarette paper around my teeth to fake a grill and painted fake jewelry with clear fingernail polish just to keep the green off my skin. I was doing the most—just to cover up how little I thought of myself and to portray the status of a kingpin when I was really only a pawn. I believed if I could trick people into thinking I had everything, maybe I'd trick myself into believing I wasn't worth shit. But all I really did was bury the version of me that needed development, not decoration. Let's tell the truth—Jeff Bezos didn't wear Gucci in that dusty-ass garage. Bill Gates wasn't pushing a Mercedes while starting Microsoft. Warren Buffett didn't own a Bentley while building Berkshire Hathaway. Why? Because when you're really on the path to something big, you ain't got time to be flashy—you're too busy being focused.

Now, there's nothing wrong with believing in yourself as you go after your dream—but there's a big difference between faith and fabrication. Faith builds foundation—faking it just builds a front that eventually collapses. So, no, don't fake it till you make it—faith it till you make it. Just believe you will achieve it. Work with what you've got. Show up broke, honest, and hungry. Show up in your truth, not in your costume. Because the grind will always outshine the gimmick. And people may laugh at where you are now, but they'll never forget how real you kept it. Image fades—character scales. You weren't made to be a dressed-up disappointment. You were made to be a raw, uncut rise. So take the filter off. Drop the act. Let the process shape you. Because when you finally arrive, it'll mean something—and it'll last. It's always better to preserve who you are than to pretend to be someone you're not.

Growth Affirmation: I will **GROW** out of the mindset of "Fake it till you make it." I'm showing up for growth. My journey don't need a costume, just consistency.

ReTHINK this cliché: "*You complete me*" sounds romantic, right? But that phrase is one of the most dangerous lies people wrap in love. If someone has to complete you, then you came in broken. That ain't love—that's dependency. "I don't know what I'll do without you"… "I'll be lost without you"… "There's no me without you"—those lines ain't sweet, they're scary. Stop telling people you can't live without them like it's cute. That ain't love—that's a leash tied to your own insecurity. They might complement your growth, but they were never supposed to be your glue. And if you fall apart every time someone walks out, that ain't a loss—that's proof they were holding together what you never built yourself. Nobody should have that much power over your existence. If you don't feel whole without somebody, you ain't ready to have anybody. You need to be working on yourself. Fixing what's broken. Relationships are supposed to elevate you—not resuscitate you. If you still need somebody to complete you, you're a damn parasite, not a partner. You don't need a soulmate—you need a soul check.

For me, it wasn't a person that I thought completed me—it was pills. If I didn't pop something, I couldn't eat. Couldn't smile. Couldn't sleep. Life without them felt like walking without bones. They became my escape, my ease, my engine. I truly believed I couldn't function without 'em. I'd tell myself, "This is just who I am." But the truth was, it was just who I settled to be. That lie wrapped around me like comfort—but it was a coffin. Every time I reached for that pill, I was reaching for something to fill the hole I refused to face. I wasn't addicted to the pill—I was addicted to the idea that something outside of me could make me feel alive inside. And that's what this cliché really is—a spiritual addiction to being saved by somebody else. The day I finally sat in the pain—the cravings, the silence, the truth—I realized I didn't need to lean on pills, people, or anything else to stand tall. I didn't need a damn thing to complete me. I just needed to reclaim what I walked away from: My own worth.

Let me be clear—if you still walking around waiting for a person to "complete" you, how pathetic. You ought to be ashamed that you gave someone else the job to finish what only you were born to start. No man, no woman, no partner, no friend, no damn vice is supposed to be the missing piece. That's your responsibility. You weren't created to be half a person—you just been living like one. Stop using love as a crutch for your lack of identity. Stop calling it romance when it's really weakness. Grow yourself up before you ask someone else to grow with you. You are not to be built by love but to show up built for it. Because if they gotta complete you, they'll eventually control you. And when they leave—and, trust me, they will—you'll fall apart like a house that was never built on its own foundation. Stop chasing people just to feel whole. That's not a relationship—it's a rescue mission. Free yourself from needing to be saved. Reinforce your value. Rebuild your soul. Completion starts with you—whoever joins is a bonus, not a backbone.

Growth Affirmation: I will **GROW** out of the mindset that says, "You complete me." I don't need someone as a crutch—I need to stand on my own.

ReTHINK this cliché: "*Once a cheater, always a cheater*" is a lazy way to write someone off. It don't call out cheaters—it locks them in a cage and throws away the key. It assumes people are trapped in the moment they failed, like growth can't exist after guilt. But that ain't truth—that's bitterness trying to pass for wisdom. And let's be real—some of the same folks screaming this line are the ones who pushed somebody to cheat, then hid behind that weak-ass slogan. Truth is, that mindset's probably why your ass got cheated on—your negative ass spoke it into existence. You out here cursing people, convinced nobody can evolve, then act shocked when that same energy circles back. Your own mouth keeps manifesting your misery because of your belief in that cliché. That phrase don't protect people—it punishes anyone who's trying to evolve. It paints brokenness as permanent, like mistakes are shackles instead of wake-up calls. But who are you to chain somebody to who they used to be? "Once a cheater, always a cheater," is no different than, "Once a dope fiend, always a dope fiend." If people can become addicts and still recover, why can't they mess up and still evolve? Not everybody who messed up stayed messed up. Some of us got fed up with lying to ourselves more than we ever lied to anybody else. And truth be told, the people who scream that line the loudest are usually the ones too scared to believe in growth—'cause if they did, they'd have to admit they're capable of evolving too. And that means no more excuses.

Despite the fact that I had given up pills, there was this one person who would still call me a dope fiend every time he got mad. "Pill head," "Junkie," "You gon' always be an addict"—he kept that ammo loaded like it was his only way to feel powerful. I had walked away from that life, but he couldn't. Not because I was still stuck in it—but because he was stuck needing me to be. Some people can't handle your healing, so they try to drag your ass back into the dirt they met you in. Where they're most comfortable. Growth threatens people who ain't done none. I didn't ask to be seen as perfect—I just expected not to be punished for progress. I'm not always what I was—but he needed me to stay that way, so he could stay superior. Every time he opened his mouth, it was like my transformation meant nothing. Like my recovery was invisible unless I came with a receipt. But I knew who I was. I knew what I came out of. I knew how many nights I sweat that poison out my body, how many mornings I chose discipline over relapse. I didn't get clean for his applause—I got clean to live. So keep your labels. Keep your low blows. I'm not living in your remembrance—I'm walking in my redemption.

Once a cheater ain't always a cheater. Once a liar ain't always a liar. Once broken don't mean forever busted. That mindset don't build people—it builds prisons with no parole. If you keep locking folks inside who they used to be, don't act shocked when they stop trying to become anything else. People evolve. Not because it's easy, but because staying the same starts costing too damn much. Growth don't happen in judgment—it happens in grace. Not the kind that ignores what was done—but the kind that sees who they're becoming anyway. So before you toss out that tired-ass line, ask yourself—are you speaking truth, or just echoing your own unhealed hurt? Because I'm living proof—you can fall, and still rise. You could've once been a menace, and still mature. You could've once been evil, and still evolve. Don't roll your eyes at somebody else's second chance. Another man's mercy shouldn't make you bitter—it should make you nod in respect and bold enough to seek your own. If someone's redemption offends you, maybe it's 'cause you've never had the guts to earn your own.

Growth Affirmation: I will **GROW** out of the mindset
that says, "Once a cheater, always a cheater." The past
don't get to chain me—I've changed the locks.

ReTHINK this cliché: *"Boys will be boys"* is a dangerous excuse to dismiss bad behavior. It tells young men they can do dumb, destructive things and just call it growing pains. But when we let that slide, we raise men who don't take responsibility—we raise storms. That phrase gives immunity to immaturity. It protects predators, excuses aggression, and shrinks the standards for manhood. It's a hall pass for harm and a get-out-of-jail-free card for entitlement. You mean to tell me if someone told you your 10-year-old son was out here grabbing little girls' butts, your response would be, "Boys will be boys"? That ain't parenting—that's passive participation in their downfall. When boys grow up thinking their damage is excusable, they turn into men who cause casualties—then call it character. And the cycle keeps spinning: Broken boys become broken men who build broken homes. "Boys will be boys" ain't cute—it's cultural poison made to tolerate foolishness. That mentality teaches them that an apology is optional, consent is confusing, and chaos is just part of their charm. But there's nothing charming about a man who never outgrows his excuses. He only learns to excuse himself from accountability.

In prison, I saw many little boys in grown men's bodies. I watched men throw tantrums over phones, fight over snacks, and stab over shoes. They weren't men—they were boys in bigger clothes. And I realized something: We don't have a masculinity problem; we have a maturity problem. These weren't evil men. They were underdeveloped ones—never taught discipline, never forced to take accountability. They were emotionally stunted, because somewhere down the line, "Boys will be boys" let them off the hook. I saw men crumble when told no. These men spiraled when challenged. These men exploded when asked to take responsibility. That wasn't strength. That was arrested development in its rawest form. When boys ain't taught to master their emotions, they don't grow into men—they mutate into miscreants. And those miscreants don't just make noise—they make headlines, heartbreak, and havoc. The world had told them that their behavior was expected, excused, even natural. But nature ain't the problem—nurture is. And when nobody ever nurtures emotional growth, you don't get men—you get time bombs.

Let's rewrite the standard: Boys will be held accountable, taught boundaries, and raised into men who heal, not hurt. Don't hand out excuses and expect growth. Teach boys that emotions aren't weaknesses, that it's okay to cry, that control is strength, and that being a man ain't about dominance—it's about discipline. Stop telling boys to man up when no one ever taught them how to grow up. A real man doesn't just own his actions—he outgrows the version of himself that made excuses for them. Because if boys will be boys, then men will be made of the mess they were never forced to clean up. Men who take the weight off their women. Men who build homes. Men who face their reflection and fight the little boy still hiding in their pride. Boys who ain't taught to be men don't just grow up—they grow dangerous. You can let boys be boys if you want to. But don't be shocked when the next man down is you—taken out by a grown-ass boy who was never taught to man up.

Growth Affirmation: I will **GROW** out of the mindset that says, "Boys will be boys." I refuse to be a grown man with a little boy's habits and a grown woman's burden.

ReTHINK this cliché: "*It is what it is*" gets tossed around to claim that surrendering makes you wise. But more often than not, it ain't wisdom—it's emotional laziness. That phrase is a resignation letter to your own power. It tells life, "Do whatever—I'm done trying." It don't bring peace—it buries potential. It turns victims into volunteers. You don't rise from rock bottom by shrugging your shoulders—you rise by swinging your fists. "It is what it is" keeps you stuck in what was, too numb to push into what could be. It's the anthem of defeat, coated in fake depth. People cling to it because giving up don't hurt as bad as growing up. But say that line long enough, and life will keep slapping you with reruns. Acceptance without action is just quitting with a ton of makeup on. You say, "It is what it is," like that closes the case— but all it really does is close the casket on your comeback. You ain't accepting reality—you just scared of responsibility. And look, it's understandable if you've been hit with something like a terminal illness or a forced amputation, yeah—some things are unchangeable. That ain't weakness, that's reality. But most of what folks throw that line at ain't terminal—it's just tolerated.

"It is what it is" was my mantra. I slept in a garage. "It is what it is." I popped pills every day. "It is what it is." I scammed people out of money. "It is what it is." I'd stare at that wall, watching the clock bleed hours, thinking maybe if I said it enough times, I'd make peace with my pain. The more I said it, the more I sank. But the moment I stopped saying that and started saying, "It ain't how it has to be," things shifted. I realized I still had a say in how the story went, even if I couldn't erase the past chapters. The truth is, I was using that phrase to dodge my own responsibility—to excuse staying stuck instead of facing the fight to move forward. That weak-ass mindset kept me in mental handcuffs long after the physical ones came off. Just because something *is* doesn't mean it's how it *has to stay*. I wasn't chained to my choices—I was chained to the mindset that told me I couldn't make new ones.

Declaring that "It is what it is" is how people settle for suffering instead of stepping into change. Stop using that phrase like a peace treaty when it's really a prison. It ain't what it is—it's what you've chosen to let be. People out here settling like struggle is their soulmate. Settling for mistreatment like loyalty means staying where you're unloved. Settling for a job that drains your soul because you forgot you had options. Settling for disrespect like you forgot you were worth more. You gave up on your value, so now the world just reflects that. Don't be shocked when people step all over you—you the one laid out the welcome mat. You stopped asking for more. Stopped demanding better. Started calling your comfort zone "reality" like it was the only route. But reality didn't trap you—your approval of it did. And every time you say that weak-ass line—"It is what it is"—you give suffering squatters' rights. Because every time you say it, you turn temporary pain into a permanent tenant—who don't pay rent, but lives large in your head.

Growth Affirmation: I will **GROW** out of the mindset of "It is what it is." I will drive out "It is what it is" by saying, "Enough is enough."

ReTHINK this cliché: "*Let bygones be bygones*" is often said by people who don't want accountability—they just want you to shut up about the foul shit they did and let them off the hook. It's a lazy shortcut around the hard work of repair. People love to scream, "Let's move on," when it's their dirt that needs cleaning up. But buried pain doesn't just stay buried—it rots, it stinks, and sooner or later it crawls out to collect its debt. You can't sleep with someone's girl and think it's business as usual. You can't snake your boy for a couple dollars and expect loyalty to magically grow back. You can't bring harm to someone by spreading a false rumor and believe time's gon' wash that blood off your hands. You can't disrespect someone, rip their trust apart, and think a weak-ass apology erases the wreckage. Real healing doesn't start with silence—it starts when every filthy truth gets dragged into the light. Until you face the mess you made, there is no "moving on"—there's just a fake peace built on broken glass, and one day, everybody bleeds. "Letting it go" doesn't mean letting it slide.

A friend close to me who had betrayed me—by giving me counterfeit money for some drugs I had sold him—came back around acting like nothing happened. Like we were good. Because I never let him know about what he did, every conversation felt fake. Every laugh had a limp because we never dealt with the issue. We never talked about what happened. He cracked jokes like we were back to normal, but my heart wasn't laughing. I held my tongue, tried to be the "bigger person." But all I did was grow bitter in silence. I'd smile on the outside and scream inside because time didn't heal it—truth would've. I thought maturity meant moving on, but I learned that real maturity means being bold enough to pause and unpack the pain, not just pass off the same old bullshit. I carried that weight, hoping it would get lighter, but it just settled deeper. And every time I looked at him, I didn't see a person— I saw the resentment that sat in my heart.

Letting bygones be bygones only works when there's been acknowledgment, amends, and accountability. Otherwise, you're not letting go—you're letting the damage sit and rot. Real peace doesn't come from pretending pain didn't happen. It comes from processing it, talking about it, and building something stronger on the other side of it. If we don't face it, we repeat it. You can't rebuild trust on silence. If nobody talks about what happened, it festers underneath the fake peace. Don't let bygones be bygones. Let truth be told. Let wounds be cleaned instead of covered. Choose to attack it head-on—not hide behind it. And if that makes someone uncomfortable, good—because pain should never be comfortable. Growth doesn't come from brushing past betrayal—it comes from breaking it down brick by brick and deciding to rebuild or walk away. Don't hand out forgiveness just to keep the peace. Closure doesn't happen if someone chooses not to open their mouth and take accountability. Don't close the book or turn the page unless you know the chapter is done and there are no more lines to be read between. When someone ducks accountability with, "Let bygones be bygones," look them dead in the eye and say, "Cool. And how 'bout I let yo ass be gone too."

Growth Affirmation: I will **GROW** out of the
mindset that says, "Let bygones be bygones." Without
taking responsibility, nothing gets restored.

CHAPTER 2

MISS THE MESSAGE, REPEAT THE MISERY

"These ain't bedtime stories—they're alarms for the parts of you that've been rocked to sleep by lies."

DION PARKER

BEFORE YOU READ THIS CHAPTER:

This chapter ain't entertainment—it's confrontation.

Don't come in here looking for comfort. These stories weren't written to make you feel better—they were written to make you *see* better.

You survived the fire, but did you learn the lesson? Or did you just drag your pain into the next season and call it strength?

Pain that isn't processed turns into patterns. And if you don't pause to face the message, life will make you repeat the misery.

These stories are alarms—raw, loud, and necessary. If you read them right, they won't just remind you of what happened… they'll show you what to *do* with it.

So before you flip the page, ask yourself one question:

Are you ready to stop bleeding from what you never healed… or are you still addicted to surviving?

THINK about this story: Jennifer was a single mom doing everything she could to keep her son from becoming a statistic. He was knee-deep in the streets—dealing, reckless, spiraling toward a casket or a cage. Out of options, she called her five brothers. One said, "I got my own kids." Another said work came first. The third? "Ain't my damn responsibility." The fourth blamed his wife. The fifth told her straight up—she should've aborted him. Three days later, her son was gone. Dead. Same five brothers? She asked them to be pallbearers—and they agreed. At the funeral, she stepped to the mic, looked each of them in the face, and said, "It's a damn shame how y'all came to lift him up when he's gone—but none of y'all raggedy asses came to lift him up while he was still breathing."

I was that son. The one who had his mama living in fear, waiting for a knock at the door or a call from the jail—or worse, the morgue. I racked up mugshots, relapsed more times than I can count, and crashed in places built for broken people. Most gave up on me. Hell, I gave up on me. But my mom? She stayed in the ring even when I was fighting her love with my pain. She showed up. She prayed like her life—and mine—depended on it. Again. And again. She saw something in me that I didn't. She didn't let my mess scare her off. She didn't cosign my chaos, but she also didn't cancel me when the world turned its back. Without her, my name would be on a headstone instead of this book.

Moral to the Story: Jennifer's story and mine crack open a hard truth: Most people are more loyal to people's funerals than they are to people's future. They'll help carry your coffin but won't help carry your crisis. They'll help lower you in the ground but won't help lift you off the floor. People will show up in suits for your funeral but they won't show up in sweats for your fight. They dress for closure, not for rebirths. Don't bury someone when they're broken.

A burial is reserved for the dead, not the living. Too many treat pain like a coffin instead of a construction site. They confuse healing with hopelessness. People don't need you showing up when they're finally at rest in peace. They needed yo ass when they couldn't rest and were in pieces. They need presence while they're gasping for help. A letdown isn't a lost cause—it's often just a low battery nobody bothered to recharge. People can be powered back up, but not if everyone keeps pulling the damn plug too soon. Carrying a casket is easy. Carrying someone through their chaos? That's the real weight—and most can't handle it. People want to show up for the funeral because it's cleaner than the fight. Death makes them feel useful without getting their hands dirty. They wanna act like a hero when someone is in a hearse, but they didn't give a damn when they were hurting. Flowers don't erase the fact you went missing when they needed breath, not bouquets. Don't have the nerve to take flowers to a grave you helped dig by not doing shit—when you should've taken your ass over to their house or called to check on them when they were alive.

Growth Affirmation: I will **GROW** out of the mindset of cutting people off too soon. If I can't show up when someone's crying in their fight, I sure as hell won't show up crying at their funeral.

THINK about this story: Tianna was fed up—tired of being overlooked while lazy coworkers gossiped, scrolled their phones, vanished for long lunches, and somehow still got promoted while she sat in the same damn chair. Ready to quit, she stormed into her boss's office and complained about the actions of her coworkers, but he didn't respond. He just handed her a coffee cup filled to the brim and said, "Do me a favor before you go. Walk to the break room and get me a fresh cup. Don't spill a drop on your way there or on your way back." Tianna weaved through the office like it was a minefield, dodging distractions, watching every step, and made it back without losing a single drop. "Did you notice anyone slacking off this time?" he asked. "No," she said. "I was too focused on the coffee." "Exactly," he said, sliding a check for $1,000 across the desk for staying locked in. Tianna yelled, "You're giving me this for just that?" "Yes," said her boss. "Tianna, when you focus on your own path, you stop worrying about others—and the payoff always comes to the one who stops looking sideways and stays locked in on what the hell they're doing."

As militant as I was, I always complained about how someone else had it easier, or how the world was set up to hold me down. I blamed the system. Blamed society. Blamed the white man. Blamed anybody but me. But none of that changed where I was. All it did was lock me in a loop of anger and excuses while time kept moving without me. I kept pointing at the game instead of writing a playbook. It wasn't until I turned the spotlight inward that I realized I'd been tripping over my own complaints. Wasting energy watching others instead of investing it in my own grind. Real talk? I wasn't overlooked—I was outworked. And I did most of that damage to myself.

Moral to the Story: Like Tianna, I spent years running my mouth—mad that life wasn't fair, pissed I wasn't further along, too busy watching everybody else instead of working on myself. But here's the part I had to choke on: Life don't cut checks for crybabies—it pays executors. If you don't know why you losing, it's 'cause you too busy keeping score on other folks' wins instead of earning your own. You loud about what you deserve, but quiet on what you ain't done. That victim speech you keep rehearsing? Ain't nobody clapping for it. Complaining is a broke man's hustle—it pays in pity and bankrupts your progress. You mad at the world, but the world ain't even thinking about you. You pressed over the next man's plate while you get spoon-fed by the government and look at your cup as half empty. Every motivational quote and plate of food you post on social media could've been action taken. But, nah, you too loyal to your limitations. You care too much about showing the world what you eatin' on Facebook, and then you have the nerve to complain about how you're not being fed by the world. That's backwards as hell. Here's your wake-up call: Life don't pause 'cause you pouting. It don't slow down for your soft spots. It moves. With or without you. And if your life tastes bland? That's on you—you're the one who has been seasoning it with the same weak-ass excuses for years. You wanna win? Then shut your mouth, clock in, and make some noise with your execution. Watch less. Work more. Lock in like your life depends on it—'cause it do. Ain't nobody in your damn way but the crybaby you keep protecting in the mirror. Period.

Growth Affirmation: I will **GROW** out of the mindset that blames everybody else for where I'm not. Crying over crumbs ain't gettin' me nowhere—but making my own bread will.

THINK about this story: Two powerhouse preachers—Pastor Hawkins and Pastor Parker—led the two biggest churches in Ohio. Both were respected in public, but behind the curtains, Hawkins carried a grudge. He mocked Parker's preaching, called him fake, and tried to tear down his reputation piece by piece. Parker knew about the backbiting. He could've clapped back. He didn't. Before a major conference where Hawkins was being honored, a reporter asked Parker what he thought about Hawkins receiving the award. Without skipping a beat, Parker said, "It's well deserved. Pastor Hawkins has reached lives and uplifted his community." Later, Parker's assistant asked why he praised someone who clearly disrespected him. Pastor Parker's answer hit different: "The reporter didn't ask what Hawkins says about me—she asked what I had to say about him."

One of my childhood friends had a reputation for being with a lot of women. Guys admired him. Girls chased him. But his reputation flipped fast when someone bitter spread a rumor that he had AIDS. People distanced themselves overnight. Instead of chasing the lies, he kept it moving. He didn't fight back or beg people to believe him. He let silence speak. But me on the other hand—when a guy I thought I was cool with started calling me a pill head behind my back, I didn't stay quiet. I confronted him, and then I got grimy with it. I started running my mouth to anyone who'd listen, telling them how his own sister once told me that when they were little, he used to force her to have sex. While my boy played the silent game, I played dirty defense. I thought I was winning because I had louder ammo, but really all I did was throw myself in the mud with him. He walked away without a stain, and I walked away with blood on my hands that wasn't even mine to spill.

Moral to the Story: Unlike Pastor Parker, I wasn't going. You said something about me, I was getting right back with yo ass. But feeding drama makes it grow—starving it makes it die. Every time you react to a rumor, you hand it oxygen. Every time you respond to shade, you invite people to bask in a light they don't deserve. Keeping clowns relevant only turns your life into their circus. People who talk behind your back are already behind you, so turning around to deal with them just slows your ass down. You want to win? Starve the drama. Truth don't chase crowds—it outlasts noise. Silence is a sniper— it hits harder without making a scene. Power moves quietly, but its impact echoes. Strength ain't in swinging back—it's in walking through the fire without spitting fire of your own. Retaliation might feel good for a second, but it takes you out of the light by responding to people who throw shade. Some attacks are bait, and responding is how you get reeled into drama that was never yours to carry. The more you respond, the more you advertise your enemy. The more you retaliate, the more you recycle the chaos. The bigger they bark, the more they reveal how small they really are.

Stay focused on your mission—not their messiness. If you know who you are, you don't chase lies—you outlive them. Silence is power. It tells them, "You ain't even worth the words." Real strength is knowing that it's easy to tear down somebody's name, yet choosing to keep building theirs up. Ignore their ignorance. Keep stepping high when others keep stoopin' low.

Growth Affirmation: I will **GROW** out of the mindset of retaliation. When people talk behind my back, I will remember that that's a good place for them to be. Behind me.

It's no coincidence that the first letter in Unique is U.

THINK about this story: Daniel hated who he was. He wanted to be like his hustler G-dad, his athletic brother, and even his spoiled friend. Daniel spent so much time chasing their lives, he never lived his own. He prayed nonstop—"God, make me like them." Sadly, Daniel died in a car crash without his prayers ever being answered. In heaven, he faced God and said, "I prayed to be like my G-dad, my brother, my friend. You never answered. I was a faithful boy." God looked at him and said, "That's because I didn't know you were talking to me. I'm God—not Xerox. I don't make copies. I make only originals."

Growing up, I had copycat syndrome. I wanted the life I saw in front of me, even if it came with death or prison. Drug dealers had the money, my uncle had the women—and I wanted it all. I thought that made them men. I prayed to be like them. The problem? I was never built to be a rerun of someone else's life. The more I tried to imitate, the more I lost the real me. It took many years—and a lot of pain—to learn that chasing someone else's identity doesn't just delay your growth… it erases your voice. What makes you distinct is what makes you divine. Most people bury their potential playing dress-up in somebody else's reality. Real power comes from owning who you are without apology.

Moral to the Story: Daniel's story and mine come with a warning label: Every time you try to be them, you bury you. Your difference ain't a defect—it's your advantage. Trying to imitate someone else is like using their fingerprint to unlock your phone. No matter how hard you try, it won't open. Your potential only unlocks when you do what is programmed for you. But most people too busy pulling off identity theft—swiping pieces of folks they watch on stage, on screens, and on social media. You out here trying to wear their shoes, but you were called to walk a whole different path. The greatest loss isn't failing to be like them—it's never discovering the power in being you. While you're busy rehearsing their role, your spotlight fades. The world ain't hungry for another version of them—it's starving for the real version of you. You'll never show up fully until you stop shrinking yourself to fit somebody else's mold. That little butt you got? God gave you that. Damn that BBL— sit your real ass down with pride somewhere. That huge gap in your teeth? God gave you that. Damn getting veneers whiter than a toilet bowl—show the world the grin that survived your struggle. Those crooked toes you hide? God gave you those. Damn the shame—stop wearing sneakers on the beach. Put them flip-flops on and walk proudly. That big ass nose you hate? God gave you that. Damn the surgery—use it to sniff out the bullshit around you. Your flaws are your power. You weren't born to blend in. Every detail of your life, even the messy parts, is part of God's greater plan. The most dangerous thing you can do is spend your whole life auditioning for a role you were never meant to play. Don't waste your potential trying to be a parrot— wanting to repeat others. You were born an original painting—don't die trying to be a printed poster. The world don't need mass-produced people—it needs masterpieces. God made you an original—so why the hell you wanna die a remake? Unique starts with U for a reason.

Growth Affirmation: I will **GROW** out of the
mindset of trying to imitate others. I refuse to settle
as a second-rate version of someone else.

THINK about this story: Rah'ara and her son were in the grocery store, walking through the aisle no one likes to shop in—the damaged goods section. Crushed boxes. Dented cans. Bruised fruit. Everything that looked like it had been through something. Her son looked around and asked, "Mom, why are you buying from this aisle? Everything here looks messed up. Nobody else is even over here." She was unfazed. "That's the problem," she said. "Everybody wants pretty packaging. But truth is, the dents don't change the nutrition— just the perception. People walk right past it like it's worthless. But I've been buying from this aisle since you were a baby—and you've been eating good off it ever since and growing stronger."

After everything I've survived—addiction, prison time, being shot, hit by cars, stabbed, betrayed, and left behind—I used to look at myself like I belonged on the clearance rack. My body's marked up like a crime scene: Bullet wounds, knife scars, busted joints, stapled incisions. I spent years believing those marks made me less than, like I had too much damage for anyone to see value in me. Hell, I didn't even see it myself. I felt like I was too broken to be worth anything. But somewhere in that mess, I started seeing myself differently. I realized my scars didn't erase my worth—they proved it. They weren't signs of failure; they were proof I made it out. A snapshot shows your dents; the full picture shows your depth. While I was too busy focusing on the outside, I forgot the value that still remained on the inside: a good heart.

Moral to the Story: Like Rah'ara, that mother in the store, I had to stop looking at my damage like it disqualified me. Scars don't diminish value— they prove survival. But for whatever reason we let the bruises in our past convince us that we're no longer worth the shelf space. Truth is, what you've been through didn't cancel your worth—it confirmed it. A cellphone with a cracked screen still rings. A car with a cracked windshield still gets you home. A bruised apple still has nutrients. Damage don't mean done—it means durability. You out here hiding your story like it's shameful when it's the very thing that makes you strong. The world wants perfect packaging, but power comes from people who've been bruised, crushed, and still deliver. Don't let anyone—or anything—label you as less than because of what you've survived. You're not broken—you're battle-tested. When you think you're too far gone, then you've gone too far. Know that you're still worthy, despite what you've been through. You're not disqualified—you're exactly what someone else needs. There's value in your vulnerability, power in your pain, and beauty in your bruises. The ones who've been through the most and still show up? Those are the real difference-makers. You don't need to look new to be useful. You're not marked "Best if used by." Purpose don't expire just because your packaging took a hit. And the right ones? They'll see it. They won't run from your bruises—they'll reach for them first. Value ain't about condition—it's about purpose. And if you're still breathing, you've got both.

Growth Affirmation: I will **GROW** out of the mindset that my past damage erased my value. My scars are just reminders of where I've been, not indicators of where I'm going.

THINK about this story: Daryl lived a boring life but with good ideas. Every idea he had, he'd kill it before anyone else could. "Honey, I think I want to write a book," he'd say. "That's great," she'd respond. "Yeah, but I don't have the education." "Honey, I think I want to open a restaurant." "You'd be amazing at that." "Yeah, but it's too risky." He had ideas, but he also had excuses—and they always won. Eventually, he retired, took out a life insurance policy, wrote a will, and a year later he died. At his funeral, while looking over the casket, her son asked his mom, "Did Dad leave a will for when he died?" His mom whispered, "Yes son… but unfortunately, he never had the will to live."

Where I come from, making wills are rare, and so are fathers. Mine chose heroin over fatherhood. He died in a cold New York cell with nothing to his name. No assets. No legacy. Just pain left behind. Later, I repeated his pattern—addiction, prison, self-destruction. I wasn't living—I was existing with no aim, no ambition, no plan to make it out. The darkest moment came when I truly believed the world would be better off without me. That's how deep it got. But then I looked at my daughters and my grandchild. Was I really about to pass down the same silence, the same absence, the same void I had lived with? That was the moment I decided that my only impact wasn't going to be the ink on a will. Most people plan on leavin' behind physical property like a Bentley in a will—I'm leavin' behind intellectual property like a book, powered by the will I had to survive. A Bentley may impress the eyes and then depreciate, but my book will empower forever and appreciate in value every time it's read.

Moral to the Story: Just like Daryl and what I almost did, too many people bury their ambition long before they bury their body. Dreams get treated like hobbies instead of lifelines. But your will ain't some fancy paperwork for after you're gone—it's the grind, the hunger, the fire that proves you ever showed up at all. A silent life full of fear and excuses ain't living—it's a slow funeral. Without will, you ain't alive… just awake. And sadly, most folks document a will for death but never give people a reason to document how they had the will to live. They pass down houses but not hope. Debt but not drive. Furniture but not fire. Life insurance might cover the funeral, but it'll never cover the life you buried on this earth by committing dream-suicide. No attorney on earth can draft a legacy for someone who never lived with one. So break the cycle. Defy the patterns. Be bold on purpose. Live so loud with meaning that your kids don't just inherit your assets—they inherit your ambition. If you're gon' leave anything behind, let it be the formula for defying the odds. Let it be your will to rise, to fight, to rewrite what was handed to you. A last will and testament don't mean shit if you never had the will to live or gave anybody anything worth testifying about. The worst tragedy ain't dying without a will—it's dying without ever having a will to live.

Growth Affirmation: I will **GROW** by building a life worth inheriting, not just leaving an inheritance. A will ain't just paperwork for death; it's the drive that keeps me alive till death.

THINK about this story: The Bloods and Crips had war in their DNA—they were rival gangs locked in a constant battle for the streets of California. One day, the Bloods challenged the Crips to a showdown on neutral turf. When the smoke cleared, all the Bloods were wiped out—except one, who was captured. The captured Blood was dragged in front of the Crips' leader. "OG, how should we kill him?" the soldier asked. "Let him choose his death," the OG said coldly. "You can either shoot yourself with this gun… or walk through that door behind you marked 'UNKNOWN FEARS.'" Without thinking twice, the Blood took the gun and killed himself. The soldier stared at the door. "What was behind it, OG?" he asked. The leader smirked. "Freedom. But most people would rather die than face their fears of the unknown."

Pills weren't my escape—they were my captors. They held me like rival soldiers who had me cornered, gun to my head, daring me to choose. Every swallow was me pulling the trigger on myself, thinking I was buying peace, when really I was surrendering freedom. Pills didn't just numb my pain—they declared war on my soul, and for years I laid down and let them win. They kicked my ass, chained my will, and turned me into their prisoner. And then came the door. A friend offered to send me to rehab on his dime. All I had to do was walk through it. But I refused. Why? Because fear had me hostage. Not fear of dying—I'd already been dancing with that. It was the fear of living. Fear of feeling the pain I'd buried. Fear of losing the one comfort I thought I could count on. So like that captured soldier, I picked the bullet I knew instead of the freedom I couldn't see. I chose the poison because it was familiar, even though it was killing me. That's the trick of fear—it convinces you the cage is safer than the open road. One day, though, I hit bottom so hard I couldn't stay down. Shaking, broken, half-dead, I crawled to that door. And when I finally walked through, I realized freedom was never locked—it was waiting on me the whole time.

Moral to the Story: Like that Blood chose a bullet over the unknown, I used to choose destruction over deliverance. That's how fear works—it locks you in a room with no bars and dares you to escape, threatening you with, "I wish yo ass would. You bet not move." It whispers lies until you believe pain is permanent and healing is hopeless. The truth? Most people ain't stuck because there's no exit—they're stuck because they too scared to reach for the doorknob. That door marked "Unknown"? That's not your enemy. That's your escape. Fear is slick—it dresses comfort in chains and makes freedom look like a setup. It don't need a cage; it just needs your consent. And you just hand it the keys, roll out the red carpet, and decorate the cell like it's home. Every excuse you make? Fear. Every delay? Fear. Every "maybe later" you hide behind? Fear. You've been calling it protection, but it's just polished paralysis. You keep praying for change while ignoring the door. You keep saying you want more, but you won't walk through what scares the hell outta you. The battle ain't on the outside—it's in your head. The monster ain't real. But the fear you feed is. So let me ask you straight: What are you afraid of? Are you scared of what's behind the door—or scared you might actually become who you were always meant to be if you walk through it?

Growth Affirmation: I will **GROW** out of the mindset of fear. Fear is a master illusionist—it makes freedom look fatal and captivity feel comfortable. It's done tricking me.

THINK about this story: Dionne had dreams of becoming an Olympic swimmer—but no clear path on how to succeed at it. Everyone around her had advice. Her dad said, "Go to college," but Dionne knew that was a damn lie—her dad finished college and still worked at KFC. Her brother said, "Practice every day," but Dionne knew her brother trained seven days a week and still rode the bench. Frustrated, Dionne hit the gym to clear her head. That's where she met Vince. Seeing the dismay in Dionne's face, Vince asked what was weighing on her. Dionne vented—she didn't know how to succeed at being an Olympic swimmer. Vince told her to follow him to the pool. Moments later, Dionne was under the water, kicking and fighting for breath as Vince held her down. When she finally broke free, furious and gasping, she yelled, "You could've killed me!" Vince stared back and said, "Now you know what it takes, Dionne. When you want to succeed as badly as you want air, you won't be denied. You'll kick and fight like hell to get to the top."

Success was never something I feared—I chased it. I always had a hustle. Whether it was selling drugs, running a prison commissary, flipping gear, running a tire shop, or selling merch out the trunk, I knew how to get to a dollar. Even while racking up cases and catching time, I stayed grinding. I graduated high school and earned college credits from Penn State—short for penitentiary, not university. Still, I kept pushing. I became a certified personal trainer to help build people physically—and a life coach to help strengthen them mentally. Now I'm an author using my pain as a platform. I've taken losses. I've tasted quick wins. But none of it came easy, and none of it came from just being "smart." What moved the needle wasn't IQ—it was "I will." It was the decision to keep showing up, even when everything around me screamed, *Quit.* I wasn't polished—I was painstakingly relentless.

Moral to the Story: Like Dionne, I had to learn the hard way—success don't come from theory, it comes from teeth-gritted, chest-burning, lungs-collapsing drive. I knew hustlers who couldn't spell "success" but lived in penthouses. Their will crushed every weakness. Truth is, you don't need to be brilliant—you need to be relentless. You don't need to be Hooked on Phonics, just hooked on your dream. It ain't academics that equals success—it's ambition. You can have the highest IQ in the room and still lose to the one who refuses to tap out. Saying you gotta be smart to win is like saying a dog needs a degree to win a dogfight—it just needs to want to survive. The ones who rise ain't always the most gifted—they're the most hardheaded when failure comes swinging. Success don't reward pretty plans—it rewards bloody, sleepless hustle. Seventeen-hour shifts. No vacations. Just grind, grit, and the guts to keep going when everybody else quits. Every excuse you make is just hesitation with a fresh coat of logic. And every time you justify quitting, you're writing your legacy in invisible ink. Comfort is the devil in disguise. Hesitation is the hitman. And success? It's only faithful to the ones who bleed for it. It ain't about how much you know—it's about how bad you want it when you know nothing else is promised. Intelligence don't guarantee shit. But desperation? That's the *mf* that don't give a fuck—one that'll drag you through hell, break its chains, and kick a steel door off the goddamn hinges just to taste tomorrow.

Growth Affirmation: I will **GROW** out of the mindset
that says success is reserved for the educated—grind
beats grades when hunger's in the driver's seat.

THINK about this story: DJ lived for the Boys and Girls Club. It was his escape after school—the one place he could laugh, play, and just be a kid. But recently that walk became a nightmare. A new neighbor had a mean dog that chased him every time he tried to pass. Fear took over. DJ stopped going, started making excuses, and let that barking dog own his afternoons. One day, sick of missing out, he finally decided to face it. He picked up a heavy rock, stuffed it in his pocket, and made the walk. Just like clockwork, the dog came charging—barking, wild, ready to scare. But DJ didn't run this time. He stood firm, cocked his arm back like he was about to launch the rock—and that's when he saw it. The dog had no teeth.

I remember a similar dog at work—only this one walked on two legs. A loudmouth with fake bravado. Every day he flexed like he ran the building. Talked like a boss, walked like a bully, but never backed up anything. Fed up with him running his mouth, I stepped to him and told him we could take it outside if he had something real to say. Out of anger, I yelled, "Your momma should've swallowed yo dumb-ass." He folded on the spot and ran to management. That's when I knew—he was just noise. All bark, no bite. He moved like a pit bull but panicked like a poodle. Everything about him screamed tough, but when the pressure showed up, he got the hell out of there. He better have run to HR, because I was about to send his ass to the ER. If you don't learn nothing from this story, learn this: Folks with no backbone always need words to back them up.

Moral to the Story: The toothless dog and that loudmouth at work had the same infection—diarrhea of the mouth. The ones who bark the loudest are usually the quickest to bitch up when it's time to bite. Their bark ain't strength—it's broken confidence on full blast. Noise is their armor—a hollow sound meant to distract you from the fact they're soft as Charmin. They bark not 'cause they're dangerous, but 'cause they're scared you'll get close enough to see they can't bite—and that exposes their hoe card. All that yapping? That's insecurity in surround sound. Diarrhea of the mouth comes from a steady diet of fear and ego—people talk heavy to cover up how hollow they really are. It's overcompensation for what they ain't got inside—heart. Tough talk is cheap when it can't survive eye contact. If barking made you a threat, every keyboard thug with Wi-Fi would be a mob boss. But real danger don't talk—it don't need to. It just shows up and shut shit down. Barking ain't power—it's panic. Car alarms go off all day, but nobody runs. Same with loudmouths. They want attention, not confrontation. So the next time somebody talks like they built for war, don't jump. Just stare 'em down like DJ did—and watch how fast they ass take flight and get the hell outta there when they realize you ain't scared of sound effects. 'Cause the ones who talk the hardest? Usually are the softest.

Growth Affirmation: I will **GROW** out of the mindset of fearing people who bark. I will remember that if they gotta announce it, they ain't about it.

THINK about this story: For his daughter Tyler's sixteenth birthday, a widowed father promised to take her to the wealthiest place in the world. She lit up, thinking it was the trip of a lifetime. "Is it Africa? Where the diamonds are? Or Dubai—because of all the oil?" she asked eagerly. They drove in silence until he pulled into a quiet cemetery. She looked confused. "Dad? Are we visiting Mom?" He stepped out slowly, eyes fixed on a familiar headstone. "Yes, baby. We're going to see your mother." Tyler smiled softly. "That's sweet, Dad, to go visit Mom before we leave, but what about the richest place in the world?" He looked around, voice low but sharp. "You're standing in it. This ground is full of songs that were never sung. Books never written. Ideas never built. People who died with their purpose still inside them. Like your mom—the novel she talked about for years? She never got around to it. Now it's in the dirt with her. The richest place ain't full of money—it's full of untapped potential."

There was a point when I was on the floor—literally and mentally. Dope sick, desperate, and broke. I'd already pawned everything of value I owned, which wasn't much. I had nothing left but a hammer and a plan. So I crushed Tylenol, mixed it with baking soda and sleep medicine, bagged it like it was fire, and sold it to junkies too green to know better. From their funds, I went to buy real pills. Even though that was a twisted way of thinking outside the box, I was dead serious about surviving. I told myself it was chess, but the truth was I was checkmating my own future. I was starving for a high, but what really got high was my capacity to survive by any means. And that same ruthless hunger—the willingness to find a way even when nothing made sense—that's what I tapped into when it came time to finish this book. Different addiction, same desperation. I just had to channel it toward something worth dying for. I was cognizant that creativity dies in coffins—so I had to use it before I was in one.

Moral to the Story: That mother in the grave who never wrote her book? She didn't think outside the box. That was almost me. What about you? Are you waiting for everything to fall into place? Newsflash: It never will. If you got a dream, you better get creative. Ain't no point in saving your ideas— pine boxes don't honor brainstorms. Playing it safe ain't courage—it's costly. The price? Legacy. And you can't afford that. A dream buried in fear is no different than a body buried in dirt—both are silent, still, and forgotten. You breathing, but your gift? That's already in a casket. And why? Fear? Doubt? Waiting on validation from people who ain't even validated themselves? The graveyard don't just hold the dead—it holds the unused potential. It's packed with masterpieces that never made it out the mind. World-changers who stayed quiet. Innovators who kept hesitating. Legends who got lazy. Impact don't happen by accident—it happens when you empty yourself out on purpose. You think you got time, but time don't think about you. Every day you wait is another step closer to the cemetery—with your best work still locked inside you. Holding on to your dream till death is like owning a brand-new iPhone and only using it as a flashlight. There is so much inside you. Don't let the dirt silence what you were born to say. Die empty. Leave proof that you were here. That you gave it your all. That you ripped the lid off the box and let your gift disrupt, uplift, and outlive you. You were never supposed to leave this earth on "maybe." A wasted gift is a caged bird—it had wings, but not the freedom to fly. Dreams don't die in cemeteries because they had to. They die because their owners never had the guts to set them free. The real cemetery ain't just in the ground—it's in the mind that buries its own vision alive. Don't let your head be the gravesite of your dream.

Growth Affirmation: I will **GROW** out of the mindset
that my gift can wait. I will dream *outside* the *box* now,
before the *pine box* locks every dream inside me forever.

THINK about this story: On Halloween night, a local church hosted "Hallelujah Night"—a wholesome alternative with candy, gospel, and truth louder than any costume. Each kid left with a bag of sweets, and a peppermint stamped "Sweet Jesus" and "John 3:16." But the real test didn't come in sugar or scripture—it came through the doors. A man dressed as the devil stormed in, what looked like a bomb strapped to his chest. "If you love Jesus," he shouted, "you're about to die!" The sanctuary exploded in panic. People screamed. Ran. Tripped over pews and others to get out. But one woman didn't move. Still. Calm. Unshaken. "Didn't you hear me?" he yelled. "I heard you," she said. "And I still love Jesus. Ain't nothing changing that." The man ripped off the mask, unstrapped the fake bomb, and smiled. "Let's have church," he said. "I'd rather worship with one real Christian than a hundred fakes."

My first marriage? Straight-up performance. I was headed to prison and thought a wedding ring would make me look like a man with structure. She got a ring that sparkled, but the shine was all show—cubic zirconia from a mall kiosk. She never questioned it, because the amount of money I made off selling drugs justified the purchase. She promised to wait for me. Claimed that no other man was worth her time. That's all I needed to hear. That she would hold me down. Once I got locked up, the truth unraveled. Three months in, she ghosted me. I've always believed she tried to pawn the ring and found out what I already knew—it was fugazi. Not the ring. Not the bond. Not her loyalty. That ring wasn't built for pressure, and neither was she. The shine fooled us both, but it was counterfeit from the jump. That whole situation taught me something the streets, the cell, and the pain couldn't—even if it looks solid, that don't mean it won't snap under pressure.

Moral to the Story: Both the panicked churchgoers and that fake ring cracked under pressure. Fake people are like cheap jewelry—they look good until they turn on you. *Like four quarters, they'll change for a dollar.* Your circle is only as strong as the people you let in, and you can't build something real with those who'll crumble when pressure hits. Gold don't get tested in sunlight—it gets refined in fire. So don't be fooled by sparkle. A cubic zirconia flashes just like a diamond… right up until life applies pressure. Then it cracks. Then it fades. Then it shows you the truth. Don't mistake temporary shine for lasting value, because appearances can deceive even the sharpest eyes. Pressure is life's diamond tester—it don't lie. It exposes what's real and what's fake. Real ones don't run when the storm hits—they stand. They hold it down. They don't just shine with you in public—they glow with you in the dark too. Loyalty ain't loud, but it shows up when everything else falls apart. Let your circle of friends be so solid that you'll never have to question if they're real or fake. The quality of your life is a reflection of the quality of your circle. Real recognizes real, and pressure will make sure of it. Wearing cubic zirconia is okay—having them as friends ain't.

Growth Affirmation: I will **GROW** out of allowing unproven people into my circle. I now realize that pressure separates the priceless from the worthless.

THINK about this story: Sister Victoria had been at the same church for 22 years—faithful, present, and proud of it. But lately, she'd grown irritated. "Every week, it's the same sermon," she thought. "I need something fresh." Before jumping ship to a new church, she decided to speak with her pastor out of respect. "Pastor White," she said, "I've decided to attend From the Heart Church to hear fresh preaching every week. It's been six weeks now, and I'm *seeing* that you're *saying* the same message." Pastor White looked her in the eye and calmly said, "Well, Sister Victoria… when I start *seeing* the message, I'll stop *saying* it."

My first time in rehab, I noticed a trend. After the usual introductions, it was clear this wasn't a lot of guys' first rodeo—second, third, sometimes even their eighth. No exaggeration. But who was I to judge? I had my own VIP pass to the prison system's revolving door. People swore rehab was a joke, a waste of time. And every complaint was met with the same tired-ass response from counselors: "Trust the process. It works if you work it." The truth? They were right. But nobody was really working it. My dumb-ass repeated the process because I didn't apply what I heard or read. Standing in a library doesn't make you smart, and sitting in a church doesn't make you obedient. Rehab taught me that proximity to wisdom doesn't create transformation—action does. Stop bragging about how much you know and start proving how much you can apply. The world don't pay for potential; it pays for proof. Don't just keep learning workouts—go fucken exercise. Don't just keep copying quotes—live them the hell out. Information don't mean shit if it never turns into transformation.

Moral to the Story: Sister Victoria and I both heard the information, but hearing isn't learning—application is. Think about how much info you've consumed versus how much you've actually used. Information is everywhere—you're drowning in it. Quotes on your timeline, sermons on YouTube, motivational reels on TikTok. But information supplied without application is intellectual constipation. You keep stuffing yourself with words, but nothing's moving through you, and that blockage is stunting your growth. Don't brag about being "well-informed" if your life stays untransformed. A battery-operated game is useless if the batteries are never put in it, and the same goes for the lessons you receive in life. You can be surrounded by power and still walk around powerless if you never activate what's been given to you. Some folks don't need a new message—they need to stop sitting on the one they've already heard. Most people don't need deeper sermons, they need deeper obedience. What good is eating if you never digest? What good is hearing wisdom if it never hits your walk? You keep begging for a new word, when the last one still ain't walked out in your life. You're not underfed—you're underapplied. Exposure ain't execution. Just because it hit your ears don't mean it activates your body. Knowing where the medicine is don't cure you—taking it does. You've been taught enough to evolve, but you ain't moved. And until you do, you will stay in your misery and the same lessons will keep circling back. The truth don't need to switch up—your response does. Until your feet follow what your ears heard, you're not being discipled—you're being entertained. Growth ain't measured by how many notes you take, but how many steps you make from the notes. Because you don't grow by what you know—you grow by what you do with what you know.

Growth Affirmation: I will **GROW** out of simply listening and start living out what I've learned, turning information into transformation every day.

CHAPTER 3

UNFILTERED. UNAPOLOGETIC. UNCOMFORTABLE. WORDS WITH BRASS KNUCKLES.

*"This struggle? It's your
origin story, not your obituary."*

DION PARKER

BEFORE YOU READ THIS CHAPTER:

This chapter don't come with sugar, sympathy, or spiritual safety nets.

These are the kind of words that swing wild and hit real. And yeah—they'll probably make you uncomfortable. But that's the point. Too many people been pampered into paralysis. You've been motivated, inspired, hyped up, and yet you're still stuck. Why?

Because nobody told you the truth without putting makeup on it. These quotes weren't written to coddle—they were written to confront. To slap. To sting. To wake you the hell up from the dead state you're in and can't seem to escape. Since you made it to this page, warning: Going beyond this point will require you to have on steel-toe shoes—because from here on out, the words ain't walking on eggshells; they're stomping on toes. Damn stepping on 'em. If you ain't ready for any real growth, you bet not dare turn this page—'cause all you gon' do is get your little feelings hurt.

Take this day to **THINK** about why you keep putting up with what you say you're sick and tired of. We've all said it: "I'm done." "I can't do this anymore." "I'm tired of this." "I'm sick of you." And in the heat of the moment, we mean it. But that phrase—"sick and tired"—ain't as strong as it sounds. It feels like a breaking point, but it's really just an emotional façade that tricks you into thinking you're tough—when you're really weak as hell. Deep down, you know you're gon' crawl your soft ass right back to what you swore you were so sick and tired of. Think about it: When you're sick, you take something for it. You treat it. You rest. Then what? You get better. It passes. You're no longer sick. Same thing with being tired. You nap. Recharge. Then what? You're not tired anymore. "Sick and tired" is a phase—not a finish line. It fades, and what fades always returns. That's why people go back. That's why habits come back. Because "sick and tired" is a complaint. Hating it—that's a commitment. When you hate something, you don't treat it. You kill it. You cut it off. You wash your hands of it. That's the difference. A boomerang always comes back—unless you break it before you throw it. And most people just keep throwing theirs with frustration instead of breaking ties.

Too many times I've said, "I'm sick of living like this." Sick of popping pills. Sick of chasing a high that leaves me low. Tired of waking up not knowing what I said, what I did, or where I was. Tired of overdosing. Tired of losing jobs. Tired of losing people. Sick of hurting myself just to feel nothing. And I meant it every time. But I kept going back. I detoxed and relapsed. Prayed and still used. I said I was done, but kept the back door cracked—just in case. Why? Because I didn't hate it yet. I feared it. I regretted it. But I didn't despise it. And as long as I didn't hate it, I still gave it access. I still flirted with what I swore was destroying me. Real change didn't come until I was disgusted by it. Until I saw it for what it was—not a coping mechanism, not an escape, but a slow, daily death. That's when I stopped throwing the boomerang and started breaking it. That's when I stopped saying, "I'm sick and tired," and started living like I hated it.

Hate ain't always hell—it can be your healing. Stop believing the lie that hate is a bad word. Hate is what seals the exit. It don't leave doors cracked. It don't miss what was killing it. Hate ain't about bitterness—it's about boundaries. When you finally hate something for what it's done to you, you don't touch it, taste it, or tolerate it. You shut it down completely. Don't think I'm trippin'—look at it. When you hate somebody, you don't just ignore their calls—you block their number. Their voice irritates you, their presence makes your skin crawl. You don't even wanna fuck wit 'em. Hell, you even convince others to avoid them. That's the same energy you gotta give to that habit, that person, that poison you keep running back to. Hate burns the bridge, boards up the path, and throws away the map. It makes sure there's no way back, even if your weakness tries to retrace the steps. So if you keep catching what you thought you threw away, maybe it's because you never broke it. Maybe it's because you only complained about it but never cut it off. You can't be free from what you still flirt with. You won't kill the craving if you keep breaking bread with it. You sick of him? You tired of her? You done with it? No, you ain't—or else your sick and tired-ass wouldn't still be puttin' up wit it.

Growth Affirmation: I will **GROW** out of the mindset that being sick and tired is enough to change. Real change begins when I hate what's been holding me back.

Take this day to **THINK** about how weak your excuses sound when your "why" ain't strong enough to shut them up. Motivation comes from within, and if you don't have anything to get you moving, that's sad. You keep chasing motivation—videos, quotes, speeches, life coaches—but hype don't move your feet, purpose does. Books and people can inspire you, but they can't motivate you. If your grind depends on someone yelling at you or posting quotes on your feed, what happens when they go silent? If your trainer dies, are you quitting on your health too? Hell no. That's why your "why" can't be a person—it's gotta be a principle. Something deeper. Something permanent. Your "why" is your health. Your children. Your peace. Your God. You ever seen a car stuck in a ditch? That's your life without a "why"—spinning your wheels, burning gas, going no damn where while everyone else passes you by. Your "why" don't make things optional—hell, it's your oxygen. It's what you live and breathe for. When your "why" becomes nonnegotiable, your grind becomes automatic. If your "why" don't set you on fire, it'll never be strong enough to pull you outta hell.

Mine wasn't just one "why"—it was a squad of reasons kicking down my excuses. First, my health. Living with a bad heart, every pill I popped felt like Russian roulette. I wasn't just numbing pain—I was betting against my own life. Then came my mother. She needed me, and I knew I couldn't keep showing up halfway. You can't protect someone else if you keep self-destructing. Then came the thought of not walking my daughters down the aisle. That vision haunted me. The thought of another man doing it because I overdosed or dropped dead? Unacceptable. I had to grow up to see them grow old. That's when my "why" stopped being a feel-good phrase—it became a damn bouncer. My "why" started checking excuses at the door and silencing distractions on sight. If it didn't match my purpose, it didn't get in. I wasn't just quitting drugs—I was guarding my legacy. To marry off my daughters, I had to divorce my addiction.

A strong "why" don't just wake you up—it makes sleep feel like sabotage. Your "why" ain't just motivation—it's muscle. It shapes everything. Who you let around you? That's your "who." If they don't fuel your purpose, they're in the way. What you do daily? That's your "what." If it don't build you, it's breaking you. Where you go, when you move, how you respond—every single part of your life bows down to your "why." If your schedule's full of things that drain you, your "why" ain't strong enough to check them. If you're still tolerating mediocrity, your "why" hasn't slapped your ass hard enough yet. But when it finally hits, it changes everything. No more asking, "Can I do this?"—you just do it. Because now every move, every minute, every mile is tied to something bigger than your comfort. Your "why" becomes the gatekeeper of your grind. Because when your purpose starts swinging harder than your problems, there's no more hype needed—you won't need to be motivated, you'll *be* the damn motivation.

Growth Affirmation: I will **GROW** out of the mindset that motivation is enough—my "why" is the fire that makes quitting feel like betrayal.

Take this day to **THINK** about how much attention you give to your phone and not your life. People will run around like a chicken with its head cut off trying to find a charger, asking everyone they see, "What kind of phone you got?" "You got your charger?" But what does that say about us? It shows we give our phones the attention we should be giving to our lives. We sprint to save our phones but won't run the marathon required to be great. We lose our rabbit-ass minds at 10% on a screen but stay calm while our purpose remains at 2%. How insane is that? Don't let your battery bars get more attention than you raising your personal bars. Don't save your phone from dying while leaving your spirit and life dead. If only we'd scramble this hard to connect with our own purpose. If you spend your energy worrying about your device's charge more than your own growth, you got your priorities fucked up. Your life needs a charger too, but too often you're fine letting it drain and won't dare to ask someone to help you recharge it as you would your phone.

During my struggle with addiction, I was obsessed with keeping my phone charged. I was living in my building's garage, crashing in a busted-down car, and when that battery icon dipped low, panic set in. I'd make up lies to tenants just to get access to an outlet, begging for a little juice to keep my lifeline alive. I'd keep my phone off for hours to stretch a few percent, dim the screen, anything to save that last bit of power—because if my phone died, my connection to my supplier died with it. It wasn't just about a phone— it was about feeding a habit that was slowly killing me. And the wild part? I fought harder to keep that phone on than I did to keep myself alive. Later, the irony hit me like a ton of bricks: I scrambled to save a device from dying while letting my own life drain to nothing. Now every time I plug in my phone, I ask myself: *"Am I charging my life with the same urgency, or am I still fading while distractions thrive?"* Because if you ain't actively recharging your life, it's only a matter of time before you're empty on the inside, even if your phone stays fully charged.

People will sprint to charge a dying phone, but won't lift a finger to charge a dying life. Really? Why are you okay with letting your job drain you, your vices drain you, and people drain you—but won't fight to unplug from them and plug into the Source of life Himself—God? Life is no different than that phone you panic over when the battery's dying. You treat a low battery like an emergency but treat a low purpose like it's normal. Every day you stay disconnected from your purpose is another step closer to shutting down completely. If you find yourself drained, it's time to treat your growth and well-being with the same urgency as saving your devices. Plug into purpose—prayer, discipline, vision, and hustle—and watch your spirit charge back up. And before you power down at night, make damn sure you've set a plan to power up tomorrow. Life requires constant connection. Stop leaving your soul on Low Power Mode. You'll charge your phone to get through the day—so why won't you charge your spirit to get through life? A dead battery can inconvenience you, but a dead spirit will destroy you. 'Cause 100% on your screen don't mean shit if your soul's walking around on 1%.

Growth Affirmation: I will **GROW** out of the habit of keeping my phone charged while letting my purpose fade. My soul deserves the same power I give my phone.

Take this day to **THINK** about why you can't make something happen out of all that's happened to you. You've been molested. Neglected. Beaten. Deceived. Rejected. Left to raise yourself in a house full of people who got high and ran it like a hoe house. You cried. You screamed. You carried secrets that shattered you. And now, all these years later, you still telling the same sad ass story with the same sad ass tears, expecting different results. You got a right to be hurt—but you don't got the right to build your identity around it. You ain't the only one who been through hell, but if you don't do something with that hell, it'll end up burying you. Life ain't fair—never was and never will be. It handpicked you to go through what you went through. But you don't honor your pain by preserving it. You honor it by producing from it. Your ancestors—especially those of African American heritage—didn't just survive pain—they turned it into power. While you out here trapped in a cycle of complaining, they were out there converting scraps into survival. They didn't have degrees, therapists, or time to feel sorry for themselves. What they had was fire. So don't tell me you carry their strength if you won't carry their struggle. You weren't just born from pain—you were born from perseverance. Act like it, damn it.

Life hit me with the whole hell package—poverty, pain, prison, and pills. No dad. No discipline. Just dysfunction. I was addicted, abandoned, arrested, and ambushed by my own actions. I got shot, set up, sold out, and shackled. My life was one long rap sheet of recklessness. But I learned to turn my messes into messages, my scars into stories, and my pain into power. Life happened to me in the form of addiction—but now I use my recovery to help others heal. Life happened to me when bullets tore through my body—but now my survival is proof that purpose still breathes through pain. Life happened through fatherlessness—but I became the father I never had. Life happened in prison—but that's where I fell in love with fitness, and that fire turned me into a trainer. And just when I thought I'd lost it all, I found my voice. I went from being an inmate to being an impact—standing in the same prison that once held me captive, preaching purpose to the same kind of men I used to run with. And they gave me a standing ovation. Not because I was perfect, but because I was proof. Proof that out of everything that's happened to you—something greater can still happen through you. What you're reading is a scrapbook of the scraps life gave me—full of pictures that ain't pretty, but every one of 'em was necessary to frame the man I am.

Life's challenges are like the scraps that were thrown to enslaved African Americans—undesirable cuts of meat meant to humiliate, not nourish. But they flipped it. Took pig feet, neck bones, intestines—turned what was supposed to be nasty into nourishment. They turned struggle into soul food. You turned yours into sob stories. They had chains—you got choices. Stop holding press conferences about your pain and start producing from it. You've talked enough. You've cried enough. Now you owe it to yourself to do something with it. You been abused? Now what? You been betrayed? Now what? You been raped? Now what? Pain don't get the last word unless you let it. Turn your tragedies into triumphs. You're not powerless—you're just undisciplined. You wanna be honored like your ancestors? Then act like you've inherited their spirit, not just their pain. You too can make a feast from the scraps of your life. They made a feast outta famine. You making excuses outta fear. They made everything with nothing. You doing nothing with everything. They had nothing and made something happen. You have more and make less happen. They made history out of hardship while you out here making excuses—with YouTube University, Google, and ChatGPT in your fucken back pocket.

Growth Affirmation: I will **GROW** out of treating my history like a handicap—what I've been through should build me, not bury me. Shame on me if I can't make more when my ancestors had less.

Take this day to **THINK** about why you keep holding tight to people who keep holding you back. You say you're ready to soar, but you won't cut loose from the ones content with crawling. Some folks don't hate you—they just hate how far you're willing to go without them. They call it loyalty, but it's really limitation that looks like friendship. You can't elevate while staying attached to those who fear altitude. And let's keep it real, some of the ones you're calling support systems are nothing but anchors. They only clap when you stay on their level. The moment you try to rise, they roll their eyes, crack jokes, and question your ambition. You can't build with people who panic every time you dream past their ceiling. You ain't leaving them behind—they just never planned on leaving the ground. Truth is, there are times when elevation demands isolation. You have to be willing to do it alone, even if no one wants to go along. It's okay to outgrow their level. Not because you're better—but because their sorry asses refuse to rise. Some people never had the lungs for high altitudes in the first place—they start hyperventilating the moment you take off.

Michael Jackson, my favorite musician, lived this truth. I "Remember the Time"—no pun intended—when my mother took my sister and me to see the Jackson 5. From that day on, I studied his life. When Michael first tried to join the group, his own brothers mocked him, saying he sounded like a girl. Even after proving himself, the doubt didn't stop. Michael had a dream of becoming a solo artist. His brothers said he'd fail—that nobody wanted just one Jackson. But Michael refused to let their vision dictate his future. I believe his song titles were born from the words he fired back at his brothers. I imagine him telling them this: "The Way You Make Me Feel" is really turning me off. Y'all living too much "Off the Wall," always "Wanna Be Startin' Somethin'," making my life a "Thriller," so I'm telling y'all to "Beat It." Michael took a look at the "Man in the Mirror" and went after his dream. When he finally succeeded, I pictured him at Neverland Ranch, thinking, "I'm Bad," as he "Remember[ed] the Time" his brothers doubted him. He didn't need their permission to rise—he needed space. And when he went solo, he didn't just walk into history—he moonwalked past every limit they put on him.

Altitude strips off everything—and everyone—that can't handle the pressure. It's like rocket boosters: They're designed to help a rocket launch, but once it reaches a certain height, the boosters fall away—not because they're bad, but because they're no longer built for the next level. If they were to remain attached to the rocket, it wouldn't reach great heights. The same goes for some people in your life. They were only meant to get you started, not to go the distance. But you keep trying to hold on to folks whose purpose expired at ground level. And the more you fight to keep them attached, the more drag you put on your own flight. You want greatness? You wanna make history? Then let go of people who gripe about your growth. Some folks will never understand your vision because they're too busy guarding their ceiling while you're trying to break yours. You weren't born to stay in formation—you were born to take flight. And not every seat on your journey will stay filled. This ain't coach—it's purpose. You're not abandoning people—you're accepting that some can't go where you're going. Don't delay your flight just to make crawlers feel safe. Take off. Rise up. And if you've gotta ride solo to reach that next level—so be it. The air's thinner at the top for a reason: Less noise, more clarity. Go high, even if it means going solo. Because when it's time to rise to greatness, let go of anyone who's afraid of heights.

Growth Affirmation: I will **GROW** out of the
mindset that letting go is betrayal—some folks
are just rocket boosters, not copilots.

Take this day to **THINK** about how your family shows up—only when someone stops breathing. Think about the cousins you ain't seen in years until there's a casket involved. The uncles that don't pick up the phone but show up dressed in black like they've been holding the family together. The same folks who won't come to a birthday, a graduation, or a baby shower suddenly make time when there's a burial. That ain't togetherness. That's tradition soaked in guilt. If the casket's the only thing bringing you together, y'all ain't a family—you're just familiar strangers in matching black. We cry over bodies we ignored while they were breathing, then hug each other in church lobbies talking about, "We need to come together more." But we never do. We go back to our cities, our corners, our silence—until the next name gets called. That ain't love. That's laziness wearing all black. We take more pictures with tombstones than we do with each other. And half the time, the people in the funeral program ain't even got a photo with half the people in the room. Funerals ain't reunions—they're reminders of everything we didn't do while there was still time. You don't need a eulogy to say what a phone call or an occasional visit could've.

To this day, my family still hasn't had a real family reunion. Not one. The only "reunions" we've had were funerals. And every time, like clockwork, someone gets up during remarks and says, "We need to stop meeting like this." And everybody nods. People cry. Some even hug. But it's all temporary. Once the casket closes, so do the hearts. We go right back to being strangers with the same blood. Right back to scrolling and strolling past each other like we ain't got the same last name. I've watched this cycle repeat itself over and over—tears, prayers, promises… then silence. No phone calls. No cookouts. No checking on Grandma unless she's hospitalized. We say we love each other, but love ain't loud in action—it's quiet in absence. The truth is, we're reactive, not connected. Death brings us together for a few hours, but love should've kept us close before it ever came to that. To my family—are we ever gon' have one? Or are we gon' keep acting like funerals are good enough? 'Cause the same food we pass around after a casket closes is the same food we could've shared while they were still alive.

It's time to call it what it is: dysfunction masked as grief. If the only time we check on each other is when the hearse pulls up, then we're not a family—we're just a funeral club. You say you love your people? Then show up before the obituary gets printed. Flowers mean more when they're smelled, not buried. Hug people while they're still warm. You don't need a church and a coffin to make a connection. We say, "Life is short," but act like we've got forever to fix things. And by the time we realize we don't—it's too late. If you really care, stop waiting for a funeral to have a family gathering. Come together more often. Start making plans before the pain forces you to. Don't let your only reunion be a recap of regret and unspoken apologies. A casket shouldn't be the RSVP that finally brings us together. Don't let the only time you come together be during death. That ain't family—that's a pattern of pain we keep passing down. Start planning family gatherings. It's better to pull up to the park and eat some ribs with your loved ones while they're living than to pull up to their wake expecting to eat some there.

Growth Affirmation: I will **GROW** out of the mindset
that love can wait until loss. I choose to show up now—
while hearts are beating and while laughter still echoes.

Take this day to **THINK** about how fast people grab backup when their truth ain't strong enough to stand alone. Especially the ones who scream out: "Facts." "On God." "On my momma." "On my kids." "I swear." "You can take that to the bank." All that mouth movement just to package poison and market it as medicine. Real truth don't need no hype men or background dancers. It don't need your voice cracking, your blood pressure rising, or your chest poking out. People who mean what they say don't need accessories on their honesty. The louder you yell, "Real talk," the more people wonder what fake shit you're tryna cover up. 'Cause half the time, your "real talk" ain't nothing but fake news. The stronger the swearing, the weaker the truth. Like a diamond doesn't need to shout that it's bright, truth don't need to shout that it's strong. If your words carry weight, they don't need a name-drop. If your word was really your bond, it wouldn't need a cosigner. People who stand on truth don't need to stand on names. Integrity don't need insurance. Don't borrow God's or anybody else's name to cover what your character can't.

Got into it at a dice game one time—dude jumped bad about what he was gon' do to me, yelling, "On God," "On my momma," "On the hood." But I'd seen this same clown cuss out his own momma like she was trash. Called her a "fat bitch" behind closed doors. Now suddenly she holy when his ego's on the line? That wasn't truth—that was theater. That wasn't conviction—that was camouflage. Trying to scare people with borrowed honor when he got none of his own. All that hype didn't make him look serious—it made him look shook. He bench-pressed his mom's name because his own word had no weight. That stuck with me. People with no backbone always borrow someone else's name to boost their bluff. But truth? Truth don't need no damn disguise. It don't perform—it proves. Truth stands alone. It don't need Secret Service to back it up.

Nobody's taking what you say to the bank if your name is insufficient.

Truth don't ask for backup—it brings receipts. You out here swearing on God but don't even know Him. Putting it on your momma but ain't called her in months. Putting it on your kids but don't even claim 'em. Swearing it on your soul, knowing damn well you going to hell. Claiming "on the hood" but selling it poison. Talking "Word is bond" when your word ain't worth a damn. You swear on everything you love, but you don't even show love to anything. Not even yourself. Truth don't need volume—it needs value. And if you ain't got that, shut up. The louder your mouth, the lighter your message. Real ones don't yell—they don't have to. You wanna know if somebody's truthful? Watch how quiet they stay when they speak. If your truth needs background singers, it's just a lip-sync act—your mouth moving, but nothing real is coming out. If your story can't stand without a shout, it ain't strong. Your name should be the stamp—nothing else. Integrity don't beg for belief. It don't need God, momma, the kids, or the hood to verify it. Loud talk don't equal real talk—it just sounds desperate. Being loud don't mean your word is legit. If you can't keep it real, keep it quiet. Stop bringing your momma into your lies. If your name ain't strong enough to carry your truth, then your truth ain't strong enough to carry your name. In other words, your words should make your name respected—and your name should make your words believable. If neither do—shut the hell up. 'Cause you ain't gon' do shit.

Growth Affirmation: I will **GROW** out of the mindset that truth needs backup. My word will carry weight without name-dropping, swearing, or shouting. Real truth stands tall—alone.

Take this day to **THINK** about why you keep giving people bread who wouldn't even toss you a crumb. You keep handing out pieces of yourself to people who treat you like a vending machine—push a button, take what they want, and walk the hell off without a second thought. They don't check on you. They don't sit with you. They don't ask how you're holding up. They just pull up empty, take everything you got, and dip until they need a filling up again. And your thirsty ass let 'em. Over and over. Out of guilt. Out of desperation. Out of loneliness. They don't care about your presence—just what your presence can provide. You ain't a drive-thru. Stop letting people order your love to go. You better start putting a limit on how much you give. Because takers are never gon' put a limit on how much they take. Being surrounded by takers don't cure loneliness—it deepens it. Silence might sting, but leeches will starve you. Eat you out of house and fucken home. It's better to be alone than eaten alive. Relationships aren't supposed to feel like transactions. If they can't pour into you, feed your spirit, or sit down long enough to know what you're going through, then they got no business touching your plate. You're not a pit stop. You're not an ATM. And you damn sure ain't free refills for people who never pour into your cup.

My grandmother loved playing *Trouble* and watching *Dancing with the Stars*, and despite my struggles, I made time to sit with her. Sure, I'd occasionally ask her for money, but I also gave her something back—my presence. Despite my struggles with addiction, I'd pop in on her regularly, sharing laughs and creating memories that I still cherish. I'm thankful I did, because now that she's gone, I have no regrets about how I showed up for her. That contrast? It exposes the ones who only come around when they're hungry, never when you're hurting. People who can't even sit across from you to ask how you're doing got no right draining your resources. They ain't friends.

They're freeloaders—loading up on your time, your money, your peace—like bandits with no mask. But because you so thirsty for company, you mistook being looted from for being loved on. Ain't nothing noble about letting people nibble off your generosity.

If your presence ain't matched with presence, then your absence better be permanent. Start evaluating who's eating with you and who's eating off you. People who don't feed you emotionally, mentally, or spiritually don't deserve a seat at your damn table. Love, time, energy—those are investments, not giveaways. If someone only hits you up when they need something, hit them back with silence. Protect your peace like it's gold, because it is. If they can't pour into you, they don't get to pull from you. Your table ain't a buffet for the ungrateful. You ain't nobody's backup battery or bottomless wallet. If their loyalty expires when your benefits run out, then their access should too. If they don't check in when you're low, they don't deserve you when you're high. Be done feeding people who leave you starving. Your soul ain't a soup kitchen. Your time ain't disposable. And your heart ain't a free sample. If they can't match your presence, stop tolerating their pattern. Either they come correct—or they don't come at all. If the only thing they feed is their appetite, you're the full course meal—not a friend. You weren't born to be eaten off— take yourself off their menu. Shut the fucken soup kitchen down.

Growth Affirmation: I will **GROW** out of being everybody's refill—I'm not a fountain—I'm a force. If they think I'm a drive-thru—then let 'em keep on driving.

Take this day to **THINK** about why one bad result sends you running like you never wanted it in the first place. One "no," one brick wall, and you throw your hands up like life robbed you. But it didn't. Your failure is an inside job. Truth is, you never committed—you just flirted with the idea of success until it got hard. You was all in until shit got real. You say you're "tired," but tired of what? You ain't even put in the pain required to be exhausted. You call yourself a fighter, but every time the dream swings back, you flinch—with your scary ass. You'll chase a relationship through heartbreak after heartbreak but won't chase your purpose past the first rejection or failure. Why give that raggedy ass partner more chances than you give your goal or dream? The truth? You don't fail because life's unfair—you fail because you're weak. Edison ain't build the light bulb in no clean streak—he failed thousands of times. But he didn't cry. He clocked every miss as one more reason to swing harder. Edison didn't discover light by being lucky; he wrestled the dark until it coughed up respect. If he had quit after a few setbacks, we'd still be surrounded by candles and oil lamps. Success don't reward the first to try—it rewards the last to quit. Every reputable success is born from repeated failure.

My mother was built different. Dropped out young to take care of family—no complaints, just survival mode. Many years later, she decided to chase that GED. First time? Failed. Second? Failed. Third? Same story. Each time knocked her down a little more, made her question if she was built for it. But she didn't break. She walked back in that testing center after every L, feeling the stares, hearing the whispers, but refusing to fold. She studied at night, worked all day, and kept pushing through the fog of doubt. And on that fourth try? She passed. Not just a test—she passed every excuse, every reason to give up, every lie that said she couldn't. She walked that stage in my graduation cap and gown—and that moment wasn't about paper, it was about power. Her failure didn't hold her back—it sharpened her will. Her grit and grind produced greatness. And that cap? It didn't just fit me—it crowned her.

Why won't you give yourself another chance on that goal or idea? Did you quit seeking love after the first couple of relationships didn't go well? No. Sometimes you gotta go through two or three relationships to find the right one. Same with your ideas—you might fail a few times before you find the right fit, but keep trying until it clicks. You only need to get it right once. You benchin' yourself after two bad tries like the dream's supposed to hand itself over? Cry all you want, success don't hand out tissues. It don't want your feelings—it wants your fury. *A sign of failure ain't never a stop sign—it's a yield.* Let what didn't work blow past, then punch the gas. Next time failure pulls up, don't freeze—fight. Edison ain't fold. My mama ain't fold. So what's your excuse? Failure ain't a wall—it's a weight room. Every rep of rejection builds resistance. Every fall trains your balance. Every miss is a warm-up. Every "no" is preseason. Every loss is leg day—training you to carry the load. You don't get strong by skipping the struggle—you get strong by showing up sore and swinging anyway. You'll hand out second chances to failed relationships like it's government cheese, but you won't do the same for your vision? What kind of shit is that? If you had the guts to try love again after heartbreak, don't you dare act like your goals ain't worth the same fight. Don't be brave for somebody else's heart while staying a coward for your own. If you had the grit to give love another shot after the last one fell apart, you can damn sure give your purpose another round. Stop showing more loyalty to failed relationships than you do to your own future. The path forward is lit by folks who got knocked down and said, "Run it back." So lace up. Bite down. Lock in. And swing like your bloodline got something to prove.

Growth Affirmation: I will **GROW** out of the mindset
of quitting when things get hard. Life's an experiment and
every reputable success is born from repeated failure.

Take this day to **THINK** about how reckless your mouth can be when your emotions run the show. You pop off without pause, then wonder why relationships crumble. Don't act like you didn't know your words carry weight—you just didn't care in the moment. You call it venting, they call it venom. Angry words hit harder than fists—and leave bruises you can't see but never forget. You think letting it fly makes you real? Nah. Real strength is shutting the hell up when silence protects what your mouth would destroy. A sore tongue don't compare to a broken relationship. Biting your tongue stings for a second. Chewing someone out stuns for a lifetime. Restraint ain't weakness—it's wisdom. You gotta ask yourself: "Is my pride worth the fallout?" Because chewing someone out might taste good now, but later it'll leave you choking on guilt and spitting out apologies that won't always fix what you broke.

There was a day I let my mouth run through my sister like a blade. She was a recovering addict, and instead of meeting her pain with understanding, I met it with ego. I tried to one-up her suffering like it was a competition. Didn't even pause. Just snapped. Every word I said landed like a hit—and I saw it. Her face crumbled, tears falling, and in that split second I knew I had crossed a line I couldn't uncross. The worst part? I wasn't wrong—I was just ruthless. I weaponized my words and aimed them straight at her heart. That moment still sits heavy. Not because I snapped—but because I aimed to hurt. Love requires restraint. And that day, I failed the test. Grateful we healed, proud of the woman she became, but that moment? Still real. I had to learn the hard way: Silence saves more than feelings—it saves your own character. Tisha, if you're reading this, know that I see you, I respect you, and I love the mother, daughter, and grandmother you've become.

Before you **run** your mouth and let harsh words **fly** out of it, be sure there are words you won't wish you could **walk** back later. Words build or break—there ain't no neutral. When your blood's boiling, silence ain't weakness—it's a weapon. That pause? It's not about being passive—it's about being powerful. Your mouth ain't meant to outrun your mind. Slow it down. Think first. Then speak like you actually care about what survives. You think you're just "keeping it real," but real ain't reckless. Restraint ain't soft—it's savage. It takes more power to hold back than to lash out. Anybody can bark demands. Not everybody can breathe deep. One wrong outburst can burn a bridge that took years to build—and once it's ash, don't think your "sorry" is gon' rebuild it. Your mouth can make messes that no apology is strong enough to clean up. Bite your tongue now or choke on your own words later. One hurts for a moment. The other lingers for life. Pick your words wisely, or get used to going to cemeteries talking to tombstones or ashes sitting on a mantel that can't talk back.

Growth Affirmation: I will **GROW** out of the mindset of letting my emotions dictate my words. To preserve my relationships, I will swallow my pride before I chew someone out.

Take this day to **THINK** about why you pass out trust so freely to people who haven't earned it. Your trust is valuable. It's not a piece of cheese with a toothpick stuck in it—laid out on a tray for anybody walking by. You pass out trust passes like a soup kitchen hands out meals, without questioning who's receiving them. You're so thirsty for friends or a mate, you let the same untrustworthy people walk in and out of your life like a revolving door. Don't you get tired of being betrayed—or have you grown addicted to disrespect and lies? Trust isn't something to be given lightly; it's a VIP room meant for Very Invested People, not Very Inconsistent People. Your life is not a run-down motel where anyone can check in and out at will. Stop letting people in who haven't proven their worth. Thoroughly check their credentials. Their character. Their résumé of friends. How they treat others, especially their parents, spouse, or partner, is how they will treat you. If they'll lie to them, you don't stand a fucken chance. When you stop running your life like a motel, you start living with meaning. The more selective you are about who gets in, the fewer betrayals, heartbreaks, and disappointments you'll face.

When I went to prison for the first time at 18, I met an inmate who had no filter for who he trusted. He allowed anyone to get close, failing to see the dangerous agendas that existed around him. Smiling faces hid malicious intentions, and his lack of discernment made him vulnerable. One day, a dude he called "his boy" turned on him in the most violent way imaginable by taking his manhood. Dude was no longer "his boy"—he was now "his man." Watching his pain made me realize that being too trusting is not just naïve—it's dangerous. It's a lesson I'll never forget. From that, I've learned to filter people, to demand proof of loyalty and integrity before granting access to my life. Trust is a bank, and it's a currency too valuable to give out as a loan to people with a history of defaulting.

Stop passing out your trust like Halloween candy—to people who always trick you out of something and treat you to nothing but lies. Face it, when it comes to trust, you move like a prostitute—giving it up too easy to anyone willing to pay you… no attention, that is. You're quick to believe lies, fall for manipulation, and excuse betrayal like it's love. You're so naïve it's pathetic. You keep letting the same people hurt you, hoping for a different outcome, like pain's going to magically teach them how to love you right. Get this through your thick-ass skull: You can't get people to change. Stop being so thirsty for connection that you ignore the contamination. The ones who deserve to be close will earn their way in—no shortcuts, no free rides—while the wrong ones will expose themselves the moment you set a boundary. And if someone's all words and no action, believe what they do, not what they say. Apologies don't mean shit without action behind them. Trust ain't a pass—it's a privilege. And when misused, that privilege gets revoked. It's time to give the wrong people who have checked in a wake-up call. It's checkout time. Pack yo shit and get the fuck out.

Growth Affirmation: I will **GROW** out of the mindset that love means access—my heart ain't a hotel, and trust ain't an open-door policy.

Take this day to **THINK** about why you're wasting your time playing cleanup for karma. Would you clock in at your friend's job just to make sure they get paid? No. Then why keep stepping in to do karma's job like it's your responsibility? You ain't the universe's hitman. You ain't karma's assistant. Every time you chase revenge, you prove how little control you actually have. They hurt you, and now they're squatting in your mind while you out here plotting comebacks, losing sleep, fucken up your peace. All while they're out eating wings and watching Netflix. Let that sink in. You don't win by getting even—you lose by putting your life on pause. Revenge is a boomerang made of blades—it cuts you coming and going. Meanwhile, karma's just sitting back, clocking every detail like a sniper with patience. It don't need help. It don't need speed. It just needs you to stay the hell out the way. Karma don't miss. But you? You'll miss your whole future trying to hit back. Let go of that fake power trip. Release yourself from that weight. Vengeance might feel good in the moment, but peace feels better for a lifetime.

There was a dude I trusted to help around my tire shop—gave him a shot, paid him fair, fed him when he needed it. Then one night, he broke in and robbed me blind. I saw red. Took matters into my own hands like I was some street-level avenger. All that did was blow up in my face. Next thing I knew, I'm dodging charges and ducking heat like I'm the one who broke the law. All because I wanted to make sure he "felt it." But karma? Oh, it played the long game. A year later, he got locked up for beating his girlfriend bloody. Skipped court. Warrant out. Now he's the one hiding. That moment made me realize something that still cuts deep—I didn't have to get my hands dirty and get myself caught up in the court system. Karma had it the whole time. And all I did was wreck my own peace trying to play God.

Karma is a two-faced professional: part accountant, part cold case detective. It keeps life's books balanced, and it files cases labeled "pending" until justice is served. Then, when you least expect it, that bill comes due—with interest. It don't call ahead. It don't leave warnings. It just shows up and collects. And if you're too busy trying to write your own revenge script, you'll miss watching karma burn them without you lifting a finger. You don't need to clap back. You need to fall back. Because karma ain't forgetful—it's fervent. Free yourself from the chokehold of bitterness. Let them think they got away with it. Let 'em gloat. Let 'em flex. Let 'em laugh. Karma don't chase people—it chastises them. Karma ain't loud—but it always lands. And when it does, it won't just humble them. It'll remind them who they fucked with. The universe don't ignore mistreatment—it just returns it later with interest. Karma don't knock—it kicks the door off the hinges. So relax. Just chill the hell out. You don't need insurance or a tracking number when karma's handling the delivery—might not be overnight, but best believe it knows the exact address where to drop off revenge, no signature required.

Growth Affirmation: I will **GROW** out of the mindset
that justice is my job—karma never forgets an address,
and I don't need to deliver what's already in transit.

Take this day to **THINK** about how silence ain't neutral—it's an answer. Every time you keep your mouth shut about something foul, you're giving it permission to breathe. From day one, we're taught to mind our business. "Don't tattle." "Stay out of it." "Ain't got nothing to do with you." "Don't be a snitch." "Ain't none of your business." That kind of thinking not only leaves you speechless—it makes you spineless. It conditions you to turn a blind eye until it comes back around and bites you in the ass. Standing by while wrong happens don't make you innocent—it makes you complicit. You ain't innocent—you just quiet with blood on your tongue. It's like watching someone break into your neighbor's house and acting shocked when they show up at yours next. Every time you stay quiet about the darkness, injustice grows teeth—and your neck is next. If you ain't willing to call it out, don't act surprised when it calls on you. Because if you ain't stepping up to blow the whistle, you're basically standing by and handing it your blessing. Whether your hand lit the match or not, if you ain't running to get an extinguisher, you're part of the blaze.

One of the hardest moves I ever made was telling my boy, who was locked up, that our other homie was messing around with his baby mama. I hesitated. Telling him could wreck his mental state while he's behind bars, but staying silent made me feel like I cosigned the betrayal. Every day it ate at me. I knew if the roles were flipped, I'd want someone to say something— whether it hurt or not. So I told him. He spiraled. It crushed him. Less than nine days after getting out, he was back in for puttin' hands on her. That truth sent him into a rage, and part of me questioned if my words had pushed him over the edge. But truth be told, he deserved the truth—even if it cracked him. That pain wasn't my doing. But the betrayal would've been if I'd just kept quiet. Because silence would've made me just as dirty as the ones doing him wrong. Silence ain't passive—it's permission.

Here are two million-dollar questions for you: If your spouse was cheating, would you want somebody to tell you? Or if you were being molested by your father, would you want somebody to speak up? Stop acting like your silence is harmless. It ain't. It's an accomplice. Every time you stay quiet, you're stamping approval on whatever goes unchecked. You ain't "staying out the drama"—you're signing off on it. It's easier to look away than speak up, but easy choices lead to ugly outcomes. You think you're avoiding conflict, but you're really feeding cowardice. There's acquiescence in your silence, as my friend Harry would say. Life will put you in moments where comfort and conscience go to war—and your decision will say everything about who you are. You don't need a megaphone to speak truth, but you better stop using silence as a muzzle. Because silence screams. It screams approval. It screams agreement. And it screams weakness. When you see wrong and say nothing, you're just another voice in the chorus of cowards. If you see something, say something. Especially if it violates the care of another human being. You may be their only voice to freedom. You either stand up and stand against the persecution of others, or you stand aside. You ain't protecting peace—you're preserving poison. One day, that silence you used as a shield will stab you in the back when it's your turn to need a voice. People don't just remember what you say—they remember when you didn't say shit.

Growth Affirmation: I will **GROW** out of the mindset
that silence is safe. My voice has value. By biting my tongue
on injustice, it will only come around to bite me.

Take this day to **THINK** about why your mouth is always moving but your feet never follow. You've become the spokesperson for broken promises about moves you never make. You say, "I'm about to lose weight," while you're still eating cake, chips, and candy like they're weight loss pills. Newsflash: Running your mouth ain't cardio—it don't burn calories. You say, "I'm leaving his sorry ass because he don't know how to treat me," yet you're still there catching punches. To pull you in, he told you his love language was *physical touch*—but his hands don't hold, they hit. Why are you still interpreting an ass beating as love? That ain't devotion—that's delusion. Quit broadcasting what you're gon' do and just do it. Success don't need a preshow. You must love the sound of your voice. Because your mouth moves more than your feet ever have. You all fucken talk. You don't need a mic—you need a muzzle. As soon as you tell people you gon' do something, you don't follow through—you fall off. The oxygen you waste bragging could be fueling progress. You're not on a mission—you're misleading. If you were a business, you'd be getting sued for false advertising. You make claims that aren't true. You out here leaking trailers for a movie you keep saying you're going to produce but never do—that's why your name never shows up in the credits.

Had a deaf friend I fell out with over a drug issue—haven't spoken since, and truth be told, I don't give a damn if we ever do. But one thing I can't knock? He got to the bag and still does. For a while, that was me too. Silent hustle, loud results. But somewhere along the way, I stopped letting my hands talk and started running my mouth. I became Mr. "I'm about to." Told everybody I was quitting pills, becoming a trainer, writing a book. All bark, no bite. Sounded solid—but while my mouth ran a marathon, my body never left the starting line. You ever notice how the ones doing the most talking usually got the least to show? That was me. And chances are, it's you too. Every week, a new plan. Weeks pass. Nothing changes. You got high off hype. Talking made you feel productive. Problem is, talk don't build empires. Only your hands can do that. And mine? They weren't building anything—they were just busy stuffing pills down my throat.

Stop announcing what you're about to do and start letting results introduce you. Stop talking loud and moving like a whisper. Inflated words leave your world deflated. You've run your mouth long enough. When you gon' admit you've been lying to yourself and commit? Words alone are good for conversation, not elevation. The longer you keep blowing smoke, the longer you'll stay in the ashes of your own potential. Words don't carve muscle. Words don't cash checks. Roll up your sleeves and bleed for it, because success don't answer to speeches—it answers to sacrifice. If mediocrity feels like home, don't act surprised when success stops inviting you in. What you deserve is on reserve, waiting for you to act. It's on lock until your hands show up with the key. You keep preaching purpose with lazy hands. Nobody's clapping for potential anymore. Dreams don't come true for fakers—they come true for finishers. You ain't unlucky. You're undisciplined. You want applause before you even audition. But this stage ain't for the talkers—it's for the tenacious. Kill the commentary. Show up in action, not announcements. Let your hands do the talking—and let the results do the shouting. You can't keep campaigning for success but be too scared to hit the streets and knock on doors. Make your hands perform what your mouth keeps promoting. The road to success isn't easy, and you have to decide: Are you ready to pay the high price it demands, or is mediocrity just easier for you to afford because talk is cheap?

Growth Affirmation: I will **GROW** out of the mindset
of talking about what I'm about to do. Lip service without
servicing my words makes me a product of failure.

Take this day to **THINK** about why success always slips through your fingers. It's not a mystery—you quit on every damn thing you start, or worse, you tiptoe into it with weak effort and expect great results. Keep it real. You never got high halfway. You never drank halfway. You never had an affair halfway. You never indulged in your vices halfway. You'll go out of your way to produce all kinds of lies to succeed at cheating on your partner. But now, when it's time to build something that matters—your goals, your peace, your purpose—you start slacking like effort's optional. You love halfway because it lets you say you tried without ever risking real failure. You give halfway because full effort scares you half to death. Your life ain't whole because you partially commit. Half-hearted hustle don't bring full blessings. Either go all in—or move out the way. You want to live a full life with a half-ass work ethic? That math ain't mathing. You gave your vice 100%—now give your recovery, dream, or goal the same energy.

I used to say I wanted to quit pills—but the truth was, I wanted the pain to stop without giving up the high. I didn't want freedom—I wanted comfort without the cost. I walked into rehab like it was a hotel lobby, not a war zone. Checked in. Got cozy. Checked out. I wasn't chasing change—I was thawing out. Half of me wanted healing, but the other half still romanticized the escape. That's why nothing stuck. I was swinging with one arm while the other hand held the very poison I claimed I was done with. You can't fight a demon you're still feeding. Pills didn't just numb me—they owned me. And as long as I kept showing up halfway, they kept taking full advantage. I had to decide: Was I trying to impress people with my effort, or actually trying to live? Because halfway wasn't just stalling me—it was slowly erasing me. The moment I gave it everything—mind, body, soul—that's when things changed. That's when the withdrawals, the cravings, and the self-hate started to lose power. Not because it got easier—but because I got ruthless.

If you don't get ruthless about your purpose, you'll stay romantic with your ruin. Commitment is the fuel that ignites every success story. You can't bake a cake halfway and expect it to rise—it'll stay flat like your progress. Half-hearted effort breeds only empty-handed results. Stop clapping for your own distractions and start starving your excuses. Greatness don't walk toward you— you gotta run to it without looking back. You're not failing because the dream is too big—you're failing because your effort is too small. Half-hearted effort is like trying to light a match underwater—it'll never spark success. Greatness don't negotiate with weakness. You can't climb halfway up the mountain and expect the view to come to you. Until you go all in, don't cry about how your life is turning out. Halfway effort don't build nothing but halfway results, and nobody celebrates a man who almost made it. You gave your addictions, your lies, and your vices everything you had—so why do your goals only get the bare minimum? If you can go all out for your destruction, you can damn sure go all in for your destiny. Effort is the difference between living a story worth telling and dying a disappointment. So either push every chip to the center of the table—or shut the hell up about what you almost did. 'Cause almost don't count for shit.

Growth Affirmation: I will **GROW** out of the mindset that trying is enough—until I get ruthless about my goals, I'll keep losing gently instead of winning aggressively. Evolution don't bargain with laziness.

Take this day to **THINK** about why you keep sugarcoating the truth like it's doing anybody a favor. You ain't helping out—you're holding back. You lie to protect feelings, then catch an attitude when nobody protects yours. That's backwards as hell. Truth ain't supposed to tuck you in—it's supposed to wake you up. You want to be comforted more than corrected, and that's why growth keeps ghosting you. What starts sweet in the mouth ends bitter in the soul—that's the poison sugar hides. When you soften the truth, you're not sparing someone—you're stalling their breakthrough. If truth rattles you, it's 'cause you'd rather stay blind than face what the mirror's been screaming. I'd rather be told that I have a booger in my nose or my breath stinks than walk around mocked. Better to be bruised by honesty than hugged by a lie. But let's be clear: Truth ain't a license to humiliate. Deliver it raw, but don't drag folks through the mud just to flex your honesty. There's a difference between being real and being reckless.

While I had a friend locked up, I wrestled with a truth I didn't want to share. Before going in, he asked me to look out for his girl—and I did, but in more ways than one. We crossed lines we shouldn't have, and the guilt was eating me alive. I debated whether to tell him, because I knew it would hurt, but I also couldn't stand laughing in his face like everything was fine. That fake smile, that fake friendship—it bothered me more than anything. In a world where "real" is rare, I decided to be a realist. I told him the truth. As much as I didn't want to, I needed to keep it real. Raw truth was needed. It broke both of us. He was hurt, I was ashamed, and things between us haven't been the same since. But here's the deal: I'm not sayin' it was always like this, but I'd rather face the fallout of honesty than live with the poison of deceit—even if it stings. The truth can burn, but it heals faster than lies ever could.

Stop feeding people candy-coated lies just to keep the peace. The truth should punch, not pacify. Growth don't come from comfort—it comes from confrontation. Don't water down your words to protect egos that need breaking. *Have the nerve to strike a nerve.* They'll get over it. And if they don't, oh well. Move on. You tried to help they sorry ass. Sugary words rot relationships the same way candy rots teeth—slowly and silently. So don't get mad when somebody hands you the mirror; thank 'em for not letting you walk around with your mouth smelling like dumpster juice. Breath that ain't halitosis—but "hellatosis." The truth may slap you, but at least it will awaken you. The truth might crack your pride, but lies will crush your character. You don't build strong bonds by pretending. You build 'em by bleeding truth, even when it's messy. Stop looking for sweet talk and start listening for sharp truth—it's the only kind that cuts deep enough to evolve you. Truth should always be unsweetened, not full of artificial sweetener. The truth don't need sugar—it needs guts. Tell people what they need to hear and not what they want to hear. And if someone can't handle it pure, raw, unfiltered, unadulterated, and straight to the vein? That just means they're too damn sensitive—and that ain't your problem.

Growth Affirmation: I will **GROW** out of the mindset of sugarcoating the truth. When it comes to telling others what they need to hear, I will always go sugar-free.

Take this day to **THINK** about why you keep entertaining people who've already disrespected you. How many black eyes, white lies, red flags, and emotional breakdowns does it take for you to finally walk away? They've shown you who they are—again and again—and you keep hoping for a miracle, like they gon' flip the script one day. But let's keep it real: They're not confused, they're consistent. You're just ignoring the proof because you're scared to be alone. You ain't loyal—you thirsty. Desperate for attention, for love, for someone to tell you you're something, even if they treat you like you're nothing. That ain't love—that's addiction to dysfunction. You don't love them—you love the version you created in your head. You ain't waiting for change—you're volunteering for chaos. You romanticize pain and call it patience. You excuse bad behavior and call it loyalty. And every time you do that, you teach people exactly how to treat you: Like trash they know you'll never throw out. Stop hoping people will heal in your presence while bleeding all over your peace.

During my darkest days, I was the one showing my true self—and my intentions weren't pure. Pills consumed my every thought, and manipulation became second nature. I fought people who wouldn't give me what I wanted. I lied, calculated, and charmed my way into situations that benefited me. I moved from one person to another, only staying as long as they served my purpose. Every conversation, every compliment, and every kind gesture was a strategy to get what I needed. Behind my words was always an agenda—never real care, never real connection. I even remember meeting a nurse once. She was kind, soft-spoken, had a good job—but I had zero interest in her as a person. I only saw her as a potential plug. I opened her car door like a gentleman—shit, I would've laid my jacket over a puddle just to convince her I had chivalry. But underneath? I was calculating. Every move was a con. I wasn't dating—I was deceiving. I was hoping she'd slip up, drop a hint, maybe get me access to a prescription pad. That's how twisted my thinking was. Stepping on people instead of seeing them as stepping stones. I didn't love—I leveraged. I didn't bond—I baited. I didn't respect—I reeled. And they ignored the warning signs, because they wanted to believe in the version of me I pretended to be, not the person I really was.

Why do you keep praying for potential while ignoring the proof? People lie with words, but they scream with patterns—and you keep covering your ears and closing your eyes. "They're changing," you say, just because they apologized. "They've been through a lot," you say, just because they had it rough. Hell, who hasn't? Self-respect starts with walking away when the actions don't match the apology. If their apology is a routine, their growth is a lie. Stop cradling grown people's dysfunction because you're scared of being uncomfortable. They gave you black eyes, had you seeing red, gave you the blues, told you white lies, and robbed you blind of your green—and you still don't see their true colors? Let it go. Their colors aren't going to paint a different picture. Peace ain't a gift—they don't give it to you. You protect it, or you lose it. When folks reveal their pattern, quit pretending it's potential. Every time you ignore who they are, you lose more of who you're supposed to be. Stop looking for who they used to be. When people keep showing you red flags, don't act like you colorblind—raise your white one and get the hell outta there.

Growth Affirmation: I will **GROW** out of the mindset that people will change just because I hope they do—they been screaming who they are, and I'm done being colorblind to protect my denial.

Take this day to **THINK** about what really keeps you up at night. Not monsters. Not death. But the cold, cruel grind of barely scraping by. You know what's scarier than a casket? Being fired. An eviction notice. Scarier than dying is opening the fridge and seeing nothing but light—provided the electric is on. It's watching the bills stack up while your check barely covers survival. That's a different kind of horror—a slow bleed that never stops. Barely making ends meet don't just bruise your pockets—it breaks your spirit. You start questioning your worth. Wondering if you'll ever catch a breath that ain't laced with panic. Living check to check ain't just exhausting—it's humiliating. It's pressure that doesn't let up, a silent war nobody sees but you fight every day. People talk about fearing death, but the truth is, most of us fear dying a little more every day from a life that never lets us live. Survival ain't living— it's creating a one-page obituary to be read in three seconds at your funeral.

The second time I got shot, I remember watching the shooter stand above me, trigger aimed like it was the last thing I'd ever see. Blood leaking from the first shots, body going numb—and yet, I wasn't scared. No life flashing before my eyes. No panic. Just stillness. That's just what it was. Growing up, death wasn't something to be feared—it was woven into my reality. I saw it firsthand. For me, selling dope wasn't rebellion—it was survival. I didn't see another way to escape the weight of poverty. The drug game brought danger, but it also brought dinner. It kept the lights on when nothing else could. And that's the part most people don't get—dying didn't scare me. Hell, it felt familiar. But starving? Struggling? Watching bills pile up while the fridge stayed empty? That's what had me shook. That slow grind of never having enough— that was the real monster. It barely scared me to meet my end. What scared me more was barely making ends meet.

Struggle is real—but it don't have to steal your soul. Keeping it real, the reason we're barely making ends meet ain't just income—it's impulse. You can't complain about being broke if you keep buying your own bondage. We buy Clorox instead of generic. We drop rent money on Jordans instead of grabbing Skechers and stacking the rest. We prioritize image over increase, pride over progress. Let Netflix go. Tubi is just as good. Stop DoorDashing your future away. You keep robbing Peter to pay Paul, but you never pay yourself—and that's the real robbery. It's time to stack and starve—starve the habits that drain you, the luxuries that lull you, the comforts that keep you broke. Starve the spending so you can feed the savings. Declare boldly, "This won't be my ending." Budget that five dollars. Shop at thrift stores. The goal ain't comfort—it's control. Survival might be the season, but strategy is the shift. You've suffered enough. Keep robbing Peter to pay Paul and you'll end up in debt to both apostles. Instead of robbing Peter to pay Paul, skip paying Paul—he ain't the one struggling. You are. Pay your damn self first! You ain't gotta be rich to build. Just relentless. The world already bet on your failure—don't cosign it. *This struggle? It's your origin story, not your obituary.*

Growth Affirmation: I will **GROW** out of the mindset of letting poverty define me and focus on making the most of my situation, taking small steps toward a better future.

Take this day to **THINK** about who really makes the world go round. Not CEOs in glass offices. Not boardroom members sitting around an oval oak table. It's the workers—the overlooked, overworked, underpaid. Without them, this world wouldn't just slow down—it would shut down. You ever heard of a company shutting down because a CEO decided to strike? Hell no! During the COVID pandemic, it wasn't the bosses who saved us—it was the ones who opened up the businesses while the world was locked down in their homes. Nurses, cashiers, janitors, truck drivers—real ones who didn't ask for praise—just a paycheck. They didn't post about hustle—they *lived* it. And like in basketball, not everybody hits the game-winner—but without the rebounds, screens, and assists, there's no win to begin with. Michael Jordan wouldn't have won championships without Scottie Pippen and Dennis Rodman. Without you, nothing scores. Nothing moves. Nothing works. Every role matters. Just 'cause you ain't in the spotlight don't mean you didn't help light it.

I used to think clocking in was a form of captivity. That working a job meant you were settling or selling out. But that mindset came from watching people hustle backwards—glorifying the fast life while secretly drowning in it. I saw too many dudes flex stacks on Friday and be flat broke by Monday. They laughed at 9-to-5s but cried over court fines and casket costs. Truth is, I confused freedom with recklessness. But prison humbled me. On the outside, I complained about working. On the inside, I worked for a measly $18 a month—what we called "state pay." Those same jobs I once thought were beneath me became my therapy. In a place built to break you, work kept my sanity intact. It gave my days structure and my soul something to stand on. Now, I see it different. Instead of society carrying me, I carry my share. And truth be told, working a 9-to-5 is far more rewarding than doing a 10-to-20.

With all these books, infomercials, seminars, and gurus telling you to "Live your dream" or that working for someone else makes you weak—you start feeling like your 9-to-5 means you failed. Like if you ain't launching a business, selling a brand, or preaching on a podcast, you're behind. But here's the truth nobody wants to admit: If everybody's building empires, who the hell's laying the bricks? Who's wiring the power? Who's keeping the floors clean, shelves stocked, and systems running? The world don't spin on CEOs—it spins on the backs of workers. Janitors, drivers, security guards, baristas—real ones who keep the whole show alive. You're the reason that tired mom comes to the drive-thru for her kids. You're the reason someone gets their medicine on time. The work you do matters more than the applause you don't get. You don't need a title to matter. You already do. You're not beneath anyone—you're the backbone. Without your role, there is no dream. There is no luxury. There is no empire. Here's something worth knowing if you ever start to believe that what you do in the world don't matter: The lightbulb for the business may have come on in the entrepreneur's head, but you're the one who keeps the lightbulbs on in the business. Stop questioning your damn worth. You are not optional. You are not replaceable. You are the reason the world works—without you, it shuts down.

> **Growth Affirmation:** I will **GROW** out of the mindset of thinking that my work ain't essential. Real impact don't wear suits—it wears scrubs, boots, aprons, and name tags.

Take this day to **THINK** about why your progress stays tucked away while others keep shooting upward. Let me shoot it straight: The problem ain't luck—it's nerve. They took their shot while you stayed holstered, letting good ideas rust inside your mind's chamber. You're fully loaded with potential, but too scared to cock back and fire. They land shots 'cause they fire on sight— but you still fumbling with the safety. And when you do take your shot, you shoot out blanks. You're not out of chances—you just ain't brave enough to use 'em. You keep blaming your background, your parents, your job, your environment—but the truth is, the only thing holding you back is your hesitation. Life doesn't hand out success; it hands out shots. But you keep ducking yours. The worst kind of failure ain't missing—it's never firing. Keep hesitating, and you'll be outlived by someone with worse aim but better nerve.

People taking their shot ain't new to me—literally. I've been shot at twice. And I've been hit a total of seven times. First time? .38 pistol. Second time? .45. Two different calibers, two different shooters, one common trait—they didn't hesitate. Although those were tragic events, both men showed me what it looks like when someone decides to pull the trigger and follow through. They had an idea, they aimed, and they executed. Period. They weren't standing around wondering if their aim was good enough or if now was the right time. They didn't ask for a sign or crowd approval—they just acted. The .38 may have been smaller, but it still tore through me like it had something to prove. The .45? That one barked louder and bit deeper. But size didn't determine damage—action did. Success works the same way. Ain't no perfect timing. When you have the shot, take it. It don't matter if your "caliber" is small—you pull that trigger with focus and intent, you'll make an impact. Because whether it's a .22 or a .45, hesitation don't make hits—action does.

In life, we're all given the same shot—the same 24 hours, the same 1,440 minutes, the same 86,400 seconds. The difference ain't in the time—it's in what you do with it. Life don't play favorites—it's just a firing line, and we all get a turn. Some aim with focus and fire with intent. Others panic, fire wildly, and wonder why nothing hits its target. You still lining up your shot, second-guessing yourself while someone else already emptied the clip. It ain't about resources—it's about resolve. If you're stuck, it's because you've packed your mind with blanks: fear, excuses, overthinking. Every second you stall, somebody else reloads. You don't have to be a *sharpshooter*. Because the ones winning ain't always *sharper*—they're just *shooters*. Stop watching. Stop waiting. Pull the damn trigger. You don't need the biggest caliber. You just need a big heart. Life don't reward hesitation—it honors the one bold enough to squeeze. All the ideas in the world can be loaded in your mind, but if you won't take the shot, you'll stay jammed up, and life will keep backfiring on you.

Growth Affirmation: I will **GROW** out of the mindset of placing my life on safety and not taking my shot. My shot is not wasted by missing—it's wasted by not firing.

Take this day to **THINK** about how many times you've let obstacles stop you dead in your tracks. Somewhere along the way, we forgot how to fight. As kids, we didn't overthink failure, nor did we care how others looked at us. We fell, got bruised, got back up, and kept going. Failure wasn't a wall—it was a step. But life teaches fear. Fear of looking stupid. Fear of not being good enough. Fear of falling so hard that you never recover. Now you sit in excuses like they're protection—thinking stuck is safer than swinging. But let's be real—failure don't kill you; excuses do. Your excuses ain't harmless—they're the hitmen you hired to assassinate your own future. Either you bury them, or they'll bury you—and they won't even send flowers. Every time you refuse to challenge an obstacle, you choose to stay in the same place. You've replaced the joy of rising with the fear of falling. That's why you ain't growing. You're so scared to fail that you've stopped giving yourself a shot to succeed.

I didn't think I could ever quit popping pills. But then came a defining moment. I was home, withdrawals ripping through me, watching my favorite show from prison—*American Ninja Warrior*. I loved that show because it wasn't just about strength—it was about resilience. Some crushed every obstacle, others fell short. But what struck me was how the ones who fell didn't quit. They came back the next season, refusing to let failure get the last word. That was the mindset I needed. If they could fight through their seasons of failure, so could I. I challenged myself to push through the withdrawals, the cravings, and the lies I kept feeding myself about why I couldn't change. Day by day, I fought. Step by step, I climbed. But keeping it real, I failed the challenge of sobriety more than one season, but I kept showing up; fighting like an *American*, kicking like a *Ninja*, and climbing like a *Warrior*.

Every challenge that comes your way, you act powerless. But let me jog your memory—did you forget who the fuck you are? Forget what you've already overcome? You act like this obstacle is your first *rodeo*. That's *bull*! You've been through worse, and now all of a sudden you think this is the one that's gon' take your ass out? Hell no! Use your past as proof. Didn't you pass a test you once failed? Survive a breakup that left you in pieces? Land another job after you thought it was over? Get over being betrayed by a friend? Didn't the loss of your parent or child become more manageable? Get your child back after you thought you lost them to the streets? Restore your marriage after infidelity? You survived all that tried to take you out. Damn it, use those comebacks to fuel every come-up. That's not history—that's evidence. That's résumé material. You've been built for pressure. Built for bounce back. Life ain't asking for perfect—it's daring you to remember who the hell you are. You don't need motivation—you need a mirror. Look at the person who's already made it through hell. Stop acting new to the struggle. These obstacles don't disappear—you destroy them. The strength that got you through before? Still in you. Your fight don't guarantee victory—but quitting guarantees failure. Win or lose, have some backbone. You weren't built to back down—you were built to bounce back.

Growth Affirmation: I will **GROW** out of the mindset of quitting before I try to face my obstacles. My fight doesn't guarantee victory, but if I surrender, it guarantees failure.

Take this day to **THINK** about why you never achieve your goals. Every time you set one, it falls flat, and deep down you know why. It's because you don't take the time to spell it the hell out. And now to achieve it, you're left to read between the lines. A goal without a plan is just a wish, and wishes don't create progress. Imagine baking cookies. You can't just say, "I want some cookies," and expect them to appear. To bake them, you need two things: ingredients and directions. The ingredients tell you what you need; the directions tell you how to use them. It's the same with goals. If you ain't writing down the what and the how, then you're just staring at the oven, hoping heat satisfies your sweet tooth. Success doesn't come from desire alone; it comes from a process that supports the outcome. When your goals are vague, they're dead before they ever begin. If you won't write it down, don't act surprised when life erases it.

My New Jersey partner spent years dreaming of owning a tire shop. He was inspired by his uncle who ran a successful one. In prison, that dream consumed him—it was all he talked about, vowing to leave the streets behind and run an honest business someday. Sadly, that time never came. After his release, he was shot 13 times and put on life support. His family had to make the heart-wrenching decision to remove him from that machine, and when he died, his dream died too. Seeing his dream unfulfilled left a lasting mark on me. In his memory, I made it my goal to open a tire shop of my own—Parker's Tire and Automotive—and I did. Although the shop no longer exists, I brought it to life because I gave it structure by writing down actionable steps on how I was going to build it from the ground up. That experience taught me a painful but necessary truth: Unwritten objectives keep your goals hooked on life support, waiting for you to decide if they'll live or die.

Having a goal without a plan is like ordering a pizza but never giving your address—it ain't ever pulling up. I ask clients all the time, "What's your goal?" and their reply is, "To lose weight." Duh. You can say, "I want to lose weight," all day long—but without spelling it out, that goal is on life support. No plan? Then stop lying to yourself—your ass won't lose weight. You're watching your dreams die because you refuse to hook them up to objectives that can keep them alive. Start using the SMART method when goal-setting—Specific, Measurable, Achievable, Realistic, Timely. That's not some acronym for school—it's the oxygen mask your dream needs. Saying, "I want to lose 20 pounds in three months by exercising five times a week and cutting 500 calories," is how you keep the goal alive. Objectives give structure. They give direction. They stop your goals from getting smothered under all the daily noise and nonsense. Your goals are the engine, but objectives are the fuel. No fuel, no forward motion. Writing them down is how you resuscitate what you say you want. The reason your life feels unstable is because your goals are stuck in the waiting room—still gasping, still ignored—just waiting on you to write the prescription. Be smart and set SMART goals—or keep living like the damn cover model for *Smart Goal-Setting for Dummies*.

Growth Affirmation: I will **GROW** out of the mindset of neglecting my goals. I will commit to creating clear objectives that give them life and a chance at succeeding. It's dumb not to set SMART goals.

Take this day to **THINK** about how, when life puts you at a standstill, your first instinct is to complain, point fingers, and act like the world did you dirty. Why are you walking around defeated when you still got the one thing that matters—life? You're still breathing. Still standing. Still in the ring. A standstill doesn't always mean you're being slowed down on purpose—sometimes it's just life doing what life does. Being unpredictable. Ruthless. Out of your hands. But here's what ain't out of your hands: how you respond. Just because things ain't moving doesn't mean you're finished. Even standing still is a position of strength when you use it right. Don't waste the pause. Don't mistake stillness for failure. Sometimes the best move is just staying on your feet until it's time to take the next step. A little pause don't mean a lack of power.

Prison is a warehouse of lost time—a place where it feels like your life is on pause while the world keeps spinning without you. Men pass the hours glued to the "idiot box," laid out on the yard at what we called Peter Beach, soaking up the sun, or arguing with their girls on the phone when they didn't pick up on the first ring. In those moments, I often found myself thinking that death had to be better than that emptiness. One day, I broke down on the phone with my mom, telling her how trapped I felt. That's when she did something that changed everything: prayed. That prayer shifted my thinking. So many of my homies never made it to that phone call. They didn't get a pause. Life didn't let up, but that day taught me the power of prayer—to give thanks to the Man above for giving me another day to breathe.

Life shouts nonstop—"Keep pushing!" "Stay strong!" "Grind harder!"— like momentum is the only thing that matters. Yeah, all that sounds good. But sometimes life don't just knock the wind out of you—it sits a goddamn elephant on your chest. There are days you lose people you love, face battles you ain't built for, and wake up feeling like the only thing you've accomplished is making it through another 24 hours. That's real shit. It ain't weakness—it's life.

And in those moments, don't fake strength—feel what you feel. It's okay to be overwhelmed. It's okay to cry. It's okay to be angry, depressed, confused—those are human responses to hellish seasons. Just don't confuse a pause with a period. You're not finished—you're figuring. When life slows you down, don't falter—start asking, "What now?" That's where the win lives. Gratitude isn't about ignoring the struggle; it's about acknowledging that as long as you have life, there is still hope. The fact that you're still standing—even if barely—is proof the next move is still yours. You don't have to be at full speed—just hold your ground until the light changes. Life is like standing at a red light—it pauses you, but it doesn't park you. So when things change—and they will—your job is simple: Take the step and make your next move your best move.

Growth Affirmation: I will **GROW** out of the mindset of hopeless delay. Stillness is not the end—it's the setup for my next step.

Take this day to **THINK** about why you're so quick to view life's challenges as permanent defeats when they're really just pit stops—momentary breaks meant to refuel, to reset, to prepare you for the next lap. Pit stops might feel like punishment, but they're part of the process. When you're in it, it's easy to think you're stuck, but ask yourself this: "If I were driving a race car, would I call pulling into the pit lane a loss?" No, because without that stop, the car doesn't finish the race. The tires need changing, the engine needs tuning, and the driver needs a moment to catch their breath. You ain't stalled—you're being serviced. Your faith is being recalibrated. Your strength is being tightened. Life wants to tighten the loose screws that shook during your race— the very ones that could've caused your breakdown—so you can keep moving forward. The real question is, will you sit there thinking it's the end, or will you use the time to get yourself back in the race?

In rehab, I had a roommate whose struggle was so raw it made me forget my own. Two days into the program, we were both wrecked—withdrawals kicking our asses, cravings consuming every thought. But his desperation hit a level I hadn't seen before. He somehow snuck in a syringe and decided to inject his own urine, hoping to squeeze out whatever heroin traces might still be there just for a high. I couldn't believe it—part of me wanted to laugh, but the other part wanted to cry because I understood it. We were both in what felt like life's pit, stripped of every coping mechanism, and left with nothing but the pain we'd been running from. But here's the thing: That pit wasn't the end for either of us. It was the place where we started to strip away the damage, face our demons, and prepare for the next lap. Just like a race car in a pit stop, we were there to repair the broken pieces and get ready to drive forward. That pit wasn't our grave—it was our pit stop to be tuned-up.

Life might feel like a race, but even race cars pull over. Not because they're quitting—but because they're smart enough to know they can't finish broken.

A pit stop ain't a setback—it's survival. When life chokes the hell out of you—when you lose a child, bury a parent, or hit a wall so hard it shakes your soul—that ain't weakness. That's wear and tear. And wear and tear needs work. But here's the line you can't cross: Don't let your burden become your burial. Fix what's loose. Refuel. Reset. And yeah, cry if you need to—but cry while you tighten your bolts. Because the pit ain't the end of the race—it's the reason you'll finish it. Everyone needs a pause. But don't confuse that pit stop for a pity party. Don't let a delay turn into your downfall. Don't let life's *pitfalls* cause you to *fall* into depression and land you in the *pits*. You ain't falling behind—you're gearing up. Don't die in the pit because you mistook it for a grave.

Growth Affirmation: I will **GROW** out of the mindset of seeing life's pauses as setbacks and embrace them as opportunities to refuel, reset, and realign to keep running my race.

Take this day to **THINK** about why humility is the only thing in life that truly fits everyone. From the Victoria's Secret model to the biggest sumo wrestler. Unlike the clothes we wear, humility doesn't need to be altered, stretched, or hemmed—it's universal, one-size-fits-all. It doesn't matter if you're black, white, red, yellow, rich, poor, tall, short, fat, skinny, or somewhere in between; humility wraps around you without asking what size you wear. Humility ain't a flex—it's like Polo: always clean, always classic, and never screaming for attention. Too often, we're taught that strength means standing alone, putting on a tough exterior, and never backing down. But humility offers a different kind of strength. It's the strength to connect, to admit when we're wrong, or to be able to learn from others. Humility don't shrink you—it strips off the ego and makes room to grow. When you approach life humbly, you're embracing a strength that ain't about power but about resilience, empathy, and understanding.

Growing up in the hood, I wore pride like it was high-end gear—I could've won "best dressed" every year just by the way I carried myself. I put on a show, hiding my demons behind fresh clothes and flashy swagger, even while I was popping pills behind closed doors. I thought nobody knew the truth, until one day I was cruising back to my old block, dressed in Polo from head to toe, when the neighborhood bum came up to me asking for a few bucks. I sneered, "When you gon' get your shit together, man?" He looked me dead in the face and said, "I might be broke, but I ain't beneath you. Everybody knows your ass out here popping pills. In fact, you keep your damn money, because you probably gon' need it to buy pills. Pill head." He checked me. His words were truly a punch in the gut. My pride shattered on that sidewalk. That was the first time I realized wearing humility didn't strip me of my identity—it allowed me to rebuild it.

Humility is universal—and you ain't gotta drop pounds, just pride.

Anybody can wear it. It don't care about your title, your tax bracket, or your street cred. Humility is a designer label—it's designed for the ones who wanna label themselves humble, but it only fits if you strip the ego first. Pride will have you acting loud, wrong, and alone. Humility will have you quiet, right, and respected. That's the difference. It ain't about looking strong—it's about being solid. Humility opens doors, arrogance slams shut. It lets you connect instead of compete, admit instead of argue, learn instead of lie. You think being humble makes you look soft? No—being too proud to grow is what makes you look foolish. With humility, your character becomes a bold fashion statement. Don't be the loudest in the room with nothing to show for it. Pride wears flashy chains; humility forges unbreakable ones. And anyone clothed in humility wins "best dressed" every time. If humility feels too tight, it's not your body—it's your ego that's overweight.

Growth Affirmation: I will **GROW** out of the mindset of ego. I don't need to look hard to be strong—real power shows up quiet, dressed in humility, not arrogance.

Take this day to **THINK** about what emotional cargo you keep dragging that's draining your spirit. That worthless man—lying, leeching, leading you nowhere. That promiscuous girl—laying up with every Tom, Dick, and Harry… but mostly with Dick. It makes no sense why you put up with people who only want to shack up instead of shake things up. That fake-ass friend who brings nothing but drama, envy, and negative energy. Old habits, stale mindsets, tired excuses—you're clinging to what's killing you 'cause it's familiar. You keep telling yourself you need them, but what you really need is an amputation. Like a surgeon slicing off an infected limb, you gotta cut off anything that's contaminating your peace. If it ain't helping you heal, it's holding you hostage. Stop babying what's breaking you. Let it go before it guts your future. You ain't stuck—you're just too scared to pull out the damn knife. Don't you get that the longer you leave the infected limb untreated, the more likely it is to destroy you? I'm telling you now, do what you gotta do. Cut the damn infection off. Amputate the bullshit so you can finally breathe.

During a high-speed chase with police, a good friend of mine, known for running track in school, was in a car accident that damaged both his legs. Sadly, he was told he had two options: amputate his legs, or die. Losing his legs meant losing his freedom, his mobility, and part of the identity he'd carried for years. But holding on to them would have cost him his life. Not wanting to die, he chose amputation. Watching him go through that experience was brutal. I knew how much he loved to run. But it taught me that sometimes letting go of what's been a part of you—what you think defines you—is the only way to survive. Holding on would have killed him, but letting go gave him a second chance. It wasn't just his legs he had to leave behind—it was the life that brought him to that moment. Letting go allowed him to rebuild, even when it felt like he was losing part of himself. He couldn't walk on two legs anymore—but he sure as hell could still roll with two arms. His legs gave out, but his arms still carried him forward.

Amputation, whether physical or emotional, don't feel good—but it's necessary when survival's on the line. Whatever or whoever isn't propelling you is paralyzing you. Flat out. You might feel attached to a friend, a habit, or a belief, but if it's draining you, delaying you, or damaging your growth—it's got to fucken go. It ain't gotta go home, but it damn sure gotta get the hell away from you before it kills you. This ain't about being coldhearted—it's about protecting your peace and your purpose. If it ain't amplifying you, it's slowly amputating your future. Stop dressing up dysfunction just because it's familiar. Call it what it is—dead weight. You wouldn't walk around with a gangrenous leg just because it's been with you for years. So why hold on to something that's been killing your momentum? Your excuses are protecting what's poisoning you. Cut it off. Save your mind. Save your energy. Save your damn life. Letting go isn't weakness—it's wisdom. You're not losing—you're clearing space for something better. Until you get bold enough to amputate what's hurting you, you'll never heal. Either you amputate what's killing you, or you keep hanging from the noose you constantly mistake for a hug.

Growth Affirmation: I will **GROW** out of a mindset that clings to what no longer serves me. I will release what holds me back, knowing that letting go is the path to new.

Take this day to **THINK** about why you keep sinking your own ship, then expect someone to show up in a lifeboat. You lose your way and expect the world to stop what the hell it's doing, form a search party, and come find you and bring your lost ass back to your senses. You indulge in bad vices, hook up with the wrong woman or marry the wrong man, then act shocked that no one's coming to drag you out of the mess you walked into. Newsflash: Nobody's coming. Nobody can help you until you help yourself. You're not stuck because of what happened to you; you're stuck because you're waiting for someone to come pull you out. You think everybody's AAA, ready to tow you out every time you break down, jumpstart you when you're dead, or patch you up when your life goes flat. No. Stop expecting people to rescue you outta the messes you made. You're searching for clarity. But clarity doesn't come from waiting; it comes from beginning the search to discover where you took that wrong turn. Like misplacing your keys—you're the only one who knows the places to look, so it's on you to retrace your steps. Stop waiting for a lifeline that's never going to show up. Some lose their way because their mind betrays them from diseases like Alzheimer's or dementia—what the hell is your excuse when yours is intact?

During my addiction, I was waiting to be saved by others. I expected counselors, therapists, sponsors, family, and friends to restore me. I convinced myself that if they all just played their part, I'd eventually find my way back to normal. I remember one session blowing up on a counselor, cussing her out because I didn't see a damn change in me. I questioned her credentials, barking, "Why the hell you even here if you can't fix me?" I was mad at her for not saving me, but truth is, nobody could. I had to help myself. No amount of outside help could move me forward until I aligned my own actions with the values I had abandoned. I wasn't lost—I knew exactly where I was and what was wrong; I just lingered in the same destructive behaviors, hoping for some breakthrough. The change came only when I stopped waiting for others to carry me and started moving in the direction my moral compass pointed. I began making decisions that reflected the man I wanted to become—not the one addiction had made me. It wasn't easy, but every right step made the path out of hell a little clearer, until I finally found my way back by following the trail of truth and broken pieces I had left behind.

Why is this hard? You can't light a smoke signal and expect the world to save you from a blaze you keep feeding. Stop sitting there waiting for someone to notice how lost you are when you the one causing the confusion. The world ain't sending a rescue team. No search party is coming with a flashlight. It's your path. Your pain. Your problem to solve. Nobody owes you a map—you gotta make your own. Finding yourself starts with owning your part in the mess and doing something about it. Stop wishing for a fix and start working the damn problem. Motivation ain't coming to save you—it's waiting on you to move. People can inspire you, but they can't carry you. That's your job. So ask yourself: "What's my reason to fight?" What's the one thing that keeps you moving forward when everything says, "Quit"? Hold on to that and start walking. Step by painful step. Clarity don't come from crying foul—it comes from crawling forward. Lost keys don't crawl back to your pocket—and neither will your right mind if you keep sitting still. You can send up smoke signals all you want and set off all the flares you want, but don't expect rescue helicopters or search dogs. Here's the shocker: You're not lost—you keep throwing dirt on your own name and burying yourself so deep you wonder why nobody can find you. You built a whole damn bunker out of your lies and locked yourself inside.

Growth Affirmation: I will **GROW** out of a mindset
that waits for others to rescue me. It's okay to ask people to
help me find my way, but I still have to take the steps.

Take this day to **THINK** about how failure isn't something embedded in your DNA—it's a choice, a pattern that can either continue or be broken. Too often, families accept failure as if it were a family heirloom, passed down like eye color or hair texture—when in reality, it's learned behavior. Failure seems to run in families because no one in the family runs toward success. Instead, they avoid risks, settle for less, and repeat the same cycles, convincing themselves that greatness is out of reach. But here's the truth: Failure is not hereditary. It's not something you're born into; it's something you step into when you refuse to challenge the status quo. It's the result of choices, habits, and mindsets that are learned and repeated across generations. Breaking free from it requires courage, determination, and a willingness to rewrite the story your family has been telling for generations. The curse ain't in your bloodline—it's in your mindset.

In my family, Type 2 diabetes is everywhere—an epidemic dressed up as inevitability. What frustrates me isn't the disease, it's the defeat. They treat it like a birthmark, not a battle. As if being sick is the standard and getting better is some fantasy. I've watched them ignore solutions, reject discipline, and embrace decay like it's tradition. And sadly, this is exactly how families treat success. They exchange rationalizations. They bequeath brokenness. They defend dysfunction. They normalize quitting. Not because they can't win—but because nobody's ever dared to try something different. Complacency becomes culture when no one chooses change. Just like diabetes, failure might run in the family, but it doesn't have to finish with you. Reversing it takes more than motivation—it takes rebellion. You've got to be willing to be the one who breaks what everyone else calls normal.

Unlike disease, failure ain't coded in your genes—it's coded in your habits. It doesn't pass through blood—it passes through belief. It's not something that gets passed down—it's just that success keeps getting passed up. It stays in the family because nobody wants to outrun it. They pass limitations like batons and treat ambition like it's out of reach. Imagine a relay race where success is the handoff—but every runner fumbles it out of fear. And now here you are, staring at the same damn baton. You can pick it up, or you can walk past it like the rest. If failure looks familiar, it's because it's been rehearsed. But just because they rehearsed it don't mean you gotta perform it. You either break the cycle or you become it. Your last name ain't a tragedy—it's a title waiting for your Michael Jackson to make it sing. This ain't about what runs in your blood—it's about who finally stops running from the work. Just because failure lived in your house don't mean it has to live in your head. You're not doomed by your DNA—you're paralyzed by your patterns. Quit treating failure like it's Grandma's pearls—some things ain't meant to be passed down. Be the first in your family to flip the script—be the first to graduate college, the first to build a business, the first to buy a home, the first to write a book. Somebody's gotta stop passing down excuses and start passing down examples. Might as well be you.

Growth Affirmation: I will **GROW** out of the mindset of thinking that failure is my family's DNA. Family habits might've raised me, but they ain't gotta raise my kids.

Take this day to **THINK** about why you insist on dulling your mind with nonsense when you have every opportunity to sharpen it. You scroll aimlessly, gossip like your name is Wendy Williams, and binge-watch shows like they're gon' pay your bills. Why? Is it easier to stay average than to put in the work to be better? Your mind ain't some cheap tool you throw away when it's dull—it's your sharpest weapon, but you treat it like junk. Every minute you waste filling it with garbage is another minute you could've spent making it sharper, stronger, and more prepared for the battles of life. The mind doesn't wear out with use; it gets sharper. But you'd rather fill it with porn, mindless social media, addiction, and excuses than equip it to break out of the life you claim to hate. That's not just lazy—it's self-sabotage. Why do you insist on not sharpening your mind? Stop treating your brain like a dull pencil. It's not going to sharpen itself, and the more you ignore it, the harder it'll be to make progress.

In prison, I wasted years talking about nothing. Day after day, I'd sit around telling war stories—bragging about how much weight I moved, which girls I smashed, and who ain't got what. It was a pissing contest with no prize. We weren't building—we were reminiscing. Feeding off past war stories like we should've earned Purple Hearts for wreckin' our own lives. We were sharp, but we dulled our minds with recycled ignorance. Instead of reading, learning, or planning, I was performing for a crowd that wasn't going nowhere fast—just like me. Contrary to what people may think, prison is filled with brilliant minds. Men with trades and talents that sustain the inside economy—electricians, chefs, artists, clothing designers, bookies, and even grocery store owners, like I was. But many of us on the inside used our gifts for selfish or destructive gain. We had what the free world needed—time. We just chose to waste it. Prison should be the sharpener. With all that time and reflection it could produce problem-solvers, business plans, and future millionaires. But too many let their minds rot while glorifying a life that already failed them.

The mind doesn't get sharper by accident—you gotta put it to work. Your mind ain't like a pencil that gets dull with use—it sharpens every time you put it to work. But if you keep feeding it TMZ headlines, porn sites, social media trends, and gossip, don't act surprised when you can't think your way out of a wet paper bag. That ain't stimulation—that's sedation. You numb your potential with garbage, then wonder why your life stinks. You scroll through other people's fake lives, chasing clout and chaos, but won't invest ten minutes into sharpening your own damn mind. That's not entertainment—that's enslavement. And the algorithm is your warden. You ain't being held down or held back—you're just mentally sedated, overdosing on distractions. Trade the filth for something that fuels you. Learn a trade. Crack open a book. Stream a documentary that actually teaches you something. Listen to a podcast that can elevate you. Every scroll you waste is a stroke against your own evolution. You've fallen into the trap satan set for you—to waste the most powerful thing God ever gave you: your mind. You're digitally possessed, chained to a screen, and proud of your own bondage. As long as satan can keep you from sharpening your mind, he knows you'll never be a threat—never add anything of value to this world. So go ahead—scroll your life away, drink your life away, smoke your life away. But understand this: By being consumed by scrolling and not sharpening your mind, you're not living—you're just livestreaming your downfall for the whole world to see.

Growth Affirmation: I will **GROW** out of the mindset that feeds my mind garbage. By not sharpening my mind, not only will I stay stuck in life—I'll die stuck on stupid.

Take this day to **THINK** about how many times your mouth murdered your message. You ain't wrong about what you're saying—but the way you spit it? That's the problem. Truth with no tact hits like a slap, not a save. Some people talk like drill sergeants—barking commands, swinging their opinions around like a sword, thinking just 'cause it's true, they're justified in slicing folks open. That ain't wisdom—that's ego with a megaphone. Telling somebody, "You need to stop doing that," might be true, but your tone made them feel attacked, not advised. If you sound more like a warden than a witness, don't act shocked when they don't hear you. A closed heart don't care how true your words are—it only hears the tone. Instead, try saying, "Have you thought about…" or, "You might want to consider…" That ain't being soft— that's being surgical. You're planting, not pounding. Your delivery decides whether your truth heals or harms. A brick in your hand can build a house— or break a window. Same brick. Different intent. Different impact. What you say can either open the door or slam it shut. Say it like a bridge, not a bulldozer. It's not about being right; it's about being effective.

People's truth screamed at me like it came with handcuffs. "Dion, you need to quit doing pills." "You better change your ways." And here's the truth, they were right—but it felt more like they were putting me on trial than pulling me up. They weren't reaching down—they were looking down. Like they were trying to flex their clean hands while pointing at my dirt. That ain't help—that's humiliation. And it pushed me deeper into denial. If your delivery burns bridges, don't be shocked when nobody crosses over. I wasn't running from the truth—I was ducking the disrespect. The way they said it stripped me of my power, like they knew better and I was just some case to fix. But if somebody had slowed down and hit me with, "What do you think this leads to?"—that would've hit different. Truth should stretch you, not strangle you. It should convict, not corner. Truth delivered wrong becomes another wound to heal from. People remember how you made them feel longer than they remember what you said. Knowledge dropped right is likely picked up.

Stop weaponizing the truth like it gives you license to lecture. You ain't the authority on nobody else's path. Don't lead with what they "need to" do. Don't start barking out "shoulds," "betters," "musts," and "have tos" like you got it all figured out. Nobody's gon' hear your truth if they feel like they're being shoved in a corner. You think facts alone change people? Nah. Respect does. If your truth comes with heat but no heart, don't expect applause— you're just showing off how smart you are while being mean. Your tone can be the right map but give the wrong directions. Real leadership ain't loud. It listens. It plants seeds without pounding pavement. You don't need to dominate a moment to make a difference. Say less. Ask more. Let people breathe around your advice. Because even if your truth is perfect, but your tone is poison, all they'll taste is venom. Don't just be right—be heard. Droppin' knowledge is different from droppin' bombs.

Growth Affirmation: I will **GROW** out of the mindset that being right is enough. Before I speak, I will ask myself, "Are my words about to be a bridge, or are they about to burn one?"

Take this day to **THINK** about why you're so quick to snap at somebody for checking your mannish-ass child, knowing damn well your child is outta control. You act like correction is disrespect—but what's really disrespectful is letting your kid run wild with no guidance, no accountability, and no consequences. You're not your child's best friend. You're the one responsible for shaping their life, not cheering them on while they stir up bullshit. Today's parents wanna be cool so bad, they forget to be effective. You got mothers competing for "most viewed" while not giving a damn about viewing their child's report card. You got dads posting selfies in gyms while their sons are sitting in jail waiting on them to post their bail. Parents care more about comments than commenting on what needs to be done about their disrespectful-ass child. Parents wanna dress young like them, go to clubs with them, and get high with them. And now we got kids out here raising hell because the ones who were supposed to raise them got too scared, too soft, or too selfish to do so. Yes, we live in a world where discipline is judged—but guess what? So is a child with no home training. Child Protective Services ain't the biggest threat. The streets are. The prisons are. The graveyards are. And if you don't wake up, your child might be the next one who gets put in either one. Beat their ass if you have to. Because your absence plants the pain that buries them.

Growing up, my neighbors were allowed to whoop my ass without recourse from my family. Today that's not the case. A close friend of mine is now doing life because his parents didn't raise him—they entertained him. His mama smoked weed with him like they were college roommates. His dad took him to gambling spots and taught him how to throw dice when he should've taught him how to throw a fucken a baseball. They bragged about being the "cool parents" while the streets shaped their son into a monster. No boundaries. No accountability. Just good vibes and bad voices. And it cost somebody their life. Now he's locked up, and they're left visiting the version of their child the world created in their absence. They gave him too much rope—the judge hung him with it. Prison got him bound because his parents had no boundaries. They didn't raise him—they released him. If you don't build yo child, the system will break them. You wanna be cool? Cool don't keep your child off a T-shirt. Not being connected to your child is like having a broken Wi-Fi signal—they'll search for connection somewhere else. And that "somewhere" might be a gang, a predator, or a group of kids just as lost as them. A child left unchecked becomes an adult no one can correct. And once that world slaps them with charges or a casket, it's too late to wish you had been more involved.

You thought being their friend was enough. You let them run the show—and now the judge or mortician has center stage. You gave the spotlight to your child early—now the only light on them is from a police officer's flashlight or from a camera crew at a crime scene. You wanted everybody to like your child, and it worked—now everybody's wearing their face on a T-shirt. You wanted a child star—now their fifteen minutes of fame is a news report on their death. Look, not knowing how to parent ain't a free pass. Learn. Ask. Reach out. Programs like Big Brothers Big Sisters exist for a reason—use them. There's help out there. What's not acceptable is using your pain as an excuse to pass down chaos. Kids without correction become headlines with consequences. You don't raise them? The world will—and trust me, the world don't love your child the way you should. Talk to your kids. Set the standard. Correct their steps while you still can, because the cost of neglecting your child today will be paid in tears tomorrow. Be their parent now—or be their visitor later, in jail or at their grave. You gave your child all that freedom, so the system came and took it. Don't beg for sympathy when they're locked up or laid out—you the one handed them the handcuffs and the fucken gun.

Growth Affirmation: I will **GROW** out of wanting to be liked
by my child—they don't need a fan, they need a foundation.
My silence today could echo in a courtroom tomorrow.

Take this day to **THINK** about why your life feels like reruns—same problems, same drama, same excuses. You ain't evolving, you just old school in the worst way. Still preaching principles that ain't never paid off. You wear stubbornness like it's a badge, when really it's a chain. Still talking about "back in my day." You'd rather stay broke than admit your way ain't working. You treat advice like offense, feedback like disrespect, and truth like betrayal. You talk like your way works, but you ain't got no results to show for it. You act like you allergic to progress—every time someone hands you a better way, you swat it like disrespect. Nobody can correct you, coach you, or convince you, because you'd rather stay loyal to an era than be educated. And while the world moves on, you stay in your little bubble, proud of how unchanged you are. You don't want better—you want familiar. And the sick part? You'd rather stay behind than admit you've been wrong. That's why you ain't evolving. Not because life's unfair—but because your pride don't fit in progress.

In the streets, there's this thing called the "street code." This unwritten rule requires absolute loyalty—no ratting or snitching, no matter what. The consequences of breaking it can be dire. I had a falling out with a friend over this exact thing. He was convinced I betrayed him, but I saw it differently. To me, it wasn't snitching—it was setting shit straight. The problem with the street code is that it demands unwavering loyalty, even when that loyalty is not reciprocated. But some guys are so rooted in this mindset that they go as far as tattooing "Death Before Dishonor" on their bodies, signaling they'd rather die or go to prison than break the code. But here's how naïve they are: If they really believed in "Death Before Dishonor," they may as well have killed themselves a long time ago. The day they chose to live a life of crime was the day they dishonored themselves and their family. They choose the streets over them. Are you saying that your stubbornness to the street code is important to you, but your family ain't? Too many people are so consumed by this mentality that they can't escape it—they're stuck in a way of thinking that keeps them from freedom.

Being hardheaded ain't strength—it's sabotage. You treat your outdated beliefs like antiques—thinking the longer you hold on to them, the more valuable they'll become and fetch you millions by advertising them on *Antiques Roadshow*. Newsflash: Your old-ass principles ain't even garage sale worthy. Your stubbornness is nothing but recycled ignorance. You still living by rules that never respected you in the first place. That code you swear by? Ain't built nothing but chaos. You ain't principled—you're petrified. The truth? You'd rather be stuck than stretched. You defend your stubbornness like it's your legacy, but all it's done is leave you isolated and irrelevant. You out here swearing by loyalty, but it ain't loyalty if it's to a lifestyle that's choking your growth. It's the same mindset as elders holding onto house phones like smartphones are the devil, or churchgoers acting like God cares more about your suit than your surrender. God don't give a damn about somebody coming to church in holy jeans—you do. Nobody says a word about that dusty-ass hat you keep wearing, but you quick to run your mouth about what somebody wearing to church. So what their jeans got holes? At least some part of them is holy. You love comfort so much you'd die before you grow. Let that sink in. And maybe that's why you still where you are—because you treat information like an insult and progress like punishment. It's no mystery that when you die, history won't call it a death—it'll call it an extinction, 'cause you were too damn stuck in the Stone Age to ever evolve.

Growth Affirmation: I will **GROW** out of the mindset that being stubborn makes me strong—real power is in being teachable, not untouchable.

Take this day to THINK about how long you gon' keep punking yourself out of the life you swear you want. You cry, "I can't," when you ain't even tried. You let somebody else's weak, "You can't," chain you up like a mutt, and you don't even bark back. How long you gon' let fear pimp you, make you lay down for failure, sell your soul, and call it fate? The reason you're starving in life is because you don't hate the lies. You should be embarrassed living like this—walking around acting powerless when the truth is, you just too damn scared to bet on yourself. "I can't" is a straight-up bald-faced lie from your own cowardly mouth. "You can't" is the trash others toss at you hoping you'll choke on it. And you've been foolish enough to swallow both. Stop being proud of paralysis. Stop pacifying lies that are robbing you blind. The moment you stop listening, you'll discover the freedom to act and prove those lies wrong.

After I got hooked on pills, people didn't just lose faith in me—they buried me alive. Said I'd never bounce back. Said I was too far gone. And I couldn't even blame them. I was burning every bridge behind me just to light the way to my next high. Manipulating anyone who got too close. Using charm like a weapon. Wearing the same outfit for a week. Losing jobs left and right, showing up late—or not at all. Calling in with lies I didn't even bother making believable. I was a shell of who I used to be, and they said the real me was dead and buried. And truth be told, I started believing it too. Thought I'd crossed a line you don't come back from. That lie became my leash—tight around my neck, pulling me deeper into that pit. But the day came when I realized that just because you got written off doesn't mean the story's over. I had to cut that leash and kill the echo of their doubt. "You can't" is just a mirror reflecting their failures, not your future. The biggest threat to your progress ain't your circumstances—it's the lies you let live in your head.

"I can't" leaves you sitting on the shoulder of the road because you didn't want to get gas. "You can't" slaps your hand off the pump before you can put gas in the car. Together, they've parked you and convinced you that it was fate. But you ain't out of gas—you just stopped fighting. That lie in your head? It ain't truth—it's trauma talking. And that lie from others? It ain't real—it's their reflection replying. Stop asking permission to be great. Rip the "I can't" out your damn mouth and replace it with "Watch the hell I do." Shatter the "You can't" by doing exactly what they said you wouldn't. The engine's still good—you just forgot how to hit the gas. Every small step forward becomes undeniable proof that the lies were never true. Success don't require leaps— it starts with a single step forward, repeated over and over again until the lies lose their hold. You don't need perfect conditions, you don't need a certain amount of money, you don't need a ton of resources, yo ass need motion. Start where you are, use what you got, and prove every lie wrong, one gritty step at a time. You can make things happen—you just keep talkin' to liars. And one of 'em lives in your mirror.

Growth Affirmation: I will **GROW** out of the mindset of believing the lies of, "I can't," and, "You can't." The lies may echo, but your actions will silence them.

Take this day to **THINK** about why you keep living beneath your potential. Inferiority ain't something you were born with—it's something you picked up along the way and started wearing like it was designer. You decided greatness was for them, not you. That success was some exclusive nightclub you couldn't get into. But let me put you on game—there ain't no bouncer standing at success's door stopping you from getting in. You're not too messed up, too broken, or too late. That'd be like standing outside a party with no guest list, swearing you weren't invited. You're just too used to standing outside. Most people ain't being rejected—they're rejecting themselves before they even try. *Superiority ain't about thinking you better than everybody—it's about refusing to accept that you're less than anybody.* You ain't beneath nobody unless you bow to that mindset. You can't claim royalty while treating yourself like a peasant. Either you start believing you belong at the table, or you keep begging for scraps from it.

Boy, I had an inferiority complex like a mug. Sat there quiet when I should've spoken up, hung back when I should've stepped up—'cause I didn't think I had it in me. I remember this one girl, bad as hell. I wanted to shoot my shot, but fear had me shook. Wouldn't even look her way, let alone say something. She was from the hills, I was from the hood. It felt like the movie *The Outsiders*—a Greaser tryin' to holler at a Social. But get this—I get a note slid to me from her friend. Open it, and boom—it's her. The same girl I was scared to even glance at. She asking if I wanna be her man. Told me to check the "yes" or "no" box if I wanted to be her boyfriend, as if we were in grade school. That was the day I learned that inferiority ain't real—it's just a lie you keep rehearsing till it sounds like truth. Soon as I snatched that lie off repeat, I turned into a problem. Casanova with a mission. No chick was off-limits. If I wanted her, I was shootin' my shot. You couldn't tell me I wasn't him. The only thing ever disqualifying me was that inferior voice in my head I kept givin' the mic to.

The only reason you feel beneath others is 'cause you keep bowing to fear and ducking greatness. Living with an inferiority complex is like dragging around a balloon with no air—useless, sad, and sagging. But the second you fill it with belief, grind, and guts? That same balloon starts rising like it had potential the whole time. Stop letting people convince you you're not enough. Somebody says you're fat? Don't pay them no mind—you're not overweight, you're under construction. Somebody calls you ugly? Don't pay them no mind—you're not unattractive, you just ain't stepped in front of eyes that know what beauty looks like. But one day you will. People who stay trapped in small mindsets sit in the bleachers of their own life—clapping for everybody else, too scared to realize they had front-row seats to their potential. But the truth is, your life's been on pause, not because of lack of opportunity, but because you keep seeing yourself less than. Stop walking past closed doors like they're sealed shut. Most of them ain't locked—you just never had the guts to test the handle. You ain't unqualified—you just have no belief in yourself. Your worth isn't up for debate unless you're the one on the debate team. Get rid of that stage fright. The stage is set. The lights are on. The mic is hot. You belong on that damn stage—but you've got to stop sitting in the nosebleeds. Ain't nobody ever said you couldn't; *you* just never said you could.

Growth Affirmation: I will **GROW** out of the mindset
of inferiority. I ain't beneath nobody—I just been
bowing too long. It's time I stand up and stand tall.

Take this day to **THINK** about why you keep chasing comfort over connection. You say you want unity, but you're too busy scanning people for similarities instead of substance. If they ain't from your hood, your background, your brokenness—you shut down, like truth needs to be identical twins. That ain't unity—that's masked insecurity. You're not looking to build bridges, you're just looking for mirrors. And that's why you never get ahead—because your circle ain't a team, it's a group of clones. Real unity don't come from copy-pasting yourself into a room—it comes from stomaching the discomfort of being different. But you don't want different—you want predictable, safe, and soft. And safe don't sharpen you. Nor does it elevate you. All you're doing is surrounding yourself with yes-men who throw parades for your plateau, nod at your nonsense, and cosign your complacency. You'll never grow by leading a parade of puppets. If you only commune with people who think like you, don't call it a community—call it a cult.

Walking into recovery spaces, I didn't see a single counselor who looked like they'd ever got high a day in their life. No one had done time, lost family to addiction, or seen the street corner turn into a graveyard. I sat with my arms folded, already convinced they couldn't teach me nothing. I thought, "_If you ain't touched it, how can anything you say touch me?_" But I was dead wrong. The wisdom they had wasn't born in my world, but it still had weight in it. Every time I actually listened, something clicked. Their stories didn't match mine, but the lessons hit all the same. I realized recovery wasn't about finding somebody who'd walked in my shoes—it was about walking with somebody who could help me gain my footing. What mattered was that I was ready to quit, and they were willing to help me. Damned if they hadn't been through what I went through—I wanted the hell out. And if that meant teaming up with people who were different but had the same goal as me, then let's make this shit happen. For the longest, I was looking for twins instead of a tribe, and that's why I wasn't growing. I needed to unify with people who could help me. Not a fan club.

Unity is like an orchestra. Ain't no power in everybody playing the same note—that's noise, not music. Real harmony happens when violins, trumpets, flutes, and drums all play different parts but build the same melody. Your life's the same way. You don't grow by echo chambers—you grow by exposure. And you don't need someone who talks like you to teach you—just someone committed to truth, growth, and purpose. Stop dismissing people because their struggle don't match your scars. Find common ground in the goal, not in the grind. Growth don't come from mirrors—it comes from merging perspectives into momentum. So quit expecting people to mirror your story and start appreciating those who magnify your future. Unity don't mimic your life—it multiplies your purpose. Harmony ain't about everyone playing the same note—it's about making a note that unity is forged, not in likeness, but in the commitment to grow and succeed together, despite differences. Unity don't echo opinions—it elevates outcomes.

Growth Affirmation: I will **GROW** out of the mindset of thinking everyone has to be like me to stimulate growth. I will embrace the beauty in others without judgment.

Take this day to **THINK** about why you're still frontin' like you've got it all together when everything in your life is falling apart. Pride's been lying to you—telling you it's strength when it's really your straightjacket. You walk around like you don't need nobody, like asking for help is weakness, but that tough act ain't toughness—it's torment. Your pride ain't protecting you; it's punishing you. You're duct-taping a cracked windshield and swearing it's road ready—but you're one bump away from it caving in. That's why your life's in shambles—because you'd rather choke on your pain than swallow your pride. You'd rather bleed out in silence than scream for help—that ain't strength, that's stupidity. Pride keeps you broke, bitter, and bound. But hey, if pretending you're good while everything's crumbling is your definition of strength, then by all means—more power to you. Just don't cry when everything crashes, 'cause real growth don't come with a mask on.

During my addiction, pride was the armor I wore to hide the chaos. I acted like everything was cool, like I had it under control, but behind that fake smile was a man drowning. I refused help, dodged honesty, and ran from reality because I thought admitting my mess would make me look weak. What it really did was delay my healing. The shift came when I had to come clean to my daughter—no script, no lies, just truth. I laid it all out: the pills, the pain, the lies I told to protect the image I thought I needed to keep. I thought she'd hate me. But instead, she hugged me tighter. That moment wasn't the end of my strength—it was the beginning of it. No more pretending. Just vulnerability, truth, and connection. Dropping my pride helped me pick up the pieces. That pride I kept holdin' on to was the same thing that was holdin' me back.

Pride don't pay bills, fix relationships, or rebuild broken men—it just delays the downfall. Your image might impress people, but your honesty is what'll actually save you. Pride don't protect—it poisons. And you keep chuggin' it like it's strength in a bottle. Pride is a terrible bodyguard—it'll block the ones trying to heal you and let in everything that's killing you. If pretending fixed problems, you'd be perfect by now. The cracks in your ego? That's where the healing gets in. You think you're protecting yourself, but all you're doing is building a prison with no doors. Strength ain't in silence—it's in surrendering to the truth. You can't fix what you keep faking. If pride's the poison, humility is the antidote. Let pride die so you can finally live. You ain't gotta keep collapsing behind a mask. There are people waiting to help you. Stop hiding the fact that you're hurting. Drop the pride and the tough guy act. Your ass ain't hard—you're just hiding. The more you fake strength, the further you get from real healing. Get help. *Let go of the front and let others have your back.*

Growth Affirmation: I will **GROW** out of the mindset of being prideful. I will swallow pride whole in order to digest any information or tools needed to better myself.

Take this day to **THINK** about why you're drifting through life, letting your brain collect dust like it's some antique instead of the most powerful tool on earth. You're walking around with a supercomputer between your ears, but you treat it like a paperweight. Don't say it's hard—truth is, you've just stopped thinking. You'll waste hours chasing distractions, chasing drama, and chasing everybody else's life—but won't give ten minutes to fixing your own. If you cleared the junk in your head like you clear storage on your phone, you'd finally have space for progress. If you protected your thoughts like you protect your passwords, negativity wouldn't hack into your purpose so easily. You're not a victim of your environment; you're a prisoner of your passivity. The brain wasn't given to you just to survive—it was given to help you create, innovate, and elevate. But instead of activating it, you've turned it off like airplane mode, then wondered why your life ain't taking off. You ain't mentally dead—you're just sitting on a live mind acting like it's a corpse.

You want to hear the irony of my life? One of the shows I used to watch was *The Walking Dead.* Zombies stumbling around in a lifeless daze—that hit different for me, because it felt like I was watching a reflection. I was a walking void. Pills had hijacked my mind, held my thoughts hostage, and turned my life into a numb routine. There were stretches of time when my brain wasn't worth two cents—completely consumed by addiction. The pills didn't just want me high—they wanted me helpless. And for a while, they got what they wanted. My body was moving, but my mind wasn't. I wasn't thinking critically, planning anything real, or making decisions that could pull me out. But I started thinking seriously the day my dude got shot in the head. He ended up brain-dead, machines keeping him barely hanging on. And seeing him laid up like that—unable to speak, move, or even blink—something in me woke up. I thought: His brain was gone, and here I was wasting mine.

That moment cracked me wide open. That day, a piece of me started thinking straight—when I realized his thinking days were done.

It's comprehensible when the brain dies and the body stops. But when the brain works and the mind still quits? That's beyond comprehension. *Understand that the body cannot go where the mind won't take it.* A mind left unused is like a dead phone—full of power, but useless if it never gets charged. Here's what's sad: We're quick to update apps, but when it comes to updating our minds, we stall. We put more effort into clearing space on a device than we do clearing space in our own heads. It's time to download discipline, upload wisdom, and delete every excuse. Stop treating your brain like a junk drawer. Your brain is not a decorative organ—it's a divine engine. Stop walking through life like a zombie. Power up, plug in, and use what's already in you to think your way out of the miserable-ass life you're living. Get your brain out of sleep mode. Take the Do Not Disturb sign off your mind so information can come in and do some cleaning. A powered-down brain is the cause of a powerless life. You'll never live fully while your mind stays logged off.

> **Growth Affirmation:** I will **GROW** out of the mindset of running on autopilot. My brain is a supercomputer, and I refuse to let it sit in sleep mode.

Take this day to **THINK** about how your life feels uninspiring, filled with unmotivated moments and a lack of direction. Let's be honest—boredom isn't just about having nothing to do; it's about choosing to do nothing. You sit there with nothing on your mind, letting time slip through your fingers like sand, complaining about how nothing ever changes. But how could it? You're too busy counting distractions when you could be counting achievements. Stop letting boredom be your game plan—it's time to draw up a playbook for the life you want. Boredom isn't harmless; it's the quiet thief that steals opportunities, kills ambition, and keeps you stuck in mediocrity. You say you want more, but are you doing more? The truth is, you'd rather sit in a room bored than put yourself in a boardroom where decisions are made and futures are built. And that's why nothing is changing. It's wiser to be in a room full of decisions than in a room full of distractions. Boredom wastes moments that could've been used to build momentum.

Spending six months in a prison hole, I was trapped in boredom within four walls. Each day, the arts-and-crafts cart came by offering books and supplies, but I ignored them. I was too busy asking the porter to sneak me in some contraband. I was so deep into boredom that I resorted to counting the Rice Krispies in my breakfast cereal—that's how empty it got. Eventually, I realized that staying in that mental state would do me more harm than good. One afternoon, I finally took the porter up on his offer. I picked up art supplies from his cart and started putting together a picture of what I wanted my life to look like. I created a vision board. That small act was a defining moment. It gave me vision. I put up a picture of T. D. Jakes because of his ability to reach people, a gym because I wanted to become a trainer, and a plane to remind me I'd travel one day. And I have accomplished them all. Today, my life is no longer spent in "rooms bored." The difference between a "boardroom" and a "room bored" isn't just about location—it's about the mindset you choose. It's the difference between me sitting in a room bored, popping pills and staring at the walls, or sitting in a boardroom, popping out ideas and staring into my future.

Let's be real—the reason your life looks like nothing is 'cause you do nothing. All. Damn. Day. A part of me can only hope that you reading this book is the end of your days being idle. 'Cause if not, as soon as you're done reading, you gon' go right back to being unproductive as fuck. To transition from a bored life to an engaged one, creating a vision board can be liberating. A vision board isn't just a collage of dreams—it's a contract with yourself to pursue them with no room for negotiation. Don't wait—do this as soon as you can. Go to Walmart. Hell, hit Dollar Tree. Grab a piece of construction paper, scissors, and glue, and find some magazines. Cut out the life you want, paste it on the paper, and start staring at it daily like your future depends on it—because it does. Each time you glance at it, you're reminded of what you're working toward and why it matters. It's not just about motivation—it's about strategy. Like a boardroom full of decisive plans, your vision board becomes the space where you strategize your next moves. One decision, one action at a time—choose ambition over apathy and purpose over passivity. The boardroom mindset starts with you stepping into the role of CEO—Chief Execution Officer of your own life. Because ideas don't free you from boredom—execution does.

Growth Affirmation: I will **GROW** out of the mindset
of passive comfort. Some people sit in boardrooms.
Others sit in rooms bored. I *must* choose my chair.

Take this day to **THINK** about why you're so caught up in competing and comparing yourself to others, and ask yourself: "What exactly am I winning?" Competing with others doesn't make you stronger—it makes you smaller. You always feel like you gotta prove you're better than somebody. Comparison robs you of peace, progress, and potential, leaving you stuck in a cycle of proving yourself to people who don't even fucken matter. Competition and comparison are nothing more than distractions. They keep you worried about what somebody else got, so you don't even realize what you could be building yourself. They keep you with a crook in your neck 'cause you keep looking sideways in someone else's business instead of forward, wasting energy you could use to build something meaningful. Collaboration and cooperation grow gardens; competition and comparison build walls. You build more by linking arms than throwing fists. Stop looking to outdo others. Cooperation and collaboration will always lead to more significant achievements than comparison and competition ever will.

Early in my fitness career, I fell into the trap of thinking I had to be the best. Like I had in the streets. Back then, it was all about outshining the competition. In my mind, winning meant proving I was superior to everyone else. But that mindset didn't make me better—it had me bound. The moment I stopped trying to outdo others and started collaborating with people who had strengths I didn't, my life began to evolve. Partnering with other trainers who were certified in nutrition, rehabilitation, and specialized exercises allowed me to elevate my training and help my clients in ways I couldn't have done alone. The same thing was true on the streets. When I aligned myself with people who had complementary skills instead of competing with them, we accomplished more together than I ever could have on my own. Working with others achieves more than working against them. Collaboration multiplies what competition only divides.

Why are you so consumed with competing with or comparing yourself to others anyway? The truth is, the mirror is your rival. Stop wasting energy worrying about who got this or who got that—that's not where growth happens. Don't hate them because they doing better than you. They doing shit you ain't willing to. Progress begins when you focus on competing with the fears, doubts, and procrastination that keep holding your nosy-ass back. You should ask yourself every day: "Did I grow? Did I learn? Did I take even one step forward?" If the answer is no, the problem ain't someone else—it's you. The world doesn't need another bitter person tearing others down to feel superior. It needs builders, collaborators, and visionaries who understand that the greatest wins come from working together. Use that energy of comparing and competing to create something bigger than yourself. Together, you can build mountains of progress instead of fragile castles of insecurity. Growth happens when you stop trying to outshine others and start learning how to light the way for yourself and those around you. The only opponent you should be competing against and comparing yourself to is you. Want a real win? Stop shadowboxing strangers and square up with the man in the mirror. You keep worrying about rivals, but the only one stopping you is that sorry-ass reflection. The real competition ain't with them—it's with the sorry version of you that keeps quitting. You wanna beat up somebody? Beat his ass. He's the one who got you believing you ain't shit.

Growth Affirmation: I will **GROW** out of the mindset
of comparison. I'm done measuring myself by others
when my only rival is the man in the mirror.

Take this day to **THINK** about why you keep begging for a future you won't lift a damn finger to build. A clock's hands stay moving forward, counting hours like they matter. Yours? They're too busy digging in chip bags, stuffing Oreos down your throat, turning up bottles, lighting crack pipes, shooting up with needles, pushing buttons on your remote, or putting your hands all over people you know belong to somebody else. You swear you want change, but your hands stay on everything but your purpose. A clock uses its hands to count the hours; you should be using yours to make the hours count. Life don't hand out rewards to people waiting on "perfect timing"—it throws them at people who clock in and grind. But you? You're just posting, playing, pouting—wasting time like it don't run out. If your hands ain't building, fixing, or creating something that'll outlive you, you're not just wasting time—you're throwing your own life in the trash one hour at a time. Tick, tick, tick. Time's constantly moving. Why the hell you ain't?

For years, my hands were just as foul. They stayed full but never with anything worth keeping. I had pills to pop, dice to throw, guns to grip, and women I had no business touching. My hands weren't shaping my future— they were sealing my fate. Every quick high, every fight, every dumb move was me writing my life story in permanent failure ink. Then came the cell. Concrete bed, steel bars, a clock on the wall ticking while my potential sat in a coma. That's when it hit me: Time was working, my hands were worthless. I had two choices: Keep letting my hands ruin me, or make 'em start redeeming me. Nobody was coming to pry the destruction out of my grip— I had to drop it myself. Time wasn't waiting, but as long as I had two hands and a heartbeat, I had a shot at something different.

Question: Do you ever stay up late watching infomercials with their over-the-top slogans urging you to "ACT NOW" or miss the opportunity? That's how life is—to win you must "ACT NOW!" There comes a time when what it offers expires. Every hour you waste with your hand pushing the buttons on a remote instead of on your grind, every night you're laying hands on people you know ain't yours, every minute you spend turning up instead of turning your life around—you're proving that time's outworking you. The clock don't need motivation—it just moves. Think of farming: A farmer plants seeds with his hands, grinds through dry seasons, and earns the harvest. But you? You want fruit from a field you never even touched. Get your hands moving! The results won't always be immediate, and the grind might feel thankless, but you must keep putting in the effort until you see the harvest. You'll never see the fruits of any labor if you just sit back and refuse to do a damn thing. Stop acting like tomorrow owes you something. Time don't wait on talkers—it remembers doers. Don't let the hands of time tell a story that says you lived lazy, loved sloppy, and left this earth with nothing built. If a clock's hands never stop moving, neither should yours—unless yo ass is sleeping. One day the hands of time will quit for you, and when they do, the question will be simple: When the clock stops, will you clock out having wasted your life?

Growth Affirmation: I will **GROW** out of the mindset of idleness. I was born to use my hands to shape the future, not to scroll all day in the present.

Take this day to **THINK** about the condition of your life. Are you in a miserable relationship you don't even recognize yourself in anymore? Are you battling addiction? Sitting in rehab or prison wondering how the hell you ended up there again? Are you broke, bitter, burned out, but still pointing fingers at everybody but yourself? You know why that is? Because your thoughts wrote checks that your life is now being forced to cash. You're not a victim of life—you're the editor of it, and God, the Author, allows you to make certain changes. Your life is the beneficiary of your mind's policies. Your mind is writing the policy, and your life is inheriting it daily. If your thoughts are sloppy, lazy, negative, or rooted in fear, then your life inherits that same energy—frustration, confusion, delay, and struggle. But if your thoughts are focused, determined, hungry, and disciplined, then your life starts pulling in power, direction, and momentum. Every thought is a deposit, every belief is a clause, and the fine print is simple—you get out what you put in. Keep feeding your mind trash-ass policies, and your life's going to keep inheriting garbage. If your thoughts ain't premium, your life won't be either.

For the longest time, my life was cashing out on the reckless policies my mind kept writing. When I filled my thoughts with the streets—selling drugs, gambling—my life inherited bullets. When I let my mind feast on addiction—Percocets, Vicodin, OxyContin—my life collected withdrawals and pain. When my thoughts were consumed with shortcuts—insurance fraud, receiving stolen property—my life inherited long stints in prison. My life wasn't premium because of the weak policies my thoughts held. I thought incessantly about mischief, but my body and soul paid the price. My thoughts wrote the will my life inherited. It wasn't until I made the hard decision to rewrite that policy—to deposit better thoughts—that I started seeing real change. I switched insurance carriers because the cost of having satan as my agent was taxing my soul. I stopped paying premiums on pain and started investing in purpose, sobriety, and growth. The day I fired hell's agent and signed on with God, my coverage changed—and so did my life. Slowly but surely, my life began to reflect those new investments. Dysfunction was no longer listed as my beneficiary.

You keep saying, "Life ain't fair"—but maybe it's just paying you exactly what your mind has been inheriting. You're the policyholder. Your mind is the underwriter. Your thoughts are the premiums. And your life? That's the payout. You don't get to fake your way into a better future—you have to fund it with focused thoughts. Make daily deposits that feed your future, not rob it. Stop signing off on the same dumb-ass excuses. Make the cancellation. Rewrite policies that will insure you a better life. No more naming gossip, bitterness, distraction, or doubt as your life's heirs. It's time to put discipline, drive, clarity, and self-respect in those slots. Because the payout is coming. The only thing standing between the life you're living and the life you want is what you're willing to think. You don't get what you wish for. You get what you think about. Make your mind pay out what your future is worth.

Growth Affirmation: I will **GROW** out of the mindset
of feeding my life negativity. I can evolve. My life is just
following the policy my thoughts signed off on.

Take this day to THINK about why you keep convincing yourself that your past takes you out of the game. You think a rap sheet rips up your royalty? You think one dumb move deletes your whole mission? You think because you were a prostitute, a scammer, an inmate, or an addict that it's over for you? Think again. Malcolm X sat in a cell before he stood on stages. Martha Stewart did time for insider trading and came back on the outside triumphing. Their pasts were checkered too, but they didn't sit still—we ain't talking saints here, we're talking survivors. They didn't sit in shame—they stood on it and made power plays. But you? You're sitting there like the game's already lost because you gave up a few pieces. You keep staring at the board, crying crocodile tears, while time keeps ticking and the crown keeps waiting. You ain't disqualified—you just too damn stubborn to get over what you did, too prideful to pivot, and too poisoned by pity to play. Life don't crown cowards. It crowns the committed. And if you ain't ready to jump over your mistakes, don't blame the board—blame your goddamn self.

One of my favorite pastimes in prison was playing checkers with Mr. Mobley—a man who had been locked up since 1984. The world had evolved, but he found peace in this game. And through that board, he schooled me. He'd lean back, grin, and say, "You know why I like checkers over chess? 'Cause in checkers, kings are made by pushing forward—in chess, kings get taken off the board." That line stuck with me. I saw my life in those moves: sometimes boxed in, sometimes forced to jump, always trying to survive. Jumping over cars to avoid bullets wasn't so different from jumping over traps on that board. Being boxed in a cell wasn't so different from being boxed in on that board. But each move taught me something: How to see ahead, how to wait, how to strike. I didn't lose the game just because I made mistakes. I lost when I refused to keep playing. And that's what Mobley helped me realize—my checkered past didn't disqualify me from being crowned. It qualified me for it.

The goal in checkers is simple: Reach the other side and become a king. But that don't happen if you freeze every time the game gets tough. In fact, miss a jump in checkers and you lose your piece. Life ain't any different—it'll snatch opportunities when you fail to see your next move. Checkers teaches you that losing pieces don't mean you lose the game—it just means you adjust, adapt, and keep jumping over obstacles and pushing forward. Life will corner you. Life will try to double-jump your confidence. Life will smack your pieces off the damn board and dare you to pick 'em up. But if you want that crown, you gotta play smarter, think sharper, and stay hungry. Your past is the board—but your future? That's the crown. And it don't go to the person who played perfect—it goes to the one who didn't fold when the board got bloody. So stop blaming your past. Stop staring at the pieces you lost. If you're breathing, the game's still on. And you've still got moves left. The question is—do you got the guts to make 'em? Kings ain't made from perfection. Kings are made on checkered boards, by players who keep attacking. So keep moving. And don't stop pushing forward until that crown is on your fucken head and you yell out, *King me*!

Growth Affirmation: I will **GROW** out of the mindset
of being trapped by my past and commit to making
moves that lead to transformation and victory.

Take this day to **THINK** about why you assume feedback is an attack, when it might actually be a lifeline. Not everyone who offers advice is out to get you. Some people genuinely want to see you succeed because they've been where you are or have knowledge that can help you grow. You ought to be grateful somebody cares enough to correct you—most people would rather watch you fall on your fucken face. Not everyone has that luxury. Criticism isn't a prison cell—it's the key to unlock your potential. But too often, pride blinds us to the help that's being offered. Instead of treating feedback like it's meant to tear you down, start asking yourself if it might actually be trying to build you up. Feedback can be rough like sandpaper, but it smooths out the edges for a polished result. It don't feel good 'cause it's performing surgery—not a massage. The choice is yours: Will you use it to improve, or will you get in your feelings and let pride block your growth? Feedback isn't an offense, but an opportunity, offering insights that sharpen your skills, enhance your performance, and help you avoid future pitfalls as you journey towards your destination.

As a new hire at Planet Fitness, a fellow trainer approached me to offer feedback about my training methods and choice of exercises. He told me that my workouts reflected prison yard exercises. The words stung because they carried more truth than I wanted to admit. I was out of prison, but my mentality was still doing time. Feeling disrespected, I "checked" him, dismissing his advice. Two days later, while training a client, I pushed them too hard, and they became extremely exhausted and needed attention. That's when I realized what the trainer had been trying to tell me—I was training clients as if they were inmates, running them through routines meant for prisoners. My pride was protecting my feelings but punishing my progress. I wasn't being shamed; I was being sharpened. I learned that the correction you resist today is the regret you repeat tomorrow.

The only thing standing between you and growth is your refusal to listen. Stop seeing feedback as a personal attack. The ability to embrace feedback without letting it crush your spirit is what separates those who grow from those who stay trapped. The word "criticism" has unfairly had a negative connotation, and, sadly, it has prevented a lot of people from reaching their full potential. Criticism is the smoke alarm—you can get mad it's loud, but it just might be the reason you make it the hell out alive. It's not there to annoy you; it's there to guide you out of the fire. The key is learning how to discern constructive feedback from destructive criticism. Constructive feedback focuses on your actions and offers solutions—it pushes you toward improvement. Destructive criticism, on the other hand, is vague, personal, and meant to tear you down to persuade you not to pursue what you're after. Thank those who give you useful feedback, even if it stings. Because you don't need fans clapping—you need critics coaching. Stop thinking when people give you feedback they're throwing shade—it's sunlight. Let it grow you out of darkness.

Growth Affirmation: I will **GROW** out of the mindset of rejecting feedback. If feedback offends me, it may be that I need it. Correction could be my elevation.

Take this day to **THINK** about why you keep letting your breaking points feel like the end of the world when they're actually the beginning. Breaking points are your starting points. They're the wake-up calls screaming at you to stop pretending, stop running, and confront what's breaking you down. Haven't you been beaten enough? Haven't you abused your body enough? Haven't you had enough of being stepped on, dragged through the mud, and overlooked? You know you're at your breaking point, but instead of using it to break free, you choose to stay where you are, letting the weight break you down further. How much more do you want life to take you through? Damn. Does pain just turn you on? What are you waiting for? A mental breakdown? To be so far gone that ending it feels easier than escaping it? You better get a grip before you lose your mind—if your stressed-out ass ain't already. Sometimes it takes damn near losing it all to finally see what you should've left behind. Breaking points are good because they alert you to things you need to get the hell away from. Without them, you're slowly killing yourself. Let your breaking point launch you to your breakthrough.

Living at the lowest I ever had, I was at my breaking point. Pills had stripped me of money, family, jobs, and nearly my life. They didn't just cost me; they consumed me. I was stuck in a cycle of popping Percocets to feel alive, all the while watching them slowly kill me—physically, emotionally, mentally. My liver was failing, my relationships were shattered, and my sense of self was nonexistent. I was sleeping in my mom's busted-up car, parked inside the garage of my rental building—the same car I totaled in an accident while high. I used a bucket as a toilet, ate dollar store crackers for dinner, and watched TV through the cracked screen of an old phone with barely any service. It was hot in the summer, freezing in the winter, and humiliating every single day. That was it—my breaking point. That moment didn't just wake me up; it slapped me in the face. I realized I wasn't just addicted to the pills—I was addicted to the lies I told myself to stay in that prison. Breaking free wasn't instant. It took admitting my failure, facing the shame, and deciding that even if the climb out was hard, staying broken down was worse. Breaking free didn't just save my life—it gave me a new one.

Here's the truth you don't wanna hear: You're at your breaking point 'cause you let yourself get dragged there—you stayed in that busted relationship while they dogged you out, you kept letting them drive you crazy, and now you got the nerve to yell, "How could you do this? I gave you all of me!" That's the damn problem—you gave them all of you and lost yourself in the process. You keep handing people and vices the hammer and acting shocked when they smash you to pieces. But no matter how you got there, breaking points are crossroads: You can break down or break free, but freedom won't ever show up if you keep choosing chains. You're crying over pain you signed up for, begging for peace from people who profit off your misery. At some point, you either stop surviving on scraps of fake love and take your life back, or you keep letting fools drag you to the edge, blaming them while it's really yo simple-ass for keeping the door open. Breaking free requires you to be brutally honest with yourself and take action, even when it feels impossible. It means recognizing that the things holding you back—fear, doubt, addiction, people, or pain—don't have to own you. They can be overcome, but only if you're willing to fight for your freedom. At your breaking point, breaking down is always optional. But breaking free is essential and must be intentional. If your breaking point don't wake your ass up, it'll wipe your ass out. Life will get hard, and when it does, know that you ain't broken—you just ain't broken free yet.

Growth Affirmation: I will **GROW** out of the mindset of breakdown. Hitting my limit ain't my end—it's my signal to break free, not fall apart.

Take this day to **THINK** about why you keep spilling your soul to anyone with ears. Every time you hand your secrets to someone who hasn't earned them, you gamble with your privacy and your peace. You need to treat your life like a privately held company—exclusive, selective, and protected. In business, privately owned companies don't just hand out access to their day-to-day operations or earnings. They don't go public with private information, and they sure as hell don't let unqualified shareholders influence their decisions. Why isn't your life operated the same way? Keep your affairs private. Stop exposing them to the public. Not everyone should be a shareholder—some aren't interested in holding your secret, only in sharing it with the world. Every time you confide in the wrong person, you're listing your pain on the gossip stock exchange—people exchanging shares of your secret with everyone who will buy into it. Not everyone is investing in your healing—some are betting on your misery to take the focus off of theirs. If you wouldn't put your secret on a billboard, then don't hand it to someone who will. The wrong ears can turn your confession into a block party. Don't mistake fake concern for true confidentiality. Some people don't carry secrets—they carry megaphones.

Two moments in my life drilled this into my skull. First time, I told a dude I rocked with heavy about a side piece I had. He then went behind my back and told my main girl just to try to smash her. That betrayal didn't just cut—it carved deep. And the stupid part? I didn't learn. I did the same thing in my addiction when I exposed it. I told them everything, thinking they'd protect it. Instead, my troubles became tabloids. My lowest moments got recycled as jokes for the same streets I was trying to escape. The pain wasn't just in the exposure—it was in knowing I gave them the bullets and watched them load the clip. After that? My personal life turned into Fort Knox. If your silence ain't tighter than my struggle, you don't get a key to the vault. Most people ain't vaults, they're jukeboxes—drop a coin in and they'll sing your business on request.

Your personal business ain't a defective vehicle that rolls off an assembly line—you don't get to issue a recall once it's out in the street. Once it's rolled off your lips, it's out of your control. Before you open up, ask yourself if their loyalty runs deeper than your pain. A real confidant is a vault, not a window. A real confidant don't let others peek in when you ain't around. Sharing with the wrong person isn't vulnerability—it's voluntary exposure. And the proof? If they'll leak someone else's truth to you, your shit ain't safe either. Trust ain't built by how they act with you—it's revealed by how they speak about others. Stop treating your story like it's on clearance and your peace like it's disposable. Your life ain't reality TV—quit giving people episodes. Protect your story like your sanity depends on it. If someone's loyalty don't match your level of trust, then shut the hell up. A real confidant guards your secrets like their own. The fakes treat them like a press release. You better learn quick that the only way to hold onto your peace is to hold your tongue.

Growth Affirmation: I will **GROW** out of the mindset of confiding in the wrong people. They don't want to know my pain to help me—they want to know my business to spread it.

Take this day to **THINK** about why your life isn't turning out so great. If you're searching for the answer, look no further. Stop looking at the sky and start looking in the mirror—and, more importantly, at your grind. Truth is, you're not unlucky—you're undisciplined. The moment you decide to do something great, yo ass stops. You say you're gon' lose weight, but the first time your stomach growls, you treat it like it's a five-alarm fire, panicking and running for the cookie jar. You swear you'll quit drugs, but the second withdrawals hit, you withdraw your attempt. You want greatness to pull up without sending an invitation. Expecting great outcomes without putting in great effort is like hoping to win the lottery without buying a ticket. You say you're tired of losing, but are you even playing the game? Greatness doesn't happen because you wish for it—it happens because you work for it. It's born in the mud and achieved through the storms. Stop blaming bad breaks and start checking your pulse. If life's not giving you maximum fulfillment, maybe you're giving it the bare minimum. You can't expect to get muscles without lifting weights, just like you can't expect greatness without lifting a finger.

Words are a passion of mine, but I never thought it would translate into a book. While in prison, I forced myself and challenged other inmates to learn five new words a week just to elevate our vocabulary and replace saying, "Yah mean," "You feel me," or, "Know what I'm sayin'," all day. But writing a book? That felt impossible. I thought, "Who the hell was I to think anyone would care about my story?" That self-doubt kept me parked in neutral. But eventually I had to shift. It wasn't about fame or becoming a bestselling author. It was about proving to myself that I could do something great—that I could "write my wrongs." And if you missed that wordplay, let me break it down: I wasn't just writing a book—I was doing right by using words to rewrite the mess I'd made. That decision wasn't just about creativity—it was a declaration. A decision to stop settling. A choice to show up for my potential. And that's what greatness demands.

Too many people confuse noise with greatness. You think being seen is the same as being great. It's not. You do everything to appear successful—loud clothes, louder captions, chasing clout like it's currency. But let's get something straight: Wearing designer clothes ain't doing nothing great—that's dressed-up insecurity. Posting your whole life online ain't greatness—it's weird-ass shit. Being flashy don't expose greatness—it exposes how empty you really are. Fake nails, wigs, fake butts, painted-on six-pack abs, weaves, and filters don't reflect confidence—they just show how far your fake-ass will go to *look* like you got it. You do all this to look like you've arrived, but the truth is you ain't even left the driveway. You ain't showcasing greatness—you're showing desperation. Thirsty to be admired. Starving to be seen. But here's what you missed: Greatness is contingent upon your grind. You can't expect greatness to show up if your effort's a no-show. You can put all the success you want on your registry, but if you won't shower yourself in the grind, baby, don't expect greatness to bring you a damn thing you wished for.

Growth Affirmation: I will **GROW** out of the mindset of expecting greatness without effort. If I don't have greatness, it's not that I'm unlucky, it's that I'm uncommitted.

Take this day to **THINK** about how quick you are to react when someone crosses a line, as if every offense requires immediate retaliation. You're so sensitive—ready to put people in check over minor slights. But have you ever taken the time to check on the people you've put in check to see if they were okay? You're quick to correct, but slow to connect. The truth is, most of the time people's actions ain't about you. That drive-thru attendant who messed up your order might be holding back tears because she gotta go home to an abusive man. That dude who cut you off in traffic might be rushing his pregnant wife to the hospital—or racing there because he just got the call his son's been shot. That friend who didn't text back could be curled up in the dark, battling depression heavy enough to take their life. You don't see all that—you just see the slipup and make it about you. Instead of pausing to understand, you rush to put them in their place. Why? Because pride tells you that being tried is unacceptable, while empathy reminds you that people sometimes act out or lose focus because they're hurting. Instead of always assuming violation, maybe it's time to assume they need grace. Checking on people doesn't make you weak—it makes you human.

Growing up, I had a habit of putting people in their place the moment they rubbed me wrong. In high school, there was this one girl I kept clownin' because of her nasty attitude and how conceited she seemed. All the guys called her "stuck up"—like she hated dudes. Every chance I got, I hit her with slick lines like, "You ain't all that," or, "That's why your breath stinks." Truth is, I wasn't checkin' her—I was covering for my own rejection. Mad she ain't give me no play, so I masked my bruised ego with pride and sarcasm. Years later, when we actually started dating, she told me something that rocked my soul: Her own father was the first man to ever have sex with her. All those times I thought I was "putting her in check," I was just piling on to pain I couldn't begin to understand. Instead of checking with her to see why she thought guys were toxic, I labeled her as bitter and treated her like the enemy—never realizing I was confirming everything she was trying to protect herself from. It was a wake-up call that changed how I saw people and their actions. Not everyone needs to be put in check—some just need to be checked on.

Putting people in check might feed your ego, but checking in on people proves your strength. Checking in on people can make a world of difference when a person's world has become different. A wellness check—in law enforcement—is not about accusation, but ensuring safety. The same applies in your daily life. Checking in on someone isn't about judging their actions, but understanding their situation. Putting people in check is like pointing a finger at them. Checking in on them is like extending a helping hand. One approach accuses, while the other offers support. The next time someone rubs you the wrong way, pause and ask yourself: "Are they really out to get me, or are they struggling with something I can't see?" Most people ain't looking for a fixer—they just want to know they're seen. By checking in on others we don't know, we offer them support rather than suspicion, a moment of understanding rather than confrontation. For those we do know, don't wait to post "RIP" online after they're gone, when yo ass could've posted up with them while they appeared to be out of line. Don't check for their name in the obituary section of the paper, when you could've checked for their pulse while they were here. It's too late to care after they're in the coffin. That's why it's imperative we check in on people before they check out.

Growth Affirmation: I will **GROW** out of the mindset of quick judgment. I don't need a badge to do a wellness check on others, just a heart. I will call someone today.

Take this day to **THINK** about how costly mistakes demand full payment upfront—no payment plans, no partials. You slip up and have unprotected sex, you end up pregnant or with AIDS. You swing too hard at your kid, you end up with Child Protective Services at your door, taking them. You make the mistake of having an affair with your wife's friend, and you lose your family. These ain't accidents—they're choices with consequences that charge interest from the moment you make them. When we make mistakes, life sends us a bill immediately. These aren't charges you can put on a credit card or defer. Mistakes come with penalties that must be paid in reality checks—cold, hard, and nonnegotiable. The cost of our actions is due the moment it happens, and there's no option to pay in installments. Just like committing a personal foul on the football field triggers an automatic penalty and a loss of yardage, life's mistakes come with consequences that we must accept and deal with the setback. The tuition for life's wisdom is paid in pain—make the degree worth it.

Mistakes drained me in more ways than one—thousands in hospital bills, stacking up in six-figure sums. Thousands spent in court fees, fines, and legal filings, each one adding another burden. Thousands of lost wages, gone with every missed shift and every opportunity I wasted. Thousands in overdue child support payments, debts deepening with every setback. And that's not all; I served thousands of hours locked away in jail cells and prison blocks, with even more time spent in rehabs, fighting for a freedom I almost lost. Each mistake cost me something—financially, emotionally, physically—but these losses taught me valuable lessons I couldn't ignore. Either cash in your mistakes, or keep going bankrupt on growth. Every mistake makes a withdrawal— make sure wisdom is the deposit. Each wrong choice became my financial advisor, forcing me to realize the real cost of every decision I made. It was a steep price to pay, but at least it bought me wisdom. Now, I can invest and deposit into others from the mistakes I withdrew from life.

Costly mistakes can feel overwhelming, but they also offer invaluable lessons that can shape a better character. Mistakes demand full accountability, not avoidance. When life hands you a reality check, there's no dodging the payment—you either face it or let the debt of regret grow. Regret's expensive. Learning from it? That's priceless. Each mistake is a brutal teacher, but its lessons are life-changing if you're willing to learn. A reality check isn't just a bill—it's an investment in who you're becoming. Pay once, learn once, and move forward stronger. Mistakes are inevitable, but how you handle them defines your worth. They can become your greatest investments in your personal growth. Life doesn't cut deals, but it does reward those who turn setbacks into comebacks. Every costly mistake is a down payment on the character you're building—so make it count. Because if your mistakes don't pay you back in growth, they'll rob you twice—once when they happen, and again when you stay too ignorant to learn from 'em.

Growth Affirmation: I will **GROW** out of the
mindset that keeps taxing my potential—I'm done
making costly withdrawals with cheap decisions.

Take this day to **THINK** about how you seem to always come up with an excuse to avoid doing what needs to be done. Why is it that every time opportunity knocks, you come back with some lame-ass story about why it's not the right time, why you ain't ready, or why you can't do it? The truth is, excuses are just lies you've dressed up to make yourself feel better about staying exactly where the hell you are. They're not reasons—they're refusals. They're the costumes you put on to avoid facing the hard truth: You're capable, but you're scared. Excuses are like counterfeit money—they might look convincing at first glance, but they're worthless when they are put to the test. You're not fooling anyone but yourself. Stop lying to yourself and calling it logic. The only thing those excuses are buying you is more time in the same miserable-ass place you claim you want to escape. Stop telling yourself lies just because you too damn scared to improve your quality of life. Success doesn't come from masking the truth—it comes from stripping down the lies and putting in the work.

I spent years feeding myself excuses, each one as convincing as the last. I told myself I couldn't quit pills because the withdrawals were too painful. That was a lie—it wasn't the pain; it was my refusal to endure it. Many people have overcome addiction despite the withdrawals. I told myself I couldn't write a book because nobody would care about my story. That was a lie too— the truth was, I was too scared to let the world judge me. Many people have written bestsellers based on traumatizing lives. When I wanted to become a certified trainer, I told myself I wasn't good enough, that people wouldn't trust me, and that I might have an agenda other than training them. Another lie. Many people who now train in the gym were once in bondage. The real issue wasn't my past; it was my refusal to step into my future. And when it came to relationships, I told myself I couldn't be faithful—that it wasn't in my nature. Yet another lie. It had nothing to do with my nature, but everything to do with me being nasty. Every excuse I made was just a way to delay the inevitable truth: Nothing about your life changes until something about you does.

You're not trapped because you can't—you're trapped because you won't. Believe in yourself the way you believe in the lies. Enough people lie to you as it is—why lie to yourself? Excuses don't solve problems; they multiply them, feeding your fears and starving your future. The next time you catch yourself building barriers out of lies, stop and ask: Is this a fact or just fear? Stop dressing up hesitation as logic and laziness as obstacles. Excuses are nothing but Halloween costumes—open the door to them, and they'll trick you with lies or treat you to loss. Rip off the mask, put in the work, and take control. The only thing you should be dressing up in is action, discipline, and the determination to become who the hell you think you can't. Every excuse you make is one more lie you'll have to live with. Quit fucken feeding yourself lies about why you ain't where you're supposed to be. Life don't give a damn about your sob story. Your job don't give a damn you had a rough night, your bills don't give a damn you're tired, and your kids' stomachs sure as hell don't give a damn about you being full of excuses when they're still empty. Excuses don't raise your family, excuses don't pay your fucken rent, excuses don't bury your brokenness. You want results? Kill the excuse before the excuse kills you and drops your ass in the dirt.

> **Growth Affirmation:** I will **GROW** out of a mindset
> that feeds me excuses disguised as truths. I now realize
> that my excuses are only real lies—mirages. From a
> distance they look real, but up close they disappear.

Take this day to **THINK** about why you ain't contributing more to life. You waste your days gaming, getting high, scrolling your phone, standing on the corner, or running your mouth—pure fucken laziness. You're like a powerful engine stuck in park. Full of potential, but going nowhere. Some of y'all even fake disability checks, chasing Social Security when you never worked long enough to secure a bag. You're content with that first-of-the-month check, those food stamps, and free healthcare, like the world owes you for breathing. All you're doing is wasting time and resources, adding nothing of value to the life you're living or the people around you. You claim you want more out of life, but your actions scream otherwise. You're not stuck because of circumstances—you're stuck because of comfort. Assets grow through action; liabilities linger in laziness. And right now, you're just a liability to yourself and everyone else. Why are you okay with that? If you want to be more than just a drain on life and mooching off of it, quit pretending like the world owes you something.

Section 8 kept a roof over our heads when rent was a joke we couldn't afford to laugh at. But somewhere down the line, survival turned into sabotage. I became a drug dealer—poisoning the same streets that raised me. I wasn't just harming myself—I was harming the block. Then came addiction. Crashing cars high. Wasting bed space in rehabs I wasn't ready to take seriously. Burning out the patience of everyone who tried to help me. No job. No plan. Living off free healthcare. And when I got locked up, I became a number the state had to feed. A body the system had to house. A tax burden for hard-working citizens. Truth is, I could've been claimed as a dependent on taxpayers' returns. I was taking up space while giving nothing back. But those days are over. I went from draining the system to contributing to it. I'm paying taxes now—supporting the same structure I once leaned on. Somebody's gotta help fund the next man's rock bottom until he finds his rise. So if you're comfortable being a liability instead of an asset—if you'd rather take than contribute… you're welcome. People like me are the reason you can walk into that hospital and get seen for free. Yeah—thank me. Somebody's taxes are carrying your ass the same way they carried me.

Life doesn't hand out participation trophies just for living. The world is not your parent that's responsible for taking care of you. It don't owe you shit. You want to be an asset? Start proving it and get off your ass. Learn a skill, contribute to your community, and stop depreciating your own value. You're not like a car that loses its value once it drives off the lot. Your value increases the day you roll out of your mother's womb. Every lazy day is another lost opportunity to invest in your greatest asset: yourself. Get off your ass, stop being lazy, and do something that makes your life—and the lives of others—better. It's not about being perfect; it's about being purposeful. You don't have to be the most talented, the smartest, or the strongest— you just have to be willing to work, to grow, and to give more than you take. Life isn't about what you can get for free—it's about what you can give and how you can leave things better than you found them. An asset adds value to the world, but right now all you're doing is subtracting from it by being a liability. Get yo ass off your momma's couch, out of your grandmama's basement, and start adding value to the world. Sitting too long on your ass only produces mediocrity and hemorrhoids.

Growth Affirmation: I will **GROW** out of the mindset of laziness. I ain't built to be a burden— I'm built to add value, not just take up space.

Take this day to **THINK** about why you keep chasing shortcuts in life, acting like the grind is optional. You skip the hard work, dodge the sacrifice, and then wonder why you're trapped in the same place or suffering the consequences. Shortcuts ain't solutions—they're scams dressed up as opportunities. You don't want to study, so you cheat your way through. You don't want to grind and raise the money, so you scam people out of theirs. You don't want to clock in and work, so you poison your own community, selling drugs like it's a career path. You don't give a damn about the damage you do, as long as you get what you want, leaving others to crawl through the pain you caused just so you could sprint past the process. What you think is progress is often digging a deeper hole, and you're the one holding the shovel. Every time you avoid the hard work, cheat the process, or look for an easy fix, you're trading long-term success for short-term convenience. Like running a red light to save a minute, the risk of collision can cost you everything, including your life. Those split-second decisions may feel like momentum, but they're just a fast lane to a casket viewing or a courtroom verdict.

Cutting corners took me down long, painful roads. I wanted greatness without the grind, the prize without the perseverance. Chasing the so-called American Dream by taking shortcuts led me into an American nightmare. What looked like the cheat code ended up being a self-destruction button. And the worst part? I wasn't just ruining myself—I was influencing others to do the same. I remember this one kid from the neighborhood, eager, wide-eyed, just looking for a way out. I told him what I believed: that street money could make him more than what his teachers were bringing home. That dealing was fast, easy, and smart. But shortcuts come with contracts—fine print written in blood. Two weeks after I put that idea in his head and him on the street, he got shot and paralyzed over a couple hundred dollars. That day still haunts me. Because my shortcut didn't just cost me—it put someone else in a wheelchair for the rest of their life. Looking back, I realize that shortcuts don't just steal your future—they can end somebody else's. What seemed like the easy road turned out to be the hardest, most exhausting journey of my life. Easy life now. Hard life later. That's the shortcut contract. Shortcuts don't lead to success—they just put you in a hearse quicker.

Every shortcut signs your name on a consequence you can't outrun. They sell you speed but serve you suffering that drags on way longer than the grind you're too scared to face. Stop playing gangster with your life. Stop selling drugs, stop stealing, stop scamming folks out their hard-earned money— and get your ass a job. You think you're slicker than an oil can, thinking you'll escape the consequences, like you know something every other fool who took shortcuts didn't. But it's just a matter of time before those consequences catch up and collect their payment in full. Because every so-called "shortcut" you're taking got a long prison stint waiting with your name on the paperwork. Convenience ain't free—it taxes your time, robs your health, hijacks your peace, and sometimes snatches your life. It's like juicing up on steroids to skip the struggle of building muscle—you might look big for a season, but you're one bad side effect away from losing everything that really matters—your strength, your sanity, and even your girl—'cause your lil man can't stand up to the job. Success don't come from skipping steps—it comes from bleeding through them, sweating through them, crawling through them if you have to. The hard road hurts, but at least it don't handcuff you. Keep chasing instant gratification, and watch how fast it turns into permanent consequences. Every shortcut feels fast until you realize you've been running laps in hell with no finish line in sight. You think you're saving time, but all you're doing is buying pain on credit.

Growth Affirmation: I will **GROW** out of the mindset of chasing shortcuts. If I cut corners long enough, eventually life will cut me out the picture.

Take this day to **THINK** about how broken people prefer company that matches their brokenness. We live in a world that craves "breaking news"—especially when that news involves someone else's downfall. Think about it: Have you ever seen the media interrupt your favorite scheduled program to share something positive? Never. They'll cut right into your life to deliver tragedy, as if you don't already have enough shit going wrong. And it's not just the media—people do it too. We'll call and interrupt someone quick just to tell them about someone's fall. For some reason, we love turning the struggles of others into our entertainment. Let a pastor, politician, or athlete slip up, and watch the world sprint to the headlines. We tune in, not to learn, but to laugh—mocking their failure like it's a halftime show. Their breaking news distracts us from our brokenness. It's a twisted validation—a way to mask our own pain by laughing at someone else's. As the saying goes, misery loves company, because it distracts people from their own shattered pieces. It's easier to cheer for someone's downfall than to confront your own suffering.

In less than six months at US Foods, I was climbing fast—became a floor trainer, joined the safety committee, got employee of the month, was nominated for employee of the year, and even received a recognition plaque of excellence. On paper, I was thriving—killing it at work and becoming the face of the company. But behind the scenes, I was battling demons. My addiction to pills controlled me, and one day it all came crashing down. High on the job, I collapsed. An ambulance rushed me to the hospital, and the news spread faster than wildfire. My failure became their entertainment; my breakdown became their "breaking news." People were thrilled to see me fall, because it gave them safety and something to talk about. But what they didn't know was this: That moment didn't destroy me—it saved me. It forced me to face my demons head-on. I turned their gossip into my greatest glory. The best way for me to silence their cheers for my failure was to succeed loudly. That tragedy became my triumph, and my ruin became the foundation for my redemption.

Your brokenness should never become someone else's breaking news. But if they insist on celebrating your downfall, give 'em a reason to hate you for surviving what they thought would destroy you. Their gossip is just noise; your growth is the real response. Prove that their joy in your failure was just the opening act for your success story. The same people who celebrated your breakdown will be speechless at your breakthrough. You ain't got to clap back—just come back stronger and make 'em choke on the silence. Transform their whispers into your win. The best way to respond to those who celebrate your failures is to rebuild yourself stronger and help others do the same. When you see someone's downfall, don't revel in their brokenness—rise to the occasion and help them heal. Be a participant in their healing, not their hurting. Life has a way of cycling back, and the same people you laugh at and make fun of today could be the ones standing tall tomorrow. Turn their mockery into your motivation. They wanted a front-row seat to your ruin—now make 'em pay for season tickets to your redemption.

Growth Affirmation: I will **GROW** out of the mindset of letting others affect me through tragedies. Failure made my headlines. Now I will let my healing make history.

Take this day to **THINK** about why starting from the bottom earns respect, but getting off your bottom deserves praise. You sit around, glorifying people who "made it out," but you never take a hard look at why you still got your thumb stuck up your ass. Maybe it's because you've convinced yourself you have a valid reason—those "buts" you embrace like a favorite teddy bear: "I would, but I don't have the time," or, "I could, but I don't know where to start." These "buts" are nothing more than self-inflicted chains keeping you exactly where the hell you are. Justifications are nothing but adorned lies. The only things holding you back are the butt under you and the "but" in you. One keeps you planted, the other keeps you paralyzed. Kill 'em both— 'cause greatness don't sit, and it damn sure don't stutter. Success doesn't start at the bottom; it starts when you get off yours. Growth doesn't happen where you're comfortable—it happens when you challenge yourself to stand up to fear and step out on faith. The only thing that grows from staying seated is regret. So either get yo ass up now—or stay seated and watch your future get handed to somebody who actually stood the hell up.

The day I finally got off my butt and "buts" to become a personal trainer was the day my life transformed. Trust me, I had every excuse in the book: "But I don't have resources," "But I've been to prison," "But I'm just a street thug." I even told myself, "But I don't talk like those professionals; I'll never fit in." My "buts" were just barriers I built to justify staying broken. So I stood up and got off my butt—literally—and decided to act. I didn't know everything about becoming a trainer, but I knew how to exercise and help people transform their bodies. Deciding to get started, I enrolled in classes, studied, and practiced until I earned my certification. No, it wasn't easy, but every step I took crushed another "but." The climb starts when you no longer cling to your "buts." Today, I'm not just a certified personal trainer—I'm living proof that your "buts" don't define you unless you let them. Take the leash off your comfort zone.

Starting from the bottom is admirable, but staying there because of your "buts" is a choice. Success isn't about waiting for you to have everything figured out; it's about making the moment you're in matter by taking action. Think of your "buts" as dead weight—the longer you carry them, the more they drag you down. You don't need permission to move—you need the guts to. Waiting for the right time is just procrastination in a tuxedo. The shift happens when you stop saying, "But I can't," and start asking, "How can I?" Progress don't come from planning—it comes from pushing. Respect the bottom, but don't get comfortable in it. The ones who rise ain't lucky—they just had a fucken nuff. And if you ain't fed up yet, maybe you ain't been hungry enough. You know what's crazy? You'll get off your ass real quick when it's time to start a rumor. You'll get off your ass real quick to chase drama. You'll get off your ass real quick to be nosy. But when it comes to starting a business, chasing discipline, or running your own life—you glued to the couch like it's got chains on it. Don't tell me you ain't got energy. You just spend it on bullshit. If you can stand up for gossip, you can damn sure stand up for growth. The problem ain't that you can't start from the bottom—it's that your quitting ass made peace with poverty and started calling comfort a blessing.

Growth Affirmation: I will **GROW** out of the mindset of excuses. My future don't start when I rise to the top—it starts when I get off my "but" and move.

Take this day to **THINK** about how every new day gives you a chance to make the right choice. Your yesterday ain't got shit to do with today. So what—you cheated on your taxes. So what—you betrayed your friend. So what—you stole from your job. So what—you pulled the trigger and can't take it back. It happened—let it go. Forget about the mistake you made or the wrong you've done. Today is a new day. When we fuck up, it's tempting to think we need to restart, to scrap everything and start over. But restarting often means throwing away the progress and lessons we've already gained. Resetting, on the other hand, allows us to pause, reassess, and correct our course while keeping our foundation intact. It's like taking a test: Resetting is erasing the wrong answer and fixing it, while restarting is tearing up the whole test, losing every right answer along with the wrong ones. Life isn't about wiping the slate clean every time you stumble; it's about making corrections and moving forward with the wisdom you've gained. Your wrongs aren't endings—they're checkpoints, pointing out where you need to check yourself. Each reset is a chance to build, not abandon, what you've already accomplished.

When I first came home, I didn't know how to be a father—I was too busy trying not to be hated. I tiptoed around my daughter like I was on parole in her life too. Guilt had me soft. I bought her stuff, let her slide when she needed correction, and laughed off behaviors that needed discipline. I wasn't parenting—I was pacifying. I was so scared she'd resent me for the time I missed that I tried to be her homeboy instead of her dad at home. Then one day, she caught an attitude. Her face said it all—"Who are you to say something now?" That's when I knew: I'd been trying to restart. Pretending I could show up new by erasing the old. But that just made me a stranger in her life with no voice. Because I had set our relationship in reverse, she had no reverence for me. So I reset. I didn't need a clean slate—I needed a clear stance. That's when things started to shift. Not overnight, but over time she stopped testing me and started trusting me. I wasn't trying to be her favorite anymore—I was finally being her foundation. Resetting wasn't easy—because it meant realizing fatherhood ain't about being liked, but being respected. I couldn't hide behind gifts or guilt—I had to get back to guidance.

The ground beneath you isn't an eraser—it's a foundation you can rebuild on even stronger. Learn the difference between resetting and restarting. Starting over is running from the mess—starting again is learning how to clean it up. Resetting isn't easy; it demands courage to face your mistakes, honesty to accept where you went wrong, and determination to adjust your path without giving up on everything you've built. Restarting might feel like a fresh start, but it's often an escape from accountability—a way to avoid dealing with what needs to change. Don't let the evil shit you've done take you out the game; let it write you a new playbook on how to win. Every reset is your shot to get yo act together, fix the shit you kept running from, and build the backbone you should've had the first time. Stop crying about starting over—start swinging with the strength you lacked before. You don't need to erase your story to rewrite the next chapter—just make edits and keep building. Every day you wake up is proof that you have another opportunity to start again, not over. The power to change isn't in starting over—it's in beginning again, right where you are. Stop tearing up the whole test just because you missed one answer. You ain't broken—you just need to diagnose why your check engine light is on. Quit acting like you need a new engine when all you need is a tune-up.

Growth Affirmation: I will **GROW** out of the mindset
that I can't get it right. Growth don't require a restart, just
a realignment. Each sunrise is my reset button.

Take this day to **THINK** about how coming out of character ain't them exposing you—it's you exposing yourself. Ain't nobody made you cuss out your mama. Ain't nobody made you disrespect your boss. Ain't nobody made you crash out. That wasn't their hand on your strings—you got tripped up by your own. Stop blaming other people for dragging the real you to the surface. They didn't make you do shit—they just yanked the mask off and showed the real you. Your reaction isn't a response to them—it's a reflection of you. Your ass is just out of control. They didn't pull you out of character; they just unlocked the truth you hid inside. Like logging into a locked phone, only you have the passcode to unlock what's hidden. What you constantly rehearse is who you are. If you're snapping, lashing out, or losing control, you've practiced that your whole life, and that's the person you portray very well. The world can provoke you, but it's your choice to decide how you respond. They didn't write your lines—you chose your script. Your external actions are governed by your internal condition, whether your uncontrollable ass likes it or not.

There was a time in prison when I swore up and down to another inmate that this clown who bunked a couple doors down made me act out of character for running his mouth. I was standing on the top tier, heated over something petty, and I snapped—issued a threat that I knew damn well I shouldn't have made. In prison, that ain't a game. You don't throw threats—you throw hands or stay silent. But I let my pride and anger speak, and seconds later I was diving off the second tier to dodge a boiling splash of baby oil from a hot pot. After it was all over, I remember thinking, "He didn't pull me out of character—I pushed it out on my own." That rage, that recklessness, that lack of control—that was mine. All he did was press a button that was wired to explode anyway. That moment taught me something cold: People don't pull you out of character—they just shine a light on what's already inside. I didn't get exposed because of him. I got exposed because of me.

Listen, you're never provoked—you're exposed. Character isn't a reaction—it's a reflection of who the hell you really are. The hardest part about managing your emotions is realizing that you are in control. Like a thermostat, you set the temperature, no matter how hot the environment gets. If your character slips, don't blame the audience—blame the actor. No matter how chaotic the scene gets or the roles people play, stay calm and don't break character. Anger, frustration, and pride might try to hijack your performance, but don't let them dictate your actions. If you don't like what's being revealed, it's time to rewrite the part you play. Stop playing multiple characters—one day you a madman causing horror, the next you a crybaby stirring up drama. Instead, choose to respond in a way that reflects the person you aspire to be. Stop saying the devil made you do it and people made you come out of character, when it was just your lack of discipline and control that did it. Truth is, you ain't out of character when someone upsets you—you in character, and the whole damn crowd just finally saw the show.

Growth Affirmation: I will **GROW** out of the mindset that my triggers are stronger than my self-control—I control the thermostat, not the temperature outside.

Take this day to **THINK** about why you keep letting your trauma run your life—like it's your manager, your mouthpiece, and your map. Trauma isn't something you carry to stay strong—it's something you carry because you haven't learned to let go. What the hell are you actually gaining from holding on to your trauma? What is it doing for you—besides wrecking your peace and robbing your joy? You got raped—now what? You were molested, abused, betrayed, abandoned, lied on—now what? Are you gon' keep dragging it through every chapter like it's your identity? This might sound cruel, but somebody's gotta say it: Are you that thirsty for sympathy and attention? Truth is, people don't give a damn about what you've been through—and they're fed up with hearing about it. They got their own shit going on. It's time for you to confront it and get on with it. You replay your trauma like a highlight reel, reliving the worst parts of your life like it's who you are. But pain ain't a personality. Trauma doesn't make you real—it makes you stuck. And you keep justifying the weight like it's preparation, but really, it's paranoia. It's comfort in chaos. Holding on to trauma is like holding in doo-doo—you get bloated with pain, constipated with emotion, and more uncomfortable by the minute.

The trauma from being shot had me locked up long after the hospital let me out. I wasn't just trying to survive—I was planning retaliation like it was my purpose. Every day was a new way to scheme on revenge. I wasn't a father—I was a ghost in my kids' lives, present in body but consumed in spirit. My obsession with payback was killing everything good in me. I kept telling everyone I crossed paths with that I was going to get him back come hell or high water. But to keep it real, I needed to let that pain go before it finished the job the bullet started. And I did. Not because I felt strong. Not because forgiveness felt right. But because I was tired of watching my future bleed out while I stayed loyal to the past. When I finally let go, the pain didn't vanish—but the grip it had on me did. I stopped living like a victim and started showing up as a father again. That was my freedom.

Letting go don't mean forgetting—it means remembering without relapsing. Acknowledge what happened, but stop wearing it like it's all you got. You're not healing—you're hosting your hurt like it pays rent. Your trauma ain't your truth—it's your trap. You ain't weak for letting go—you're strong for refusing to be ruled. Healing ain't soft. It's violent, it's messy, and it takes everything in you. But it's better than staying shackled to yesterday. Therapy. Journaling. Prayer. Screaming into your pillow. Whatever the fuck it takes—do it. But stop feeding the pain and acting surprised when it grows. Your trauma ain't your pet—stop acting like it won't turn on you. Your trauma has had its fifteen minutes of fame—it's done, it's over, it's played itself out. Stop giving it exposure like it's still relevant. Pain might've built you, but it shouldn't be crippling your potential. You're not your trauma—you're just someone who's overdue for peace. And just like having to take a dump real bad, once you finally release all that backed-up crap, you'll feel the relief you've been dying for and feel five pounds lighter.

Growth Affirmation: I will **GROW** out of the mindset
that letting go means losing something—what I'm really
losing is the weight that's been holding me hostage.

Take this day to **THINK** about why you're still dragging around people, places, and mindsets that have already expired. That church you sit in out of tradition, not transformation? Dead. That relationship built on gossip and convenience? Dead. That business idea that ain't ever gon' work? Dead. That old belief system that's been poisoning your mind since childhood? Dead. And yet, you keep breathing life into what's been lifeless. You say you want peace, but you entertain chaos. You're not miserable because life isn't fair, you're miserable because you keep holding on to dead weight. You've convinced yourself it's easier to stay chained than to break free, but all you're doing is letting the dirt from others—or yourself—bury you alive. If it's not bringing you up, it's bringing you down. If it keeps tearing you up, it's tearing you down. Get rid of the tears. All that water in your eyes is not allowing you to see clearly. A life that always hits a dead end ain't cursed—it's overpacked with corpses. And until you bury the dead, you'll keep living like the walking dead.

For me, it wasn't until I decided to stop popping pills that I began cutting the dead weight out of my life. Every time I got out of prison or rehab, I went right back to the same people, places, and patterns that enabled my old habits. It was as if life had hit pause while I was in rehab, but as soon as I got out, I'd press play, and the same self-destructive movie would start all over again. The depression, the addiction, the bad decisions—it all came rushing back because I refused to cut the ties that were dragging me to the bottom. Finally, when I came to a dead end, I got serious. I deleted numbers, blocked people, and started showing up in places where I knew temptation wouldn't follow me—like church. Every sermon became my new high, giving me the clarity and strength I had been craving all along. God's Word was the only thing that could fill the emptiness that pills never could. It was then I realized that the dead weight wasn't just killing my potential; it was killing me.

You keep visiting graves and wondering why nothing grows. You hold funerals for your future every time you choose to keep what's been killing you. It's evident in your statements: "I've come too far to let it all go," or, "If it wasn't for the kids, I would've been left." That's a goddamn lie. Them kids ain't got shit to do with it. If the distance you've traveled has only dragged you deeper into dysfunction, what exactly are you protecting? You think you're staying for the kids, but the truth is—you're teaching them to normalize pain. They don't need your presence if all you're passing down is poison. And you didn't come this far just to stay miserable—you came this far to finally stop. You're not proving strength—you're proving you'd rather die loyal to pain than admit it ain't worth it. Pride got you locked into a path you should've buried years ago. And every time you keep what should be gone, you delay what could be great. The longer you keep holding the casket, the less life you have left to live. A dead life don't end till you end the dead weight. Damn… don't you ever get tired of having to find something black to wear to your own funeral every day?

Growth Affirmation: I will **GROW** out of the mindset
of holding on to dead weight. If it's not lifting me, it's
lowering me—and I ain't going down with it.

Take this day to **THINK** about how wearing brand names may make you look good, but making your name a brand will make you—and your future generations—look even better. You rockin' Louis Vuitton, but in life you still losing. You rockin' Gucci, but your name still generic. Wearing a label shows clout; building one shows character. It's easy to invest in appearances—spending your hard-earned money to showcase someone else's name across your chest. You out here braggin' on a $5,000 shirt that cost less than a Happy Meal to make—congratulations, you just raised the value of another man, while yours is still worthless. But what about the name you were born with? What does it stand for? Fashion is fickle; one minute it's in, and the next, it's out. But a name with value lasts forever and never goes out of style. The value of a name isn't in what you wear; it's in what you represent. Brand names cost money; making your name a brand costs determination. A brand name can be bought—a name that becomes a brand has to be built. It's not about the label on your chest—it's about the legacy in your heart.

Majority of my life, I wore Polo from head to toe. It made me feel like I belonged to something bigger. Ironically, I didn't even know how the game of polo was played—but wearing the name Ralph Lauren gave me a sense of celebrity… until it didn't. I thought I was somebody just because my collar had a horse on it. But what's wild is I've got a friend pushing damn near sixty who swears that's all he'll ever wear; he once told me, "Man, they gon' bury me in Polo." And that's the sad part—he's so focused on what he'll be buried in that he don't even see how he's digging a financial grave for his children's future. He'll leave them a closet full of outfits before he ever leaves them a slice of ownership in the company he's obsessed with. That's the kind of delusion that keeps grown men caring more about what's stitched on their chest than what's secured for their family's tomorrow. It's no longer about fashion for me. It's about designing a name my family can wear proudly. It's hard work, but I've learned that a brand name may cost money—but making your name a brand costs blood, sweat, and tears, and that's the price I'm willing to pay.

How can you care more about wearing the latest drip when your name remains dry? At some point, your name gotta mean more than the ones you're wearing. Designers have made millions off their name—yet you're still making excuses with yours. Building your name as a brand requires daily dedication. Building your name as a brand isn't about quick fixes or shortcuts—it's about commitment. You're repping success, but are you actually building any? Building a legacy means showing up when it's hard, sacrificing when it hurts, and staying consistent when convenience tempts you to quit. It requires you to weave integrity, trust, and excellence into everything you do. Each small step—every sacrifice—becomes part of the fabric of a name that carries real value. You've already invested in wearing brands. Now it's time to invest in becoming one. Their brand went global—your name ain't even known past your block. Fix that. A designer's name may decorate your wardrobe, but your actions today will determine whether your name decorates a legacy tomorrow. Wear your name well—it's the only brand guaranteed never to go out of style, the one with power to last for generations. You rock designer threads—now design a future your kids can wear to school proudly.

Growth Affirmation: I will **GROW** out of the mindset that clout is currency—I'm chasing character, not couture.

Take this day to **THINK** about how the thoughts that run through your mind determine the people who walk into your life. A person doesn't just stumble into the wrong crowd—they invite that crowd in by the thoughts they entertain. Your army of friends didn't corrupt you—your thoughts recruited and enlisted them. Your mind is like a bouncer who determines what thoughts get in, stay in, or get kicked out. If you let negativity slip past unchecked, don't be surprised when the wrong crowd is sitting in your VIP section. If negativity, self-doubt, and reckless desires fill your head, don't be shocked when the people around you mirror those same traits. Your thoughts are the ringmaster of your life—change them, and the circus of clowns surrounding you disappears. The crowd you attract ain't random; it's a reflection of what's playing on repeat in your mind. You don't run with the wrong crowd—they run to you 'cause your thoughts look familiar.

During my drug days, I didn't run with the wrong crowd by chance. I attracted them because my thoughts matched theirs. When I started popping pills, my mind became a magnet for others doing the same. If I thought about getting high, people with the same energy appeared. If I thought about wild nights, I found company that shared the same reckless mindset. My thoughts were the bouncer letting negativity past security and straight into my life—with guns, knives, and all. But once I hired new bouncers, they started throwing toxicity out. When I thought about getting sober, my circle changed to include those who supported that journey. When I thought about success, I found people striving for more. My thoughts cleared the peanut gallery of my life, making room for those who actually deserved VIP access. I didn't follow the wrong crowd—they followed the trail of my thoughts. The people ain't the problem—your thinking is. Until your thoughts change, your crowd won't.

Don't blame the company you keep for showing up. Your thoughts sent the invitation to those who just RSVP'd. The wrong crew don't corrupt you—they just confirm you. Stop telling people they need to cut someone off as if it's that person who is the problem. It's not the people they're hanging with, it's the thoughts they're holding on to. You keep cleaning up the crowd, but you never clean up the thinking that called them in. That's like mopping up a flooded floor while the faucet's still running. You trying to clean up the mess without shutting off the source—your mind. The people you're running with ain't to blame for the way you're living. Success, peace, and progress don't come from wishing for them; they come from changing the energy of your thoughts. The mind attracts its equivalent. Whatever you think about is what you produce in your life. Think broke, and you attract broken. Think reckless, and you attract ruthless. Think small, and you'll attract people who are small-minded. If your mind is messy, don't wonder why your circle keeps you in mess. The wrong crowd doesn't pull you in—they come visit you 'cause your thoughts sent them a postcard, and they saw it as the perfect vacation spot.

Growth Affirmation: I will **GROW** out of the mindset that invites confusion, chaos, and counterfeit connections. My thoughts will no longer make the guest list for my party of friends.

Take this day to **THINK** about why we let bad blood simmer until it explodes, creating messes we later regret. Too often, we allow minor issues to snowball into major conflicts, all because pride and anger drive our responses. Bad blood can creep into any relationship—friends, family, even strangers on the street. But here's the truth: Not every disagreement has to become a declaration of war. Instead of fueling the fire, we have the power to turn down the heat before it scalds everyone involved. The only thing a bloodbath guarantees is more blood to clean up. And when you're the one holding the knife, you run the risk of also getting cut. Bad blood doesn't have to boil over into destruction—it can cool down into understanding if you're willing to step back and let clarity take the wheel. Matters seen as minor can turn into a major scene, leading to a bloodbath.

On Cincinnati's Westside, there were rivalries between neighborhoods like Millvale, Fairmount, Fay, Moosewood, Cumminsville, and English Woods. Loyalties were defined by where you lived, and tension between groups was always simmering just beneath the surface. One day, bad blood between the Fay and English Woods boiled over into a shootout. In the chaos, my good friend Cheese was killed. The tragic twist? It wasn't even the "opps" who shot him—it's widely rumored that someone from our own hood mistakenly pulled the trigger. Cheese lost his life because nobody was willing to pause, talk, and let cooler heads prevail. It wasn't about who was right or wrong anymore—it became about a feud that got out of control. This didn't have to happen. Like the Hatfields and McCoys or the Bloods and Crips, these situations show how bad blood can lead to hot heads when no side chooses to cool down. Not every feud needs a funeral—some just need forgiveness.

Conflict is inevitable, but destruction doesn't have to be. Like a rope being pulled in a tug-of-war—bad blood only strengthens the tension, but letting go eases the strain. Start practicing emotional control—pause and calm yo ass down before reacting, and let your emotions settle. Think about the impact your actions will have, not just on you but on everyone involved. Seek dialogue instead of division. Truce instead of tragedy. Sometimes, a conversation is all it takes. And if the situation can't be resolved immediately, don't be afraid to walk away. Space can bring clarity and allow tempers to cool. Some people die trying to prove a point that wasn't worth the coffin. Not every grudge is worth a grave. Being right don't matter if you're *dead* wrong. Anytime bad blood starts boiling, turn down the heat before it overflows. Life is too short to let bad blood cause a bloodbath. Real strength ain't in pulling triggers—it's in pulling back. Nobody's winning if everybody's wounded. Choose peace, not pride. Because in the end, what matters isn't who was right or wrong, but whether everyone made it out alive.

Growth Affirmation: I will **GROW** out of the mindset of letting my ego escalate conflicts. Minor grudges make major graves when nobody cools off.

Take this day to **THINK** about why you let where you are dictate where you stay. Whether you're in a prison cell, sitting in rehab, drowning in depression, or suffering in a toxic relationship, your race begins where you stand—not in some dream scenario. You're not the only one who started off life unfairly or who found themselves in hellish circumstances. The difference between those who rise above and those who rot where they are is action. They executed while you made excuses. They faced the pain while you hid from it. The harsh truth is, nobody's coming to save you, and the only thing worse than starting at the bottom is staying there. The journey doesn't care about your complaints; it only cares about your commitment. The problem ain't that you don't have the tools—it's that you're too busy waiting for perfect conditions to use what you've already got. It's like being handed a shovel in a pit and saying, "Now all I need is a ladder." You weren't given a way out— you were given a way to start digging. But instead of moving dirt, you're day-dreaming about elevators. Stop waiting on a lift when you were born to climb. You've got tools—you're just too focused on what's missing to use what's in your hands. And as long as you ignore what's in them, you'll stay buried by what's around you.

My life started out bad. I was raised in the projects with no father, no guidance, and every excuse in the world to give up. Years of pain, bad choices, and running from reality eventually landed me in rehab. But what felt like the bottom turned out to be my beginning. Sitting in that room, surrounded by silence and consequences, I picked up a pen and started writing out my thoughts. That simple act would evolve into me writing a book. I had nothing but a broken spirit, a pen, and a notebook—but I made a decision to get started. As I wrote, I thought about my rough start in life and realized something powerful: My start doesn't matter—my finish does. Even in a jail-based rehab with nothing, I could still take the first step toward something. Greatness isn't reserved for those who start strong—it's for those who find the courage to even start at all.

Rock bottom ain't the end—it's the basement of your breakthrough. Your past ain't a prison—it's a platform. Your current position isn't a life sentence—it's a launchpad. The pain you're standing in is just wet cement—move now, or forever be stuck in the same damn spot. Don't let your current condition convince you that you're set back too far. You don't need a map to move—you need the guts to get going. Are you in rehab? Start rebuilding. Are you in a dead relationship? Start planning your exit. Are you drowning in depression? Start reaching for help. Are you thinking about losing weight? Waiting is the enemy of winning. Evolution doesn't come from pity parties—it comes from purposeful planning. You don't get out of the pit by whining about how deep it is—you dig, crawl, and bleed your fucken way out. You don't care about busting your knuckles or breaking your fingernails. The first step don't have to be big—it just has to be taken. Growth begins the second you stop accepting the basement as your ceiling. It ain't about neat exits—it's about getting the hell outta there.

Growth Affirmation: I will **GROW** out of the mindset that I need perfect alignment to begin—waiting for clarity kept me in chaos. To leave the war zone, I gotta walk outta the waiting room.

Take this day to **THINK** about why you keep giving people front-row seats and backstage access to your reactions. Every time you let someone provoke you, you're handing them the remote to control you. Letting them pause your growth, mute your voice, or rewind your progress. You're not standing up—you're laying down your power. While you're trying to prove you don't take disrespect, you're being played like a pawn. But there's a better way to take control. Smile. Someone cusses you out—smile. Someone insults you— smile. Someone gets in your face—smile. Unless they put their hands on you—then you kick they ass. But aside from that? Even if it's fake, smile. That burns them the hell up. That eats them alive. Know this. Every time you lash out, you're not defending your power—you're auditioning for *The Muppet Show*, and they're the puppet master pulling your strings. You think you're clapping back, but you're clapping for them—on a good job they're doing at controlling you.

A dude I was locked up with made it his daily mission to get under my skin. He'd say slick stuff, move funny, try to provoke me like I was his personal entertainment. I used to bite every time. I thought my alpha mentality made me look strong, but it made me look owned. Until one day, another inmate pulled me aside and said, "You know he told me, 'Watch me get Dion to snap.'" That cut deeper than any insult. That was the moment I saw it—I wasn't being macho, I was being manipulated. I wasn't in control—I was being controlled. He was playing chess while I was throwing checkers. I thought I was standing on business, but really I was just reacting on command like a damn puppet. That day, I took the remote back. Suddenly, he became bothered because he could no longer bother me. Every time you hold your peace of mind, they lose a piece of their mind.

Every time someone pushes your buttons, understand it's not random—it's rehearsed. They've studied you. Your insecurities. Your breaking points. Your hot buttons. They're running plays on you. They want your reaction because it feeds their ego and confirms their power. You talk a good game when you say, "Don't nobody control me," but every outburst proves they already do. If they can control your mood, they already own your mind. Walking away isn't weak—it's brutal warfare. Real power is when you stay calm in chaos, when you don't flinch under fire, when you refuse to dance to the beat of someone else's goddamn drum. Every reaction you give is currency. Don't make them rich off your rage. If they don't pay your bills, don't let them press your fucken buttons. In fact, it's even better if you don't have buttons. Then controlling you becomes impossible. The second you get out of character, they win. Stop saying, "They made me mad." Each time you say that, know that you've given up control. You're a person, not a puppet. Choose better. Choose control. Choose peace. Smile when they hate. Laugh when they bait. Stay solid when they expect you to become soft. Let your silence scream louder than their noise. Every time you keep your cool, it burns them up inside.

Growth Affirmation: I will **GROW** out of the mindset
of emotional surrender. Nobody holds my remote—I
control the volume, the channel, and the outcome.

Take this day to **THINK** about how crazy it sounds to tell someone to remain upbeat while life is beatin' they ass. Imagine telling a child to stay positive while being molested by a relative, a woman to smile while being battered by her husband, or someone who's just lost a job and they don't know how they're going to feed the kids. It feels cruel, even absurd, to suggest finding light in such darkness. Pain is personal and paralyzing, and the idea of staying hopeful in those moments feels like a slap in the face. But here's the raw truth: Life will kick yo ass whether you're ready or not. It doesn't discriminate. When it comes to pain, it is an equal opportunity employer. You can't stop the punches, but you can decide to keep your hands up and stand your ground. Staying upbeat don't mean you're blind to the pain—it means you won't let it beat the hell outta you. Bruises ain't the evidence of defeat—they're the birthmarks of survival. The bruises say you've been hit—your breath says you ain't done. Life mighta got hands, but you got heart.

I've felt the sting of life's hits day after day. As a kid, it was the switch my mom made me go pick from a tree for a whooping. And it better not been a flimsy one. For reasons I don't understand, every whack came with a word: "Didn't... I... tell... you... to... stop?" One whipping, she hit my ear, and I shouted, "Mama, stop, I can't hear!" Her reply? "You gon' do it again?" I yelled out, "No!" She said, "I thought you couldn't hear." Later, the beatings weren't from switches—they came from the streets. Pills drained my body and mind. Prison crushed my spirit. Bullets nearly took my life. Each hit felt heavier than the last. But here's what I learned: Every bruise, every scar, every ounce of pain didn't just show what I'd been through—it proved I was still here. Surviving wasn't about avoiding the blows; it was about rising after each one and daring to keep going. The beatings didn't ruin me—it revealed me. If life wants to fight dirty, then you fight filthy. Let pain know it picked the wrong one.

Life might be stomping your neck right now, but your spirit better not break. Staying strong while suffering is the ultimate rebellion. It's saying, "You can mug me, but you can't move me. You can punch me, but you can't possess me. You can hit me, but you can't have me." Just like a punching bag stays steady when struck, you were built to absorb the blows without breaking. The bag doesn't fall apart under pressure—it remains stable, taking the hits and staying anchored. You're no different. Every hit you take is another reason to stand tall, another reminder that you've survived what others couldn't. Pain is proof that you're alive, and surviving it is proof that you're unbreakable. Life doesn't get easier, and the punches don't stop coming—but with each one, your resilience grows, allowing you to stand firm when life decides to check your chin. When life swings, don't run from it—stand toe-to-toe with it, take the hit, and bounce back. Let your scars tell the story of a victor, not a victim. Bruises fade, but the strength you gain from surviving them lasts forever. The hardest fights don't crown the strongest—they expose the ones who refuse to fold. Show life that no matter how bad it beats you, it'll never beat you.

Growth Affirmation: I will **GROW** out of the mindset of defeat. Life may rock my bells, but I'll still be standing when the bell rings.

Take this day to **THINK** about why you keep clinging to the dumb shit that poisons your peace and drains your power. Why you keep acting like your survival depends on the same thing that's been slowly killing you? You ain't come out the womb with a pill bottle, a liquor bottle, chocolate chip cookies, or somebody's fist in your face. That pain you're holding on to wasn't born with you—it was picked up, tolerated, and now you defend it like it's a conjoined twin. You've worn those chains so long, you convinced yourself they're accessories. Let's kill the fluff—if it ain't building you, it's breaking you. If it don't pull yo ass up, it's pulling yo ass under. That lie you can't live without? That's fear dressed in your own voice. And you can't hide fear behind filters. Loving yourself ain't about quotes, captions, or catchy hashtags—it's about declaring war on what's been quietly killing you. Stop flooding Facebook with motivation you don't even live. You're not posting power—you're posturing for strength you don't even have. Hashtagging "grind" while staying glued to the same garbage that's grinding you down. Every sip, every snort, every mindless scroll, every disrespect, every punch in the face you endure is just you signing a new lease with your chains.

After my release from prison, I reached out to a guy I bonded with in there, only to hear that he had killed his girl and himself. Their relationship was toxic—cheating, lying, fighting—but they clung to it as if their survival depended on the very thing killing them. He stressed over her behavior in prison. He'd explode when she didn't answer his calls. When I asked why he didn't just let her go, he always told me he couldn't live without her. His situation reminded me of a girl I used to argue with constantly. I remember it like yesterday: We were goin' crazy under the sheets, she looked me dead in the face, and said, "You gon' give this up?" I stopped right there, mid-stroke, and said, "If it's gon' drive me fucken' crazy—hell yeah." Her sex wasn't worth walking through hell. I wish I had that same mindset when it came to pills. What he held on to in her, I held on to in pills—same poison, different bottle. I told myself I needed them to cope, to feel alive, to function. But every pill I popped dragged me closer to the grave. Letting go hurts—but holding on was killing me. The high wasn't worth the hell it took me through. The pills weren't the problem—it was my lies. I wasn't addicted—I was just afraid to be powerful.

You got a whole brain, but letting brainless habits own you—make that make sense. Pills don't think. Ice cream don't think. Porn sites don't think. Alcohol don't think. You the one picking it up. And yet you acting like it's got more control than you do. You acting like the demon's driving when you the one holding the keys. Every time you say, "I can't let it go," that's a bald-faced lie. Keep being scared to piss off your poison, and it'll keep pissing on you. Strength ain't in holding on—it's in letting go of what's weakening you. You weren't born to survive on poison; you were made to thrive on purpose. The cure to your pain begins with letting go of what's causing it. Stop handing over power to the same poison that's been punking you for years. Start using the strength inside you to claim the life you deserve. It's not about cutting off your external weakness—it's about turning on your inner strength. Destroying what's trying to take you out. The poison ain't in the pill you keep popping or the drink you keep sipping—it's in the lie you keep swallowing.

Growth Affirmation: I will **GROW** out of the mindset of clinging to what's killing me. I'm done normalizing drinking, justifying addiction, and tolerating abuse. It's over! I'm done!

Take this day to **THINK** about why you're so damn quick to call out everybody else's flaws while frontin' like your own shit don't stink. Maybe you think it really don't, or maybe you just hope no one notices the smell trailing behind you. The truth is, your doo-doo stinks just like everyone else's—it just might stink differently. We're all flawed, but instead of owning that, we magnify others' faults to make ourselves feel better. It's like telling someone their fart stinks while insisting yours is a squirt of Febreze. The problem isn't seeing others' flaws; it's failing to acknowledge your goddamn own. We build entire stories around other people's shortcomings just to distract ourselves from our fucked up truth. When we criticize others, it's often because we don't want to face the mess in our own lives. We'd rather focus on their cracked mirrors than look into a clear one that reflects our true selves. The less we recognize our imperfections, the more likely we are to exaggerate those of others.

Sadly, I used to call people dope fiends as if I were somehow better. I thought that since I wasn't walking the street late at night, looking for dope on the ground, or stealing from my family, I wasn't a junkie. That denial became my defense mechanism. As long as I could point out how far gone they were, I didn't have to face my own addiction. My addiction didn't seem like a problem because I could always find someone "worse." The day I stopped comparing myself to others was the day I saw the truth: I was no different. I was using their visible flaws to cover up my own mess. It wasn't until I acknowledged my reality that I began to heal. Judging others didn't make me less of an addict—it just kept me in denial, clinging to a false sense of superiority while my life continued to crumble.

Everybody's dirty—you just better at wearin' clean clothes over it. It's exactly what my grandmother meant when she said, "The pot calling the kettle black." Every flaw you spot in someone else usually mirrors the flaw you refuse to face in yourself. When you finally own your issues, their issues stop being your obsession. Seeing your flaws don't make you weak—it makes you wise. You can't guide someone else's path if your own compass is cracked. And here's the kicker: Everybody's compass is cracked. So instead of tearing people down, focus on building yourself up. As raggedy as your life is, you don't got no business talking about nobody else. You ain't holier—you just hide your hell better. And hiding from your truth only delays your healing. The louder you call out their mess, the more obvious you make your own. Before you call out what's foul in someone else, clean up the funk in your own life. Because no matter how loud you shout about their doo-doo, your shit still stinks—you're just immune to it from being around it 24/7. The moment we accept that we're flawed, we can stop pointing fingers and start fixing the person we see in the mirror. People may call out how bad your life is or everything wrong with you, but trust—they're just as fucked up as you.

Growth Affirmation: I will **GROW** out of the mindset that calling out others' flaws hides my own—judging them won't justify my mess.

Take this day to **THINK** about how pathetic it is to sit around crying over what you don't have when people with disabilities—or with far less—are making more happen than you ever will. If seeing a man with no sight, no hearing, no limbs, or no voice still making power moves doesn't light a fire under your lazy ass, then you're sorry as hell. People with less vision, less strength, less education are lapping you—not because they're lucky but because they work what they've got until it works for them. They sharpen scraps into swords. They turn limitations into leverage. Meanwhile, you're sitting there with a whole toolbox of abilities you haven't touched in years because you'd rather talk about your obstacles than tackle them. It's easy to dwell on what's missing, but life has a way of compensating—amplifying something else to keep you moving. God don't weaken you in one area and not strengthen you in another. You might not see what's ahead, but that don't mean the route ain't real. Like walking through smoke in a burning building—the visibility's low, but the exit's still there if you keep moving. You don't need to see the way—just move like you believe there is one. Vision is never about what you see; it's about what you believe.

Blind Bob was my bunkie in prison—blind as hell but sharper than most with perfect vision. He wasn't in there for weakness; he was in there for assault. One day, he walked into the cell and asked, "Did you take a dump?" I said, "Yeah, like two hours ago." He smirked and said, "I may not see worth a damn, but I can smell real good." Just like that, he reminded me—what you lack don't matter if you know how to sharpen what you got. Bob didn't need eyes to read energy or defend himself. He didn't cry about what was missing—he mastered what remained. That stayed with me. I watched a man with no sight navigate hell better than people with full vision. Just like Edison—nearly deaf—lit the world. Just like Ray Charles—blind to the piano keys but still touched hearts with every song he wrote. They didn't beg for a new set of tools—they built masterpieces with broken ones. That's what it means to stop complaining and start building. Success isn't only for the fully equipped. You'll never have everything you think you need—some things you gotta build with what's left. You don't need more senses—you need more sense. It ain't about someone's disability; it's about their disbelief.

Edison and Charles didn't excuse their limitations—they turned them into legacy. So what's stoppin' you? It's not that you're handicapped—it's that you're handcuffed to comfort. Your problem ain't that you're missing something—it's that you refuse to master what's left. You'd rather rehearse your restrictions than reach for results. You spend too much time staring at roadblocks and listening to nobodies, like they've got all the answers. People out here are taking their disadvantages and turning them into discipline, while you're using your advantages to excuse your average. The hard truth? You ain't tired. You ain't broken. You ain't "waiting for your chance." You're just not willing. You've gotten comfortable hiding behind a story that's old, safe, and sad. You hold onto it because it keeps you from facing the reality that you're capable but too damn lazy. You've convinced yourself the grind is for other people while you sit on potential so long it's starting to rot. You have all you need. You've got to be blind to the pain, blind to the past, blind to the limitations you keep focusing on. You've got to be deaf to the critics, deaf to your addictions, deaf to that scared little voice in your head telling you you're not enough. The world doesn't need another sob story—it needs proof that limitation can produce legacy. And if Blind Bob can see his way through hell without sight, you've got no damn excuse for dying with 20/20 vision.

Growth Affirmation: I will **GROW** out of the mindset that disabilities are stop signs. I don't need vision or hearing to succeed; all I need is heart. It ain't about what I lack—it's about what I'm willing to amplify.

Take this day to **THINK** about how you let one hard moment punk your whole life. One slip and you fold like the fight's already finished. You treat a bad day like it's the end of your damn destiny. Newsflash: The day ain't weak—you are. If a single stumble kills your momentum, it ain't the fall that's the problem—it's your sorry-ass refusal to stand strong. Too quick to crumble. A bad day should be a bump, not a breakdown. It's a fire drill, not a funeral. You don't throw away your life 'cause one piece of it caught heat. Some days are gon' punch harder than others—that don't make them bad. That makes them necessary. They press you, test you, and reveal if you're built to handle more than just good vibes. You keep calling it a bad day when it's just a challenging one. Stop confusing pressure with punishment. If you fold over a rough morning, what the hell are you gon' do when life really comes for you? Bad moments don't ruin you—*you* do, when you let one turn into many. You weren't built to break down—you were built to break through.

One of the worst days of my life happened when I was driving my mother's car high. I hit a car on the highway, and a state trooper came to check things out. Thought I got lucky. The other driver and I exchanged info, and I pulled off relieved—only to rear-end *the same state trooper's* car just minutes later. That time, I wasn't so lucky. I was arrested, the car was towed, and I ended up back on the news—again. That day didn't just sting—it smothered me in shame. My face on every screen. My mother's car gone. Another blow to my already bleeding dignity. But guess what? I got through it. Not because it didn't hurt, but because I stopped letting it have the last word. That's when I realized something: There's no such thing as a bad day. Just challenging ones. Some days are more challenging than others, but that don't make them bad. It's like checking my blood pressure—one moment it's 120 over 80, the next it's higher. Not every reading is perfect, but that don't mean I'm dying. Same with life—every day ain't gon' feel smooth, but a spike don't mean you kill your damn self.

Bad days don't ruin people—what ruins people is giving one bad day permission to turn into seven. A bad day is like a fire alarm—it's loud, it's disruptive, but it ain't the damn fire. It's just a warning to handle what's heating up before it burns your whole life down. Don't freeze, don't fold—grab the extinguisher or find the exit. Preparation don't just ease the blow—it keeps yo ass from going down in flames. Start acting like someone who's already survived the worst. You've survived losing a parent. You've survived heartbreak, betrayal, addiction, eviction. You've survived days where you didn't want to wake up. You've survived being broke, being broken, being abandoned. You've survived days you swore would kill you—but they didn't. They didn't win. You're still here. You don't just have a survival record—you've got a survival résumé. So why let one rough day punk yo ass out now? Temporary pain don't deserve permanent power—evict it before it unpacks. Let bad days remind you of what you've made it through, not make you forget what you're made of. Don't break down because of a bad day—break through. You can't control everything throughout the course of your day, but you can control whether or not you let it throw you off course.

Growth Affirmation: I will **GROW** out of the mindset
of letting a bad day ruin my week. Bad days are like
the common cold—I will eventually catch one, but I
won't let it infect my mindset or stop my progress.

Take this day to THINK about how quick people are to idolize the outcome but ignore the origin. Everybody wants the glory but skips the guts it takes to grind from the bottom. They want success to put his arm around them, but are too damn scared to lift a finger, break their back, and go out there and break a leg. You waiting for signs, blessings, handouts—but the real ones started at ground zero with ten toes down, clawing their way through dirt, doubt, and dead silence. Stop glamorizing success and start respecting the suffering it took to get there. Ground zero don't hand out silver spoons—it hands out shovels. And if you ain't willing to bleed in the build, you ain't ready to stand on anything. The seed of an oak tree grows in silence, under pressure, through dirt. It don't cry about the dark—it pushes through it. You want to rise? First, you gotta stop being afraid of the dirt you're buried under. Starting at ground zero means you got no room for excuses—just enough space to get to work.

My ground zero was walking into a restaurant I didn't even work at, acting like I was bussing tables, just to steal tips to fund my next high. I was low—real low. If I'm being honest, I didn't just swipe dollars… I might've grabbed a half-eaten biscuit and washed it down with somebody's leftover Coke like it was mine. That's how deep I was in—starving for a high, not food. I knew I was spiraling. I knew I looked pitiful. But that was the day I didn't let fear hold me back from reaching out to a friend. I had felt like I'd gone too far to be helped, but something in me said to try anyway. I wish I could tell you everything changed after that—but I fell short again. Point is, even at ground zero, I didn't surrender to fear. I didn't let shame keep me buried or guilt stop me from trying to rise. Even when I was covered in dirt, I had just enough fight in me to start clawing back. I didn't just sit in rock bottom—I started building from it.

Listen, you either start from the bottom or stay at the bottom. There's nothing wrong with starting at ground zero. Again, ain't that where oak trees get their start? Ground zero strips away every excuse. It don't care about your sensitive-ass feelings, your fake-ass fears. It dares you to move with no map. It forces you to bootstrap, white-knuckle, and outlast. That's where real growth happens—in the mud. Not when it's pretty. When it's gritty. So stop acting like you need more clarity, more support, or more time. What you need is more heart. You either let the dirt bury you, or you let it build you. Ain't no middle ground. The road might be long, and the weight might feel heavy—but every inch you crawl proves you ain't built to stay buried. So stand on your ground zero with grit in your gut and fire in your chest. The top don't belong to those born with silver spoons in their mouth. It belongs to the ones who turned butter knives into machetes, hacked through their fears, and carved their way to the top.

Growth Affirmation: I will **GROW** out of the mindset
that there's nothing wrong with starting at ground zero. But
everything's wrong with never getting off the ground.

Take this day to **THINK** about how goals aren't achieved by stating them—they're achieved by starting them. Goals don't get achieved by writing them down in pretty journals or shouting them out to your friends—they get achieved when you decide to get off your ass and put in the work. If you're serious about what you want, you'll act like it. You won't take your sweet ass time like you got all damn day. As soon as you build up the nerve to set a goal, you set your ass right back down. But you'll move quickly when it's something you can't ignore. Think about it—when you're hungry, you'll find food. When you order a package online, you track it obsessively until it's delivered. Why don't you treat your goals the same way? Goals, like hunger or urgent needs, require immediate and focused action. If you delay watering the seeds of your ambition, they'll die before they even get the chance to bloom. Starting isn't just the first step—it's the most critical one. Write it down, then run it down. Because a goal without action is potential scribbled on a things to-do list.

My rock bottom had gym hours. Because I was living in my building's garage, I had to sneak into Planet Fitness—not to lift weights, but to lift funk off my skin in the locker room showers. That gym was my Bath & Body Works, my spa. I'd walk past treadmills like I belonged there, clutching my plastic bag of soap and socks, trying not to look homeless. At the time, I was piecing together early sobriety—no pills in my system, but still poisoned by embarrassment. Then one day, standing barefoot on that cold tile, I looked in the mirror and made a decision. "Two months," I whispered. "I'm done showering in a place that ain't mine. I'm done living in a garage like I'm a damn storage item." That wasn't just a goal—it was a vow. Every application I filled out, every odd job I took, every time I walked past temptation—I reminded myself of that mirror, that locker room, and that man I refused to be again. And you know what? I hit that goal right on time—by landing on my mama's couch. I'd cleaned up my act just enough for her to crack the door and let me in. Might not be luxury, but I had a tub and didn't have to worry about catching athlete's foot in the gym's community shower. Progress is progress—don't judge the upgrade. Commend the goal being achieved.

Do this—think about the goals you've been putting off. Now think about a full bladder. When you gotta piss, you don't wait for the perfect moment—you move now. You'll squirm, squeeze, break a damn door down, or even go outside to do it. You'll do whatever it takes just to find relief. That's urgency. So why the hell you treat your dreams with less urgency than your bladder? You'll sprint to piss but crawl to progress? How backwards is that? Goal setting should feel like having to pee real bad—but for whatever reason, you don't see it that way. When your mind fills up with purpose or a goal, that pressure should be damn near unbearable. Don't sit on your goal like you can hold it in—act like you're about to explode. The longer you wait, the more uncomfortable it gets. The sooner you act, the sooner you get relief… that sweet *ahhhhh* that comes from progress, not procrastination. Proclamation rivals procrastination—one gets you started, but the other keeps you stagnant. You ain't waiting for ideal conditions—you're leaking opportunity every second you hesitate. Give your goals the same urgency, the same discomfort, the same immediate reaction. Don't just dig them out your head and set them—track their progress, nurture their growth, and commit to seeing them through. Whether it's losing weight, learning a skill, or building a better life, don't wait to feel ready. Move the moment you set the goal to gain traction and get the relief you seek. Momentum dies quick if you let it sit. If the goal don't make you move like you gotta pee—you'll keep pissing away your potential.

Growth Affirmation: I will **GROW** out of the mindset that writing goals is enough—if I can chase a high with urgency, I can chase my healing the same way.

Take this day to **THINK** about how your mindset determines whether you'll soar in life or be eaten by it. It's sad, but most people live their lives thinking like turkeys, content to stay grounded, settling for crumbs, and never daring to rise above. Are you one of them? I know I was. Be honest. Do you spend your days looking down, too scared to aim for something greater? Binge-watching trash TV, liking strangers' posts more than your own life, stalkin' exes on social media, diggin' in your nose and up yo ass all day—wastin' time like your future's not on the line? If you're not flying high, it's not because you can't—it's because you refuse to. Choosing to think like an eagle means trading the safety of the barnyard for the freedom of the open sky. If you keep thinking like a turkey, don't be shocked when life serves you up for everyone to eat off of. Forget the coop—build a cockpit. If you're still grounded, don't blame gravity—blame the mindset that clipped your own wings. You're the one refusing to think higher and to see further. The sky's wide open, reserved for those with the vision to rise above—but as long as your turkey-ass thinks small, the sky will always feel too far.

I'll never forget the time a CO called me a birdbrain. I severely cussed him out. But while sitting in the hole, I started thinking. If I was going to be a bird-brain, then I'd make damn sure it was the brain of an eagle, and not a turkey. Back then, my mindset was trash. I was a jive turkey who wasn't going nowhere. Stuck in the barnyard. That made me think. Turkeys live for safety, for comfort, for what's easy. Eagles? They live for the sky, for the hunt, for the freedom to go where others can't. When I made the choice to start thinking like an eagle, everything changed. I stopped worrying about what the turkeys said about me. Now, I look at them from above as they watch me from below fly circles around them. Once you start thinking highly of yourself, you'll discover that the sky ain't the limit when you think like an eagle—it's just the runway.

You got real dreams but spend all day watching reels and scrolling comments like success gon' DM you first. You wasting time like you got a spare life in your trunk. And you wanna know what's crazy? It's bad enough your wings ain't flapping—but you let people with no wings tell you you can't fly. Be careful with people. They clip their own wings, then call you crazy for flying. The Wright brothers got called birdbrains too—but they flapped back, and their "crazy" became everybody's runway. While everybody else was laughing their ass off, they were lifting off. They refused to let gravity, doubt, or others' limits keep them grounded. They weren't content to dream small like turkeys—they dreamed high and dared to chase it. And now we have planes. That's what thinking like an eagle looks like. It's not about wishing or hoping—it's about daring to go where others won't. Most people will never get off the ground because they're too afraid of what's above. But fear is for turkeys. Eagles don't waste time listening to turkeys—they fly higher where the noise can't reach. Stop thinking small, stop settling, and stop being okay with the barnyard. Eagles don't belong on the ground, and neither do you. So, what's it going to be? Are you going to keep pecking in the dirt, or are you going to take flight? Damn what they say. Let 'em call you a birdbrain—just make sure it's the kind that flies, not fries.

Growth Affirmation: I will **GROW** out of the mindset of listening to turkeys. I won't let people who never left the coop talk me out of the clouds.

Take this day to **THINK** about why you keep breaking your back in that relationship or job, convincing yourself you're climbing somewhere—when really, you're jogging on a busted treadmill. That treadmill life got you stuck in the same damn view: Cheated on, lied to, disrespected—and you call it "progress" 'cause they throw you a date night every once in a while or drag their ass home five nights outta seven. That job? Same scene, year after year—no raise, no real respect—but you tell yourself you're moving forward 'cause they slap a shiny new title on you and let you rot in the same parking spot. Treadmills trap you in routines that exhaust you without results. You sweat, you struggle, but the scenery never changes. Trails, on the other hand, push you to explore, challenge you with obstacles, and take you somewhere new. Trails will show you there are people who will actually value you, places that will actually grow you, and challenges that will actually change you. If your life feels trapped, it's time to ask yourself, "Am I running in place, mistaking motion for movement?" It's time you realize that treadmills wear you out—trails build you up.

There was a stretch when I thought I was killin' it—off the pills, clocking into work, eating microwave meals like I was thriving. But really, I was just the CEO of Going Nowhere Fast, Inc. Wake up, same routine. Work, same drama. Home, same sad dinner with a plastic fork. I wasn't living—I was looping. That was my treadmill. I used to brag about staying clean, like I deserved a trophy, but all I was doing was running in place and sweating mediocrity. The highlight of my week was buying different flavors of ramen noodles—chicken and shrimp—and mixing them together like I was a chef cooking a gourmet meal. One day I thought, "Bruh, this your 'better life'?" I had gone from chaos to cruise control—but forgot to hit the gas. So I finally stepped off. I traded that treadmill life for a trail: I started writing, healing, stretching beyond the safe and predictable. It wasn't glamorous, but at least it wasn't bland. Stepping off the treadmill was the only way to change my direction. On it, I was only going one way. Real progress only began when I discovered that if the ground beneath you ain't changing, then neither are you. If it's not a trail—it's a trap. Treadmills shrink your waistline—but trails stretch your backbone.

Now it's your turn to reflect. Are you stuck in the same routines, hoping for change while repeating the same patterns? Staying on a treadmill is like eating the same meal every day—it keeps you alive, but it's dull as hell. Trails are the buffet of life, offering endless opportunities to explore. The treadmill might feel safe, but it's a prison. Trails, though unpredictable and challenging, are where transformation happens. Trails build strength, endurance, and resilience. Trails don't baby you—they break you down and rebuild you stronger. Out there, you'll trip over rocks, grind up steep hills, and wrestle with sharp turns—but that's exactly where your grit, endurance, and purpose show up. Life on a treadmill is predictable but stationary. Trails will exhaust you, but they'll also evolve you. Don't waste another second running in place, hoping the view will change. The treadmill tracks your steps—the trail tracks your growth. Life's best rewards aren't found in the safety of repetition—they're waiting for you on unbeaten paths. Leave the treadmill behind and take the trail ahead. The treadmill keeps you running in place; the trail takes you places. In life, don't just run—run somewhere. Treadmills burn off the fat—trails burn off the fat lie that keeps you stuck in place.

Growth Affirmation: I will **GROW** out of the mindset of running in place. Treadmills move my feet. Trails move my life. Treadmills train my legs—trails train my life.

Take this day to **THINK** about why you waste energy fighting about shit today that won't even matter tomorrow. You'll fight over a man that ain't yours but won't fight for your son to grow into one. You'll fight about somebody breaking in line but won't fight for breaking the cycle in your bloodline. You'll fight about someone stealing yo seat but won't fight for a seat at the table. You'll fight about somebody stepping on yo shoes but won't fight for stepping into your purpose. You throw hands about drama but won't lift a hand for yo dream. Arguing over small things is like using a fire extinguisher to blow out birthday candles—it wastes resources you'll need for real emergencies. The things you fight about reveal vanity, but the things you fight for reveal value. The battles you pick prove what matters most to you—and for too many, it ain't worth the bruised knuckles or the wasted breath. Every petty fight is proof you've abandoned a bigger one. Nobody gets remembered for what they argued about—only for what they stood for.

During my time in prison, men—myself included—fought over the most petty things. Fights broke out over who got the remote, who had next on the microwave, or who cut in line at the commissary. One man got beaten senseless over a weight bench; another was stabbed over a phone call. But none of those fights were about what they seemed. Beneath every fight for control of a microwave or TV remote was a deeper desperation—the fight for respect, for validation, for a sense of power in a powerless environment. And yet, while we wasted time brawling over nothing, we neglected the battles that actually mattered—the fight for freedom, redemption, and becoming better men. Looking back, I see how those meaningless battles stole energy I could've used to fight for what mattered. Fighting over trifles keeps you mired in the shallow end of life, while the deeper battles—the ones for peace, purpose, and progress—go unfought. You can't fight for your destiny if you're busy fighting over distractions.

It's sad that you'll go to war over the dumbest things but back down when it's time to fight for your future. You'll fight about your place in line but won't fight for your place in life? You'll fight about a parking spot but won't fight to get outta that fucked up spot where life has you parked? Are you fucken serious? What you fight about shows what you live for. Fighting about nonsense only proves you've got nothing real to fight for. Fighting over petty shit is like shadowboxing—you waste all your energy swinging at nothing. The fight ain't worth it if it don't feed your future. Use your energy to fight for your dreams, not to waste it on drama. Instead of squabbling over who's right, fight for what's worth it. The next time you feel pulled into a trivial argument, ask yourself, "Is this worth my time? Is this taking me closer to my purpose, or is it just taking time away from it?" If it ain't building your legacy, it ain't worth a battle. Don't fight about a rumor—fight for your respect. Don't fight about a post—fight for your potential. Don't fight about pettiness—fight for your peace. The battles worth fighting are the ones that shape your future, not the ones that shift your focus. Save your strength for battles that build, not brawls that break. If it won't matter in five days, five weeks, five months, or five years—don't give it five fucken minutes of your energy.

Growth Affirmation: I will **GROW** out of fighting over petty things and focus on fighting for what truly matters— my family, my dreams, and my peace of mind.

Take this day to **THINK** about how quick we are to call a parent's absence abandonment when we were really being provided for in silence. Some parents didn't go AWOL—they were deployed to the front lines of survival. A dad working doubles, skipping family dinners—not because he didn't care, but because he's out there fighting bills to keep you clothed, fed, and housed. A mom missing recitals—not because she forgot, but because she's holding down two jobs to keep the roof from caving in. Love don't always come home for dinner—it clocks in early, skips birthdays, and trades tuck-ins for time-cards. You call it absence, but they were out there making sure you had a bed to sleep in and water to wash your ass. You ain't gotta like how love looked, but you better respect what it kept you from losing. Some parents get judged for what they missed while being forgotten for what they made possible. And by the time you finally see it for what it was, the years are gone, and, "I get it now," is all you've got left to say.

Growing up, my mother's absence felt like rejection. No school assemblies, no bedtime stories, no talks about life. It felt personal—like she didn't want to be there. But I never asked why she wasn't around. I never stopped to consider what her absence meant. As I got older, I realized she wasn't gone—she was just buried in survival. She left before sunrise, came back after dark, and collapsed into sleep just to do it all again the next day. Her love was in every light that stayed on, every meal that showed up, every sigh she exhaled after a 14-hour shift. I used to be bitter. I thought I was missing something. She didn't join me at school for Muffins with Mom. She didn't pick me up often, but she held me down. And now? I carry that sacrifice with me every time I clock in, every time I show up for others, every time I grind when I don't feel like it. She loved me the best way she knew how—with every tired bone in her body. My mom's absence didn't mean she didn't love us—it meant she couldn't afford not to.

The fact that you can't see the callouses on your dad's hands or the blisters on your mother's feet don't mean the love wasn't there—it means you were blind to how it showed up. Love ain't always soft; sometimes it's sacrifice in steel-toe boots. Stop crying about what you didn't feel and start honoring what you didn't notice. Just because a chef ain't sitting at the table don't mean they didn't provide the meal. Don't confuse an empty chair for an empty heart—some love cooks the meal but eats last. Some love shows up in dirty hands, sore backs, and barely enough gas in the tank—because they gave their all to make sure yo ungrateful ass didn't go without. Kids, recognize love in your parents' effort, not just the embrace. Drop the attitude. Just because your parents couldn't be there every moment; they were making sure you could wear Nikes instead of Sikes. It's easier to remember who wasn't at the game than to understand who was behind the scenes paying for the uniform. Parents, your life is in the sacrifice. You didn't need to be in the room to still be in their future. Drop the guilt trip that you're failing to be present for your child—you're doing what you have to do so that your children can do what they want to do. You're the backbone that keeps clothes on their back. That's not neglect—that's legacy.

Growth Affirmation: I will **GROW** out of the mindset
of thinking that my parents neglected me. If they missed
the moment, it's 'cause they were working to pay for it.

Take this day to THINK about how much you're clowning around—performing acts that bring no real purpose, no growth, no future. You love to play games—entertaining people with gossip, jumping through hoops to impress people who don't give a damn if you die tomorrow, and juggling habits that do nothing but drag you down. You're playing with fire every time you choose comfort over progress, and you're walking a tightrope every time you fake happiness while walking on eggshells, afraid to address the elephant in the room for fear of getting punched in the face. You keep running in circles, putting on a show, and for what? So the crowd can cheer? So you can feel like you're doing something, when deep down you know you're going nowhere? Stop lying to yourself. The crowd doesn't care, and they're not going to be a safety net when you fall. The longer you perform for others, the more you lose yourself in the act. The loudest applause often comes when you're furthest from your purpose.

I remember taking my youngest daughter to the circus, and she was mesmerized by the performers—the tightrope walkers, clowns, and acrobats. But watching them reminded me of my own circus days when I was running the streets. I was the clown, juggling lies and hustling for fast money. Selling drugs was my act, and getting high was my escape. I walked a tightrope every day, knowing one wrong move could send me to the grave or back to a cell. I played with fire, thinking I was invincible, but the flames always burned me. My audience? They laughed every time I fell off my tightrope. They clapped while I destroyed myself. I let the streets control my show, and it cost me my freedom, my family, and my peace of mind. That's the truth about the circus—you think you're the star, but you're just the entertainment for people who don't give a damn about you.

The more praise you get, the more off-track you actually are—because people love the show, not your growth. You lose your identity every time you trade authenticity for applause. The circus only continues if you keep performing; the moment you walk away, the show ends. Remember, the same people who clap for you on the way up won't hesitate to laugh when you hit the ground. Remove the makeup from your face and stop living a life that's made for laughs. Shut down the circus act and take control. Stop performing for people who don't care if you fall. Ask yourself, "Am I living for my advancement, or am I living for their admiration?" You're not here to juggle others' expectations, burn yourself out, or walk a tightrope just to keep the crowd entertained. Focus on what truly matters, cut loose the acts that don't serve your growth, and build a life where you're living for you, not the audience. Life is too short to be a performer in your own story. Step out of the ring, take off the clown makeup, and start living a life that's real, balanced, and yours to control. Real life doesn't need applause—it needs accountability. You're the ringmaster, not the clown—take the whip and tame the chaos.

Growth Affirmation: I will **GROW** out of the mindset
of performance. I'm done clowning for applause—this
life is mine to command, not theirs to consume.

Take this day to THINK about the engine in your head that's got two sides: The left handles logic, the right fuels creativity. But let's be real—you out here wasting both. You don't lack logic—you just apply it to the wrong things. You'll strategize for hours how to get revenge on people who you got problems with but won't spend five minutes solving your financial problems. You'll use every ounce of reasoning to defend your dysfunction, justify your laziness, or stay in a relationship you know is draining you. That ain't logic—that's ludicrous. That's left-brain energy used backwards. And your creativity? That right side of your brain that was built to imagine, invent, and build something meaningful? You've been using it to invent lies, sneak around, and come up with new ways to cheat, scam, or stunt on people who don't even matter. You'll dream up 20 ways to hide your dirt, but zero ways to clean your life up. You're not uncreative—you're just creative in all the wrong directions. The truth is, your mind is still working—it's just working against you. You've trained it to survive instead of evolve. You build stories instead of solutions. You imagine betrayal instead of building vision. That's why nothing in your life feels aligned—because the engine between your ears is firing in the wrong direction.

For a while, my brain was scrambled. Not because it didn't work, but because I was working it in all the wrong ways. On the left side, I used logic to justify destruction. My thinking was, "They gon' get high anyway. Might as well get it from me." That was my twisted business plan. Pregnant women. Mothers with toddlers. Didn't matter. If they didn't have money, I got creative. Told 'em I'd give 'em $20 worth of dope for $40 in food stamps. And they went for it—because addicts don't do math; they do desperation. Meanwhile, I convinced myself I was just helping them get by. That was my right brain working—just not for good. Instead of using it to write books, start businesses, or build anything that mattered, I was out here creating new schemes and survival tactics like a sick genius. That creativity didn't die—it just got corrupted. The same brain I used to destroy my life became the one that helped rebuild it. I didn't move forward in life because both sides of my brain kept taking me in reverse and parking me in places like jail, prison, and rehab. Piece by piece, thought by thought, I reprogrammed my mind and gave both sides a new job: to help me grow.

Your brain is just like a car engine—if one side misfires, the whole system struggles. The same is true for your mind. If you've stopped creating out of fear or let others think for you because it's easier, your life will stay in neutral. To move forward, you have to engage both sides of your brain. Feed your logic by learning, solving, and building; fuel your creativity by dreaming, risking, and doing. When both sides of your brain are firing, your life stops idling and starts accelerating. The key to unlocking your potential isn't in your hands—it's between your ears. If you keep ignoring the engine, don't cry when your life won't start. You've got a mind that could cure your chaos, but you let it collect cobwebs. Your left side's being used to overthink, not overcome. Your right side's being used to create evil, not evolve. That's why your life's miserable—it ain't a lack of brainpower; it's misplaced power. Both sides still work—you just don't make 'em work for you. You got horsepower under the hood but won't mash the gas and hit the open road 'cause you still think that on the right side ain't nothing right, and on the left side, ain't nothing left.

Growth Affirmation: I will **GROW** out of the
mindset of allowing my brain to sit idle. I'm not out
of options—I'm just not out here thinking.

Take this day to **THINK** about the truth—your body gon' rot one day, but your name don't have to. And right now? You ain't doing shit worth remembering. Nobody gon' talk about the designer clothes you wore, the car you drove, or the house you flexed in. Nobody gives a damn about what you had—they only remember what you did. What you do today is writing the story the world gon' read tomorrow. So what's it gon' say—that you were just another nobody who pissed away potential, or somebody who broke the mold and carved a mark into history? Your purpose is like a streaming service: When you put out the right content, the world replays it long after you've logged off. Purpose ain't measured by the moment—it's measured by the echo it leaves when you're gone. The way you're living, your name won't mean a damn thing. Martin Luther King Jr. lived out his purpose by standing for justice and equality, creating an unshakable legacy. Walt Disney's imagination gave the world characters that still live in our kids' dreams. Whitney Houston's voice became a timeless gift that still cracks hearts wide open. Their names are so loud the grave couldn't silence them. Keep living the way you are, and your name gon' die the same day you do.

I once sat in court, shackled, as the judge read off my charges like a biography. No talk of my heart, no mention of my hurt—just my history. My name sounded like a lost cause on a docket sheet. And I thought, "Damn... is this how my obituary gon' read too?" Would my family have to print a bunch of lies just to make it sound like I had a name worth remembering? That bothered me. I wouldn't let paperwork write my legacy. I'd write my own. So I decided to become a trainer and an author. Now, the only time my name gets called is to train clients, sign books, or speak truth into people ready to evolve. Training clients wasn't just exercising—it was elevating. Writing my book wasn't just therapy—it was testimony. Both achievements are ways to make sure my name outlived my mistakes. I built a name my daughters can say with pride—not pity. And if I die tomorrow, my obituary don't need to be embellished—my life already speaks loud enough long after I'm gone. That shift from destruction to purpose showed me that your physical body may die, but your body of work can live forever.

If you're only living for today's satisfaction, you're robbing tomorrow of its potential. Every choice you make today lays the foundation for how you'll be remembered tomorrow. What story will your name tell? Living out your purpose ain't about clout, likes, or chasing fame—it's about creating something that slaps time in the face and refuses to fade. You don't need to be a global icon to make an impact. Purpose is found in the everyday choices that shape your life and the lives of those around you. It's in how you lift others up, how you keep going when it's hard, and how you turn your struggles into strength. You don't need a million followers to be remembered—you just need one purpose you refuse to walk away from. Your obituary won't list your likes and followers—it'll echo the life you chose to live. Live in a way that your name becomes a movement, not just a memory. Live so loud in your purpose that even death can't turn down your volume. Don't let your obituary be a recap—make it a relay baton. Your tombstone should mark where you rest—not where your impact ends.

Growth Affirmation: I will **GROW** out of the mindset that my name has to die with me—I'm building a legacy that outlives the grave.

Take this day to **THINK** about how toxic habits and choices don't just rob you of material things—they strip you of your values. Vices don't give a damn about your stuff, just your soul. They don't care about your materials, just your mind. Drugs, gambling, alcoholism, pornography, or any other vice aren't worried about your possessions—they're after something far more precious. These vices creep into your life like silent burglars, promising escape or pleasure, only to rob you of your self-respect, morals, and the essence of who you are. Unlike burglars breaking into houses, they don't stop at your valuables—they target your soul, stripping away everything that makes you whole. They make you empty your pockets, but worse, they empty your character—where your values used to live—leaving you to barely recognize who you used to be. Drugs are like termites; they gnaw away at the foundation of your character, leaving behind a hollow shell of what once stood strong that even you can't stand to live in.

Drugs didn't break into my temple—they broke into my life. They didn't stop at taking what I owned; they stripped away what I valued—my relationships, integrity, and self-worth. I used to rob myself. Every pop of a pill was a stickup of my own soul. I wasn't breaking into houses—I was breaking into my future every time I pawned something just to feed my high. I sold the flatscreen, the jewelry, my car scanner—but worse, I sold off my values. I told myself, "It's just for now"—knowing damn well that whenever I got money in my hands, it was going to buy pills, not reclaim my items. I was trading my dignity for dope, my morals for moments. I was the thief and the victim, emptying out my life one piece at a time, until the mirror stopped showing a man and started showing a ghost. I didn't just need rehab—I needed to change the locks on my life. I couldn't rebuild anything if I kept leaving the door cracked for destruction. It was like leaving stuff at an ex's place just to have an excuse to get back in.

Either you protect your values like Fort Knox, or your vices will rob you blind—like a thief in the night with your eyes wide open. Just like you'd protect your home from intruders—locking windows and doors, setting alarms, staying alert—you've got to guard your soul with that same urgency. Build mental deadbolts. Set internal tripwires. If a toxic thought, person, or craving comes knocking, don't even ask, "Who is it?" Let they ass sit right outside that damn door. Peek through the peephole of wisdom before you let anything enter that wishes to do you harm. Install alarms that scream when anything tries to steal your peace. Because if you don't, vices will slither in like friends, rob you like foes, and leave you wondering why you ever let them in. Your mind is sacred ground, not a crash pad for chaos. Fortify your boundaries with clarity, conviction, and consequences. Guard your values like they're the last thing you own, because once they're gone, so are you. If you don't secure your soul, your vices will strip it down and sell it piece by piece to the highest bidder—and drugs, alcohol, and sex will pay top dollar.

Growth Affirmation: I will **GROW** out of the mindset of leaving my values unguarded. My soul ain't for sale, and I'm done leaving the door cracked for destruction.

Take this day to **THINK** about how fucken easy you've been getting played, duped, and strung along. A sweet-talker whispers, "I love you," just to drag you in the bed. A so-called friend hits you with, "If you were a real one, you'd ride with me," just to pull you into their bullshit. A family member throws out, "After all I've done for you," just to guilt-trip you into submission. Even social media got you hypnotized—feeding you fake lives to chase while your real one rots. At some point, you gotta square up to the lies. If not, stop crying—'cause it ain't on them, it's on yo ass. And you got the nerve to want sympathy? Nah—you're just sorry for staying a fool long enough to be manipulated. Quit being hypnotized by pretty faces and polished words. Quit buying lies like they truth on clearance. Manipulation doesn't need volume—it's slick, it's subtle, it's whispers of guilt, doubt, and insecurity until you have bought into it. Then you wake up living for everybody but you. You no longer even know your damn self. Don't whine about being brainwashed when you won't wring out the lies. Stop blaming manipulation for running your life when you keep leaving the keys under the mat.

To treat my pain, doctors convinced me that pills were the solution. They didn't care about healing me; they cared about hooking me—giving me ninety pills at a time. Their manipulation wasn't loud or obvious—it came wrapped in authority and trust. "Take this; it'll help you." But all it did was ruin me. I thought those pills were saving me, but they were enslaving me. Manipulation is an artificial sweetener people pour over lies to make them easier to swallow. My life was run by lies. The turning point came when I finally stopped being a pawn in their game. I stopped trusting every word and started being wise. Wisdom told me that these doctors were probably getting kickbacks from the drug companies for prescribing their bottled death. It taught me that knowledge isn't enough. Knowing I was manipulated wasn't the fix;

applying wisdom to my choices was. I locked those doors, sealed those windows, and stopped letting manipulation creep in.

You weren't made to be molded by everybody else's guilt. If manipulation keeps working, it's because you keep cooperating. You keep trading silence for acceptance, letting guilt trips reroute your life while calling it "keeping the peace." But peace bought through obedience ain't peace—it's silent control. Every time you swallow your voice to keep from upsetting someone, you shrink. That fake praise, those slick apologies, that "After all I've done for you" or "Who else is going to want you" speech—those are traps wrapped in ribbons. And you keep unwrapping 'em like they're gifts. People don't need power over you—they just need you to keep pretending you don't see the game that's being played. But wisdom don't whisper—it screams in the silence you ignore. Start checking timing, tone, and intention. Ask yourself: Who benefits from your compliance? Who thrives when you stay confused? You're not weak—you're just scared of what happens when you finally say no. But strength ain't in how long you take ass-whoopings—it's in when you decide enough's enough. You done puttin' up wit their bullshit—lies, manipulation, deceit. And if you keep giving people access to your mind without a background check, don't cry when they scam you out of who you are. Keep lettin' people put you on spin cycle, it ain't brainwashing anymore—it's you handing them the fucken soap.

Growth Affirmation: I will **GROW** out of the mindset
of mental submission. My mind ain't a sponge for lies—
it's a vault for wisdom, and I'm locking it down.

Take this day to **THINK** about how regret ain't meant to be lived in; it's meant to be learned from. And yet you choose to make it a permanent camping site. For some strange reason, you keep revisiting the crash sites of your past like there's some souvenir to pick up from the wreckage. Still replaying the abortion you never talked about. Still beating yourself up over the fact that you were a bad parent early on. Still obsessing over the opportunity you blew years ago. You have the potential to go high, but you choose to stay yo regretful ass buried in a mess that's no longer relevant. What part of "let go" don't you understand? Regret just keeps you grounded. It's like booking a flight to freedom but refusing to board the plane 'cause you're still arguing with the TSA about baggage that's already been scanned. Why you keep insisting on going on a guilt trip with regret, revisiting landmarks that brought you nothing but pain? Regret ain't nothing but a bad tour guide. Showing you only the bad spots of your life. Who you've hurt. The mistakes you've made. But regret doesn't have to be your compass. It can be a landmark—a reminder of where you've been and what you've learned, but not a place to vacation. Stop letting the pain last and the lesson pass.

She didn't cry. Didn't argue. Just stared out the window while I drove her to the clinic like we were going to the grocery store. I didn't force her, but I damn sure didn't stop her. I told her we weren't ready, that it was the smart thing to do. Truth is, I was just scared. Scared of being tied down. Scared of stepping up. We never talked about it again. But that silence? It never left me. That was a life I helped erase—and no matter how I try to dress it up, I was a coward who made it easy to end something I should've protected. From time to time, I feel the ghost of a child I didn't fight for. I can't go back and fix it—but I damn sure won't let my fear kill anything else I'm supposed to protect. It's not about what you've done but what you do from this point. Mistakes are nothing more than "missed takes," much like an actor who messes up a line during a scene. In movies, mistakes don't ruin the story—they lead to retakes. I started to view my life in that same vein. Every bad decision was a retake—a chance to run it back and learn from the fuck-up. My past wasn't a cell anymore; it was a classroom.

Mistakes aren't walls—they're windows, and it's on you whether you look through 'em or crash into 'em. Regret don't hold power until you keep giving it a microphone. If you treat your mistakes like tombstones, you'll spend your life grieving instead of growing. But if you treat 'em like missed takes, you'll stop crying over scenes and start doing retakes. Regret is only as powerful as the meaning you assign to it. Your guilt ain't supposed to be your identity—it's supposed to be your ignition. Stop living in reruns of your worst moments and start producing a better plot. Take the wheel back. Hit the gas. You can't change the scene that already played—but you can change what happens next. Regret does nothing but keep you grounded and on constant delay—circling the runway while your future takes off without you. You ain't grounded by regret—you're just refusing to apply the lesson and liftoff. Your loyalty to regret is what's holding your growth hostage. When you screw up, life don't end the scene—it yells, "Cut!" and hands you a retake. But a retake ain't about living in the mistake—it's about learning the line you fucked up and getting it right. That's it. Life will shout, "Action!" again, but if you're scared to shoot the sequel, regret will keep showing you reruns of your bloopers.

> **Growth Affirmation:** I will **GROW** out of the mindset of
> regret. Mistakes are a matter of perception. If I see them as regret,
> I'll live in them. If I see them as lessons, I'll learn from them.

Take this day to **THINK** about how both your physical and emotional scars are a testament to your strength, not a reason to be scared to live. Why are you having a tantrum over today's problems when you've survived battles that should've left you broken? Your scars are proof of that survival. The rape didn't put you in a coma. The heartbreak didn't land you in the psych ward. The abuse didn't kill you. So why the fuck are you letting fear of "what might happen" keep you from living the life you already fought to protect? Scars don't exist to remind you of your pain—they're proof you overcame it. Like a dropped phone, yeah, you show cracks, but you can still connect with others. Cracked ain't broken. Scarred ain't silenced. If your phone can still function after taking a beating from being dropped a thousand times, so can you. Every mark you carry—whether stitched across skin or stitched into memory—is a receipt for the pain you already paid in full that can't be refunded or exchanged.

I've got an eight-inch "zipper"—67 staples—running down my abdomen from being shot, a permanent reminder of a day I should've died. For years, I stared at it with shame, hating what it represented. Complications from that scar tissue could flare up anytime. That fear consumed me until I realized the scar didn't own me—I owned it. My scars became the bookmarks of my story, marking the chapters where I triumphed, not what tried to kill me. I started using it as a warning when I talked to kids about street life. I'd pull up my shirt, point at the "zipper," and say, "This is what the streets got me." My scar wasn't a weakness; it was a weapon. It was my proof that I survived what most wouldn't. It wasn't just a mark of survival; it was a mark of strength, proof that I'd turned pain into purpose. If survival is my passport, my scars are the stamps—proof of all the places I visited that tried to be my final destination.

Scars don't tell the story of pain—they prove you pulled through it. They weren't given to keep you scared; they exist to show you're still standing. Whether from abuse, addiction, betrayal, or your own damn decisions, scars only hold power if you hand it to them. You got marked but not muted. Bruised but not buried. Stop tiptoeing around your future just because your past drew blood. Scars aren't chains—they're history lessons that chronicle the battles you already survived. Don't let a past wound become your future weakness. Don't let it be the enemy to your evolution. Let every scar scream survival, not surrender. Just like my "zipper" proves I made it through something lethal, your scars prove that you made it through something scary. Healing ain't about erasing the memory—it's about rewriting what it means. Your scars might've marked you, but they don't make you. Your scars mark the battles. They show you've won the war. You have a victorious spirit. When you move beyond the fear, your scars become landmarks of triumph, not reminders of trauma. Your scars might've scratched the surface, but they never put a dent in your destiny. Your scars are evidence of your power—not reminders of your pain. They ain't proof you're weak—they're proof you won.

Growth Affirmation: I will **GROW** out of the mindset of being defeated. My scars are a signed contract with survival— the incident can't take back what I made it through.

> ***Darkness*** produces ***growth***.

Take this day to **THINK** about how darkness is always labeled as negative. We hear "dark place," "dark cloud," or "dark times" like it means death—but sometimes it means development. For some reason, we are obsessed with being afraid of the dark. But funny how we ain't scared of the dark when we're creeping into someone else's bed. We ain't scared of the dark when we're shoving that shit up our nose behind closed doors, or committing crimes. You loved the dark when it covered your dirt—but now you hate it because it's uncovering your truth? Don't call the dark "evil" just because it stopped working in your favor. Darkness ain't always a dead end—it's an open road. That pressure, that pain, that silence you feel? That's growth trying to push through. Stop cursing the cocoon just because it don't feel like flight yet. You were bold in the dark when it helped you be treacherous—now be bold in the dark when it helps you transform. The darkest places aren't here to eviscerate you; they're here to evolve you. Life ain't about avoiding the dark—it's about proving you can build in it.

For the longest time, I said, "I'm glad I went to prison—that dark place— it made me a better person." But that was a damn lie. Prison didn't make me who I am, and addiction didn't either. Those dark places weren't magical— they didn't do anything but hold me down until I decided to grow. I had to stop playing the victim and start taking advantage of the opportunities in front of me. For years, I sat in darkness—jail, prison, rehab—and did nothing with it. The bars didn't make me better, but the programs I attended, the knowledge I soaked in, and the wisdom I applied—that's what made me grow in those dark places. I had to water my own roots while sitting in darkness. Me. Myself. And I. Let's not get it twisted: Evolution ain't automatic. There are still people in those same dark places—prisons and rehabs— who won't grow, because they're waiting for the darkness to do the work for them. An inmate can sit in that dark place for thirty years, but if they don't take the time to let some light in, their dumb-ass gon' walk out the same way they walked in.

Darkness don't have to hinder growth—it can foster it, but only if you're intentional. Just like seeds are planted deep in the soil, surrounded by darkness before they sprout, our darkest moments can serve as fertile ground for growth. A rose blooms and releases its fragrance after being rooted in darkness. A baby forms in the safety of a dark womb before taking its first breath. Even our bodies grow stronger in the stillness of the dark as we sleep. The darkest places in your life are your training grounds. In the right perspective, darkness isn't an enemy—it's an opportunity for evolution. But the key lies in what we do during that time. Darkness is where you build roots so you can rise strong when the time comes. Are you challenging yourself during dark times? More importantly, are you being patient with yourself during the growth process? Just as it takes a flower months to bloom, a baby months to form, and a body years to grow, your journey through darkness will also take time. Your darkness didn't form in one night, so don't expect to grow into the light in one day. Burial and planting look the same—but what you do next proves which one it is. One conceals, one reveals. Darkness ain't a deathbed—it's a delivery room.

Growth Affirmation: I will **GROW** out of the mindset
that my worst season defines me—burial and planting
look the same, but I know I'm being planted.

Take this day to **THINK** about why you keep ignoring the "funny feeling" that warns you about certain people. That's why yo ass keep getting burned—because you dismiss your Spidey senses when they're tingling. Your gut is like your personal security alarm, built to detect bad intentions before they break into your life and rob you of your peace. But instead of listening, you let a fake smile or friendly face talk you out of what you already know deep down. You want to believe the best in people so badly that you'll override your instincts to keep the peace or avoid the truth. Ignoring your gut is like ignoring your car's check engine light—you're pretending there isn't a problem because it's still operable, then wonder why later you're having a breakdown. Because you ignored the warning sign. When someone's face says "friend" but their actions scream "fraud," trust the actions. That funny feeling isn't a false alarm; it's a flashing neon sign telling you to exit before you get burned. Two-faced friends smile on one side and wink on the other—the same mouth that praises you in person poisons you in private.

One night I picked up a dude I called my brother—he was on bad times, but, hell, he was like family. Still, something in my gut told me to leave him where he stood, since I knew how he treated others. I brushed it off, thinking I was trippin'. He wouldn't violate me. Later, as I laid up in the back with my girl, he cranked the TV loud in the living room. My gut was screaming, but I silenced it. When I finally walked back in, he was gone—along with half a kilo and ten grand. The wild part? He didn't even take it all. Left some behind, like he was doing me a favor. How considerate, right? One day, I was watching *Spider-Man,* and when I heard the line, "My Spidey senses are tingling," it reminded me of my situation. That tingle was my gut telling me, *Don't fucken take him to my home.* I had no one to blame but myself. He wasn't hiding who he was—I just refused to see it.

Anytime someone gives you that funny feeling, don't be impulsive—but don't brush it off either—inspect it. Check out why the feeling exists. Don't just trust your gut blindly; trace it back to why it's going off. Trusting your instinct without checking it is like drinking milk without checking the date— you might swallow something bad. That funny feeling is there for a reason— take a second to investigate the truth before it steers you wrong. That funny feeling is your built-in X-ray. What your eyes can't see, your instinct scans and exposes. Pay attention to how people talk when they think you're not paying attention. Listen to what they don't say. Watch how they handle others' vulnerability—do they carry it, or do they weaponize it? If their mouth says "loyal" but their moves scream "liability," believe the moves. Your gut don't speak in words, but it screams in signals. Ignoring it won't erase the fallout—it just delays the explosion. You get played because you silence the one voice that never lies: your gut. That gut feeling ain't paranoia—it's protection. Here's some game. You know why it's called a funny feeling? 'Cause by the time you hear the laughter, the joke's already on you.

Growth Affirmation: I will **GROW** out of the mindset of trusting fake smiles and ignoring my gut. My *instincts* will stop me from letting what *stinks in*. By inspecting my funny feelings, I lessen the chances of others making fun of me.

Take this day to **THINK** about why you hoard what you know like it's a treasure meant only for you. You done bought into that silly-ass cliché: "The game is to be sold, not told." You so stingy with information it's pathetic. What are you so afraid of? That someone might take what you've shared and outshine you? Someone compliments your outfit and asks where you got it— you lie and say you went shopping out of town, when you know damn well you went shopping off of Temu. You're just afraid they might rock it better than you. Has it escaped you that you are where you are because someone shared information with you? Or do your delusional-ass claim to be self-made? Newsflash: You're not. Understand that your flame doesn't dim when you light someone else's fire. Helping someone else shine doesn't make you any less bright—it makes the world brighter. Yet we live in a society where people refuse to share even the simplest information, afraid it will cost them their edge. It's the same selfish mindset that keeps people from sharing their resources, advice, or even the source of their success. But withholding knowledge doesn't elevate you; it isolates you. You don't decrease by increasing others. In fact, when you share what you know, you multiply your influence, creating a ripple effect that touches lives far beyond your own. You're not losing your light when you share information—you're lighting the path.

When I sold drugs, I had the cheapest connect in town, but I wasn't about to share that information with anyone else. I didn't want to lose my advantage or let anyone else get ahead. Fast-forward years later, when I was on a completely different path, trying to write my book. I reached out to someone I knew for guidance—someone who had already written a book. But they wouldn't share a single piece of advice with me. I got a taste of my own medicine, and it was bitter. That rejection made me realize how destructive it is to hoard knowledge out of fear. Now I see things differently. I'm grateful someone shared their knowledge with me about addiction, because if they hadn't, who knows where I'd be right now? That act of generosity reminded me of my late cousin's vigil, where I watched people light each other's candles from ones already burning—without those flames going out. Oftentimes, what you share can save someone's life, just as I now share information with other addicts that was given to me. The knowledge passed down by others is now what I use to pull others up.

Giving someone the key to unlock their potential doesn't lock you out of your own success—it just opens more doors for others to walk through. Sharing knowledge is like giving out your Wi-Fi password—you're not losing signal, you're expanding the network. As you saw from my cousin's vigil, a candle doesn't dim by lighting another—it amplifies the glow. Just like a lighter, it can fire up a hundred cigarettes and still keep its spark. So why hoard the light like it's going to run out? Every time you drop game, give guidance, or point someone to a better path, you multiply your impact. You live on. Ain't that the point of it all—to be remembered for something you left behind? You so scared somebody gon' outdo yo ass. But so what if they did? There's enough money, materials, men, and women to go around. Don't fear being overshadowed. You don't lose value by helping others level up—you prove yours. The world don't need another gatekeeper holding information hostage. It needs more fire starters willing to strike a spark. If your flame's real, it won't flicker when others shine—it'll continue to spark wildfires that no amount of firefighters can put out. The more you give light, the longer your legacy shines.

Growth Affirmation: I will **GROW** out of the mindset that sharing my wisdom diminishes my success. My value doesn't diminish by helping others succeed.

Take this day to **THINK** about why you keep letting folks who ain't done shit in their own lives tell you how far you can go in yours. You listen to sideline spectators like they've suited up and played the game. Why the hell do you let the uninspired infect your inspiration? Why let the unaccomplished write the script for your ambition? Their opinions don't come from wisdom—they come from fear and failure. The loudest mouths usually echo from the emptiest résumés. Most critics never built a damn thing—they just professional haters good at smashing other people's hope. Not every opinion deserves oxygen, and not every voice deserves volume in your head—don't matter if it's yo momma, daddy, or anybody else. You don't need their fucken validation to prove you valuable. Treat useless input like pop-ups on your screen—hit X and keep it moving. You weren't made to shrink into somebody else's fear or half-baked dream. The incredible ain't reached by people who hand the mic to clowns who never moved a needle. Let them doubt while you deliver. The unqualified don't get to disqualify the destined—unless yo ass dumb enough to give them the power.

Judges, probation officers, correctional officers, and even counselors told me I wouldn't amount to anything. One probation officer I wasn't even fond of looked me dead in the face and said, "People like you either die in the streets or rot in a cell—you ain't built for anything better." That wasn't advice. That was a verbal obituary. They saw how my life was unfolding and wrote me off like I was just another statistic. You could say that he was speaking from a place of how I was living. I was reckless. For a long while, I believed them. I let their words dig roots into my identity. I started living like failure was my only option. But eventually I realized their words were reflections of their assumptions, not predictions of my future. That's like someone calling a diamond fake just because they've never held anything real. Just because people can't see your worth doesn't mean it isn't there. Some people don't care to look beneath the surface. They believe that what you see is what you get. Nothing more. I had to realize I'm the one who defines what happens next. They didn't create me, they can't limit me—and their labels can't stop what God already destined. And if that same officer saw me now, he'd probably need supervision just to process it.

Stop letting nobodies narrate your story. Just 'cause they got a mouth don't mean they got a message. Most folks talk loud 'cause silence would expose their sorry lack of progress. Taking advice from somebody with no credentials is like letting an eighth-grade dropout grade your college exam. Their feedback ain't facts—it's ignorance dressed up as guidance. Don't let their delusion become your direction. If their opinion ain't feeding you, funding you, or freeing you—fuck 'em. Their opinion expired the second they stopped growing. Why are you letting somebody who never left the porch tell you how to fly? That don't make no damn sense. Let the words spilling out their mouth bounce off your chest. If their words don't build, they don't belong. Never confuse volume with value. You don't owe validation to the unverified. Quit giving your ear to folks and breaking your neck for people who ain't got a leg to stand on or the backbone to handle their own business. Their opinions ain't coming from a higher place—they're just yelling from the basement. Here's what you better keep in mind about life's commentators: Anybody can call somebody a nobody—but not everybody knows what the fuck they're talking about.

Growth Affirmation: I will **GROW** out of the
mindset of needing approval. I don't take limits
from people who've never left the ground.

Take this day to **THINK** about how much of your life has been wasted in the prison of overthinking. You dress it up as caution, label it preparation, call it being responsible—but it's not. It's fear in a little red dress. Paranoia with a pretty name. Your ass ain't being careful—you're being careless. You're not planning; you're panicking in advance. You ain't calculating moves— you're caught rehearsing failure like it's your full-time job. You build disasters out of dust, drown in fake storms, then wonder why nothing in your life moves. Overthinking is hearing the weather report say there's a 40% chance of rain—so you throw on rainboots, put on a poncho, grab an umbrella, but still decide to cancel your plans. Thinking it over is grabbing one umbrella and getting the hell on wit your day. The only difference between the two is action. You keep asking what could go wrong instead of what could go right.

At the time I was on probation, I had to call in every day to see if my color came up for a drug test. The day it did, I froze. I knew I was dirty. Instead of thinking clearly, I folded. My mind started spinning like a fan blade—probation violation, prison time, disappointment. I imagined every door closing before I even knocked. That fear? It took the wheel. I didn't face the problem. I ran from it. Months passed with me ducking, dodging, paranoid, sweating bullets every time a police officer looked my way. I made the mess worse than it had to be. When they finally caught me, the outcome was exactly what I'd been running from—plus interest. 'Cause I was caught with pills in my pocket. Stackin' a new case on top of my old charge. When my PO came to see me in the jail, she hit me with this: "You should've come to me. I could've helped you. My son also battles with addiction." That line stung harder than the sentence. All my running? Useless. I didn't outsmart the system—I just outplayed myself. Dragged myself through the very hell I was trying to dodge, all because I overthought my situation. In moments of crisis, it's fine to think the matter through—but don't think it to death.

There's a difference between thinking something over and overthinking it—and the cost of confusing the two is your freedom. You think things over when you finally walk away from an abusive relationship because you've started valuing your peace more than the pain; you overthink it when you're sitting in that same hell, spiraling—wondering how you'll raise the kids alone, if anybody will ever want you again, if you're overreacting, or if maybe it's your fault. Thinking it over says, "I've got to protect the mental health of my children and myself." Overthinking it whispers, "But what if the children hate me for breaking up the family?" One prepares. One paralyzes. And right now, your fear got a louder voice than your freedom. Obsessing over what might break is killing your ability to see what you still have the power to build. This ain't about clarity—it's about courage. Don't sit in that mess waiting for the right moment. You ain't waiting on a sign; you're dodging responsibility. So ask the real question: "Am I solving the problem—or just nursing my fear?" Overthinking don't protect you—it poisons progress. You ain't failing because you tried and it didn't work; you're failing because you're scared as hell to make a move. Growth don't knock—it breaks in. It shows up when you move scared but move anyway. You prepping for a hurricane, but it might just drizzle. Walk into the storm. Screw clarity. Screw certainty. Start scared. Start shaky. Just start—damn it! What the hell you waitin' on?

Growth Affirmation: I will **GROW** out of the mindset that overthinking protects me. I refuse to keep calling fear "logic" just because I'm too scared to move. From now on, I'll plan with purpose, not panic with paranoia.

Take this day to **THINK** about what your child is really asking for when they're bad as hell. You're so caught up scrolling through TikTok while your kid's childhood is ticking away. You're chasing validation from people who don't even know your middle name, while the person who bears your last name is begging for your attention. You'll keep waggin' your tail at folks who dog you, yet you won't fetch the needs of your children right in front of you. Their tantrums? That's not rebellion—it's a smoke signal. Their attitude? That's not disrespect—it's a battle cry. They don't want your money, your status, or your excuses—they want your presence. You claim you'd die for your kids, but can't even fucken live for them? They don't act out for nothing. They act out because the one they look up to is too busy looking down at a screen. Kids who feel ignored, unloved, or overlooked will find something or someone to fill the empty void. And trust me, what fills it might not feed them right. If you don't nourish their spirit with love, the world will feed them lies with a silver spoon. Every moment you miss becomes a memory they will never have.

My mother did her best—worked hard, provided food, kept us clothed. Although she should be honored for it, love ain't measured in bills paid. And while she played every role she could, the one role I needed—father—I never got. School events like "Donuts with Dad" made me feel invisible, like I was missing a part of me that everyone else had. That empty chair haunted me. The other kids grinned over glazed donuts with their dads; I just gazed over at the wall with a hole in my heart because I didn't have one. They feasted on donuts with filling, while I had a hunger no Krispy Kreme could fill. I craved connection so bad I found it in the streets, thinking the hood had love. But the hood only hugged me with handcuffs and pumped me with pills. What I needed was a role model who would model a role bold enough to call me out, keep me in check, and stay locked in before I got locked up. That's why

I say now, if you don't take authority in your child's life, the authorities will. Don't wait for your child to be sitting in a courtroom before you realize you should've been sitting with them in the living room.

Your child doesn't need a superhero—they need a parent who's present, not just posting. You stay on Facebook posting plates of what you eatin'— but you won't post up at a table and eat with your child. They eatin' in one room, you eatin' in another. No connection whatsoever. You worried about your followers while your kids waitin' on you to lead them. Put that damn phone down! Get yo ass off TikTok, off Facebook, and off Instagram. Get off social media and get social with your child—before their ass ends up in the media, for all the wrong reasons. You say you'd die for your children but won't even disconnect from social media for a fucken second to connect with them. You're gossiping, chasing drama, scrolling—while your child is sitting in silence, starving for your time. Are you really gon' let video games, rap lyrics, and social media raise your child? Get real! Your kids need you. They don't need another pair of Air Jordans—they need you to breathe air into them. They don't need more video games—they need you making more videos *with* them and playing more games *with* them that turn into timeless memories. They don't need more presents—they need your presence. Every "I'm proud of you," every real talk moment, every time you show up and actually see them—it builds armor against what's coming for them out there. You either pour into them now or watch them get filled up by poison later. Don't let your absence create a void so big the devil steps in to fill it.

Growth Affirmation: I will **GROW** out of the mindset of emotional neglect. My child needs presence, not perfection. I'm done letting the world parent in my place.

Take this day to **THINK** about the people you labeled "done" just 'cause your pride wouldn't let you make a U-turn. Maybe your friend smashed your girl or man. Maybe they borrowed money and never paid it back. Maybe they ran their mouth and exposed a secret you didn't want out. Ugly? Yeah. Unforgivable? Not always. Just 'cause the bond got wrecked don't mean it's totaled. They might've made a mess, but that don't mean you gotta let it stay messy. Too many of y'all walk away from people you should've walked back to, hiding behind pride when honest conversation could've cleared the whole road. Some shit just ain't that damn heavy to lose a relationship over. You can still deal with 'em—just don't fool with 'em in that space no more. That's all. Relationships are like road trips: Wrong turns happen—but only a fool quits the whole journey over one detour. We all flawed, we all gon' fuck up. Not every relationship gotta end in misery—some could last with mercy. Don't trip over crumbs and call it a feast. Almost everything is small shit once you step back and see it for what it really is. Don't let one wrong turn cancel the ending of a ride that still got miles left in it. If the love was real, a detour won't kill it—but your refusal to turn back will.

Back when I was deep in addiction, I lied to my mother to cover my tracks— and dragged my boy into it. I told him to back me up when she came asking questions. He didn't. He told her the truth. And I snapped. Called him a fake. Said he betrayed me. But what I was really mad at was myself—for getting caught, for lying, and for expecting him to lie for me too. That wasn't friend-ship—that was manipulation. I let that lie sit between us for years, like a stain I refused to clean. It wasn't until much later—after I got my mind right—that I reached out and gave him the respect he earned. Told him I was wrong. That he did what I didn't have the courage to do—tell my mom the truth. We didn't pick up where we left off, but the fact that I owned it was enough to close the gap. The apology didn't rewind the clock, but it realigned the compass.

Not every broken bond can be repaired—but making the effort still builds you. Don't confuse silence with healing. That gap between you and someone else could be filled with one conversation, one moment of realness, one humble turn of the wheel. Some wrecks don't need tow trucks—they need two people willing to jump-start them. Willing to pull it out of a ditch and push it forward. If it still hurts, it still matters. If a relationship meant something before it broke, it still might mean something now—but only if you're man or woman enough to face what broke it. Own your part, cut the pride, and say what needs to be said. Whether or not the relationship gets restored, you walk away knowing you didn't leave it stranded without trying to get out the impound. Real ones don't abandon the route when it gets shaky—they fix the alignment and steer it straight. Don't let your ego stop you from doing a U-turn or turning a detour into a dead end. Wrecks in relationships happen, but if nobody died, maybe it can still be salvaged. Some of the realest love stories begin after the wreck—when both drivers come back with their hands on their wheels, not on their horns.

Growth Affirmation: I will **GROW** out of the mindset
of prideful distance. If the bond mattered, I'm willing
to turn back before I let ego drive it off a cliff.

Take this day to **THINK** about why you've let life convince you that you ain't worth a damn. You think because you've been laid out in a dope house with a needle in your arm… because you can count the people you've slept with on all your fingers and toes… because you've been in and out of prison more times than you've been in a church… that your value is diminished? Hell no. You're not like a driver's license. No matter how many violations you've had in life, your value doesn't get revoked. It may get suspended for the dumb shit you did, but it's never taken from you. Wake up. Your past don't erase your purpose—it exposes it. You out here moving like trash when you're treasure that's just been through hell. Let me ask you this: If you found a $20 bill crumpled, filthy, stomped on, maybe even stuck to a bar floor, would you throw it away? Or would you still snatch it up knowing damn well it's still worth twenty? Exactly. Life might've dragged you, but it didn't destroy you. Stop walking like your worth got revoked and start moving like the full-value bill. You ain't out of circulation—you just let the lies you believe cut off your circulation.

I was that bill—folded, filthy, and left in the gutter. Addiction had me face down in the streets, nodding at red lights, my body sitting up while my soul was six feet under. Twice I woke up behind the wheel, cops banging on my window, pills in my system, shame in my chest. I thought I was done. But I wasn't done—I was dormant. Life had hit me, but it hadn't cashed me in. I stopped letting my mistakes write the story and started turning my hell into a handbook. Those same hands that held pills now hold a pen. Those same hands that shook dice now shake the hands of the broken—handing out truth like prescriptions. I took what tried to finish me and flipped it into what fuels me. Those dark moments didn't cancel my value—they made the comeback worth reading. Wouldn't you agree? I ain't a has-been—I'm proof that broken ain't the same as beaten.

Let's be clear—what you been through don't decrease your value. It defines your depth. So what they counted you out; still count on yourself. Fuck them. That $20 bill don't need to be clean to count, and neither do you. You don't need to be polished to have power. Stop acting like somebody gotta approve your worth before you walk in it. Nobody gives a damn what a $20 has gone through—they just use it. Happy as hell they found it. That's what you need to do: Get up and get useful. You already paid the price with pain—now cash out with purpose. All those hits you took? That's evidence you survived what most couldn't. You're not worthless, you're weathered. You're not tattered, you're tested. You don't lose value because of where you've been—you just forgot how to spend yourself right. Spend your days making purpose outta pain— not playing victim for pity. Spend your days being proof that the broken can still break cycles. Spend your days reminding people that survival ain't luck— it's grit wearing scars. You still have value. If a piece of paper with numbers on it don't lose value after being trampled, then what makes you think you do? Pick yourself up. Wipe off the dirt. And remind this world exactly how much you're worth. And like that $20, they'll be overjoyed they found you.

Growth Affirmation: I will **GROW** out of the mindset of unworthiness. I've been crumpled, not canceled—and my value don't vanish just because I've been through hell.

Take this day to **THINK** about why you keep watering weeds in your life. You've got people who applaud when you down but won't clap when you win, and yet you keep them around. Why? Holding on to people who don't cheer for you is like watering plastic plants—you waste your energy on something that will never grow. Either they're rooting for your come-up, or they're cheering for your downfall. That silence when you succeed? That "congratulations" with no conviction? That dry-ass, "That's good," with nothing behind it. Those are your signs to uproot the haters. They hate to see you win but love to see you lose. And as long as you stay on their level, you good with 'em. Stop wasting your energy and time on people who aren't invested in your evolution. You're not better than them, but their mindset isn't better for you. Weeds don't cheer for the flowers—they just choke they ass out. Let them be bitter while you bloom. If your audience only claps for your bad performances, they don't deserve a place on your stage.

When I got shot, the same people who claimed they loved me showed up with flowers for my hospital room. They even talked about retaliating for me, like carrying my pain on their back would prove their loyalty. But when I started evolving, putting the streets behind me, those same ones treated me like I was the weed. My growth made them uncomfortable, so instead of celebrating, they whispered. Instead of clapping, they criticized. The same people who cheered when I was losing were silent when I started winning. They weren't loyal to me—they were loyal to the chaos that came with me. They were never with me—they were just with the version of me that made them feel bigger. Leaving the streets wasn't about acting superior; it was about surviving. The truth is, some people are only loyal to your chaos. When the chaos stops, so does their loyalty. But those people aren't tied to your purpose—they're tied to your past. If they only support you when you're down, they don't deserve a front-row seat to your growth.

LeBron James, who's from my state, showed the world what this looks like. The moment he left Cleveland for Miami, fans lit his jersey on fire like he burned their dreams—just for chasing his own, wanting to get with a winning team. But he didn't fold—he flourished. Locked in, leveled up, won two championship rings, and made the world respect his grind. When he returned to Cleveland, those same fans who booed him were back in the front row, wearing fresh #23 jerseys like they never turned their backs. That's how it goes—they love you when you stay in the role they wrote for you, but the moment you flip the script, they treat your growth like betrayal. They want the version of you that stays small so they can feel six feet tall. You are their only hope at keeping the spotlight off their own shortcomings. But your purpose ain't up for debate, and it damn sure don't need their permission. Your life is soil—either pull the weeds up or get pulled down with 'em. If they only clap when you crash, let 'em sit in silence when you soar. And if they can't stand your bloom, bury them in the dirt they came from. Your circle should be fertilizer, not fungus.

Growth Affirmation: I will **GROW** out of the
mindset of keeping fake roots. If they ain't clapping
when I rise, they ain't staying when I bloom.

Take this day to **THINK** about why you're letting the absence of a piece of paper hold you back from getting what you want. Success doesn't demand a diploma hanging on the wall—it requires a declaration—and the refusal to let any wall stop you. This ain't about minimizing a degree—it's about maximizing your decree. Too many people let a piece of paper define their potential, forgetting that grind, grit, and guts outweigh a classroom every single time. A 4.0 don't mean shit if you have 0.0 faith in yourself. That 4.0 is just four goddamn zeros. To prove this point, some of the most powerful names in history didn't follow the college route—they made a decree to win and refused to fold. Henry Ford barely stepped into school, yet he revolutionized the auto industry. Levi Strauss, with almost no formal education, stitched together an empire that still clothes the world today. These two had incredible vision and relentless hustle. Degrees might crack the door open, but decrees blow the whole frame off the hinges—just like those men did. It ain't the letters after your name that matter. It's whether your name still echoes long after you're gone. And their names still do.

When I decided to write a book, the doubters were in full force. They told me I didn't have the credentials, the education, or the expertise to write anything meaningful. One even laughed and said, "You can't take on a project like that being from the projects." But what they didn't realize was that my qualifications didn't come from a classroom—they came from life. People want to hear from someone who's been through the fire, not someone who's only read about it. I've spent decades living what others study in books. When they told me I needed 10,000 hours to be considered an expert, I became a pain expert overnight—since I had 48 years of it. Don't tell me their GPA holds more weight than the scars I graduated with from the school of hard knocks. A 4.0 don't mean nothing if you ain't clocking 100% effort in the real world. If the grind ain't in your DNA, your GPA don't mean shit. They wrote essays on pain—I wrote mine in blood. Ain't a syllabus alive that could teach what I survived.

The system hands out degrees for passing tests—but life hands out pain for failing them. Which one really teaches you more? Your success ain't about what's printed on paper—it's about what's carved into your heart. A framed diploma means nothing next to a mind framed for greatness. It ain't about credentials—it's about potential. It ain't the letters after your name, but the number of hours you grind. The legends didn't wait for permission—they made a proclamation. Stop begging for validation from a system that never planned to see you win. You don't need a diploma to dominate—just discipline, direction, and the audacity to declare you're built for more. You don't need a degree on a wall to shatter ceilings. You don't need to be school tested when you've been battle-tested. Let your grit speak louder than any words on a piece of paper. You don't need book smarts to succeed—just backbone. A degree is a tool. A decree is a weapon. One proves you passed a test. The other proves you survived one. When it comes to success, a diploma or GED is good—but a decree and G-O-D is greater.

Growth Affirmation: I will **GROW** out of the mindset
that I need a diploma to prove my worth—my scars
are the credentials that make up my résumé.

Take this day to **THINK** about why your kitchen's always open to folks who refuse to cook for themselves. Then you have the nerve to scold them for their mess while bankrolling their excuses. You say you want them to change, but you keep being their crutch—then act shocked when they don't learn to walk. You're not helping them heal—you're handcuffing them to their habits. Is it that you don't want to face the fact that they ain't just struggling—they just worthless as hell. Careless. Addicted. Entitled. You know it, but denial makes it easier to sleep at night. You ain't just cosigning their crash—you're paying for the wreck. Keep feeding their excuses and you'll starve their growth. Teach them how to eat, or they'll keep eating off your plate. Now, you can't force someone to fly, but you can stop making the nest so comfortable. And to the one always asking for shit—you should feel sick to your stomach manipulating the only few people who actually give a damn about you. What you're doing is triflin'. That's manipulation made to look like struggle.

I used to be that manipulator. Playing victim while plotting my next request. "It's for rent." "It's for my cellphone." "Just until next week." Lies so smooth they felt like truth. I was out here scamming the same people I'd cry about not supporting me. But I didn't need support—I needed a slap of reality. And I finally got it. When the handouts stopped, I hit the bottom. And guess what? That bottom taught me more than anyone's money ever did. I had to admit what I didn't want to face—I wasn't just broke, I was broken. I wasn't a victim, I was lazy. I wasn't down bad, I was dragging myself there. The handouts didn't save me. The cutoff did. I stopped trying to talk cents out of them and instead allowed them to talk sense into me. That's what made me rebuild. Piece by piece. No more lies, no more guilt trips, and no more beggin' from the only people who gave a fuck about me, to support my habit.

Let's be real—if you keep giving, don't get mad that they ain't growing. Stop complaining about who they are, because you helped them become that.

You ain't helping—you just buying their coffin in installments. This message really needs to sink in with the freeloaders—and the damn fools who keep funding them. If you're the one with your hand always out, face it—nobody owes you shit. A handout might hold you over, but it'll never hold you up. Grow up. You're not a child anymore. You're not entitled to somebody else's labor while you lounge in laziness. Get over being addicted. Get over being dependent. You ain't the only one who had it rough. Stop milking sympathy and then have a cow when you don't get what you want. And if you keep monetizing the moochers: Stop calling it loyalty when it's really liability. You think you're helping, but you're enabling. Instead of giving from the fruits of your labor, teach them how to plant their own fruit garden. Give them a hand up, not a handout. You can't keep playing savior if you're scared to play surgeon. Sometimes you gotta cut people off to keep them alive. And if that truth hurts? Good—it's supposed to. 'Cause as long as you keep giving people your bread, they'll keep begging for crumbs and never learn how to make their own dough.

Growth Affirmation: I will **GROW** out of the mindset of giving out handouts. To help people better themselves, it's better to cut them off than cut them a check.

Take this day to **THINK** about why sometimes you gotta throw it in reverse if you ever plan on moving forward. Stop letting these "forget the past," "let it go" cheerleaders gas you up—some of y'all need to take yo ass back through the wreckage to figure out why you keep fucken up—repeating the same mistakes. Life ain't about running forward blind—it's about knowing exactly where you've been so you don't keep circling the same block like a lost puppy. The fact that you keep doing stupid shit shows that, somewhere along the way, you've lost yourself. Losing yourself is no different than losing your cell phone—you don't find it by moving forward; you find it by retracing your steps. Sometimes the real move forward is to rewind and snatch back the pieces of you that you left in bad seasons and worse decisions—to do what's necessary to improve your quality of life. The road to progress usually starts where you first got lost—don't be too proud to go there. Growth ain't always in the next step—it's in the one you skipped. Before you start making big moves, figure out where you blew it. Taking a step back to reassess doesn't mean you're giving up to bury yourself—it means you're gearing up to better yourself.

For the longest time while in addiction, I refused to look back. I was ashamed, confused, and scared of what I might find. But one day, while watching TV and being lost in the plot, it hit me—life is like rewinding a TV show: You go back to the scene you missed so you can finally understand what's happening and enjoy the rest of the story. If you don't, you'll move forward clueless about what's going on because you missed the plot. That realization pushed me to seek help, and, with the guidance of a counselor, I started walking back through my past. It wasn't one big event that led me to addiction; it was a series of small, overlooked moments, unresolved emotions, and bad habits that built up over time. By looking backward, I was able to move forward. I began to understand how I used pills to numb my pain and allowed small choices to snowball into life-altering consequences. Healing starts where the hurt happened—not where you pretend it didn't. The reverse journey was painful, but it gave me clarity.

If you feel lost, don't just keep walking—go back to where you think you dropped the map. The answers you need often lie in the moments you're avoiding. Reflecting on your missteps doesn't mean you're weak—it means you're finally willing to evolve. If you keep finding yourself in painful relationships, trace back to what love looked like growing up. If you can't take constructive criticism without blowing up, trace back to why correction feels like condemnation. If you keep sabotaging opportunities, ask yourself who convinced you you weren't worthy in the first place. Life is overwhelming when you stray off course, but backtracking can provide the clarity and relief you need to start fresh. Taking a step back to reassess doesn't mean you've failed; it means you're finally taking control and finding out why the hell you act the way you do. Much like finding your lost cell phone after retracing your steps, the happiness and relief you feel when you find your way again is unmatched. Backtracking ain't losing—it's locating where you went wrong. Revisiting your past is how you reclaim your power. 'Cause if you refuse to circle back in life, your life will keep going in circles.

Growth Affirmation: I will **GROW** out of the mindset that moving forward means forgetting— sometimes healing begins where I last got hurt.

Take this day to **THINK** about the difference between a fingerprint, indicating you touched something, and making an imprint, indicating you touched someone. Be honest. Are you living in a way that if you vanished tomorrow, your presence would be missed—or would life keep moving like you never existed? A fingerprint fades, but an imprint echoes. Having two million followers on social media don't mean shit. Leading two million people in society does. The world don't need more empty touches. It needs proof you left something behind that will touch people. Like an animal marking its territory, we're all wired to leave behind something that says, "I was here—and it mattered." But tagging your name on a wall isn't a legacy. Being remembered because of what you built, healed, taught, or gave—that's what legacy looks like. That's what echoing through time sounds like. Everything else? It fades like fingerprints on glass.

Growing up, I'd scrawl, "Dion was here," on desks, bus seats, and bathroom stalls like it proved I was somebody. In jail, I saw men carve their names into concrete walls, like that was the highlight of their existence. At the time, it felt like legacy. Looking back, it was just desperation—proof we were trying to matter but didn't know how. My turning point came when someone hit me raw: "If you died tomorrow, who would even feel it?" That shook me. I realized I'd left a trail of fingerprints—at crime scenes and on pill bottles— but no imprint that made anything better for anybody. An evolution mindset kicked in. I started planting seeds instead of stamping surfaces. Now I speak in youth centers, share my story in prisons, and use every scar I carry to make sure someone else avoids adding one of their own. I don't care about being remembered—I care about being felt. Without making an imprint, you're just the Invisible Man—you walked through life with no one noticing you were ever here.

Why only be remembered by family and forgotten by strangers? Just like an animal marks its territory, leaving no doubt it was there, make sure your mark on this world is unmistakable—because if you don't, how will anyone know that you ever roamed this earth? You can tag your name on every bus or wall, but if nobody's life was changed because you lived, you were just here—you weren't impactful. Your life didn't mean shit. Imprints change culture. Fingerprints just collect dust. Don't just pass time—pass something on. Whether it's wisdom passed to your kids, a business you birthed, or a mindset you helped reshape, leave proof that you didn't just breathe air—you moved it. Legacy ain't about credit. It's about consequence. It's about what breaks or builds because of your presence. The question ain't, "Did you touch the world?"—the question is, "Did the world feel it?" Make your mark. Not just a memory—but a movement. 'Cause if all you leave behind is a trace of what you've done and not impact, then you were never really here to begin with.

Growth Affirmation: I will **GROW** out of the mindset of just leaving traces. I'm not here to be noticed—I'm here to be felt, and I'm leaving imprints, not just fingerprints.

Take this day to **THINK** about how the legends you admire didn't skip steps—they took hits. They weren't born with fans, they built them with blood, setbacks, and years of being overlooked. You think greatness just falls out the sky? Fame ain't handed out—it's earned in empty gyms, late-night studio sessions, and silent seasons where nobody claps. You want the spotlight? Then respect the shadow work. Diamonds don't shine without pressure. Glory don't show up without grit. The Hall of Fame ain't a popularity contest—it's a survival list for those who outlasted doubt, defeat, and delay. Everybody wants the highlight reel—nobody wants the hidden hustle. But it's the struggle behind the scenes and the journey that earns your place in the frame. Ain't no fast track to fame. You can't cheat the grind by taking steroids, starving yourself, or faking success on social media. Greatness ain't a rush; it's a grind. It's like walking across that graduation stage after 12 long years—slow, painful, but every step says, "I didn't drop out." If it don't take time, it won't carry weight.

In the streets, I had my own twisted version of fame—infamy. It took years of bad decisions, dirty money, and reckless pride to build a name that rang in the wrong places. All that work I put in didn't get me inducted into the Hall of Fame—it got me inducted in the Hall of Shame—prison. I didn't earn applause—I earned time. My prize wasn't a gold jacket; it was a yellow jumpsuit. Walking those prison tiers, I realized I'd become known for chaos, not character. And I hated it. That's when I thought of Jackie Robinson— my favorite player of all time. He ain't make history off hype. He earned it by swallowing hate, grinding harder than anyone, and pushing through pain most can't comprehend. His name didn't rise because it was given—it rose because he never caved. And that's when I stopped giving a damn about who won in the ring—I cared more about the shit he had to box outside it. The fights with poverty, racism, addiction, doubt, and demons hit harder than any opponent. The fights outside the ring are the ones that prove if you're really a champ.

Anything that's worth something ain't easy. The Hall of Fame ain't built on flash—it's built on finishers. Everyone sees the statue—nobody sees the struggle. They don't tell you about the nights they wanted to quit, the times they were broke, the sacrifices no camera caught, or the times they played hurt. But that's where greatness grows—in the mud, not the mansion. The grind don't guarantee glory, but quitting guarantees you'll never get there. Nobody cares how fast you started—they care that you didn't stop. The real Hall of Fame is full of underdogs who outworked the odds and kept climbing. They didn't chase clout—they were too busy chasing clouds, climbing higher while everybody else stayed stuck showing off at ground level. And while everybody else's highlight reel is playing online, your real highlight will come from staying patient in the dark. Slow ain't weak—it's steady. And the ones who stay steady survive. Whether you're chasing a dream or branding your name, understand this: If you want your name in the rafters, you better be ready to bleed in the basement. The real Hall of Fame don't take applications—but it does take the application of endurance.

Growth Affirmation: I will **GROW** out of the mindset that greatness comes quick—legends ain't born in the spotlight; they're built in silence, scars, and steady steps. The shine at the top comes from the grind at the bottom.

Take this day to **THINK** about it—pain sucks, betrayal cuts, addiction drags you through hell. But at least if you're alive, you still get a swing, a breath, a chance to change the ending. Death don't hand out second rounds. A collapsed lung still means you're breathing. Broken ribs still mean you're alive enough to hurt. But the morgue? That's permanent silence. You've already survived worse—so why treat this problem like it's the one that's gon' finish you? You crawled through hell barefoot—now you scared of smoke? Pain means you're still in the game. Dead means game over. Don't let fatigue talk you into forfeiting your fight. Life don't break people like you—it just exposes who's willing to fight. You already earned your scars. What you do now decides if they become excuses or evidence. Ain't no glory in giving up. The same strength that got you this far didn't disappear—it's just waiting on you to fight like you did before. Life fights dirty. It won't hit you square—it'll catch you slipping, kick you while you're down, and smile as it stands over you. But pain is part of the process.

I remember lying in a hospital bed after an overdose—wired up, weak, barely able to breathe. Nurses hovered over me like I was already gone. I could hear them whispering like death was circling the room, waiting to see if I'd check out. My heart skipped like it couldn't decide if it wanted to keep me here. And I'll be real—in that moment, I didn't even care. I thought, "Hell's gotta be better than this shit. At least I'll get some rest." I had given up on life, but life hadn't given up on me. Somehow, I came back. That wasn't luck— that was proof it was better to feel pain than to feel nothing at all. I learned something: Even in your lowest, breathing beats being boxed up. 'Cause as long as you're alive, you still got a shot. Dead people don't get do-overs.

Life fights dirty, no question—it'll sucker punch the fuck outta you, choke the hell outta you, stomp the shit outta you while you're down, and then dare yo ass to get back up. But as long as you can groan, gasp, or grab the ropes, you ain't done. Every punch life throws is a question: *"You still want this?"*—and your answer better be, *"Hell yes, bring it on."* Some rounds, all you got left is heart—and that's enough. Don't confuse being winded and wounded with being weak, and don't mistake pausing for quitting; a standing eight-count ain't a knockout—it still counts as standing. Every ache is proof you're alive, every scar is evidence you're still in it, and suffering ain't failure—it's just the tax for breathing. And that tax is worth it, because the only ones who don't pay it are already gone. Better to cry, crawl, bleed, and rebuild than to be cold, stiff, and forgotten. So fight back even when your fists are failing and your faith is flickering—wipe the blood, not your name, off the fight card, catch your breath, lock your jaw, and keep jabbing. And when you're bruised, battered, and bleeding, wipe your face with the towel—but don't you dare throw it in, because nothing you'll ever go through alive is worse than not having the chance to go through it at all.

Growth Affirmation: I will **GROW** out of the mindset
that tired equals done—fatigue don't scare me, because
I've already outlived everything that tried to bury me.

Take this day to **THINK** about why you better learn quick the difference between being used, misused, and abused—before you confuse pain with loyalty and betrayal with love. The word "used" gets a bad rap, but being used isn't a bad thing—being valuable enough to be needed is a sign of purpose. The problem is, most people lump all three together. We're quick to say, "Why you letting them use you?"—but the real question should be: "Are they using you, misusing you, or abusing you?" Being used means your strengths are appreciated. Being misused means your strengths are being applied the wrong way. Abused? That's when your worth is being violated, not valued. Being used is a compliment—your cue you're valuable. Being misused is a warning—your cue to have a conversation. Being abused is the door—your cue to get the hell outta there. Learn the difference, or you'll walk away from every situation that could've grown you—and stay trapped in the ones that are destroying you. A tool ain't powerful unless it's in the right hands—and neither are you. If you can't separate the three, you'll either push away people who actually value you or hold on to the ones who secretly don't give a damn. Not everyone who needs you has your best interests in mind—pay attention. Stop adding people to your life who only subtract from you.

After surgery, pain pills had a purpose. First, I started using them—swallowing them for healing. Then I started misusing them—taking more than prescribed. Eventually, I was abusing them—buying them off the streets. I was no longer using pills—they were using me. I wasn't in control—I was under control. What started as relief became a prison. And that's what abuse does—it wraps itself in justification, then suffocates you in silence. Nobody wakes up planning to get abused—not by drugs, not by people. But when you don't check the shift from use to misuse, it happens fast. I had to reclaim my power one painful step at a time. I learned that use is neutral, but misuse is toxic. Abuse is when you hand over your power and forget you can take it back. You weren't built to be broken—you were built to be respected. Demand that.

You can serve others without selling your soul—just don't forget who it belongs to. You ain't supposed to be drained by your purpose—you're supposed to be driven by it. Don't confuse being used with being devalued. A gun in the right hands protects. A gun in the wrong hands destroys. Same tool, different intention. If someone uses you and both of you benefit—it's purpose. If they misuse you and only they gain—it's exploitation, and you better wise up. If they abuse you and leave you broken—it's destruction, and they don't deserve you. Learn the difference before your kind heart becomes a casualty. You're not weak for being helpful—you're just unwise if you don't watch where your help is going. Use this day to evaluate who's leaning on you: the ones who lift you while you lift them, or the ones who drain you while calling it love, loyalty, or friendship. Being used means you're being useful and have something to offer. But if you don't set boundaries, your value gets violated, and your worth gets watered down. Being used is never the problem—being used up is.

Growth Affirmation: I will **GROW** out of the mindset that loyalty means letting people misuse me— my worth deserves alignment, not exploitation.

Take this day to **THINK** about how life don't let nobody fly without some turbulence. Folks act like something's wrong just because the skies ain't smooth every second. You brag on blessings, but the second life faces turbulence, you act like the whole plane's going down. Somebody leaves you, and you think your whole future just walked out the door. You lose a job, and suddenly you're spiraling like your house just burned down. One bad week, and you act like the cockpit's filling up with smoke. The lows ain't punishment—they're proof you're in motion. You ain't having a crash landing—you're just hitting a pocket of rough air. You don't need to grab a parachute—you just need to tighten your seatbelt. You ain't out of oxygen—you just forgot how to breathe under pressure. A plane don't turn around just because the ride got rough. It keeps pushing forward because it has a destination to get to. And the higher that plane climbs, the more bumps it hits—that's the price of going places. You ain't exempt from turbulence just 'cause you think you special. Life don't give a damn about your comfort. It cares about your growth. Growth never comes on a smooth flight. You want altitude? Expect attitude from the skies. That pressure you feel? That's how pilots are made.

There've been incredible highs in my life—watching my mother proudly earn her GED, holding my personal training certification in my hands, publishing my book, birthing beautiful daughters. In those moments, I felt like I was soaring above the clouds. But then came the lows. I was on home-incarceration when my first child was born. Addiction had clipped my wings. I was so desperate for a high I faked an injury to see if I could be prescribed pills. I stole from people I loved just to chase a feeling that faded fast. Prison humiliated me. Being stripped naked and forced to spread my cheeks during a cavity search and hearing guards laugh while I stared at the wall, pretending I wasn't breaking inside. Having to shower next to grown men with no stalls. That was my turbulence. And for a long time, I didn't know if I'd ever get back up. But like a plane battling storms, I had to keep flying—had to refuel, reroute, and rise again by journaling my thoughts, leaning on trusted friends, and turning to counseling to stay grounded.

Pilots earn their wings in cockpits—*you* earn yours in life's chaotic pits. Life's not gon' always give you clear skies. And when it don't, buckle in and keep flying. Every pilot knows that turbulence ain't the end of the journey; it's just part of the process. It too shall pass. You ain't crashing—you're being conditioned. The view from the top looks good, but the lesson lives in the lows. Fight to stay alive. Grab the oxygen mask, catch your breath, and then go finish what tried to finish you—call that lifeline, write out what you're going through, breathe through the fog until the light comes back. You wanna soar? Learn how to stop shaking when the shaking starts. A plane trusts the air to hold it up—why don't you trust the fight in you to hold you together? Turbulence ain't no wrong turn—it means you're flying through what cowards avoid. And the moment it passes, you'll realize you didn't just survive it—your tolerance for altitude just got higher. Turbulence don't mean surrender. It's hours of pain in flight school to earn your wings. Elevation doesn't eliminate ups and downs. Don't believe me? Ask any pilot.

Growth Affirmation: I will **GROW** out of the mindset that turbulence means trouble. I'm not falling—I'm flying through it, and every shake just proves I'm gaining altitude.

Take this day to **THINK** about how you got so many ideas bouncing around your head like a basketball, but instead of taking the shot, you freeze, letting the clock run out. Every time a powerful idea hits, you're quick to dismiss it like it ain't worth your time. But the truth is, it ain't the idea you're scared of. You're scared of failing. Scared of being exposed. Scared that trying and failing might be worse than not trying at all. But here's the thing—you've already failed if you keep letting your own hesitation bury what could've changed your life. You'll replay the idea in your head a hundred times, fantasize about the results, even talk about what it would look like if you did it. But that's all it ever is with you—talk. The idea kept calling—but you the one who kept hittin' decline. You keep choking on "What if?" because deep down, you'd rather die dreaming than risk looking dumb trying. You don't need more clarity. You need more guts. You're not confused. You're just scared. You ain't stuck—you're stalling. That's the truth you won't say out loud.

In 1999, I started a Black historical apparel line that was sitting in my spirit. I saw the pieces, drew the designs, even imagined the success. Although I started, I stopped because I fed myself lies. "I ain't got enough money." "I don't got the right connections." "This will never really work." Eventually, someone else dropped something similar, and it hit. That's the moment I learned: If you keep hesitating on your idea, don't be surprised when it shows up in someone else's hands. Watching them succeed with an idea I let go of wasn't just painful—it was personal. I let self-doubt creep back in and choked on my own inconsistency. That experience branded something into me: Ideas are only as powerful as your willingness to act on them and put in the work to drive them forward. Your idea could've put you in position—but you'd rather warm the bench than check in the game. You don't get points for thinking of ideas. You get them for execution. Ideas ain't loyal—they'll run off to someone willing to spend quality time with them.

You think you're waiting for the right time? That's a lie straight from hell. You've been telling yourself that lie so long that now you believe it. You don't need money, approval, or another sign. What you need is to get rid of the fucken excuses. Your hesitation is the thief. Your comfort zone is the coffin. And your delay is destroying everything that idea was meant to become. If an idea keeps showing up in your mind, that's not a coincidence—it's your shot to take. Stop dribbling the idea in your head and shoot. Don't be the one in the end who says, "I had that idea." The regret of not trying is heavier than the weight of failing. Wait too long on your idea, and you'll fumble it—then watch somebody else scoop it, run it back, and celebrate in the end zone like it was theirs the whole damn time. Throw your Hail Mary before the clock runs out. Ideas don't die—they just get adopted by the bold. Quit warming the bench with brilliance. Your idea's already laced up, sweating, pacing the sideline. Put it in the damn game and let the scoreboard tell the story.

Growth Affirmation: I will **GROW** out of the
mindset that I've got forever to act—if I don't
move, my idea will find someone who will.

Take this day to THINK about why you keep chasing after someone who already slammed the door in your face. You letting your breakup give you a breakdown. You out here starving yourself, losing sleep, skipping meals, throwing up, neglecting your kids, letting your sanity sink—all because someone left you. That ain't love—that's lunacy. You're on your knees begging to be kept by someone who already replaced you in their head. Why? They don't want you no more. You keep rereading old messages and following their social media pages like they still mean something. You keep praying for a redo when all they gave you was a preview of their true colors. And the sad thing is, while you're stuck grieving over someone who dipped without looking back, what's meant for you is circling the block waiting for you to pull yourself out that emotional alleyway so they can find a parking space in your life. That person didn't ghost you—they released you. And the more you beg for what's walking away, the more you delay what's running toward you. People leaving your life are like expired coupons—no matter how long you want to hold on to them, they bring no more value. Stop having a tantrum when people *toss* you aside or *throw* you out—you're the fucken *catch*.

When my high school crush walked away, it felt like my whole world hit pause even though I was only 17 years old. I begged her to stay. I promised I'd change. But none of that mattered—she was gone. I stayed in my room for days, dragging my dignity through the dirt, until my late grandfather—may he rest in peace—snapped me out of it with one brutal line: "Son, you can't keep someone who doesn't want to be kept." That hit harder than any heartbreak. I realized I had lowered myself trying to convince someone to stay who had already clocked out. Every time someone left after that, I started paying attention—not just to the pain, but to the lesson. Every relationship got better because I took the lesson from the last one and applied it to my new one. What to accept and what not to. Letting go ain't losing—it's you finally stopping the bleeding. I've learned that the ones who walk away usually make room for the ones ready to show up.

Look, a breakup is a lot to carry—no denying that. But don't waste your strength trying to find closure from someone who already closed the door. Spend that energy on healing, not on chasing explanations that won't make you whole. You don't owe pain your curiosity—you owe peace your attention. Stop sitting in the ashes asking "why this, why that." Some heartbreaks are divine redirections. A lot of rejection is really ejection—God or the universe removing what was blocking what's next. What feels like a burden right now might be the blessing you didn't see coming. You're trying to make sense of it all, but sometimes searching for answers just leads to more questions—and in that process, you lose yourself. Don't give every ounce of your energy to what broke you and leave nothing to rebuild yourself. Don't let this heartbreak drive you insane. Let it teach you how expensive peace is so you never hand it out cheap again. Have your moment—feel it, grieve it—but don't live there. Stand back up, wipe your face, and remember you weren't created to beg for love that doesn't want you. You've survived worse. You'll rise from this too. Don't forget who the hell you are.

Growth Affirmation: I will **GROW** out of the mindset
that love should cost my dignity—anybody who leaves
me gave me a gift: space to be found by someone real.

Take this day to **THINK** about why you keep rushing into decisions without calculating the cost. You gamble with your health, relationships, and future like they're Russian roulette, only to act shocked when the consequences roll in. You don't protect yourself during sex, then stress about how you're going to cope with raising a child or dealing with AIDS. You cheat on your partner, then you got the nerve to stalk their social media page and threaten them for leaving your cheatin' ass. You sell drugs, then sit in jail worried about who's sleeping with your girl and who's raising your kids. You should've thought about that shit before you did it. Don't cry now. You gamble recklessly, then beg life for a refund like you didn't just place the bet and take the risk. Life doesn't forgive bad math—it punishes it. Skipping the math can multiply the problem. You can add up the risks before you act, or you can subtract opportunities from your life later. The choice is yours, but don't act like you weren't warned when the punishment arrives. Add up the risks, or life will multiply your headaches, divide you from freedom, and subtract you from peace.

When I first started popping pain pills after an injury, I didn't see the problem. My body was healing, the prescription felt harmless. But when the bottle ran dry, I didn't stop. I told myself, "The doctor gave them to me, so it's safe." Then I told myself, "Just one more day." That "one more day" turned into weeks, then months, until the pills weren't medicine anymore—they were my master. I never counted the cost of my choices, and the price was steep: I lost jobs, relationships, and even my freedom. The pills took over, and by the time I tried to do the math, it was too late. Each pill I popped was like ignoring the engine light on a car. The warning signs were there, but I kept driving until the whole thing broke down. Every time I didn't do the math, life wound up taxing me. If I had taken a moment to think, to add up the consequences, I could have avoided the instability that became my life. But I didn't. I was already in the aftermath, and it was too late for me to balance the books.

Whether it's with your finances, your health, or your relationships, the time to calculate the cost is before you act. Reflecting on your choices after the storm hits is like trying to put on a seatbelt after the car has already crashed. Planning ahead isn't just smart—it's survival. Counting the cost beforehand gives you the clarity to avoid unnecessary pain and loss. Before you commit an act, take the time to figure out whether it would lead you to friction or freedom. Don't wait until you're at the bottom to realize you could've stayed on solid ground. Hindsight won't heal what foresight could've prevented. Stop letting pride or impulse drive your actions. Life won't wait for you to figure it out—it'll punish you for every careless misstep. Add up the risks, weigh the consequences, and make decisions that don't leave you drowning in regret. Do the math now, or life will hand you the bill—with interest, compounding pain, and no payment plan. You better get in the habit of counting the cost before you move. Hell, use your fingers if you got to—but you better make sure you count, 'cause life will have yo ass in a situation you'll be boohooing to get out of.

Growth Affirmation: I will **GROW** out of the mindset of acting without thinking. Every time I skip doing the math, life makes me pay the price, plus tax.

Take this day to **THINK** about why strength can't be something you pick up and drop off like laundry. Life don't give a damn how tired you are. It ain't gon' stop throwing jabs just because you feel drained. And yeah, your job's a lot. Your relationships feel like tug-of-war. Your kids are raising hell. But you can't cry about exhaustion while you keep volunteering to carry everybody else's weight. You ain't exhausted—you just confused self-neglect with sacrifice. The real issue ain't your plate being full—it's the fact you keep fixing everybody else's plate first and then there's nothing left over for you. You ain't fatigued—you just ain't fed yourself in a long time. You're not drained—you're just dehydrated from pouring into everybody else who thirsts for your attention. You don't need rest—you need boundaries. Strength ain't about being unbreakable—it's about not using fatigue as a free pass to not chase your dream because you don't know how to say, "No." You running on E, wondering why your life is flat. Weak days don't announce themselves—they sneak in quietly, disguised as, "I'll get back to it," and next thing you know, your purpose is out of gas. And if you don't tighten up, those weak days become your default setting. That's how a mission turns into misery. Then in the end, you die without ever accomplishing shit.

While I was writing this book, there was a stretch when writing consumed me. I could see the impact it'd make—how it could reach people in ways I never could with my past. But I slipped. I let distractions and other people's needs knock me off course. Told myself the lie we all tell—"I'll start back tomorrow." Tomorrow became next week. Next week became next month. And the pen stopped moving. My thoughts got cloudy. My message lost its edge. It reminded me of training in the gym—you grind daily, you build power. But skip too many sessions, and strength don't pause—it leaves. Getting back felt like pushing a boulder uphill. That stretch taught me something real: You don't lose strength all at once—it bleeds out while you're busy watching TV and scrolling. Rest too long, you rot. I wasn't just falling off—I was fading. And weakness don't ask for consent; it moves in when discipline moves out.

Be tired—but don't be lazy. There's a difference. It's hard to exalt yourself when you're always exhausted. You don't get to choose your strong days—every day gotta be one. This ain't seasonal. This ain't mood-based. This is a lifestyle. Strength don't just show up when it's convenient—it shows up when you say, "Come hell or high water, I'm gon' make this shit happen," and drag it out the mud, exhausted or not. You can't skip days of watering a plant and expect it not to die. It needs steady attention and care. As do you, or deal with the consequences. Your discipline needs feeding like your body needs fuel. Being tired is human, but the more you talk about how tired you are, the more obvious it is you ain't built for this shit. If you always tired, maybe you oughta give yourself some rest from excuses—not effort. Begin to feed yourself mentally, emotionally, physically—whatever keeps you from collapsing in your own excuses. Weakness ain't a pit stop—it's a pattern. And patterns build lives. You tired? Cool. Then be tired while still getting it done. Otherwise, shut the hell up and sit down. Because for real, we gettin' tired of hearing how tired you are. We all got bags under our eyes. Difference is, some of us—even wit 'em—keep gettin' to the bag.

Growth Affirmation: I will **GROW** out of the mindset of convenient strength. Tired or not, I show up—because weak days don't work when I'm built for war.

Take this day to **THINK** about the reason your world stays stuck in struggle—it's the garbage coming out of your own mouth. Your mouth is nothing but a trash can, stuffed with busted declarations, broken ambition, and recycled doubt. Every sentence you speak is either laying bricks for your breakthrough or swinging hammers at your own foundation. You tell the world what you ain't, what you can't, and what you'll never be—then live it out like it's prophecy. You don't need enemies when your own words are at war with your future. You always talk about how others be hating on you, but you're your biggest hater. Your negative declarations are just self-hate with better marketing. You bury progress before it even takes its first breath. Your mouth is your murder weapon—and you're the victim. Stop acting like your circumstances are choking you when it's your own tongue doing the strangling. Your life's not stuck—it's obedient to your vocabulary. You wonder why life ain't moving forward? 'Cause your mouth been driving in reverse. You keep saying, "I can't," and then act surprised when you don't. Fire your inner narrator—they're telling a horrible story. Your words ain't harmless—they're habits. And habits create homes you end up stuck in.

Back when I was trying to quit pills, my biggest enemy wasn't withdrawals—it was my own damn voice. I'd say, "This is too much," and it became too much. I'd whisper, "I can't take this," and suddenly I couldn't. My mouth gave my addiction permission to keep running the show. I didn't even need a dealer—my tongue was doing a good job. Same with fitness. I liked training, but out my mouth came, "I won't pass this test," or "People outside my zip code won't relate to me—I'm street, they're structured." But I never hesitated when it came to destroying myself. "I'm 'bout to pop a pill." "I'm gon' rob that fool." "I'm gon' cheat." I spoke certainty into chaos with ease—but hesitated to speak life into purpose. My words dictated my world. That's when it hit me—if I could declare pain with confidence, I could declare power too.

My mouth had always been the architect. Once I started speaking like I was already free, already built for more, my life started following the script I finally had the guts to rewrite. Every word I spoke against the craving was like taking a brick back from the wall I had built around myself.

Your mouth drives your life—every time you speak doubt, you swerve straight into failure. It maps your future. How in the hell can anybody believe in you when you don't even believe in yo damn self? "Will I?" don't move mountains—it builds walls. "I might," don't spark fire—it smothers it. If your mouth don't believe it, your hands will never chase it. You ain't lost—your mouth has just been giving you directions to nowhere. Write a new map. Drop the weak-ass phrases. Drop the maybe mindset. Drop the uncertainty. Talk like someone who plans to win, not someone trying to survive. You've declared destruction long enough—now try declaring dominance. Never again say, "Will I?" Say, "I'm already on the way." Never again ask, "Am I ready?" Say, "I've been built for this." Words are instructions—and your life is just following orders. What you say is what you see—so if your life looks wrecked, check your tongue. You don't need magic—you need mouth discipline. You can't plant poison and expect purpose. You can't curse your progress and expect promotion. Speak like you believe you belong in the winner's circle. Speak like you're not afraid of the fight. Speak like the future you want don't have a fucken choice. Speak with fire. Speak with focus. Speak with intention. Your mouth is steering your life whether you like it or not. Your life won't translate to success if your words are fluent in failure but illiterate in growth.

Growth Affirmation: I will **GROW** out of the mindset that declaring failure protects me from it—my tongue is no longer my enemy, it's my engine.

Take this day to **THINK** about the lifeless routine you keep calling a life. You ain't trapped—you're just scared as hell to shake things up. You wake up, go to a job that don't fulfill you, come home to a man who treats you like shit, feed the kids the same processed meals, scroll the same feeds, watch the same shows, and wonder why nothing changes. That ain't living—that's early retirement from your own purpose. You've confused repetition with stability. And comfort? It's just a soft trap you got used to. You're bored because you refuse to build. Your dreams didn't die—they dried up waiting on you to water 'em. And here's the wild part? Your food got more flavor than your life. That's tragic. Just like seasoning brings bland food to life, bold moves bring excitement to your days. God let you borrow oxygen, and this is how you repay Him—wasting it on reruns and excuses? That's not just sad—it's self-robbery in broad daylight. But let some guy give you some flowers or let some female give you some sex, and suddenly you remember how to live— but only for them. If your routine ain't got flavor, stop calling it a life—call it what it really is: a slow death on a calendar.

There was a time I was pilled out, slumped on my mama's couch day after day—high, hollow, and hiding from life. That couch knew my body better than I knew my own purpose. I'd lay there in a haze, binge-watching the same shows on repeat, eating ramen noodles like they were gourmet meals—same flavor, same shame, every day. Meanwhile, my mom in her 70s, got up every morning and went to work. I watched her lace up her shoes while I lay there doing nothing. Keeping it real, I was a sorry excuse for a man. That was a shame I couldn't drown in pills. I had no job, no direction, just an addiction and a cushion that coddled it. And somewhere between the numbness and the neglect. That couch was my coffin with Wi-Fi. And the only thing deader than my ambition was my will to change—until that one morning I couldn't ignore the truth: I wasn't tired, I was a waste. And when I finally chose to move, life didn't just get better—it got explosive. I stopped playing small and started living like I had somewhere to go.

Sorry to be blunt, but if you're not ready to live, then move—get the hell out the way, as Ludacris would say. Go sit down somewhere. Let's call it what it is: You ain't living—you loitering. Just posted in life's hallway, doing nothing but blocking real movement. People walk past you all day long saying, "Excuse me," because yo ass in the way. Listen here, if you ain't ready to live with urgency, then step aside for the ones who are. Living don't mean breathing—it means breaking barriers, chasing purpose, and doing more than just waiting for the weekend to party and bullshit. You weren't given life to coast through it—you were meant to conquer it by putting the pedal to the metal. Find you a hobby, learn you a trade, go back to school—hell, buy some coloring books if you have to—just do something that drags you past mere existence. Stop wasting borrowed oxygen and start giving meaning to the breaths you take. Stop existing, and start living with intention. Existing is for passengers; living is for drivers—grab the wheel and take control. Stop calling TV marathons self-care when it's really self-abandonment. You weren't built to exist—you were built to evolve. You're not a victim of circumstance; you're a victim of complacency. Life ain't a dress rehearsal, so quit actin' like you got forever to get the damn show on the road. You don't. Your time's running like a parking meter, and one day you will expire. Choosing to stay parked in the same spot is a serious violation. Life ain't gon' beg you to move—but sooner or later, it'll stop giving you chances. And when it does, don't go looking for a refund. When God asks what you've done with your time, don't stand there looking stupid, checking your pockets like you lost the receipt—knowing damn well you never had it, 'cause you ain't never done shit.

Growth Affirmation: I will **GROW** out of the mindset that routine equals purpose—if my days don't shake my soul, I'm doing something wrong. *Existing in life is resisting to live.*

Take this day to **THINK** about how much barking you've been doing without ever breaking skin. "I'm about to lose weight." "I'm about to leave his no-good ass." "I'm about to stop getting high." You ain't had enough of sounding like a fucken broken record? 'Cause everybody around you is sick of hearing that shit. All that "about to" talk is just noise in a world that only respects action. You talk tough, but your life ain't leveled up. You say you're ready, but your habits say you're cool in your comfort. In a world full of wolves, nobody fears the one running their mouth—they fear the one that's silent, focused, and strikes without a heads-up. Barking sounds busy—but it don't change a damn thing. The more you run your mouth, the further your goal walks away. Barking makes you sound serious, but biting proves you are. Stop thinking people are against you. People ain't doubting you because they don't believe in you. They're doubting you because you do too much damn lip service, but never service your words. That ain't ambition—it's avoidance. You ain't being overlooked—folks just tired of over-listening.

Locked up in Jersey, I learned quick: Prison don't respect barkers. That place was a pit, and it tested whether you had bark or bite. One time, some dudes tried pressing me for my shit—loud, reckless, trying to see if I'd fold under pressure. They assumed I was an easy target since I was from Ohio— a state they thought was country. I can still hear one of them ask, "What's the verdict?" They thought because I was quiet, they had somebody sweet— until I soured their plans by standing my ground and fighting back. I'm not sayin' I was the toughest, but I damn sho' wasn't gon' let 'em punk me. If I had, they would've kept doing it. Eventually, they left. Real ones don't bark— they bite through the silence. That day taught me something loudmouths never understand: Talk don't protect you. Action does. Anybody can bark in peace, but pressure exposes what's real. Your bark might echo, but it's your bite that leaves the scar. And scars? They're proof that you fought for what mattered. Life ain't impressed by the noise you make—it's watching the dent you leave. The bite mark.

Having that dog in you ain't about screaming—it's about sinking your teeth in and locking your jaws until what you're after surrenders. Like a lion in the wild—it don't roar to survive, it hunts. You say you wanna lose weight? Stop chasing a double cheeseburger with diet Coke like the drink's about to baptize your arteries. You wanna leave that toxic relationship? Pack your shit and dip. You done with drinking? Flush that bottle down the toilet and fight through the withdrawals like your life's on the line—because it is. Biting means bleeding. Biting means risking. Biting means doing the stuff nobody claps for—until the results slap 'em in the face. Keep barking, and you'll stay on the porch. Keep barking, and people will keep laughing at you behind your back. As they should. You invited that. Yo ass needs to be made fun of. They ain't laughing 'cause they hate you—they laughing 'cause you still ain't done shit. You the one running your mouth about what you "about to" do—but never actually do it. You know why? Because you allergic to accountability. When you bite down and handle business, you get the last laugh. Get off the porch. The porch ain't meant for pit bulls. Bark less. Bite more. Because talk don't earn trophies—bite marks do. Barking brings about laughter; bite marks bring about legacy.

Growth Affirmation: I will **GROW** out of the mindset that I need applause to act—my bite will wake the hell up everybody who slept on me.

Take this day to **THINK** about why your life looks like leftovers—empty, cold, and lacking everything you swore you were meant for. You keep talking about what you deserve, but where's your dedication? You deprive yourself of things in this world when you never dedicate yourself to your words. You have not because you do not. You cannot because you will not. You're not being excluded—you're being exposed. Every missed opportunity, every delayed goal, every wish that never turned into work is the result of your lack of determination. You say you want more, but your actions look like less. You'll dedicate yourself to losing, but won't go all in on winning. You want a breakthrough, but you still operate like somebody who's just browsing—window shopping. You can't starve for greatness and snack on distractions. You can't demand success while offering up inconsistency. You say you're tired of struggling, but you're still married to half-ass effort. You don't get to beg for blessings when you treat effort like it's optional. Life ain't puttin' nuttin' on your plate, 'cause you keep feeding it crumbs. You're not underfed—you're under-focused. Dreams don't respond to wishful thinking—they respond to work. You can't keep screaming you deserve more when you won't deliver more.

I used to chase pills like they were purpose—broke, sweating, throwing up, dodging cops—and still found a way to feed the habit. That kind of dedication was real, I just gave it to destruction. So when I set out to earn my personal training certification and told myself I was locked in—that was a damn lie. I studied when it felt convenient, skipped when life got loud, had one foot in and both eyes wandering. I'd already failed the test once. My momentum? Gone. Progress? Stalled. Everything shifted when I told a friend who survived cancer that personal training may not be for me. He asked, "How many times have you taken it?" I said, "Once." He said, "Dion, I beat cancer by fighting every damn day—not once." That rocked me. Because truth was, I wasn't fighting—I was flirting. I wasn't locked in—I was just lingering.

That moment shamed me. I thought, "You really fought harder for a fix than you're fighting for your future?" I'll be damned if I ever give pills more dedication than I give my own damn purpose. From that point, it didn't matter how tired I was—studying became nonnegotiable. And when I finally gave growth the same hunger I gave destruction? The results couldn't hide. I passed that test after two tries—not because I was smarter, but because I finally dedicated myself. That cancer survivor showed me that determination defeats deprivation. Every. Damn. Time.

Dedication is the heat that turns rare ambition into, "Well done." Without it, you're just chewing on potential and wondering why life is tough. Having a goal but lacking grind is like owning a gym membership and dying out of shape. You want consistent results? Then show up with consistent effort. You want a better life? Then act like it owes you nothing and work like it's everything. Lock in or stay locked out—those are your only options. You can keep repeating the same cycles, or you can get disciplined enough to break 'em. Either way, life will give you exactly what you've earned. Dedication is the only currency accepted at the bank of elevation. Without it, you're broke in more ways than one. Because if you ain't dedicated, you're just decorating your downfall. Your life will never be good enough if you never want it bad enough.

Growth Affirmation: I will **GROW** out of the mindset
that effort alone is enough. Life don't pay out based
on potential—it pays out based on performance.

Take this day to **THINK** about the toxic beliefs you've been treating like long-term guests in your head. At first glance, this might sound like it's about "tenants"—like people camping in your mental space. But it's deeper than people. That's a story all in itself. This is about "tenets"—the destructive rules you've let take over your mind and dictate your life. The statements like, "I don't deserve better," so you keep being someone's punching bag; or, "It's too late for me," so you bury the fire in your chest; or, "This is just who I am," so you chain yourself to the same damn life and call it fate. These thoughts ain't harmless—they're termites, eating your confidence from the inside out, reducing you to just a shell. And the worst part? You lettin' 'em in. You handed over the master key and begged them to stay, like a toxic ex you know you need to throw the fuck out. You kept renewing the lease on your own sabotage. Now you walking around with trashed self-worth, and can't figure out why nothing's changing. If you don't evict those beliefs, your mind will become a trap house, with negative thoughts running in and out.

As a property owner, I've dealt with Section 8 tenants who left my units wrecked—holes in walls, busted plumbing, trash in every room. This is not to say that all folks who take part in that program are that way. But the nastiest eviction I ever had to do wasn't in a building—it was in my brain. I had "tenets" in my head tearing down everything I was trying to build. "You ain't ever gon' be more than this." "You're damaged goods." "You're always one mistake away from blowing it all up again." These weren't random thoughts—they were my distorted mental beliefs. They'd become the rules I lived by. And like bad tenants, I let them stay way too long. They killed my ambition. They vandalized my peace. And I still let 'em roam like they were paying rent. But once I realized I was the damn landlord, things changed. If a thought didn't build me, it was evicted. Period. Slowly, the value of my life started rising.

Your mind ain't the slums for self-sabotage—kick that mess out. Your mind supposed to be filled with meaningful projects—not the projects. Your mind is not an Airbnb for negativity. Manage your thoughts. Don't keep letting negative "tenets" live in your mind like they pay bills. Stop letting mental squatters wreck the place. Let me ask you this: How long you gon' keep letting freeloading fears trash your mind? You wouldn't let someone move into your home, punch holes in the wall, graffiti the bathroom, and sleep on your couch for free. So why are you letting guilt, shame, and doubt do that in your head every single day? You are the property owner of the most powerful piece of real estate you'll ever own—your mind. Start acting like it. Do the application screenings. Do regular inspections. And if they're toxic, it's trespassing. Thoughts that don't build you gotta go—no exceptions. If it ain't investing in you, it's infecting you. If it ain't increasing you, it's decreasing you. You want peace? Raise your standards. You want growth? Clear the clutter. You want power? Reclaim your space. Because your mind ain't a motel for misery. It's a penthouse for your promise. But only if you start evicting what don't belong there. Otherwise, you'll forever be stuck in that one-room shack, with depression raiding your fridge, grief crashing on the couch, and guilt hogging the bathroom.

Growth Affirmation: I will **GROW** out of the mindset
that lets toxic thoughts live rent-free. My mind is no longer
a home for lies—I'm raising the rent on negativity.

Take this day to **THINK** about why you feel the need to broadcast every good deed like it's breaking news. Are you helping because they need it—or because you need attention? If it's exposure you're after, you ain't helping—you're hustling for praise. You're not building someone up, you're building a résumé. Real support don't come with a spotlight. It don't require hashtags, applause, a press release, or a damn camera crew. If your help got a volume knob, turn that shit down. Real ones move in silence. If your goal is to be seen, you lookin' to stunt, not support. There's a difference. Not everything worth doing needs a megaphone. Let me paint you the picture. In business, you have what you call silent partners. People who back someone behind the scenes—money, effort, time—with zero need for clout. They move quietly, but their impact screams. Silent partners don't need to be heard to help others make a lot of noise. They're content with working from behind to push others ahead. That's the kind of help that holds weight—the kind that doesn't need to flex to be effective. Silent partners are like roots underground—unseen, uncelebrated, but essential. You don't see them, but without them, nothing grows. Their contribution is in the fruit, not the fanfare. If your help needs a standing ovation, it ain't help—it's a performance.

During my second attempt to break free from addiction, I saw the difference between performance support and real support. The first time, someone helped—but they made damn sure everybody knew. Every favor, every ride, every dime—they made it public. It stopped feeling like support and started feeling like shame—like I was a project, not a person. That spotlight blinded me, and I relapsed under the weight of it. The second time? Whole different vibe. I finally found someone who didn't say much. If anything at all. She didn't make noise. She showed up, stayed consistent, and never asked for a thank you. Her presence felt like roots—quiet, solid, life-giving. She wasn't there for credit. She was there for me. And her silence spoke louder than all the noise the last person made. That's when I learned: If your help humiliates, it ain't holy—it's hollow. Real help uplifts without humiliating. It doesn't need a stage—it just needs sincerity. Thank you, Tayoun.

Let your actions, not your announcements, define your contribution. True help is a hand, not a headline. It needs intention, not attention. Too many people offer help with a hook in it. They throw you a rope but expect to be pulled into the spotlight with you. But genuine support don't need a tag, a post, a trophy, or a, "Look what I did." When you help someone, check your motive—are you investing in their growth or feeding your own ego? Because if it's about you, it damn sure ain't about them. The loudest ones usually do the least. And the ones who move in silence? They're the ones who actually make a difference. The strongest support don't echo—it elevates. Quietly. True help is a lift, not a label. A gesture, not a gimmick. If your voice has to be heard every time you help, you're only chasing clout. When you announce what you've done, you potentially annihilate someone's worth. The impact should speak for itself. Silent partners don't reach for bullhorns—they lay bricks. Support that shouts ain't support—it's self-promotion. Noisemakers don't change lives—it's the quiet force in the background making sure others get heard. Silent support amplifies character. Every time you need credit for helping someone, you ain't making a deposit—you're bankrupting your character. Cause when your heart's in the right place, your mouth don't need to broadcast it.

Growth Affirmation: I will **GROW** out of the mindset that craves credit for my support—being the backbone means more than being the billboard.

Take this day to **THINK** about how staring at closed windows won't open new doors. Missed chances hurt, yeah—but they don't keep you closed in unless you slam the window shut yourself. Plenty of people have shattered ceilings after years of being in the basement and missing countless windows of opportunity. Life don't run out of opportunities. It runs out of people willing to keep knocking. You keep crying over the windows you didn't crawl through, like life ain't full of doors just waiting for the right knock. Missed one bus? Cool. There's another one coming—that's if your eyes ain't too full of tears to see it. Regret only wins when it paralyzes you. You ain't cursed— you're just too focused on what didn't work to realize there's still work to do. And trust—there's always work to be done. Too many folks treat failure like it's fatal, when really it's just a reroute. You lost a window? So what. Stop acting like that was the only opening life had for you. Opportunities don't die because you missed 'em—they just wait for a better version of you to catch up. So stop mourning windows and start searching for keys. Because doors ain't gon' knock on themselves. And they damn sure ain't gon' open up on their own.

With my background, I thought every door had been slammed shut for good. Too many stints in the system. Too many burned bridges. I figured no one would take a chance on me. Then one day, an opportunity popped up—solid company, real benefits. But it came with a drug test. I panicked. I wasn't clean, but I didn't want to lose the shot. So I did what a lot of desperate people do—I faked it. Pulled up with someone else's clean urine, thinking I was slick. What I didn't know? They checked the temperature. Game over. Door slammed. I left that place humiliated. Thought that was my last shot. But here's the twist—once I actually got clean, once I started moving right, I got my ass back out there and new doors started unlocking. And this time? I used my own urine. No shortcuts. Just truth, effort, and growth. And guess what? That honest version of me got hired. All those doors I thought were locked? They weren't—I was just showing up dirty, broken, and unprepared. The moment I got aligned, life responded. It ain't about if the door opens—it's about who's knocking.

You think your chances are over? They're not. They're just waiting for the version of you that's finally done fucken around. Missed opportunities don't define your future unless you keep living in the past. Reflect, sure—but don't rot there. You still got doors to knock on. There are still jobs out there, still ideas inside you. And maybe you didn't get the gig, the loan, the apology, the yes—but that don't mean you don't deserve the next one. Opportunities are never truly gone—they're just waiting for the right time and the right version of you to step through. The question is—will you be ready when they open? Life gives second, third, even fiftieth chances—but only to the ones who keep showing up. Doors don't open for the bitter. They open for the bold. So stop watching the clock. Stop replaying the loss. Stay ready, and keep knocking. You ain't run out of chances—you just ain't become the version of you who can handle them yet. You didn't miss your opportunity—it just revealed you weren't ready. Windows close, but don't stand there pressed against the glass, looking all sad and shit. Wipe your face, fix your focus, and go knock on another door. And if no one answers—kick the damn thing down.

Growth Affirmation: I will **GROW** out of the mindset that missed chances mean no future—I wasn't denied, I just wasn't ready.

Take this day to **THINK** about why your life feels like a pressure cooker with no release valve. This ain't rocket science, and it ain't no episode of *Unsolved Mysteries*—you're stressed because you won't cut the shit out that's cutting into your peace. Your problems are only multiplying because you're too damn scared to subtract what's holding you under. Keep making excuses instead of cuts, and you'll die holding what you should've let go of years ago. You keep people around because you don't wanna be lonely. You keep bad habits alive because they're familiar. You out here dragging dead weight and wondering why your back hurts. You keep hugging the very hell that's burning you alive. You didn't just stumble into it—you invited it in and offered it a seat. Stress don't just show up. It grows in the soil you refuse to weed out. The longer you take in pollution, the slower you suffocate on the fumes of your own chaos. Every time you stay attached to what's destroying you, you're signing up for another round of self-inflicted suffering. You ain't a victim—you're a volunteer. You will always suffer from the toxic shit you don't sever.

One of the dumbest decisions I ever made was hitting the road to buy dope out of town. This was a $30,000 deal. Supposed to be a simple flip. Instead, I got played with counterfeit drugs and ended up in a high-speed chase, trying to retrieve the money like something out of a movie. Only this wasn't fiction—it ended in cuffs. Out of state. Far from home. That moment wasn't just about a bad deal—it was the fallout from a mindset I refused to let go. Nothing was holding me hostage; I was a willing participant. That mentality told me I had to stay in the streets, stay plugged into people who never gave a damn about me. And that one choice? It didn't just add problems—it multiplied them. Now I had open cases in Tennessee and Ohio. I was blaming life for being heavy when I was packing bags labeled unnecessary. Had I subtracted that lifestyle sooner, I wouldn't have been sitting in a jail cell sick. That trip cost me more than freedom—it cost me time, family, and peace. And for what? Loyalty to a lie. Let me make it plain: The toxic you don't subtract from your life will divide you from what you love the most.

You can't keep pouring gas on a fire you swear you're trying to put out. You have to stop fueling what's feeding off you. Stop whining about stress if you ain't bold enough to cut the cancer causing it. Life's hard enough. You really gon' make it harder by choosing to stay attached to what's killing you? That shit don't make no sense. You want peace? Start swinging the axe—or life will keep swinging the hammer. There is no middle ground. That fake-ass friend, that toxic ex, that bad habit? They're the mold on your mentality. Let 'em sit, and they'll spread. Stop talking about needing closure. The longer you wait for closure, the longer your heart stays open for hurt. The only thing standing between your chaos and your comeback is your courage. Your peace ain't gone—it's just under the weight of everything you refuse to release. Peace is simple math. Subtract what stresses you. Multiply what magnifies you. Add what aligns with your purpose. Divide from what distracts you. The reason your peace ain't adding up is because you keep refusing to subtract the bullshit.

Growth Affirmation: I will **GROW** out of the habit of emotional hoarding—it's only cluttering my life. Peace comes when I let go, not hold on.

Take this day to **THINK** about why you keep trying to fight battles like a one-man army—like you Rambo. You say you wanna change the world, spark something real, create a movement—but you keep trying to do it all by your damn self. Let's get one thing straight: One voice can make noise, but it takes a choir to shake the ground. If your voice ain't echoing through others, it don't get loud—it gets lost. If you wanna make noise, stay solo. If you wanna make history, move with many as one. There's no movement until you move with others. Change don't fear your noise—it fears your numbers. You either build with people or get buried in your cause. You're not weak for needing help—you're foolish for thinking you don't. A single raindrop dries up before it hits the ground. But a downpour? That's pressure. That's disruption. That's movement. Raindrops don't ask for attention—they show up in numbers and flood the neighborhood. That's what unity looks like. It don't knock—it breaks through. You want real change? Then stop obsessing over what separates you, and start showing up for what connects you. Real power ain't found in isolation—it's built in collaboration. Stop being the drop that dries alone—and start being the flood that changes the landscape.

Prison is designed to divide—racially, religiously, mentally. I saw it every day. Black tables. White tables. Hispanic tables. One wrong look could spark a lockdown, and riots weren't rare—they were routine. Unity? That was a myth behind bars. But one day, something snapped. A kitchen worker—one of us— ripped open a box of frozen meat and froze himself. He was shocked to see that the label said, "Not For Human Consumption." He showed it around, word spread like fire, and that box became bigger than just meat—it became a mirror. A mirror of how they saw us. Not as men. Not as humans. But as animals to be fed scraps not even fit for strays. That was the day we stood up—together. No race lines, no gang signs—just men who realized we still had worth and wanted to eat like decent humans, not be treated inhumanely. The guards didn't know how to handle it. They tried to scatter us, but it was too late. For the first time, prison didn't just feel like punishment—it felt like a pressure point that sparked unity. That moment rewired me. I realized power don't come from chaos—it comes from collective focus. Alone, I was just another number. But together, we were too loud to ignore. We weren't just a ripple—we were a riptide.

A single raindrop gets ignored—but a storm always gets noticed. History don't lie. The Civil Rights movement, women's suffrage—both started with drops that refused to dry up. You want to move mountains? Stop acting like your hands are enough and start linking arms with others. Unity takes humility. It takes sacrifice. This ain't about your ego—it's about evolution. Don't let your small frame of mind be the reason you can't see the bigger picture. If you're frustrated by the lack of progress, ask yourself: "Am I looking to be heard, or looking to be hidden? Am I pushing for change or just posting for clout?" Because if you're really about change, you'll find your tribe, link up, and move as one. Floods don't ask for permission. They change everything in their path. So either be a drop that evaporates in isolation—or join the storm that reshapes the scenery. Because when every person decides to drop in and do their part, the impossible don't just become possible—it becomes unstoppable. Your voice ain't so low that you can't spark change—it's just too solo to multiply.

Growth Affirmation: I will **GROW** out of the mindset that I can do it all alone. I'm not powerless—I'm just not plugged into others who can help me create change.

Take this day to **THINK** about why you keep dragging your past like it signed a lifetime contract. You walk around letting your mistakes act like they're your warden—deciding when you eat, sleep, and shit. When you can breathe, how far you can climb, and who you're allowed to become. Ain't no ankle monitor on your leg, but you living like you're on house arrest. Free as fuck but chained to the past. You cry about not getting ahead but won't stop looking behind. Hell, it's a miracle your neck ain't got a crick in it from looking backwards too damn long. Your past had its run—it's you that keeps renewing the contract. Damn the negotiations. Tear that shit up. Burn the contract. Stop acting like you in some hostage negotiation with memories that ain't willing to cut you loose. Freedom's right here on the table, and you steady choosing captivity like you love the chains. Meanwhile, life lapping you. Planes taking off, trucks clocking miles, but you still stopped at the light crying that it's taking too long to change. Stop using what you went through as crutches to limp through life instead of fuel to run past it. When you gon' get it? Windows in the front mean progress—mirrors in the back mean memory. Which one you gon' stare into? The view that can change your life or the reflection that's already cost you enough?

When I was on house arrest after an assault arrest, I missed my first daughter's birth. Tianna came into the world, and I couldn't even be there to hold her. Instead, I was stuck inside four walls, an ankle monitor clamped to my leg like a shackle while my little girl took her first breath without me. That moment branded me with a shame no court could sentence me to. Unlike the ankle monitor, my past wasn't permanently attached to me—I could cut myself free from it at any time. That ankle monitor on my leg kept me out of the hospital, but truth is, I kept wearing one in my mind long after it came off. My past had me strapped tighter than any shackle—reporting to shame like it was my probation officer. The court set me free, but I kept locking myself back in.

You've turned your past into a damn museum—dusting off old heartbreaks like they're artifacts worth saving. That ex who dogged you out? Still got them on display in your head like a framed picture in the lobby. That mama who chose the pipe over you? You built a whole memorial around her absence. That fake-ass friend who talked behind your back? You're still replaying the scandal like it's your favorite movie, knowing every scene by heart. And for what? To prove you survived it? Survival ain't the goal—evolution is. But you can't evolve if you're still curating exhibits for pain that's supposed to be buried. Stop charging admission for people to walk through your ruins, and start breaking ground on something new. Here's the ugly truth: More pain's coming, and if you don't drop the dead weight now, it's gon' crush the little strength you got left. The past ain't a shrine—it's a demolition site. Tear it down. Every time you look back, you're pausing your progress. Every glance siphons gas from your grind. Rearview mirrors are for learned lessons, not long lodgings. You ain't a tow truck—let go of what broke you down. Your future ain't worried about what dragged you through the mud—it's waiting to see what drives you through the fog.

Growth Affirmation: I will **GROW** out of staring
at my rearview of the past. I was made to move
forward, which makes the rear view irrelevant.

Take this day to **THINK** about why you give a fuck about who do or don't believe in you. Why are you still sitting around waiting on people to clap for you like your dream won't move without their hands? You don't need their applause to perform. Are you that desperate for validation that their silence shakes your purpose? Their belief ain't your battery—they're not responsible for your energy. They left the stage? Good. Now the spotlight's all yours. They don't believe in you? Perfect—now you get to show 'em what unbelief built. They bailed on the blueprint? Good thing you were the architect. Let they ass walk. Let they ass doubt. Let they ass exit. Belief is a bonus—not a requirement. Keep building without 'em. People's disbelief in you ain't about you anyway—it's about them. Most of the time, it's just their own insecurity. They can't see greatness in you because they've never seen it in them damn selves. Some folks will never believe in you, because doing so would force them to confront how little they believe in themselves. So let 'em fall back. You just keep springing forward. Don't let their exit shake your evolution.

When I began writing this book, I had a friend who was all in—helping me financially and offering encouragement. But suddenly he disappeared. No explanation, no warning—just gone. At first, it hit me hard. Broke as hell and unable to push it further, I pressed pause. I was rebuilding my life, and his support had felt like a lifeline. But after about three weeks, I quickly realized his belief wasn't the foundation of my success. It was a nice addition, but it wasn't the engine that kept me moving. Their disbelief might sting, but it doesn't have the power to stop your journey. I had to remind myself that my vision didn't depend on him or anyone else. His doubt wasn't a dead end— it was a detour to find those who truly supported me. Just like people stop believing in Santa or the Tooth Fairy, people may one day stop believing in you too. And guess what? You'll still be here, still building. Support is nice. But their silence don't silence your calling, and their absence don't cancel your anointing. Their belief was never the foundation—just a voice in the crowd, not the coach who called the play.

Whether they never believed, stopped believing, or switched up midway—it don't matter. That's what fickle, funny-ass people do. As soon as they see you making moves, they get mad and wanna hate. But fuck 'em. A pilot don't need the belief of their passengers to get to their destination. Neither do you. It's not about their faith in your journey—it's about your determination to get to where the hell you're going. Don't let someone who stopped believing make you stop achieving. They can stop believing, but you must never stop becoming. You can't rely on others to fuel your dream, or you'll stay parked in the same broken-down-ass spot. Your why, provided you have one, is stronger than their doubt. When others doubt you, let that fuel your fire instead of extinguishing it. You're not too loud without them—you're finally loud enough to hear yourself think. People who believe in you are invaluable, but the most important belief is your own. Keep going and keep winning, because just because they left doesn't mean you've lost. If disbelief makes you shut down, then it was never purpose; it was ego. Your gift wasn't issued on the condition that people clap for it. Damn them. You keep delivering your gift to the world—whether they believe in you or not.

Growth Affirmation: I will **GROW** out of
shrinking when support walks out—I ain't here for
cheerleaders, I'm here for championships.

Take this day to **THINK** about why you're acting so weak when everything you've been through proves you're built for war. You've taken hits most people would've folded under—but you're still here. You've been broken, betrayed, abandoned, abused—but you survived. You outlived things that were designed to destroy you, and now you're walking around like none of it counts? Like the pain was pointless? You don't get to play powerless after everything you've pushed through. Life don't hand out strength for free. You earned yours in blood, sweat, and breakdowns. Every trial, every betrayal, every scar—that was a brick in your structure. So why you walking around like your building's about to collapse? You're not weak. You're just acting like you forgot what the hell you're made of. Skyscrapers don't apologize for their height—and neither should you. Your strength was built story by story. Your stories are the reason you're standing tall and strong.

I'll never forget the day I visited the office of FUBU in New York City. Their clothing brand, "For Us, By Us," resonated with pride and purpose in the African American community, and it was the standard I aspired to when I started my own clothing line. The offices were on the 66th floor of the Empire State Building, and as I stood there looking out over the city, I was struck by how many stories made up that iconic building. Just like that building, I've been constructed out of many stories. I've been shot. Had car wrecks under the influence. Popped pills just to function. Lost a grandson I never really got to hold. Betrayed by friends. Rotated in and out of jail cells so much it felt normal. Like I was playing musical jails. None of that is fiction—that's foundation. Every one of those moments stacked on top of the last, building me up instead of breaking me down. Just like that building, my life ain't tall by accident—it's tall because of every scar, every setback, every survival. Those truths didn't crush me—they constructed me. I don't stand tall in spite of my stories—I stand tall because of them.

Your past laid the foundation—now stack stories of success on that pain and turn it into a penthouse. Stop acting like your stories are something to be ashamed of. You've been through hell—own it. Bent but not broken. Crushed but not cremated. That pain built you, but now it's time to build on it. Every one of your stories built you stronger—you just too busy whining to recognize it. Pain leaves receipts—trees included. Cut one down and you'll see rings, each one a scar of survival. Not all of them are smooth, but every one proves the tree made it through something. Tree rings chronicle years of growth, grief, and grit. Your scars are your rings. Your struggle is your story. Quit acting like your stories disqualify you—they're the damn reason you're qualified. That trauma? That chaos? That climb? It's why you're still on your fucken feet. Shrink for who? Fuck that. You didn't bleed and crawl through hell just to make yourself small now. Your brokenness had you in the basement. Now let your power put you in the high-rise. Let the world feel every level you've built. You've been building in silence long enough. Every scar's a story, every story's a floor. Build your skyscraper. They buried you in the basement—now make sure when they open the curtains, your skyline wows them.

Growth Affirmation: I will **GROW** out of being ashamed of my scars—I was constructed through painful stories, and still I rise.

Take this day to **THINK** about why the hell you keep acting like you need a perfect setup before you move. You really think those who made it had some instruction manual, a trust fund, and a cheer squad waiting on them? Fuck no. They had nothing but a fire in their gut that wouldn't shut up. They didn't cry about missing tools—they started building with bare hands. They were itching so bad to succeed they scratched through walls. But you? The only itch you seem to acknowledge is on your hand—and like an idiot, you swear it means money's coming. You sit around whining that your ducks ain't in a row, like life is gon' pause for yo ass to line 'em up. What you're doing is crazy, and ducks don't follow quacks. Stop counting what you don't got and start squeezing the hell out of what you do. No money? Grind until somebody can't help but invest. No knowledge? Park your ass in rooms where wisdom drips, and soak it up. No connections? Show up every damn day until ignoring you feels impossible. Dreams don't pull up polished and pretty— they arrive ragged, raw, and bloody. Only the ones who bleed for it, fight for it, and refuse to fold get to hold it. Starting from scratch ain't your punishment—it's your proof. But that canvas stays blank if your scared ass won't pick up a brush. Either paint your story, or shut the fuck up about wanting one.

When I stepped out of prison, there was no welcome wagon, no blueprint, no favor waiting on the other side of that gate. But prison had given me an itch to become a trainer—an itch so bad, I started coming up with a rash of ideas of how I would do that. All I had was a fire in my gut—and no money to match it. Certification cost what I didn't have, so hustle became the only option. I took whatever jobs I could just to eat and survive. I scrubbed toilets, folded towels, and wiped tanning beds at Planet Fitness while silently studying every trainer. Planet Fitness said it was a "Judgement Free Zone"— but I felt judged every shift. That's cool though. I wasn't there for validation. I was there to turn sweat into strategy. They saw a janitor—I saw a classroom.

I was broke, overlooked, and starting from below zero, but I showed up like I already belonged in the industry. Every cheap meal, every double shift, every midnight clock-in when I had two hours of sleep—all of it was fuel. Nothing was handed to me. I earned it sweating in silence. And when that certification finally touched my hands, it wasn't just proof I passed a test—it was proof I had flipped the script. Proof I turned a mop into a microphone, a toilet brush into a training badge. Proof I refused to stay boxed in by my past, and built a body of work from the ground up.

Your dream ain't a TV dinner. It ain't supposed to be prepackaged and ready in three minutes. This is soul food. It takes chopping, seasoning, patience, and heat. It's the work that happens long before anybody gets a taste of the results. Skyscrapers start with nothing but dirt and a dream—and so do you. You don't need everything—you just need to start. Your passion has to outweigh your procrastination. Your hunger has to silence your hesitation. If the world gave you nothing, build something anyway. Stop waiting for conditions to be perfect. Not everyone who struck gold chasing their dream started with a silver spoon or a silver platter. Some started eating out their hands, dirt under their nails, still digging like they were starving for more. Dreams don't show up on your lap—they get built by people too stubborn to quit. Stop holding the itch. Scratch. Scratch until something bleeds. Scratch until something breaks open. Scratch until the thing you dream about becomes the thing you're standing in. The ones who develop an *itch* to prosper and grind from *scratch*, often *break out* in a *rash* of successes. Their commitment ensures it. People who start from scratch and claw their way to the top leave marks the world can't ignore—but you keep biting your nails from the nervousness of starting, so your climb never leaves a trace. It's better to build from scratch than to die scratching your head wonderin' why you never made shit happen.

Growth Affirmation: I will **GROW** out of the mindset
of waiting for perfect conditions. I'd rather start from
scratch than waste my life scratchin' my ass.

Take this day to **THINK** about why every disagreement turns into a full-blown fallout with you. You don't try to understand—you just try to overtalk. The second something or someone rubs you the wrong way, you explode like it's your job to defend your pride at all costs. You don't pause, ask questions, or look deeper—you just assume the worst and react like a damn fool. Instead of getting to the core of what's really being said, you let surface-level offense take over and run wild. You think that makes you strong? All it shows is that you can't handle discomfort without turning it into chaos. And that's why you keep ruining solid connections. You're too emotional to be logical and too reactive to be respected. Every situation ain't an attack. Every disagreement ain't a betrayal. But you can't see the truth when you're too busy playing victim in a battle no one else knows about. You keep calling everything disrespect just because it don't feel good. A tone, a stare, a sharp truth—you take it all personal. But your version of disrespect ain't universal. Just 'cause you feel slighted don't mean you've been disrespected. The truth is, nobody's required to respect you—as long as they don't disrespect you. Your sensitivity is the reason why you keep losing people who were trying to reach you, not hurt you.

Earlier in life, I thought every correction was an insult. One time, a close friend called me out for taking his cousin into a cemetery to have sex. Instead of hearing the truth, I felt disrespected—like he had no right to tell me what I shouldn't have done. Instead of reflecting on what he said, I tore into him and became disrespectful. I shouted something wild, like, "It was the perfect place—she was stiff anyway!" At the time, I thought I was being clever, but looking back, I see how immature and sensitive I was. My pride couldn't handle the truth, so I lashed out, turning a valid critique into an unnecessary fight. I ended up cutting him off entirely, losing a good friend over my inability to handle the truth. It wasn't until years later that I realized his words were meant to guide me, not hurt me. But by the time I figured that out, the damage was done. That moment taught me that when the truth hits a nerve, it's probably because I need to hear it.

Stop using your pride as a thermometer for how people are allowed to talk and look at you. Anytime someone calls you out, stop and ask yourself one question: "Am I mad because they're wrong, or am I mad because they're right?" If you don't slow down and get beneath the surface, you'll keep turning correction into confrontation. Stop waiting for people to package the truth with a pretty bow on it before you listen—sometimes the delivery is rough because the truth is raw. Real is rare, so when it shows up, you don't know how to take it. Instead of leaning in, you back off—treating correction like it's disrespect, when it's really a lifeline. You don't ask what's really going on, you just start throwing jabs. You'll never grow if every piece of advice turns into an argument. The real work is in looking past the offense and asking what the message is trying to show you and how you can grow from it. Master your emotions, or your emotions will master you. Stop letting your feelings lead the charge and start letting your logic take the wheel. If you can't control your emotions in a disagreement, you're not built for anything long-term—friendship, marriage, business, or growth. Stop letting your pride close the door shut on people who were only trying to open your eyes.

Growth Affirmation: I will **GROW** out of the mindset of taking offense. If truth hits a nerve, it's time to listen—not swing. Not all advice is an attack.

Take this day to **THINK** about how many people are six feet under with nothing to their name but a headstone and a handful of regrets. Not because life robbed them of something—but because they never tried to live for anything. Too many die broke in purpose, bankrupt in identity, and empty as fuck in meaning. Dying over petty beefs. Dying for approval from people who wouldn't even show up to their funeral. Dying for street reputation, clout, or nonsense that don't even get written into their obituary. You say you want more, but the second life pushes you, you give it pushback. That ain't living life—that's just leeching off of it till the day you die. Every day you wake up and don't do shit, you're not living—you're slowly dying in pieces. And when it's your time, what will your life show? What will the world tell? Because life comes with its own version of show-and-tell—and your existence is the item you bring. If your story don't show proof of life, maybe it's 'cause you never gave them shit to talk about.

As an addict, I knew I was gon' die with nothing. As someone who was petty and confrontational, I knew I was gon' die over nothing. And because I stood on no principles, I knew I was gon' die not standing for nothing. I hadn't built anything. I hadn't fought for anything. I'll never forget the time I applied for a job and they asked for professional references—I didn't have a single one. Not because I hadn't worked, but because I hadn't left a mark. I was so desperate, I scribbled down my daughters' names—since they carried the last names of their mothers and not mine. I walked out that building embarrassed, exposed, and empty. I wasn't just unemployed—I was unproven. And if that wasn't enough, it got worse. Not long after, I went to a friend's funeral and sat in the back row, numb, just hoping to feel something. But when they read his obituary, it tugged at my soul: His whole life story, accomplishments included, could've been printed on a business card. Short. Shallow. Forgettable. And in that moment, I saw my own reflection in his story—alive but irrelevant, breathing but already buried. That's when I made a vow: I will not die with a story no one cares to read. If I'm going down, I'm going down fighting—for something real. What about you?

Life is meant to be lived. All this shit the world has to offer, and this is what you choose? Nothing? You mean to tell me you've been given breath but can't find one damn reason to fight for something? To live for something? To die with something worth leaving behind? If not, you're pathetic—a wasted heartbeat taking up space. Oxygen thief. Breathing but not living. And when they lower you in the dirt, the world won't lose a damn thing, because you never gave it shit to begin with. We may not physically die today, but every excuse we make, every gift we sit on—that's a funeral in slow motion. If you're struggling to move, ask yourself this question: "What do I want to bring to life's final show-and-tell?" You don't need to die for everything, but you better damn sure live for something. Don't let the only thing people remember when you die be the suit you were buried in. Let your life be so loud, even death can't shut it up. Some people get remembered for what they did. Most get forgotten for what they didn't. Which one are you? 'Cause if your story reads like a business card when you die—then you had no business living.

Growth Affirmation: I will **GROW** out of the mindset of living for nothing—I want to be remembered for having a strong foundation, not a nice funeral.

Take this day to **THINK** about why you're sprinting through life like it's a 40-yard dash. You treat every day like it's some shit you just gotta get through instead of something you were supposed to live through. What the hell are you rushing for? We live in a world addicted to speed—minute rice, fast food, one-click shopping, shortcuts for everything. But here's the ugly truth: You treat life like you treat sex—quick, sloppy, detached, and over before you even looked it in the eye. No intimacy. No depth. No connection. You don't even stay long enough to pillow talk with your damn dreams. Like some cheap hookup, you roll over, make an excuse, and bounce. Life ain't no quickie. It ain't no, "Wham, bam, thank you, ma'am." It's meant to be loved slow, held close, lived deep. But most of us keep choosing convenience over connection, speed over substance—and in doing that, we rob life of its richness. We're moving so damn fast chasing the next thing, we forget how to even be in the thing we're in right now. That's why you keep saying, "What was I supposed to be doing?" or, "I know I'm forgetting something." You ain't forgetting something—you movin' too damn fast.

Growing up, my Aunt Hazel was the queen of soul food. She didn't believe in cutting corners, especially when it came to cooking collard greens. She let them simmer for hours with smoked turkey necks, garlic, and just the right amount of vinegar. "No Glory Greens in my house," she'd say, laughing as she gently scolded anyone who suggested canned shortcuts. Aunt Hazel believed that love and time were the most important ingredients in anything— whether it was food, relationships, or living. Those Sunday dinners were more than meals; they were moments seasoned with care, connection, and intention. She poured her heart into those greens, and every bite reminded you what it meant to truly savor something. Watching her cook taught me that life isn't about how fast you can cross the finish line; it's about the richness of the journey. Without love, time, and intention, life is just bland. No seasoning in your seasons.

A life spent racing to the finish line ain't a life—it's just a countdown. You microwave your whole life, then wonder why every season of it is bland. Slow down. Savor your time. Stop rushing toward a finish line that will come soon enough. The biggest failure isn't dying—it's getting to the end and realizing you never truly lived because you missed the opportunity to make it purposeful. I've heard it asked many times, "What is the true meaning of life?" And I've heard multiple replies. But I believe I have the answer. Are you ready for it? The true meaning of life is to truly give your life meaning. That's it. There is no other answer. Death doesn't sting nearly as much as living with the shame of never having taken the time to create meaning. Life is like Aunt Hazel's collard greens; the best parts of it can't be rushed. Sit down and eat with your family. Establish a game night. Pour your heart into the moments that matter. Living without purpose is like racing through the meal just to get to the dessert—blind to the soul food that built the flavor: the dash of paprika, the hint of garlic, the teaspoon of cumin. Season your days with love and care, because the best parts of life can't be reheated later. Life ain't a one-night stand. A quickie. Be intimate with it. Put in the time, the grind, the patience—because rushing it is like popping a Viagra with no partner. All you do is make life hard.

> **Growth Affirmation:** I will **GROW** out of the mindset
> of rushing through life. The real tragedy ain't me dying—
> it's clocking out of life and realizing I never clocked in.

Take this day to **THINK** about why you keep letting nobodies bait you into battles that ain't worth shit. You out here giving away your calm like it's buy-one-get-one-free, then crying about why your life feels chaotic. You think cussing somebody out makes you powerful? Nah—it makes you pitiful. Every time you give somebody a piece of your mind, you shrink your own peace of mind. That "victory" you brag about? It's nothing but a receipt showing how much peace you just spent on an argument that was worthless. It's like paying full price for what turns out to be a knockoff—you get cheap results at a high cost. You walked out thinking you had Louis Vuitton only to find out you were wearing Fooey Vuitton. You didn't win—you got hustled. People don't gotta steal your peace—you hand it over like a damn fool, wrapped up in your ego, just to "win" an argument that nobody even remembers tomorrow. And the wild part? They love it. Drama addicts get high off dragging you into their dirt because it proves they ain't the only miserable ones. And every time you bite, they laugh. You can't keep throwing the door wide open for chaos, then act shocked when it moves in and trashes the place. Your reactions are receipts, and they show the world how weak you really are. Stop selling out your sanity for cheap applause.

While serving time in an Ohio prison, I was temporarily transferred to Kentucky to handle a court matter. Before I left, I had to decide who I could trust to manage my commissary "store" in my absence. Ultimately, I put my trust in my bunkie to hold things down, thinking he'd keep things running smoothly. When I got back, I found out he had been handing out 2-for-1s to people who never paid back. Everything I'd built was gone—and I was furious. Without thinking, I punched the wall, breaking my hand. The cast I had to wear for weeks was a constant reminder of how I'd let my anger control me. My bunkie didn't pay for my broken hand—I did. The guys still didn't pay me back. What kind of shit is that? That moment taught me a hard lesson: Reacting out of anger only hurts you in the end. Peace isn't just the absence of conflict—it's the presence of control, and I had completely lost mine.

Don't throw away your peace just to prove you got a mouth. You lose more than your cool when you explode—you lose your focus, your dignity, and sometimes your life. You don't have to attend every argument you're invited to. You can't protect your peace and entertain every provocation—choose one. Some battles ain't worth the bruises. You don't win a war by throwing grenades in your own mind. True strength ain't loud—it's composed. Your silence in the face of ignorance is power. Your ability to walk away is wisdom. Don't lose your peace because someone cuts you off in traffic. Did you die? Don't lose your peace because a coworker gossips about you. Did you lose your job? Don't lose your peace because somebody calls you a hoe. Are you? Don't lose your peace because a family member brings up your past at the dinner table. Are you still living in it? Keep your voice, keep your energy, and most of all—keep your peace. Not every attack deserves an answer. Not every remark needs a response. Control is quiet. It moves with intention. In moments when you're heated, don't lose your cool. If you can master your reaction, you can master your world. Let them talk. Let them drown in their own noise. Because at the end of the day, it's not about proving them wrong. It's about proving that they never had that kind of control over you in the first place.

Growth Affirmation: I will **GROW** by protecting
my peace like priceless data—backed up, locked
down, and off-limits to drama thieves.

CHAPTER 4

KEEP PLAYIN' WITH GOD IF YOU WANT TO

"Stop thinking God's mercy is weakness—He's just giving you time before the consequences."

DION PARKER

BEFORE YOU READ THIS CHAPTER

God's grace is real—but so is His correction. You keep dancing on the line, daring Him to do something, like mercy means permission. But mercy ain't God's approval—it's just His delay. And if you think the spelling of *satan* is a mistake, you're wrong. I kept him lowercase in this book 'cause all he did was raise hell in my life. I refuse to capitalize someone who's capitalized off me for years.

This chapter is a warning—don't mistake God's patience for passivity. These stories aren't about religion—they're about reality. Real battles. Real rebellion. Real moments when the lights could've gone out, but grace stepped in. But keep playing? And that grace might just step back. Read this with reverence. Because God don't play games—and if you think He does, this chapter's about to remind you Who wrote the rules. You think God ain't real? Eff around and find out.

Take this day to **THINK** about what you're really modeling your life after, because whether you realize it or not, you're modeling someone. You out here modeling everything you see on social media—fake bodies, fake lifestyles, fake relationships—just to get views, likes, comments, and followers. But what are you chasing all that for if you claim you love God? You model God on Sunday, and the world Monday through Saturday. God ain't sending invites to folks who RSVP'd to the world every day except Sunday. You can't dress like hell all week and expect heaven to roll out the red carpet. You talk about heaven but live like hell and wonder why your life feels like one. God never called you to copy chaos—He calls you to model Him, to show the fruits of the Spirit, "*Love, joy, peace, patience, kindness, goodness, faithfulness, gentleness, and self-control*" (Galatians 5:22–23). To keep it real, you out here modeling everything but that. Modeling hate like it's trendy. Wearing anger like it's a designer label. Sporting impatience like it's a fashion statement. If you keep modeling your life after fools, don't be surprised when life makes a fool out of you. Keep thinking God's gon' overlook all of your mess just because you say His name every now and then. You can't model trash and expect treasure.

I remember one Saturday like it was yesterday. A dude had shorted me on a pack—padded the money and thought I wouldn't catch it. Me and an associate caught up with him in an alley behind the laundromat. No yelling. No posturing. Just straight to it. We jumped him so bad I swear I heard something snap—might've been his arm, might've been his neck. Either way, he was screaming, and we walked off like nothing happened. But here's the sick part. The very next morning, I was sitting in a church pew with my shirt tucked in, face clean-shaven, saying the Lord's Prayer like I ain't just try to cripple somebody the day before. Took First Communion that Sunday too— broke the bread, sipped cranberry juice out of a plastic cup, and whispered, "Amen," with a mouth that had just spit curses and threats 24 hours prior. I was Dr. Jekyll and Mr. Hyde—rocking a gold chain with a cross swinging from it. Listenin' to gospel one minute, then gangsta rap the next. I'd walk out of Bible study and then go study someone to victimize like God didn't know it. I was the one who always said, "God knows my heart," like that was a license for my demons to run wild. I wasn't livin' right—I was just good at pretending I was. I wasn't a disciple—I was a double agent. One foot in the Word, the other knee-deep in the world.

You've been mirroring a world that's broken, lost, and headed for destruction—and if you keep following it, guess where you're headed? God ain't playing games with your soul, and you shouldn't be, either. You could have millions of followers, but if you ain't a follower of the One true Jesus, you're just leading yourself off a cliff—and following the crowd straight to hell. "What would Jesus do?" ain't just a phrase—it's a challenge to stop moving reckless. Before you snap and cuss somebody out—what would Jesus do? Before you lay up in somebody's bed—what would Jesus do? Before you take that hit or that drink—what would Jesus do? Jesus didn't move like a fool—but you've been out here living reckless and calling it "real." You want God to bless your life while you keep spitting in His face with your actions. It don't work like that. Jesus lifted people up, and you're letting people down. Jesus healed people, and you hurt them. You want a crown? First carry a cross. You want the win? Start walking like the Winner. Model Christ for real—because playing around with the world is only gon' get you played by it. You can't live like the devil and expect to die like a disciple.

Spiritual Growth Affirmation: I will **GROW** out of the
carnal mindset of modeling my life after the world. Before
doing anything, I will ask, "What would Jesus do?"

Take this day to **THINK** about how your birth was intentional, not accidental. No matter how you came into this world, whether it was planned or unexpected, your existence has meaning. Too often, people struggle with the belief that they were a mistake, that their lives don't carry value because of how they were conceived. Maybe you were born out of a one-night stand, a secret affair, or even a tragic situation like rape. But despite how you arrived, you are here with purpose. Even if you've been told, "I wished you'd never been born," that was a wish beyond their control. They didn't intend to have you—but God intended to use you. Unlike an accidental death, there is no such thing as an accidental life. Every life serves a purpose. Despite the circumstances of your conception, your existence was deliberate. As Ephesians 2:10 reminds us, *"For we are his workmanship, created in Christ Jesus unto good works, which God hath before ordained that we should walk in them."* You came through mess, but you carry a mission. Even if you were conceived in chaos, you were created for calling. You are living proof that purpose is never bound by the circumstances of your conception. It's bound by God.

During a time when I was promiscuous and engaged, I had an affair with a woman who lived in the projects I hustled out of. We lost contact after a while, but 17 years later I received a call from someone informing me that I might have a child. Initially, I denied it, brushing it off. But it ate away at my conscience until I looked into it, and it was true. I had a daughter, and I made it my mission to connect with her. The circumstances surrounding her conception didn't diminish her value, and neither do yours. You weren't an accident waiting to happen—you were a purpose waiting to unfold. And if I can be truthful, I was just as unplanned as she was—but God still planned for both of us to be connected. The world may have labeled my daughter and me a mishap—God labeled us a masterpiece.

You might've come through broken people, but you didn't come out broken—you came chosen. In purpose, on purpose, for God's purpose. You ain't Neo or Morpheus—there was no glitch in the Matrix when God created you. There were no kinks or bugs that needed to be worked out. And don't you let nobody make you believe that there were. So what if they think you aren't supposed to be here—the nerve of them to try to write you off when the Author already wrote your name in the Book of Life. How dare they. You're not a typo in life's story; God didn't create you and then go looking for some whiteout—you're God's signature piece. There has never been a time where God said, "Oops. My bad." Don't make the mistake of not living out your purpose because you've chosen to hold on to the belief that your creation was accidental. Your life is part of a greater plan, and your purpose is uniquely yours. Embrace it, and live fully, knowing that your existence is intentional and that you are meant to be here. None of us are accidents, regardless of how we arrived. You might've been unplanned by people, but you were preapproved by God. Since they say, "God don't make mistakes," stop living like one.

Spiritual Growth Affirmation: I will **GROW** out of the carnal mindset of believing that I was the aftermath of sin—I was the aftermath of sovereignty. A setup by God, not a slipup by man.

Take this day to **THINK** about the chains you keep calling unbreakable when God already gave you the authority to snap 'em. You can break the chain of nicotine—stinking your breath, blacking your lungs, yellowing your teeth. You can break the chain of addiction—promising you a high but leaving you emptier every time. You can break the chain of rage—snapping on the very people who love you. And you can break the chain of that toxic relationship—the one beating the hell out of you while you call it love. Stop acting like you powerless—you ain't held hostage 'cause the chain is stronger, you held hostage 'cause you keep surrendering to it. Stop babysitting your bondage, giving cigarettes custody over your lungs, liquor authority over your kidneys, and pills the lease on your sanity. God already signed your release papers, but you steady begging Him for bail like He didn't already cover the cost with blood. You don't need another preacher to lay hands, another counselor to sit across from, or another sponsor to tell you what you already know—you need to stand up, speak up, and use the authority that's already living inside you. Heaven done stamped your parole, hell can't override it, but you still sitting in the cell with the key in your pocket, waiting on a guard that ain't coming. If you don't walk out, don't cry about being locked up.

I'll never forget when a friend of mine called me, deep in addiction, broke down crying. He had just lost his job, and now his car was about to be towed. Rock bottom was knocking at his door, and instead of fighting for freedom, he told me, "Man, I almost just wanna do something to go back to prison." Wow! Think about it—he'd spent nearly forty years of his life in and out of prison, so chains felt more natural to him than freedom. That's what addiction and broken cycles do—they twist your mind until captivity feels safer than liberty. Prison became his comfort zone because at least there, somebody else set the rules, somebody else held the keys. But here's the truth: God had already given him the authority to walk free. The release papers were signed in blood, but he wasn't using the power God put in him. And that's where so many of us get stuck—we sit in the cell with the key in our hand, waiting on permission God already gave. Stop crying like you're locked up when God already left the door wide open. You ain't trapped because life is hard— you're trapped because you're soft.

Chains don't need to be broken—they need to be walked out of. You don't need to go to anyone. Not even God. Heaven cosigned your release, but you're still begging for bail. Matthew 18:18 says, "*Verily I say unto you, Whatsoever ye shall bind on earth shall be bound in heaven: and whatsoever ye shall loose on earth shall be loosed in heaven.*" There you go. Now you got the memo. Whatever you want to let go of, heaven is already in agreement with it. With the world, you need paperwork, approvals, and people to cosign your freedom— but with God, you bypass all that and go straight to the Top. No middlemen. The chain breaks the second you speak with authority. No need for permission from a pastor, a priest, or a person. The authority was never outsourced—it was installed in you from the start. If you want to break free, God has given you the authority to do so—you don't need to submit a request, wait for a callback, or hope someone higher up will take notice. You don't need to call a locksmith to break the chains that have you bound when God has already handed you bolt cutters.

Spiritual Growth Affirmation: I will **GROW** out of the carnal mindset of asking for freedom. I don't need clearance to break my chains when I've already been commissioned by the Father to do it.

Take this day to **THINK** about the times you've wandered so far from God you thought there was no way back. The moments when shame whispered in your ear that God was done with you—like people who cut you off after too many mistakes. You outgrew people's patience, not God's mercy. God don't play by human rules. He don't throw people away because they fell short. You think because you were a drunk, a prostitute, an addict, a criminal, or an adulterer that God slammed the door shut on you? He didn't. Backsliding might have interrupted your fellowship, but it never erased your relationship. Like the prodigal son who squandered his inheritance and crawled back home covered in guilt, God's arms are still wide open—waiting for you to stop running and start returning to throw you a welcome home party. Thinking God won't take you back after a mistake is like a child believing their parent won't let them in the house because they got dirty playing outside. No matter how messy you are, God still wants you to come home—just like a parent longs for their child to come back inside so they can clean them off.

I remember getting locked up one time, and I straight cussed God out—yelled at the ceiling like, "You got me going through all this? Damn being a Christian." But in a cold, hard cell, I saw a dusty Gideon Bible on the floor. I picked it up out of boredom, flipped through it angry, and landed on Isaiah 1:18: "*Though your sins be as scarlet, they shall be white as snow.*" That was no coincidence. That was God. I cried—real tears, while still fiending to get out and chase a Percocet. I thought I had burned every bridge, but grace was out here building new ones. I thought I was too far gone, that God gave up on me like people did. But every time I crawled back, He was there—no judgment, no shame—just grace. He picked me up, dusted me off, and reminded me that His love never stopped. He never said, "Three strikes and you're out." He said, "By My stripes you are healed." His blood covers all your mistakes and He will never give up on you. John 6:37 says, "*All that the Father giveth me shall come to me; and him that cometh to me I will in no wise cast out.*" People hold grudges, but God holds grace. You think you're too stained? Nah—you're just too stubborn to let Him clean you up. Sin might've locked you out, but grace left the door cracked. Walk back in.

Stop slipping in sin when you can slide back into His grace. God's arms are open 24/7—there's no closing time. You weren't created to live bound by guilt and shame. Stop blaming everybody else for why you're stuck when it's you who won't walk back through the open door. What if the thing you think disqualifies you is the very reason God wants to use you? Sometimes it's your mistakes that become the story someone else needs to find their way home. Millions have read about the prodigal son and realized God still wanted them—your story could do the same. Don't sit sulking in your sins, acting like it's too late—because it's not. God don't care how far you fell—He cares that you're willing to get up. His grace has no expiration date. Before you come back, come broken—and let Him rebuild you. Even in your mess, you can still run back to the Messiah. Even in your junk, you can still run back to Jesus. Even in your filth, He still calls you family—now act like it and go home. You may have moved out of God's fellowship, but heaven still got your name on the mailbox. 'Cause you can walk a million steps from God, but one turn around puts you right back in front of Him.

Spiritual Growth Affirmation: I will **GROW** out of the carnal mindset that believes my mess is stronger than God's mercy.

Take this day to **THINK** about the misconception that you need to "get right" before coming to God. That lie has kept more people stuck than sin ever did. And let's be real—part of the reason folks believe that lie is because of the church itself. Those "holier-than-thou" Christians who look sideways at people walking in with the only clothes they've got. The men whispering about how slutty a woman looks—like, what the hell you doing staring that hard at her anyway, Mr. Deacon? The church women rolling their eyes at her, scared half to death the new girl is going to snatch their lustful husbands— when the truth is, Sister Jones, if he is that easy to take, he was never yours to begin with. Let's stop pretending gatekeeping at the church doors is godliness—that ain't holiness, that's hypocrisy. The hell with them. Stop believing that you gotta be polished before getting right with God. How you supposed to clean yourself up when you can't even stop the bleeding? If you had the power to fix yourself, you wouldn't be this broken. You've patched, prayed, and performed—and still ended up empty. God ain't sitting around waiting for you to show up complete. He's not checking your record before offering redemption or performing a background check. You don't need a spotless résumé—you need a surrendered heart.

The first Sunday I stepped back into a church after prison, I didn't look like no choir boy. I had on a pair of scuffed Timberlands, pants saggin' heavy, and a hockey jersey two sizes too big. Soon as I walked through them doors, I could feel eyes cutting into me sharper than any shank I'd ever seen. Church women clutching purses tighter, whispering like I came to make them surrender their wallets instead of me coming to surrender my hands. Truth is, I wasn't even there for them—I was there limping in with a crooked life hoping God could help me walk straight. But that's the trap, ain't it? Folks dressed in their Sunday best acting like threads make you holy, when underneath they got stains you can't bleach out. God ain't looking for people who got it all polished. He's looking for people like me, limping in busted, bruised, and barely breathing, but still willing to show up. God's grace meets you in your mess. But in order for God to cleanse you, you have to come clean with Him that you're living dirty.

You don't take a shower when you're already clean. You don't see a doctor after you've cured yourself. You don't walk into a hospital fully healed. You go because you can't fix it. So why are you trying to spiritually heal yourself before walking into the presence of the only One who actually can? The longer you delay, the more your spiritual health declines. God's grace is designed for the broken. The people who think they have it all together—most of the time He can't do nuttin' wit 'em. God can't pour into a cup that's already acting full. God's not impressed by performance—He's moved by surrender. Isaiah 42:16 says, "*I will lead the blind by ways they have not known, along unfamiliar paths I will guide them; I will turn the darkness into light before them and make the rough places smooth.*" That's a promise—not for the polished, but for the blind, the beaten, and the buried. You don't have to bring perfection to God. Just bring your pain. Bring your dysfunction, your disobedience, your disappointment—He can handle it. Stop thinking He wants the filtered version of you. He wants the one still wrestling, still weeping, still wondering how to move forward. The only thing He needs from you is honesty. You don't need to be worthy—you just need to be willing. Stop trying to stand on legs that can't carry the weight. You'll never get things right without going to the One who makes things right. Lean on the one person strong enough to hold you—God. Let Him lead. Let Him lift. Let Him straighten what you never could. Just let Him do what He does best: save lives!

Spiritual Growth Affirmation: I will **GROW** out of the carnal mindset that leans on pride instead of the Provider. My brokenness is not a barrier—it's a bridge.

Take this day to **THINK** about how much of your life runs on things you don't fully understand. You flip a light switch expecting the room to light up, though you've never seen the wires behind the walls. You watch TV without understanding how the picture and sound got to your screen. You carry a phone that connects you to anyone, anywhere, without understanding the technology. Yet that never stops you from trusting it to do what it's built to do. So why is it that when it comes to God's Word, now all of a sudden you need a tutor? God's Word ain't calculus—it's simple math: Divide from satan, subtract your sins, add Jesus, and watch your blessings multiply. You don't need to obtain a master's degree or a PhD before you can start living by God's Word. Proverbs 3:5 says, *"Trust in the Lord with all thine heart; and lean not unto thine own understanding"*—and that means God never told you to analyze His Word—He told you to just trust it. God never asked you to study the light—He asked you to walk in it. He needs your commitment—not your comprehension.

When I first opened a Bible, I didn't understand half of what I read. The words "thou" and "thee" sounded like a foreign language, and trying to figure out what it all meant was frustrating. Part of me didn't even want to understand, because the parts I did understand were already convicting me. I didn't want to hear that I had to give up sin. So I'd close the book and walk away, thinking if I didn't read it, I wouldn't be accountable. But God never let me off that easy. Eventually, I realized that God wasn't asking me to be intellectual—He was asking me to be obedient. God needed me to trust every word, not understand every word. That's when I finally stopped trying to analyze everything and started living under it, realizing that standing under God's Word puts me in position to receive what He has for me, whether I get it all or not.

You don't stop using a phone just because you don't understand 5G. You don't stop flipping a light switch because you can't explain electricity. But when it comes to God, you pump the brakes because you don't "get" every verse—or, if we're being real, you just don't want to. Obedience ain't about comprehension—it's about trust. If you can trust a man-made power source to light up your home, why can't you trust the One who made the sun to light your path? Stop waiting to understand before you trust. Just stand, and get under God's Word. You don't need a PhD in theology to walk in obedience—you just need faith. God is asking for soldiers, not scholars. Faith ain't about knowing all the answers; it's about trusting the One who does. You think you need to have it all figured out before you move? No, you need to move and let God figure out the rest. You don't have to understand the "how" to obey the "Who." You don't need to know the whole blueprint to follow the Builder. Stop stalling your life waiting for perfect understanding when God is just asking for perfect trust. Revelation of God's Word don't come from research—it comes from relationship. Flip the switch from comprehension to compliance, trust the Source, and watch God light up everything around you.

Spiritual Growth Affirmation: I will **GROW** out of the
carnal mindset that trusts electricity more than Elohim. If
I can flip a switch in faith, I can follow God in faith.

Take this day to **THINK** about how quick we are to blame satan for everything. We say, "satan is busy in my life," or, "The devil made me do it," like it's second nature. But how often do we acknowledge God's work? When was the last time you said, "God is busy in my life," or, "God made me do it?" If satan can make you do all these bad things, why can't God make you do a lot of good things? The truth is, if God ain't managing your life, it's because you haven't made Him your boss. Letting satan run your life is like staying loyal to a company that keeps shorting your paycheck and cutting your hours. You're giving your all to something that only takes from you and shortchanges you. God, on the other hand, don't force Himself into the role—He waits for you to step up, submit, and make Him your supervisor. God don't need your résumé—just your repentance. The question is, are you still working under the wrong management by clocking in to work for satan daily? If satan ain't checking your work anymore, it's because you've already been crowned his employee of the month—and he's reserved you a VIP parking spot in hell.

Almost due to go home, I remember sitting in jail filling out a reentry form, and it asked, "List previous employment." I just stared at the paper like, "Damn… what do I even put?" The only job titles I had were chaos coordinator, pain promoter, and master manipulator. That was a sad moment—satan never gave me no real job. Just missions to sabotage myself and destroy everybody around me. Selling drugs, sleeping with women, chasing status—I was satan's star employee. Clock in, cause chaos, collect pain disguised as profit. And every time I thought I was winning, I was really just losing a piece of myself. Every dollar I made came with a curse. Every high came with a low that damn near buried me. I wasn't a boss—I was a slave with perks. And the devil? He ain't care if I died, just as long as I kept doing his dirty work. But when the streets spit me out and the high wore off, I had to face the truth: I was being pimped by a system I thought I was in control of. My badge said "sinner," but God offered me a new role—with better benefits. He ain't just hired me—He redeemed me. And the package He came with? Peace. Purpose. Freedom. All the things satan could never put on my payroll.

If your benefits package is chaos, consequences, and confusion—congratulations, you're working for satan. Stop following a manager who leaves you overworked and underpaid. When Paul said, "*Whatever you do, work at it with all your heart, as working for the Lord, not for human masters*" (Colossians 3:23), he wasn't just talking about a job. He was pointing out that our purpose comes from who we serve. You can't thrive without the right supervisor. And satan don't care if you destroy yourself, so long as you stay off God's payroll. When you stop working for hell—a temporary service with permanent layoffs—you get employed by the One who never downsizes. If the devil ain't questioning your work, it's because you're already on his payroll. Get under God's supervision, and you'll find purpose that outweighs any paycheck satan could ever offer. Higher raises from satan don't increase your worth—they lower it. You no longer have to let satan run every department of your life. If the devil ain't bringing you in for evaluations, you no longer work for him—he owns you. You've been working for a liar long enough. Time to switch bosses before your benefits run out. Turn in your resignation to satan—God's hiring on the spot. No referral needed. Just walk in.

Spiritual Growth Affirmation: I will **GROW** out of the carnal mindset of working under the wrong master. I can't serve heaven under hellish management.

Take this day to **THINK** about how waking up each morning is a privilege, not a promise. It ain't the alarm clock, your playlist, or sunlight through the blinds that brought you back—it's God. Flat out. You woke up because mercy clocked in, not because you earned it. The Bible puts it simply in Psalm 3:5, "*I lie down and sleep; I wake again, because the Lord sustains me.*" That's divine investment. And what you gon' do with it—waste it scrolling, chasing clout, or reaching out to beg somebody back who left you? Keep it up. If your day don't start depositing your purpose, don't be surprised when He closes your account. God didn't wake you up to stay asleep. You were chosen to get up and grind in purpose. Every breath you take is a bet God placed on you. That means you owe Him a return. He let you see the sunrise—now show the Son you know what to do with breath. Don't you dare start another day on autopilot, doing dirt and calling it a lifestyle. God didn't wake you up so you could get high, cuss people out, tell lies, cheat on your spouse, sell poison, or keep breaking people who love you. If you think He ain't watching, He is. And if you think His silence means approval, you already lost. Stop mistaking mercy for weakness—He's just giving you time before the consequences crash in. You better stop playing with grace like it don't expire.

Getting high at work like it was just another Monday, I collapsed with my eyes wide open and dilated—barely breathing, barely present. They called the ambulance to treat me, but what I needed was resurrection. My heart had stopped. Flatline. The monitor didn't blink—it gave up. They hit me with Narcan once—nothing. Hit me again—and finally, the line jumped, my chest moved, and life slipped back in. I came to with a nurse screaming my name, but I knew that wasn't just medicine—that was mercy. That was God standing at the edge of death saying, "Not yet." And the craziest part? I still went back to the same dirt He just pulled me out of. I treated survival like a reset button, not a responsibility. But now I live like I'm on loan—because I am. I shouldn't even be here. If you woke up today, don't call that normal. That's grace. That's God placing another bet on you. Don't hand Him back an empty return.

You woke up on purpose—so stop living like God made an accident. Stop treating your mornings like a routine. That ain't a ritual—it's a responsibility. Every time your eyes open, that's heaven saying: "I still got plans for you." But instead of stepping up, you slouch into your vices. If your first instinct is a blunt, a bottle, or a body, you're abusing the assignment. You act like you've got infinite wake-ups to get it right. You don't. The graveyard's full of people who thought they had time. Your waking up wasn't accidental— it was intentional. But what's the point of being blessed with another day if you just bury it in the same sin that almost took you out last time? God ain't keeping you alive so you can keep playing with the fire He already pulled you out of. Your life ain't a treadmill—stop waking up just to run in place. Every time you hit snooze on your calling, you slap the hand that gave you another chance. You got oxygen, but no obedience. Heartbeat, but no hustle. You saw the sunrise—now show the Son why He let you see it. They say God don't make mistakes. If that's true, prove He didn't make one by waking you up this morning.

Spiritual Growth Affirmation: I will **GROW** out of the carnal mindset that abuses mercy. Grace ain't weakness—it's a warning that time is running out. If God woke you up, wake up.

Take this day to **THINK** about how much time we spend checking text messages from people who can't improve our lives one iota. We box out God to scroll through our inboxes, eager to see what others are saying, but leave God's messages unread. The Bible, His divine text message to us, often goes ignored—or worse, we outright block Him by not even opening it. You'll wake up to read about people's gossip instead of waking up to read about God's gospel. You'll check a "wyd" text before checking what God's trying to do in you. You'll scroll for hours through nonsense but won't scroll through the scriptures to gain sense. You'll scroll all day through group chats but won't scroll one minute through God's Word for growth. God's Word is an eternal message that holds the answers to life's deepest questions, far more important than any fleeting conversation in your inbox. You read every text except the one that could save your life—how does that make sense? Stop treating unread texts from people like emergencies while treating God's unread Word like it's optional.

Before I even barely get my eyes open, the first thing I do is reach for my phone—it's almost automatic. When prayer should be the first thing on my mind, my phone is. I give my phone high priority but don't give priority to the Most High. Even though it offers nothing eternal, I basically worship it. And I'm not alone—this disease hits 99% of people, including you. You want to know what addiction looks like? Look no further than your phone. If you can't put it down for five minutes, you're a junkie just like me—and maybe it's time you checked yourself into rehab. Our phones are our drugs. We prioritize staying connected with people, but what about staying connected with God? We make sure we never miss a text from friends or family, but when was the last time we read God's text? Keep ignoring God's texts if you want to—but don't get mad when He takes you off the family plan.

Your Bible is God's inbox, but most of us treat it like spam—unopened, unread, and ignored. The most powerful message you'll ever get is sitting right in your face, but you act like it's irrelevant. Matthew 4:4 reminds us, *"Man shall not live by bread alone, but by every word that proceeds from the mouth of God."* This scripture is a clear reminder that our spiritual nourishment comes from God's Word, and it's not something we can afford to push aside. Just like we need to eat daily, we need God's Word daily. Take God off "read" and give Him some FaceTime. His Word is always ready to guide, comfort, and transform you. We say we don't have time to read the messages in His text, but we somehow find hours to read everyone else's text messages. The text messages from people may be urgent, but only God's messages carry the power to give life. When life has us boxed in, we can always turn to God's inbox to find a message in His text that can bring us relief. Before we scroll out of bed and scroll through our phones, let's first scroll to our knees, then scroll through God's messages in His "text" to see how His Word can impact our lives. If you can't do that, but keep your phone glued to your hand, how you gon' call anybody else an addict when you one of the biggest fiends on the planet?

Spiritual Growth Affirmation: I will **GROW** out of the carnal mindset that puts my phone on a pedestal and God on hold. My soul can't survive on notifications—it needs revelation.

The problems God puts on your **plate** are His way
of saying, "***Eat your vegetables***." You may not
like them, but they'll make you stronger.

Take this day to **THINK** about the problems God puts on your plate. You don't want to touch them—just like those vegetables you hated as a kid. But vegetables are packed with what makes you strong, whether you like them or not. And problems work the same way. Just like a mother knows how much her child can handle when she piles vegetables on the plate, God knows how much to put on yours. He's not overloading you—He's growing you. Hebrews 12:11 says, "*Now no chastening for the present seemeth to be joyous, but grievous: nevertheless afterward it yieldeth the peaceable fruit of righteousness unto them which are exercised thereby.*" So if it's on your plate, it's meant to make you stronger, not take you out. You keep crying about being weak, but you keep running from what would make you strong. Every little inconvenience sends you spiraling—because you still ain't swallowed the struggle that God sent to grow your spine. God's not punishing you—He's prepping you. And that pain? That's protein for your purpose. Don't pray for strength, then push the plate away.

Growing up, I loved *Popeye*. I'd watch him eat spinach and get superhuman strength. My mom used to say, "Eat your vegetables so you can be strong like Popeye." But I wasn't trying to hear that. My thought was, forget Popeye—Wimpy became my favorite, because *I would've gladly paid anybody Tuesday for a hamburger today*. I'd sit at that table forever, pushing veggies around, trying to find ways to make them disappear. But no matter how much I avoided them, they were still what my body needed. And life's problems are the same. I used to dodge every hard thing God put in front of me. Thought if I ignored it long enough, it would go away. But all that avoiding did was make me weaker, not stronger. You can't pray for strength and then run from the very thing God's using to give it to you. Every problem I finally faced was like swallowing that spinach—another muscle added to my faith. The problems I encountered from addiction—strengthened my story to reach addicts. The problems I amassed from marriage—strengthened my story to reach married couples. God never sent problems to punish me. He sent them to prepare me. God ain't force-feeding you—if you don't eat, you don't grow. Simple as that.

Stop scraping God's lessons off your plate. Stop whining about what you don't want to face. You want to get stronger? Then you better start eating what God's serving. The problems in your life don't desert you—because you'd rather skip the vegetables and go straight to dessert. Problems are spiritual vegetables—they don't go down easy, but they give you the strength you're begging God for when life gets hard. You want more strength? You gotta face more struggle. You keep asking God to lift you up but won't lift the cross He wants you to carry. You keep praying for peace but won't press through the pain. You want the reward without the resistance. You think you're going to grow without grinding through what's hard? Problems are the recipe for faith that lasts. Your problems are vegetables for your spirit. They don't show up to shatter you—they show up to shape you. You want to grow, but you refuse to swallow what's meant to feed your faith. God's trying to grow your strength, but you still acting like a child at dinner. Eat your darn vegetables and stop whining!

Spiritual Growth Affirmation: I will **GROW** out
of the carnal mindset of not liking problems. God's
not punishing me—He's portioning my growth.

Take this day to **THINK** about how you're always rushing to rescue people like you're some superhero God never sent. Somebody gets locked up, and you're sprinting to bail them out. Somebody gets hooked on drugs, and you're playing counselor like you can heal what they refuse to face. You keep suiting up like a firefighter, trying to pull people out of blazes they lit themselves— like God's some rookie who needs your backup. But the harder you break your neck to save them, the quicker they'll break your heart. Proverbs 19:19 says, "*A hot-tempered man must pay the penalty; if you rescue him, you will have to do it again.*" That means if you keep stepping in to save people God's trying to teach, you'll keep having to save them again and again, because they won't learn. Maybe God wants them to sit in that pain. Maybe that struggle is their wake-up call, but you keep grabbing the phone from them and hanging it up before they get the message. You're blocking their lesson, and now you mad 'cause they ain't learning—move out the damn way! Stop standing in the middle of God's rescue mission.

When I was deep in addiction, everybody and their momma tried to save me—friends that meant well but were dead wrong. I remember losing a job because I was too high to show up. Instead of letting me sit in that mess, a friend slid me into a job where he worked. But I hadn't changed. I brought the same broken me into that job and lost it, which affected my dude's credibility. Every time somebody tried to carry me out of a hole God was letting me sit in, they only delayed what I needed to learn. Trying to fix someone else's struggle is like doing push-ups for them and expecting their muscles to grow. You can't build someone else's strength—they have to do the work and fight their own fight. I didn't evolve until everyone stepped aside and let me fall on my face—facing my own consequences is what made me realize I had to grow.

The more you keep breaking people's falls, the longer they stand in their pain. Let God be Batman—He don't need a sidekick, but you keep trying to step up like He asked you to be Robin. You out here running yourself in the ground trying to save people God is trying to save from themselves, and now you mad 'cause you tired. Nah, you tired 'cause you doing too much. God keeps sounding alarms in their life, setting fires to burn the mess off, and here you come with a bucket of water like you gon' stop what He's doing. Every time you interrupt their struggle, you cancel their strength. You ain't Captain Save a Soul—stop diving in like God needs your help. Sometimes love is stepping back and letting them drown if that's what it takes for them to finally learn how to swim. You out here sweating, stressed, and going broke trying to fix people you didn't break, when God is tearing them down on purpose to rebuild them right. You're not God's copilot—stay in your lane. It would be wise for you to get the hell out the way before God makes you part of the problem He has to fix next.

Spiritual Growth Affirmation: I will **GROW** out of the carnal mindset of trying to save people from themselves. If I keep breaking their falls, they'll never learn to stand.

Take this day to **THINK** about how life runs on a schedule that no human can rearrange. What God has set, nothing and no one can undo—not even you. Life might feel out of order, but everything that has happened, is happening, and will happen is right on time. Trying to stop God's plan is like trying to stop winter from turning into spring. It's impossible. Those things that broke you, those people that hurt you, were supposed to. And no matter how much you try to force your own plan, no matter how much you try to speed it up or slow it down, God's timing is already locked in. His schedule don't shift for tears, tantrums, or timelines. When it's time, it's time. Not a second before. Not a second after. Nothing in life is out of order. It's been ordered by God. The pain you've faced was a scheduled appointment. That depression you suffered is a scheduled appointment. That drug you got hooked on is a scheduled appointment. Everything. Already penciled in on God's planner. And trust—He don't care about you being uncomfortable or what other plans you had going on. God does not hit pause just because you hit the panic button. What God wrote in permanent ink can't be erased.

There was a time when I didn't see that. Being shot was something I had to go through. Addiction was something I had to go through. Prison and jail stints—something I had to go through. God didn't get surprised by my mess-ups—He factored them into the plan. No failure, no setback, and no bad decision I made could undo what He already had written for me. And every time I thought my life was offtrack, I was exactly where God knew I would be. It was already on His calendar. Nothing I did, no mistake I made, was strong enough to cancel His plan. And looking back, all the places I was trying to run from were places God meant for me to be—to break me, to humble me, and to shape me. Those divorces, that prison bid, that rock bottom—it was all on God's itinerary. I just didn't get the memo. All of what I went through was to help others get through what they're going through. And I wouldn't change a thing. We want to skip the hard parts, but sometimes God takes us the long way because shortcuts don't build strength.

Ecclesiastes 3:1 reminds us that "*to everything, there is a season, and a time for every matter under heaven.*" If you truly believe that, then you know His timing is perfect—even when it feels painful. Roadblocks are His way of rerouting you toward purpose. You're over here thinking life is offtrack because it hurts, but pain is part of the process. Your detours are just God's scenic routes to destiny. You can fight it, cry about it, or deny it—but it's still coming to pass. You're not lost. You're not behind. You're not treated unfairly. You're right where God wants you—whether it feels good or not. Every scar, every tear, every broken piece was placed right where God needed it to be. Stop trying to bring order to something God already ordered. You can't skip what God scheduled to shape you. Trust His timing and trust the tour He's taking you on—even if it feels like the long way around. Because nothing in your life— nothing—is wasted in God's hands. God's calendar don't come with cancellations. What's booked is blessed—even if it breaks you first.

Spiritual Growth Affirmation: I will **GROW** out of the carnal mindset that thinks pain means God's plan got interrupted. His itinerary includes the heartbreak *and* the healing.

Take this day to THINK about how reckless it is to run to everything but God when you're bleeding out spiritually. You're broken, battered, and bruised—but instead of grabbing the Word, you reach for distractions that can't even hold weight. You out here trying to patch bullet wounds with TikTok clips, Google searches, ChatGPT, crack pipes, and shots of liquor. And then you wonder why nothing changes. You trust horoscopes more than the Holy Ghost—that's why your soul stays sick. Matthew 6:33 says, *"Seek ye first the kingdom of God, and His righteousness, and all these things shall be added unto you."* That means don't seek the world before His Word. Don't seek comfort before conviction. If God ain't your first call, don't cry about the fallout. The reason you ain't healed is 'cause your Bible's still sealed. His Word ain't for decoration—it's your defibrillator. It's the only thing strong enough to restart what life tried to flatline. You're walking around dying slowly because you keep looking for solutions in the world's trash while God's truth is sitting on your shelf. First aid ain't optional when you're bleeding out—and neither is God.

Back in school, math was my greatest struggle. I'd sit there flipping through the textbook, frustrated because the answers in the back only covered the odd or even problems, leaving me stuck and guessing on half of them. Then one day, I got my hands on the teacher's edition, and it was like holding gold. It had every answer laid out, and suddenly the struggle wasn't so overwhelming. Although it wasn't the right thing to do, it still provided me with all the right answers. That's exactly how I see God's Word—it's not just a guide; it's the ultimate answer key to life. When the pressure builds, when I feel lost or defeated, I don't have to fumble around looking for solutions—searching social media or calling people who don't give a damn anyway. I've learned to go to God first. His Word is always there, providing the clarity, strength, and the wisdom I need to push through. I don't have to guess—I just have to know that in His manual are all the right answers to get me through life's tests.

Funny how you'll run to ChatGPT but won't run to grab your Bible to sit down and have a chat with G-O-D. Stop Googling for answers to your problems when God already gave you them in Genesis. You keep expecting healing from sources that don't even know your symptoms. That ain't recovery, that's insanity. You'd rather trust the world's vibe than God's voice. You treating spiritual surgery with backyard doctors—no wonder the infection keeps spreading. You've quarantined yourself from the cure. Whatever you're facing, seek God first. Stop turning to things that leave you more broken. That friend can't give you true healing. That psychic can't offer you real hope. That self-help book or podcast can't fill the void in your spirit. That drug or drink can't erase the damage. If prayer ain't the prescription you're filling, don't complain about the pain that's killing you. Too often, we treat God like the kid left waiting to be picked last for a game—only turning to Him after we've exhausted every other option. But He's the one who ensures the win. You'll never ditch your problems by making God your last-ditch effort. God ain't your last lifeline; He's your first and only guarantee. His Word ain't just sacred; it's sustaining—a source of strength that will never fail. Life will throw cuts, bruises, and battles your way, but when you go to God first, He'll equip you with everything you need to come out stronger. God's Word heals the wounds the world cannot see. Stop treating Google like God. Google informs. God transforms. Stop searching the web for what can only be found in the Word.

Spiritual Growth Affirmation: I will grow out
of the carnal mindset of running to the world first.
When I make God my plan A—not my plan B—He
gives me the strength to "C" my way through.

Take this day to **THINK** about all the alarms God has set off in your life—those moments where the chaos was deafening, the consequences were crushing, and you had no choice but to wake up. Struggles are not just random storms. They're God's alarms, blaring to shake you out of the mess you've created for yourself. When you overdosed on that drug, or when you're walking around with a black eye—that's God screaming at you to wake the hell up out of addiction and destruction. When your life starts spiraling out of control and has you tossing and turning, it's God yelling, "Wake your butt up before you wreck yourself!" But instead of waking up, you keep choosing to be covered in your mess, rolling over, and wondering why the same annoying alarms keep going off. Keep hitting snooze if you want—but just know, one day that alarm won't go off again. You'll wish you got out before the whole house burned down. Let's be real—some of the hell you're going through ain't satan, and it ain't God punishing you. It's God trying to rescue you, but you're too comfortable in your mess to see it. He's not trying to ruin your peace—He's trying to ruin your patterns. The longer you sleep through His alarms, the harder the wake-up call's gon' hit. He ain't setting off alarms to annoy you or for fun—He's trying to stop your funeral.

I hit snooze on God's alarms more times than I can count. When I was shot for the first time, it should've been enough to wake me up, but I just rolled over and went back to the streets. When I got locked up, God was practically shaking me to wake up, but I still hit snooze. Even when I overdosed, lying there at death's door, I ignored Him and went right back to the pills. Every stay in rehab, every close call, every near-death experience—those were alarms, loud and clear. But I was too stubborn, too blind, and too caught up in my own foolishness to wake up. It wasn't until my life was completely in shambles—physically, mentally, and spiritually—that I finally got up. God wasn't trying to kill me; He was trying to save me from the death

I was sprinting toward. He turned up the volume because I wouldn't turn down the vileness. He loved me enough not to let me sleep my life away—just like He does with you.

When God sets off alarms in your life, it's not to hurt you—it's to save you. If you keep facing the same struggles, the same heartbreak, or the same consequences, maybe it's time to stop blaming the devil and start listening to God. What is He trying to teach you? What is He trying to pull you out of? Your struggles are a wake-up call to stop living recklessly, to stop making excuses, and to start aligning with His purpose. Stop hitting snooze on the mess you keep making. Every alarm is God's way of saying, "You're still alive 'cause I got plans—not 'cause you're untouchable. Don't get it twisted. Keep trying Me if you want to." Jonah 1:17 shows us that God even used a fish to swallow Jonah up to wake him up and call him to his purpose. God will use whatever is necessary to wake you the hell up. He will let heartache swallow you up. He will let pain swallow you up. He will let abuse swallow you up. He will let addiction swallow you up. God will use your pain and suffering to shake you from that deep sleep of complacency. If He's still setting off alarms in your life, it means He hasn't given up on you. Get up, stop whining, and start changing. God's alarms are loud for a reason—don't ignore them until it's too late. And as long as He's not done, there's still time to get out that bed of mess you've made and make the changes He's calling you to make. If He did it for Jonah, He can do it for you. Keep sleeping if you want to—just don't be shocked when you wake up in hell. That alarm you hate is the only thing keeping your family from starting a GoFundMe for your funeral.

Spiritual Growth Affirmation: I will **GROW** out of the carnal mindset that waits for rock bottom to finally rise. If God's still sounding alarms, I better stop playing dead and get up. I ain't tryna die in my sleep.

Take this day to **THINK** about what you're wearing spiritually—not just physically. In a world obsessed with appearances, it's easy to get caught up in looking good for others, but God is looking deeper. He don't care about the brand stitched on your shirt; He cares about the truth, faith, and righteousness stitched into your soul. How often do we spend hours shopping, planning, and obsessing over what we'll wear—but barely give a thought to the condition of our spirit? We look good on the outside but ugly on the inside. While you're stressing over brand names, God is asking, "Where's your armor?" Are you more worried about impressing strangers than pleasing the One who designed you for greatness? The clothes you wear might boost your confidence temporarily, but what about when the compliments stop? God ain't checking for what's on your back; He's examining what's in your heart. It's not about covering your body with the latest trends—it's about covering your spirit with the protection and purpose God provides. Your fashion stays laced, but your faith stays lacked—what's the point? Don't die in designer clothes while your spirit's in rags.

My mother couldn't afford designer clothes, so my friends and I started hitting malls, grabbing what we wanted, and getting away—or so we thought. I'll never forget the day the school resource officer walked into class, called my name, and took me out. One of our crew had been caught and ratted us out. I risked my future, freedom, and dignity chasing a label that didn't even matter. Just to avoid being judged for not having the "right" clothes. The clothes weren't the real issue—it was about hiding my insecurity. What I truly needed wasn't another man's name on my back; it was God's name in my heart. I had spent my life chasing labels while simultaneously running from the only name that could save me. When Judgment Day hits, Michael Kors and Ralph Lauren can't replace Jesus—grace matters; labels don't.

The Bible puts it plainly in 1 Peter 3:3–4: "*Your beauty should not come from outward adornment, such as elaborate hairstyles and the wearing of gold jewelry or fine clothes. Rather, it should be that of your inner self, the unfading beauty of a gentle and quiet spirit, which is of great worth in God's sight.*" The clothes we wear might change people's opinions of us, but they don't change who we really are. Our true value comes from being adorned with a spirit that honors God. It's not the brands we wear that define us—it's the character we display. When we focus more on our external appearance than our internal spiritual condition, we're dressing up an empty shell. Think about what you're wearing today. Is it just for flex, or are you clothed in qualities that please the ultimate Designer? Instead of being covered in designer labels that fade, choose to wear the armor of God, which never goes out of style. Let your life be a reflection of the values God has stitched into your soul—truth, righteousness, faith, and salvation. Don't worry about impressing the crowd; be concerned with pleasing the Creator. Because at the end of the day, God ain't impressed by our fashion—He's moved by our faithfulness. Besides, if you're not right with God, what's the point in your family burying you in a designer suit to die, only to send you to hell—where it's gon' get burned up anyway?

Spiritual Growth Affirmation: I will **GROW** out of the carnal mindset that values brand names over being branded by grace. When judgment comes, Gucci won't save me—God will.

Take this day to **THINK** about why every time you try to change for the better, life seems to hit you harder. You decide to lose weight, and suddenly every fast-food spot offers buy one, get one free burgers. You stop drinking, and now every channel's running beer commercials. You swear off drugs, and right on cue, your old connect calls offering testers—for free. That's not a coincidence. That's a calculated attack. Pressure ain't punishment—it's proof of purpose. The devil don't bother you when you're already knee-deep in mess—but the moment you start walking toward God, he floods your life with distractions, temptations, and setups. The devil don't fight fair— he fights strategically. And if he's putting in overtime to trip you up, it's because you've been promoted in the spirit. The enemy knows the anointing on your life, and he wants to block it before you walk in it. God promoted you, and now satan's panicking—stressed the hell out. If hell's been busy, it's because you've become a threat. The devil fights hardest when you're finally becoming who God called you to be. If you're not a threat— satan won't mess with you.

I had landed a job, earned my training certification, been asked to speak at my old prison, and was paid to speak to wayward youth. But without fail, temptation waited. It felt like satan had a stopwatch—timing the moment I took a step toward freedom just to pull me back. I remember one time, clear as day: I was serious about quitting drugs; I was trying to live clean. Out of nowhere, my old connect hit me up and said he had some pills he wanted me to try—for free. In that moment, it took everything in me not to say yes. My head remembered what it had cost me, but my body remembered how it felt. I could've died that day. Those pills could've been laced; they could've ended it all. That's how satan moves; he doesn't tempt you with what you hate, he hits you with what you used to crave, studies your weaknesses, and strikes where you're still healing. The more I tried to climb, the harder he tried to drag me back. The strategy of satan is simple: to keep you bound by baiting you with what used to break you.

When you rise, expect resistance. The more determined you are to live for God, the more determined satan is to pull you down. Promotion from heaven brings provocation from hell. But just as the devil intensifies his efforts, God intensifies His protection. If satan is not bothering you, you're no longer a threat, no longer fighting back, and no longer pursuing God's purpose for your life. Every time you ignore God's call and cling to what's comfortable, you're casting your vote as to who will have precedence over your life. 1 Peter 5:8–9 reminds us, *"Be sober, be vigilant; because your adversary the devil, as a roaring lion, walketh about, seeking whom he may devour: whom resist steadfast in the faith…"* The attacks you face are proof that satan knows you're choosing God over him, and that terrifies him. Every attack is confirmation—you've been upgraded in the spirit. So when temptation, trials, and attacks come your way, know that satan sees you as a problem. If hell ain't nervous, you're not a threat. The devil don't chase folks who got his back—only the ones who turn their backs on him. It's not lost on satan that when you can no longer stand the heat in the kitchen, he's gotta add more fuel to the fire to pull you back in.

Spiritual Growth Affirmation: I will **GROW** out of the carnal mindset that mistakes the fight for failure. If I'm under attack, it's 'cause I'm walking in anointing, not weakness.

Take this day to **THINK** about what you're busy doing. Our days are packed with work, errands, social media, and everything in between. You call it "staying busy," but God calls it filling your life with junk so He can't get in. We run ourselves ragged chasing deadlines, making plans, and fulfilling every obligation except the one that matters most—our commitment to God. Stop pretending you overwhelmed—you're just overbooked with everything but God. You can't claim Christ is your main priority when your schedule says He's your side piece. You send God straight to voicemail while you're wide open for satan's every call. You pick up on the first ring. Even if he hits you from an unknown number. We claim we're too tired to pray, but we've got energy to prey on others. Your calendar's got more room for somebody else's spouse than it does for God. You spread gossip but won't spread the gospel. You got time to hit the block, hit the club, and hit send on another rumor—but you can't hit the floor and pray. Stop double-booking your life with God and the devil—choose who gets the reservation. If you don't fill your house with God, don't be surprised when the devil moves in and redecorates. Whatever part of your life God don't run, satan will ruin. We can't be so quick to say we put God first when, somehow, He's always put last on our to-do list.

When I was married, I had my side piece marked on my calendar like a dentist appointment—same time, same day, every week. She had slid into my DMs like most temptation does—smooth, quiet, and calculated. And I bit. Hard. What started as a casual convo turned into late-night meetups, secret text threads, and lies layered so deep I forgot which version of me I was supposed to be that day. I wasn't just cheating on my wife—I was cheating on God. I had time to meet up, time to sneak around, time to delete messages—but no time for prayer, no time for Scripture, no time for repentance. I said I was too busy to serve, but I wasn't too busy to sin. I was giving satan a reserved slot on my calendar while telling God to "hold on." That made me think: The more you let God occupy your time, the less time satan has to occupy your mind. My life wasn't chaotic by accident—it was double-booked by choice. And if you don't intentionally fill your days with God, satan will gladly fill the gaps. Keep your day full of God—it's the only way to block satan from sliding in your DMs.

If you don't let God fill your schedule, satan will make you an appointment—and you won't like the plans he set for you in his planner. Spending all your free time with satan can wind up costing you a lot. He'll book you for nights in jail, days in court, and weekends in the ER. He'll have you spending your time stirring up drama, and spreading lies. But there is a way out. By submitting to God and resisting satan. James 4:7 reminds us, "*Submit yourselves therefore to God. Resist the devil, and he will flee from you.*" Submitting to God ain't just about avoiding sin; it's about staying busy with His work so there's no opening for the enemy to enter. But being busy ain't the problem—it's what you're busy doing that matters. Keeping your schedule full of God makes it hard for satan to book an appointment in your life. Think about your day. How much of it is spent on things that glorify God? How much is wasted on things that leave you empty? If you're not intentional about filling your life with God's disciplines, satan will be intentional about flooding it with his distractions. Gossiping. Plotting. Stirring up hate. Wasting hours on "fun" that leaves you emptier than you started. Every empty slot on your calendar is an entry point for the enemy. Fill it with prayer. Fill it with service. Fill it with purpose. Because if your soul ain't sold out to Christ, it's up for sale to the highest bidder—and satan pays in pain.

Spiritual Growth Affirmation: I will **GROW** out of the carnal mindset that makes room for everything but righteousness. An unguarded life is an open invitation to hell.

Take this day to **THINK** about how disrespectful and cold life can really get. People will stab you in the back without hesitation, jobs will chew you up and spit you out, and loved ones—those you trusted most—will turn on you for a few dollars. It's a world full of frosty hearts and cold shoulders, and when that chill hits, most of us reach for anything to warm our hearts. Alcohol, drugs, meaningless hookups, revenge—you name it. But all that does is leave you freezing in a different way. Those quick fixes are like living in the projects and depending on the oven to warm the place—useless. The warmth you're searching for can't be found in anything this world offers because it's God's Comforter—the Holy Spirit—that truly covers you from the frostbite of life. God's love is your blanket—His Spirit is your insulation. Stop walking around bundled in bitterness, shivering in shame, and covered in chaos when you can be blanketed in God's love and wrapped in His Comforter—the Holy Spirit.

I remember those cold nights in jail, lying on a slab of concrete with nothing but a thin, pathetic excuse for a blanket that barely covered me. Men around me were just as desperate, pulling their arms into their shirts, pacing to keep their blood flowing, and hoping someone would pass down an extra blanket or long john shirt before they were released. As crowded as it was with men, it was cold as hell in there—so cold you could see our breath floating between us like we were passing a blunt around the room. But it wasn't just the cold in that cell; it was the coldness of the people in it too. The poison of their jealousy, resentment, bitterness, anger, and hatred filled the air. Nobody cared about anyone else. Everyone was for themselves, stepping on whoever they had to just to survive. As my mother suggested, I prayed those nights—not for a thicker blanket, but for something to insulate me from the cold harsh reality I was living in. And God answered. His Comforter, the

Holy Spirit, wrapped around my spirit when nothing else could. While my body shivered, He gave me peace that the cold world couldn't take away. The Comforter didn't just warm me—He covered me from what should've killed me. But my dumb butt kept taking the covers off.

People are cold-blooded and cold-hearted, and they have no problem giving you the cold shoulder. They'll serve dope to a mother with kids and not even care about how her children are supposed to eat. They'll take the information you gave in confidence and weaponize it against you the second it benefits them. They'll use you to climb their ladder, then pull it up so you can't follow. They'll smile in your face while plotting to sleep with your spouse. And the next thing you know, they're having an affair and planning to kill you for insurance money. You do not have to keep putting up with the coldness of this world. God offers you shelter, but your silly self would rather stand out in the cold. John 14:16 says, *"And I will ask the Father, and He will give you another Comforter to help you and be with you forever."* Did you catch that? It said *forever*… forever-ever… forever-ever. How reassuring is that? If we can let that André 3000 line from his song "Ms. Jackson" stick with us, why can't we let it stick in our head from the Almighty? This world will smile in your face while slowly twisting the knife in your back. That's why you can't depend on people whose hearts live in the freezer to keep you warm. If you let them, they'll strip you of every ounce of hope and leave you frostbitten from head to soul. When the coldness of the world and its bitterness feel like frostbite on your soul, let God's Comforter cover you like an electric blanket—bringing warmth to a world that's cold.

Spiritual Growth Affirmation: I will **GROW** out of the carnal mindset that settles for broken heaters in spiritual blizzards. The Holy Spirit is my heat, my peace, and my protection.

Take this day to THINK about what it means to claim the blessings that God has set aside specifically for you and that no other person can claim. Often, we hold back, doubting whether we're truly worthy of the dreams and goals we have in our hearts. But like a reservation at an exclusive restaurant, your table is already set, waiting for your arrival. Here's the difference: With God, you don't even need to call ahead or reserve your spot. As one of His, your seat is automatically secured. It's your faith and actions that prepare you to take your place at the table He's already prepared for you. The time to move towards your dream is now. Or are you too busy sitting in your La-Z-Boy, praying—expecting God to just sit your dreams at your propped-up feet? God ain't handing out gold ribbons for half-hearted prayers and bare-minimum efforts. You've got to get up, move, and meet Him in the process. Sitting down when you should be stepping up is the fastest way to miss your moment. Stop waiting for God to show up while you're still stuck in the same place, making the same excuses.

When I was a teenager, I'd spend hours calling into radio stations, hoping to be the right caller to win prizes. In order to win, you had to be a certain-numbered caller, or you had to correctly answer a trivia question. Once, I called in for a chance to win tickets to Rap Fest. I'd done everything right, but to actually claim the tickets, I had to be listening to the station at a specific time to hear them announce the winner. That's where I fell short. I got distracted, out in the streets, probably doing something I shouldn't have been doing. Later, I got a call from my boy telling me that he had heard my name announced on the radio. At first, I thought it was Crime Stoppers. But it was the radio station. I'd missed my chance to claim the tickets because I wasn't where I needed to be when the time came. Looking back, it reminds me that blessings can be reserved for us, but we have to be ready and willing to step forward and claim them. Otherwise, they slip by.

God set the table—but you're too lazy to leave the couch and go get your plate. Crying over missed blessings, when you're the one who keeps canceling your reservation. You have to be some kind of crazy to reject a blessing that God has reserved for you with no requirements other than to just show up. You don't have to be caller number nine, enter a raffle, or spin a wheel. Just answer the call. This is truly sad to see—someone throwing their dream, their blessing, and their place in this world away all because they're too scared. Coming to the table frightens them, so they're content to keep being spoon-fed by a government that's fine with handing out scraps. Afraid to move into their dream, but comfortable with remaining in their nightmare. Get the hell up! Go check into the place God has reserved for you. Go find that mate. Go start that business. Go get that education. Go apply for that job. It's already yours. God has promised that you will get what you deserve when He said, in Luke 14:17, "*Come; for all things are now ready.*" Step forward and take what's already set in place for you, knowing that when you arrive to claim your seat and find it prepared, that's God's way of saying, "Your table been ready. I was just waiting on you. Now eat—before your food gets cold."

Spiritual Growth Affirmation: I will **GROW** out of the carnal mindset that lets fear cancel what faith already confirmed. My seat is reserved—I just need to show up and claim it.

Take this day to **THINK** about how often we treat prayer as a demand, expecting God to deliver exactly what we ask for, exactly when we want it. Matthew 7:7 says, "*Ask and it will be given to you*," and we cling to that like it's a guarantee of instant results. But have you ever thought that maybe God ain't ignoring your prayer—He's igniting something in you while it's in process? He's not refusing to answer; He's refusing to rush. God ain't ignoring your request—He's inspecting the plane before He takes you up. Prayer ain't about quick fixes or instant gratification. Too often, we treat God like a vending machine: We put in a prayer and expect our blessing to drop down immediately. And when it doesn't, we lose our patience. We kick, bang, and shake on heaven's door, desperate for the answer we want, when we want it. But what if the blessing didn't drop because it wasn't ready—or YOU weren't ready? God don't operate on your timeline; He's setting the conditions for something better, something lasting. God's delays are divine preparation for a purpose greater than your expectations.

During one of my prison stints, I shared a cell with a man who only showered once a week—every Tuesday. The stench tested my faith, and his refusal to clean the cell only made it worse. I prayed constantly, "God, if You don't remove him, I'm going to lose it." I was convinced that the only way God could answer my prayer was by getting this man out of my cell. But God didn't move him. Instead, He moved something in me. He used that situation to teach me patience, endurance, and how to see people beyond their flaws. I was praying for a change in my situation—God was using my situation to change me. That stink on him was used to remove what stunk in me that God wanted to root out. While I thought I was losing my sanity, God was sanitizing my spirit. I was praying for relief, but God was giving me refinement. Turns out, after God settled my spirit, I learned he had only taken a shower once a week because he had been raped in one before. Still, it was all God's timing—not on my terms, not at my speed, and definitely not under my control. God applied pressure not to break me, but to prove I was ready for the promise.

When you pray, have you ever thought that God's "holdup" might be His way of protecting you? Sometimes, when you pray for peace, God don't just hand it over—He allows chaos to shape you, teaching you how to be peaceful. When you pray for strength, He don't just increase it—He sends all kinds of hell your way that will break you down before it builds you up, so when you face something deeper later, you won't have to run back begging for it again—your strength should've already been forged from everything you've survived. Think of it like this: When you're scheduled for surgery, you don't just walk in and go straight under the knife. The instruments have to be sterilized, the room prepped, the surgeon ready. You wouldn't want a rushed surgery—you'd trust the process, knowing that the preparation is what ensures a successful healing. God works the same way. That job you're praying for? Maybe He's still cleaning the environment by removing toxic people. If God hasn't moved you into your prayer yet, trust that He's busy cleaning house—dusting the cobwebs, sweeping out people. He's scrubbing that place clean and making things spotless so you won't end up in a bucket of tears when you step into the blessing prepared just for you. God's not late—He's just not letting you walk into a mess He's still mopping up.

Spiritual Growth Affirmation: I will **GROW** out of the carnal mindset that sees pressure as punishment. God ain't dragging His feet—He's dragging out the trash before I move in.

Take this day to THINK about how many times we approach prayer with the wrong mindset, treating God like He's a DJ. We throw up our requests and expect Him to "play our song," spinning the tracks of our desires exactly how and when we want them. "God, can You give me this? God, can You give me that? Can You do this? Can You do that?" That's not prayer—that's spoiled entitlement. Prayer ain't about getting what you want when you want it and how you want it. You think prayer is like Burger King where you can have it your way? No! It's about aligning yourself with His will and purpose for your life. Stop treating prayer like a wish list—God ain't Santa, He's the Surgeon. When we treat prayer as a way to satisfy our selfish cravings, we reduce it to a transaction instead of a transformation. James 4:3 says, *"When you ask, you do not receive, because you ask with wrong motives, that you may spend what you get on your pleasures."* And that's why He doesn't answer our prayers. We approach it selfishly, expecting God to give us quick fixes for our problems or quick thrills to satisfy our fleeting desires. We toss up requests like lazy prayers in the form of elevator pitches, expecting elevation. But God don't move off weak prayers with weaker motives. God refuses to let us pimp Him. Prayer ain't your hotline to comfort—it's your connection to the cross.

When I was in my teens, I used to sneak and call those 1-800 hotlines late at night, chasing something I thought would bring me satisfaction. I'd sit there, listening to voices on the other end, thinking they could offer me instant thrill. You could pick from a menu of women like you were ordering drive-thru—every type of fantasy right there at your fingertips. But me? I always pressed number 2—the "school teacher" option. And looking back, she could've been every bit of 400 pounds, with a mouth full of dentures, living off welfare, and chewed tobacco—but she had a voice like a Victoria's Secret model that could make you forget all that. In seconds, she'd give me exactly what I wanted, right when I wanted it. But that's the trap—it was all fantasy. No matter how good it sounded, it left me empty, my thoughts dirty, and my mama's phone bill sky-high. And that's the same way too many of us treat prayer—as if God's on the other end ready to fulfill our every request the second we "press a button." Prayer ain't designed to gratify your instant cravings—it's meant to grow your eternal character.

Too many people expect God to work like those late-night hotlines—instant response, zero accountability, and tailor-made to their selfish cravings. Prayer ain't about pushing God—it's about letting Him pull purpose out of you. Each prayer strengthens your faith, deepens your connection, and builds your endurance for the journey ahead. Too often, though, we misuse it, acting as if God is on standby to fulfill our every whim. Prayer ain't your backstage pass to blessings or a delivery service with next-day shipping for your wants; it's a development process for your purpose. You want God to speed up, but He's waiting on you to slow down. It's the tool God gives you to grow, endure, and step into who He's called you to be. God won't pick up if your prayer line's full of lust and laziness. Too many of us are selfish Christians, only concerned with what God has to give, ignoring what God may want from us. That's not how it works. God uses prayer to refine us, to teach us patience, to calm us, and to prepare us for His purpose. When you pray, don't just ask for what you want—ask for what He wants for you. It's not, "God, can You give me another job?" Instead, it's, "God, what job would You have for me to do for You?" Prayer ain't about twisting God's arm—it's about bending your knees so your walk stays straight.

Spiritual Growth Affirmation: I will **GROW** out of the carnal mindset that sees God as a genie. I'm not here to make demands—I'm here to be developed.

Take this day to **THINK** about how often we kill ourselves trying to measure up to people who don't even know what they stand for. You chasing likes from people who don't even like you, followers from folk who label you a fool, and comments from clowns who couldn't care less about you. You think your value rises with your follower count? You think the more Facebook friends you got, the more valid your existence? No. Underneath that you're still the same insecure, low-self-esteem person you've been your whole life. Understand that what's trendy today is trash tomorrow. Today it's skinny jeans, tomorrow it's cargos—then back again. One day you're celebrated for being bold, the next you're canceled for the same thing. Society's standards flip like coins—one day it's filling up your head with lies, the next it has you chasing your tail trying to live by 'em. Either way, you lose. The world's rulers keep moving. But God's ruler? Fixed. Unchanging. Genesis 1:27 says, "*So God created man in His own image, in the image of God He created him; male and female He created them.*" You're already crafted in perfection—why keep chasing an approval system built on confusion? Trying to keep up with the Joneses or the Kardashians will only have you running in circles. And even if you manage to "fit in," you'll end up losing the very identity God gave you. Stop breaking your back trying to fit into a world that's allergic to God and addicted to applause.

In prison, that same sickness ran deep and still does. Men would flip through those prison catalogs like they were scriptures—obsessed with ordering the latest kicks, the flyest thermals, the most up-to-date gear, just to step on the yard like they were walking a runway. And yeah, I got caught in that mess. Every time the new catalog dropped, I wanted to be the first one to rock something new. Couldn't be seen in last month's style—wasn't "in" no more. I did all that… just to impress men who had life bids and to proclaim that I was the first one with it. Spent all my energy measuring myself against inmates who were still measuring themselves against lies. Until one day I said, "Damn that. I ain't breaking my neck to win a fashion show in a place where nobody's free." I stopped chasing a look and started chasing the Lord. I stopped sizing myself up against men who God could bring down to size. It was best for me to compare myself to a God who never fails than men who always fall. Once you know who your real Master is, you stop dressing for slaves and start living for the one who sets captives free.

Get off social media and stop measuring yourself by those foolish challenges. You do everything you see the world do. In fact, you like challenges? Here's one: You think you got real followers? Go jump your happy ass off a cliff and see how many follow you then. That "like" button don't mean loyalty. In a world obsessed with taking selfies, here's what you need to know—God made you in His image. And since you were created to look like Him, that means your first selfie was when He brought you into this world. When you see you, you're supposed to see God. But instead of owning that, you're too busy trying to look like the world and measure up to its broken ruler. The world rewards masks—God honors the mirror. What's wrong with how God made you? Who convinced you that your Creator messed up and you needed to upgrade yourself to fit their trends? You ain't a mistake—you're a masterpiece. When you size yourself up by the world, you'll always come up short. The world says be louder, God says be still. The world says buy more, God says be more. The world says follow trends, God says follow truth. And the truth is—every time you chase the crowd, you crawl further from your calling. God's image doesn't need filters. So stop Photoshopping your spirit to please a world that can't even decide what it wants. God already gave you your value—why downgrade just to fit in with people who still don't know who they are? What's wrong with you? Get your life together. It's time you knock it off trying to be a knockoff of people who ain't even real. A fake copying a fake is still a fake.

Spiritual Growth Affirmation: I will **GROW** out of the carnal mindset that confuses applause with approval. The crowd can clap today and cancel me tomorrow—God's love stays constant.

Take this day to **THINK** about how many risks you take daily without even batting an eye. You ain't scared to meet a stranger off the internet, eat food handed to you by someone you'll never see again, or hop in a car with a complete unknown and trust they'll take you to the right spot. You'll ride in a plane flown by a pilot you don't know, who might be high, half-asleep, or halfway checked out. You'll trust unfamiliar people with your life, but won't trust the God who gave you breath? You'll risk it all for an online hookup, but freeze up when God says, "Move"? That makes no sense. You gamble your life on pills you didn't see manufactured, pilots you don't know from a can of paint, and drivers you didn't screen—but when the Creator of the universe calls you to step into purpose, now you act like you need a risk-free guarantee with no fine print and a PowerPoint presentation? Come on. Just dive in. You trust a GPS to reroute you when you miss a turn, but won't trust God to redirect your life when you take a wrong turn? Fear don't disappear just 'cause you quote a verse. But faith? Faith shuts fear up when you move anyway. If you can trust Uber with your destination, why not trust God with your destiny?

And I ain't talking from theory—I'm talking from trenches. I wasn't afraid to pop a pill I couldn't pronounce, even though it could've been laced with fentanyl. I wasn't scared to walk into some sketchy New York basement to pick up my shipment, knowing it could've been my last day on earth. When it came to sex, I wasn't worried about no protection—I went in raw without blinking. I played Russian roulette with my life daily, but somehow I had the nerve to hesitate when God said, "Go." You see the problem? I risked it all for sin, but second-guessed salvation. I wasn't scared to get high, run into danger, or move weight across state lines—but I acted like God's calling was too risky. That's backwards as hell. And the crazy part? I didn't need courage for the chaos—I needed it to chase my calling. I said I wouldn't fly in a plane because I was scared to crash, but I was crashing every day. One day, I said,

"Nah, I'm done letting fear drive. It didn't stop me from doing dirt." So I got on that plane. Scared, sweaty-palmed, and still shaking—but I got on. Now when fear breathes down my neck, I just tell it to save its breath—it's wasting it on a dead cause. Go scare somebody else. Matter of fact, that somebody else might be you—since you still letting fear call the shots in your life.

You'll put your faith in anybody and everybody, but treat God's faith like it's a scam. Like He's out to con you. It's the presence of bravery when you know God's walking with you, even when your next step feels like a cliff. His promise is worth more than the pain you will experience to get there. Having faith means moving when every nerve in your body says stay still. Peter ain't wait to feel brave before he stepped out that boat—he moved, and the miracle followed. That blind man didn't ask for a flashlight—he got up and walked without seeing. No disrespect to the blind, but you sitting up here with better vision than them but still scared to death to budge. Let me tell you something: You keep saying you're waiting on God—but truth is, God's been waiting on you. You think fear is a red light—but sometimes it's just a test to see if you trust Him more than your feelings. Psalms 56:3–4 says, *"When I am afraid, I put my trust in You. In God, whose word I praise—in God I trust and am not afraid."* Key word: When. Not if. Fear's gon' show up—but when it does, that's your cue to step anyway. Walk on your water. Move like the blind man. If you're waiting for fear to leave the room before you move, you'll die waiting. Ain't no right time. Today is the day. The day that the Lord has made. You can't get done what you need to do if you don't start doing it. 'Cause if you can have the faith to follow a GPS screen for directions, you can have the faith to follow God's voice for instructions.

Spiritual Growth Affirmation: I will **GROW** out of
the carnal mindset that waits for fear to leave before I walk
in purpose. If Peter can step while scared, so can I.

Take this day to **THINK** about why you're still in the dark, balled up in your bed, crying your eyes out. Walking through life with your head down. Why? Why keep pouting, whining, and throwing a fit about how life's treating you? What good is it doing? Nobody feels sorry for you—and to keep it real, they don't care. Maybe life's treating you like that because you keep serving the same plate of excuses. Yeah, some storms are out of your control, but if we keep it a buck—a lot of that mess has your name all over it. Stop sitting there playing the victim, hosting pity parties like life owes you a parade. Nobody's coming to hand you a pacifier. God didn't build you to wallow in weakness—He built you to win despite your struggles. But you can't win if you refuse to step beyond those four walls you hide behind all day. Life is gon' hit hard—but throwing tantrums won't change it. You need to invite God into that room and let His Word be the refreshment. Let His truth slap some sense into you, wake you up, and remind you that even when life feels over, He's just getting started.

Man, when I got out of prison, I threw pity parties like I was hosting a festival. Homies? Gone. Job? Couldn't get one. Family? Distant. Daughter? Didn't even want to look at me. And instead of inviting God, I was handing out invites to people just as broken as me—people who wanted to sit in the dark and complain. People who kept me stuck because that's all they knew. I didn't want to invite God to my pity party, because I knew He was gon' tell me to grow up, to stop crying, to own my role in my mess. I didn't want to hear that. I wanted to sit there, marinate in my misery, and act like a victim. And let me be real—I made sure I always sent satan an invite—by breaking things, cussing people out, and cursing God for not helping me. He never missed a party. But God? I didn't want Him stepping foot near me. Because I knew if He showed up, the party would get shut down quick. God don't sit around and entertain your excuses; He calls you to rise.

If you're tired of crying in the dark, stop drawing the curtains on your own deliverance. Jonah 4:10 shows us God ain't gon' let you stay in that pitiful mindset. He'll send that Word to call you out and remind you who you are, just like He did Jonah. When Jonah was sulking, God exposed that his pity party was blocking his purpose. You're busy crying about what didn't happen, but God is ready to do something new—if you'd stop throwing a fit long enough to listen. You're stuck on repeat, crying over the same old song—God's trying to remix your life. He's getting tired of mopping up all your tears that came from all your moping. God's not coming to your pity party to bring you a mop and some tissue. He's coming to bring a squeegee—to wipe up the huge puddle from all your crying, pouting, and whining you been doing, to clear your vision so you can finally see past yourself. You want to sit in misery, but God wants to give you momentum. He's ready to take that pain and flip it into purpose, turn that struggle into strength. You've been sitting in that corner too long—it's time to stand up. And when God walks into your pity party, He brings His own DJ—the Holy Spirit—to flip the vibe. David's praise wasn't polished; it was pure, and it moved heaven. By the time He's done, you'll be dancing like David danced (2 Samuel 6:14), even if you only know how to do the two-step. Stop sulking, start inviting God, and let Him serve up His Word—because that's the only refreshment that'll get you back on the dance floor, dancing circles around the enemy who tried to take you out.

Spiritual Growth Affirmation: I will **GROW** out of the carnal mindset of letting satan be my DJ at my pity party. He plays nothing but sad songs. I'm inviting God. I need this party turnt up.

Take this day to **THINK** about why you need to stop beating yourself up for not being the "perfect Christian." There's no such thing. God didn't call you to be flawless; He called you to be faithful. God ain't looking for perfection—He's looking for participation. Forget what people say about where they think you should be in your walk. They have no idea what it took for you to even get here. They didn't see the nights you fought with yourself just to choose God over your old habits. They didn't see the moments you felt like giving up but kept pushing anyway. They didn't see the days when you said to yourself, "I can't go on anymore." The hell with them. You've already made more progress than they'll ever give you credit for, and guess what? God sees all of it. It's not about hitting some imaginary mark or living up to someone else's expectations; it's about thanking God for bringing you a long way. Stop letting them trick you into thinking that just 'cause you tripped in your steps, you're not worthy to walk with God. Who are they to judge you? They don't know your story, they don't know your struggle, and they sure don't know what God has planned for you.

When I first started walking with God—more like tiptoeing, really—I was trying my best, but, man, it felt like I couldn't catch a break. The moment I stumbled, here came somebody quick to say, "And you supposed to be a Christian!" I can't count how many times I heard that. It became too much. It made me feel like I wasn't good enough, like I wasn't even worthy of calling myself a believer. I'd look in the mirror and wonder if God was as disappointed in me as I was in myself. Did He feel the same way as those who judged me? But here's what I had to learn: God's grace ain't about fixing me overnight—it's about walking with me through the process. I had to remind myself of 2 Corinthians 12:9, "*My grace is sufficient for you, for my power is made perfect in weakness.*" Those words hit me like a freight train. I realized my mistakes didn't disqualify me—they qualified me for grace. I'm a Christian in progress, not a Christian in perfection—grace is still doing the work. Grace didn't show up because I had it all together—it showed up because I didn't.

Being a Christian ain't about being perfect—it's about being real, being committed, and being willing to get back up every time you fall. Let 'em keep talking out their mouth—just make sure you keep walking in your faith. Your stumbles don't cancel your salvation—they confirm you're still climbing. Stop beating yourself up for falling short, because every stumble is proof you're still moving forward. Of course, you're vulnerable. The devil has turned up his attack because he knows you're done with him. Like a cheating man who would do everything in his power to win back a woman. Don't let anyone—including yourself—make you feel like you're failing. Being a Christian ain't easy—and if someone tells you different, they lying. It's a walk of faith, not flawlessness, and every single step counts. Forget the critics, because their judgment don't mean a thing in the eyes of God. He don't measure you by their opinions; He measures you by your obedience. This walk is about persistence, not perfection. The next time someone throws shade at your faith, remind yourself: They didn't bring you this far, and they sure don't have the authority to take you anywhere. If ever someone says to you, "And you supposed to be a Christian!" you look them dead in the eye and tell them, "You're right—I am a Christian. But I'm not supposed to be perfect."

Spiritual Growth Affirmation: I will **GROW** out
of the carnal mindset of seeking perfection in my
walk with Christ. My imperfections don't disprove
my faith—they prove my need for grace.

Take this day to **THINK** about all the stress pressing down on you right now. You got a spouse running around on you, but still expecting loyalty. You're sitting in a doctor's office waiting on news that might flip your whole life upside down. Bills stacked so high, you feel buried alive—and your phone's full of people who can't help and don't even ask how you're holding up. You're one problem away from spiraling, one bad decision away from throwing it all away, and the people closest to you don't even see the war you're fighting in silence. And you're thinking, "What the hell is God doing, trying to kill me? Does He see what I'm battling?" He does. But listen—God hasn't gone quiet because He's heartless. He's quiet because He's testing. This ain't neglect— it's a spiritual stress test. Just like doctors strap you up and throw you on a treadmill to see if your heart can handle real pressure, God straps trials on you and throws you onto life's treadmill. It feels like you're running yourself ragged, but it's only to see if your faith can keep pumping under weight. He don't test you to tear you apart—He tests you to toughen you up. Pressure reveals power. Resistance reveals roots. And if you're still standing, He will occasionally bring you in for testing.

I was living in a garage, dodging court cases, numbing myself with pills, trying to escape everything and everyone—including God. Foreclosure let- ters were coming in. My daughter barely spoke to me. I was ashamed, iso- lated, and exhausted. I kept praying, "God, just take one thing off me. Just one." But instead of easing the load, He let it stack. And now I understand why. All that time, God was doing the same thing to my spirit that the doc- tors did to my body when I went in for what I thought was heartburn. The pain wouldn't stop, so they wired me up and made me run that treadmill while they monitored how my heart handled pressure. They weren't trying to comfort me. They were trying to confirm my condition—checking for clogged arteries. And that's what God was doing. He wasn't being silent—He was studying. Watching how I responded under weight. Would I collapse, or would I keep stepping? That wasn't punishment—it was preparation. He had to know if I could endure what I was asking Him to elevate me into. Storms separate the real from the religious.

When life sits on your chest, relax—God's just checking your pulse. Before God trusts you with elevation, He'll test you with exhaustion—when your kids push your patience, your spouse gets on your last nerve, and your job feels like prison time. You want God to lift the pressure, but He's watching how you move while it's still pressing down. Don't confuse silence with absence— it's just the quiet part of the test. James 1:2–3 says, "*Consider it pure joy when you face trials of many kinds, because the testing of your faith produces persever- ance.*" God is saying, "Stop crying over the pressure—I sent it to prove you. That pain ain't pointless; it's producing something in you that comfort never could." That ain't religious talk—that's survival instructions. He's telling you to be joyful, because when greater storms come, you won't fold under them. Why? Because He already gave you just enough grief to grow through. It's your fault if you don't grow through what you go through. You praying for relief while God is training your resilience. You asking Him to cancel the fight when He's trying to condition your faith. Look here: When the load piles on—kids wildin', money short, body weak, mind racing, trust broken, and peace nowhere to be found—don't trip. Don't panic. Don't think He forgot you. God hasn't gone AWOL—He leaves no child, especially one of His, left behind. That weight on your heart ain't random—it's just a spiritual stress test.

Spiritual Growth Affirmation: I will **GROW** out of the carnal mindset that God has abandoned me when my life is falling apart. I'm hooked up to heaven's monitor. God ain't ignoring me—He's checking my vitals.

Take this day to THINK about how quick we are to act surprised when God does exactly what He said He would do. You praying for a breakthrough like He's powerful—then panicking like He's powerless when the pressure hits. That don't add up. Why are you shocked when He opens a door He built? That's like flipping a switch and acting surprised when the plugged-in lamp turns on. Of course it lit up—it's connected to the source. And you? You're connected to the Most High. Plugged into His Son, you're supposed to receive power. His power was never meant to be some rare cameo—it's supposed to be your daily reality. If God saved your life, cleared your record, brought your child back, healed you from what the doctors said you wouldn't walk away from—He just showed you favor that nobody can explain. That's not a fluke. That's faith in action. That's divine voltage. That's His hand moving and His will unfolding. Doing what only He can do. But the problem is, we treat His power like our name was called to come to the front row on *The Price Is Right* instead of a guarantee. You cry out, "God, help me," and then act shocked when He actually shows up and tells you to, "Come on down." Stop treating His consistency like a surprise. God doesn't flicker—your faith does. The only reason you're still breathing, still standing, and still sane is because you still attached to the Power Line—God.

Surviving my second shooting as the shooter stood over me was frightening. That day, I knew it was the end for me. Why did I survive after being on the brink of death? I was shocked that God would keep someone as evil as me alive. He allowed me to survive what could have easily sent me packing to meet my breaker—satan. 'Cause the way I was living at the time, I wasn't going to see the One who made me. But now I see that the shooting was more than just a lucky break—it was a sign of God's power at work. Divine intervention that was the prevention of my demise. Even when I was far from Him, God was keeping me close, connected to His power and purpose. Protecting me, guiding me, and setting the stage for something greater than I could see.

When you stay plugged into God, even your darkest night starts glowing like a sunrise. That power surge you feel? That's what happens when faith flips the breaker. Don't act shocked—expect it. His grace ain't a flicker—it's a live wire. And when that current flows, strongholds break, addictions crumble, minds shift, and hearts come back to life. Ephesians 3:20 says, "*Now unto Him that is able to do exceeding abundantly above all that we ask or think, according to the power that worketh in us.*" That power ain't out there somewhere—it's already working inside you. If God kept you from what should've killed you, showed up when everybody else dipped, or gave you peace in the middle of absolute hell—stop calling it luck. That's love. That's proof. That's power. You keep wondering why your light's dim—it's because doubt has been shorting out your switch. Flip it. Flip that thing from fear to faith. From panic to praise. From surviving to walking in salvation. The lamp don't ask questions when it lights up—it just knows it's plugged in. So should you. Stay plugged in to God, and watch how He lights your life up. If you ever find yourself shocked by what God *ain't* doing in your life, check if your faith is still current and you're still connected to Him—'cause when God cuts the power, He don't send disconnect notices. He just shuts it off and leaves you in the dark.

Spiritual Growth Affirmation: I will **GROW** out of the carnal mindset of being stunned by what God said He'd do. God's power should shock the world—not me.

Take this day to **THINK** about the times God had to sit you down to stop you from sitting yourself in a grave. You're out here mad at life because everything is falling apart—doors slamming shut, opportunities drying up, and people walking away—but what if that's God pulling you off the field before you destroy everything He built in you? Sometimes God will take everything from you just to save you from yourself. You think you're being punished, but God is protecting you from the next hit that would've taken you out for good. You ain't losing—you're being sat down so you can learn how to stand up the right way. The truth is, God will sideline you and put you under construction when you're too busy chasing your own destruction to realize you're running straight off a cliff. He's putting you in timeout before you run out of time to get it right. You weren't losing the game—you were losing your mind, and God had to step in. And you keep fighting to get back in a game He's been trying to pull you out—not to shame you, but to sharpen you. To sit you down, replay the film, and show you where the mistakes were made.

God sat me down more times than I can count. He sat me in the back of squad cars, in solitary confinement, in prison cells, and in rehab centers. Each time, I thought it was just life happening. I believed I was just "thawing out" before my next run, but the truth was, God was taking me out the game and putting me on the bench to keep me from getting a life-ending injury. I didn't see it at first—I was too caught up in the game to recognize that He was protecting me from my own destruction. It wasn't until my last prison stint that I began to understand what He was doing. God was sidelining me for a reason. He saw how satan was beating the hell out of me and knew I needed Christ, my Corner Man, to step in. He wasn't pulling me out of the ring of life—He was giving me the space to grow into who He created me to be. Repeatedly and ironically, God took me out the game so that I wouldn't lose, but win.

You mad God benched you, but He saw the play you were about to run would've ended your career. Just like a coach who pulls a player out of a game, God knows when He needs to put us on the bench—not because we're no longer needed, but because we need a moment to regroup. He sees us running on pure emotion, making mistakes, or just exhausted. He don't remove us from the game completely; He pulls us aside to let us breathe, regain our focus, rehydrate our bodies with His Word, and come back stronger. God does the same with us. He sits us down not to punish us but to help us catch our breath, reflect on our lives, and prepare for the next phase. As Jeremiah 29:11 reminds us, "*For I know the plans I have for you, declares the Lord, plans to prosper you and not to harm you, plans to give you a hope and a future.*" When you're standing on everything but the truth, God will eventually sit you down. His sideline moments are not about rejection but redirection. Being benched by God hurts—until you realize He was saving you from a hit you couldn't survive. God ain't punishing you—He's protecting His greatest investment.

Spiritual Growth Affirmation: I will **GROW** out of the carnal mindset that sees being sidelined as punishment. God pulled me off the field before my next move became my last one.

Take this day to **THINK** about how a pencil can't make a mark without losing a little of itself—and neither can you. With that being true, why do you beg for progress but run from the process of pruning and shaping that's meant to prepare you to make your mark in this world? You want purpose without pain, strength without stripping, and transformation without truth. That's not faith—that's fantasy. You swear you're ready for your breakthrough, but can't even sit still while God tries to sharpen you. The moment He goes to strip away what's killing you, you put up a hell of a fight. You fold at the first scrape. You cry when He starts carving. You want to be used by God, but you jump every time He brings out the blade. Growth don't happen in comfort zones—it happens on the edge of discomfort. Every sharpened pencil loses a part of itself to create its mark. But that's the price of being effective. That's the cost of being called. You say you're ready to be great, but you still guarding the dull parts He's trying to shave. The reason you can't shave the fat is because you won't let God strip you of the ice cream and cake. The reason you can't stop cheating on your spouse is because you won't let God strip away your lust. The reason your story ain't changing is because you keep erasing God out instead of letting Him sharpen you. Sit still and let Him scrape.

In prison, I used to keep about fifteen sharpened pencils taped together—stashed on the yard, in the school building—ready to defend myself at any moment. That was my weapon. My insurance policy. But as I think back, I learned something interesting about pencils. A pencil can't be sharpened unless a part of it is stripped away. Looking at that, parts of my life had to be shaved in order to be useful. My life stayed dull for years. No edge. No point. No purpose. I was hiding behind potential while rotting in plain sight. God had given me a gift, but I buried it under painkillers, women, and pride. Popping pills like breath mints. Blowing up on people like a grenade with no pin. Sleeping with women, confusing lust for validation. I was surrounded by friends who couldn't sharpen me because they were just as dull. And worst of all, I had a miscreant mindset that saw correction as control and chaos as character. But then God pulled me aside like a dull pencil. And He erased wickedness out of my life. He peeled away some people. Scraped every fake layer I used to survive. He carved off who I pretended to be. And every time it cut, He reminded me: "I'm not punishing you—I'm stripping you to sharpen you. To better write your story."

So yeah, being sharpened hurts. But staying dull is worse. You're so afraid to let God grind on you because you think it'll ruin your image. But let's be real— you ain't been writing nothing but confusion with that sad, dull existence you call life anyway. You keep wondering why your story won't change—but you won't let the Author edit the parts that need to be erased. You're praying for a new story—but keep protecting the same broken narrative. Isaiah 1:25 says, "*I will turn my hand against you; I will thoroughly purge away your dross and remove all your impurities.*" That means He's not coming just to comfort you—He's coming to cut. Not to harm, but to purify. To strip off everything that's been dulling your destiny. So let the process hurt. Let it bleed. Let it scrape your soul clean. Because after the stripping comes the sharpening—and after the sharpening comes the story that'll outlive the pain. God ain't breaking you down— He's making you usable. And maybe you're asking, "How do I even let God sharpen me?" Simple. By reading His Word. The Bible is God's pencil sharpener. Put your mind in it—and it'll grind away every lie, every layer of pride, every toxic thought you've been writing with. You wanna be whole? Then stop running from the Sharpener. Get in His Word and let it do what it was sent to do: strip you of evil and sharpen you so that you can make your mark on this world.

Spiritual Growth Affirmation: I will **GROW** out of the carnal mindset that fears being stripped—because to better write my story, God's gotta peel some layers. A pencil can't be sharpened unless a part of it is stripped away, and neither can I.

Take this day to **THINK** about how much of your God-given power has been reduced to ashes because you let somebody else's mouth play arsonist—drenching your dreams in lighter fluid and tossing sparks without care. God has placed fire in your spirit—but you keep handing your beliefs, dreams, and goals to folks who only carry water. How many times have you handed your self-worth over to people who didn't even know what to do with it? Every time you believe someone who tells you you're not enough, every time you let their insecurities speak louder than God's promises, you're giving them the match and you're left standing in the ashes. Ain't you getting fed up with letting people dictate your worth? Haven't you had it up to here with letting social media keep you antisocial? God didn't make you for dust—He made you for dominion. But you would rather be liked than lit. You'd rather fit in than stand out. And because of that, you're out here passing out gasoline to people who never wanted you to shine in the first place. They speak death, you inhale it. They throw shade, you camp in it. And then you cry out to God, wondering why your fire's gone. It's because you let somebody with no plan for your life tear down what heaven custom-built. Their words only burn if you believe them.

An associate I was locked up with from Dayton, Ohio, was murdered in a drug deal gone wrong. The assailants kidnapped him, placed him in his car, and set his car ablaze. In the end, his family had no choice but to cremate him. The physical body that God had created was reduced to ashes by a senseless act of violence. In a similar way, I once let others' negativity and harshness kidnap my self-esteem and allowed their words to burn my hopes and dreams down to nothing. Each time I allowed people's comments to matter more than God's calling, it was like throwing another match onto the fire of self-doubt. I was letting what God created in me be cremated by the opinions of others. In truth, their words only had as much power as I allowed. I was giving people permission to burn away the very things God had placed inside of me. God called me to be distinguished, not to be extinguished by people.

Stop giving flammable folks access to your potential. Let your dream be fireproof. Don't let someone else's limited perspective burn away your limitless potential. People's thoughts about you don't override what God spoke into you. The same ones trying to burn down what's inside you didn't create it, so they hold zero weight in defining its worth. You out here acting like their words carry power, but the only authority they have is what you keep surrendering. Why keep lettin' them blow out your fire like it's just birthday candles? God already told you in Isaiah 43:2, "*I will be with thee… when thou walkest through the fire, thou shalt not be burned; neither shall the flame kindle upon thee.*" People will always toss lighter fluid with their opinions, but the flame can't win unless you bow to the heat. The fire God lit in you was never meant to flicker—it was meant to torch doubt and fear. And anyway, if their words can burn your dream, maybe it's 'cause you stopped being on fire for God.

Spiritual Growth Affirmation: I will **GROW** out of the carnal mindset that lets critics cremate my calling. My worth ain't up for debate—it's already been declared by God.

Take this day to THINK about the natural disasters life keeps throwing at you. Storms, tornadoes, hurricanes—each one trying to take you out in a different way. A storm? That's your paycheck disappearing, your car tapping out, your relationship hanging by a thread—it shakes you, but you can survive it. A tornado? That's when life spins you without warning—pink slip on Friday, best friend in your bed when you ain't home, streets got your child— it tears through quick, but you can rebuild. And a hurricane? That's the long game—years of bad habits eroding your health, depression creeping in like rising water, loss pounding your spirit wave after wave—it's relentless, but you can outlast it. But here's where you keep playing yourself: You keep trying to fight these spiritual disasters with emotional umbrellas. God handed you a fortress, and you out here ducking for cover behind glass. You're standing in a Category 5 storm with a cardboard roof—no wonder you're drenched in defeat. You're begging the rain to let up when the rain was supposed to obey you. Stop grabbing comfort when God told you to grab control.

Nobody knows that better than me. That storm hit when I first got into drugs—thought it was just a little fun, something I could handle. But storms don't stay small when you ignore them—they grow. Before I knew it, that storm turned into a tornado—addiction ripped through everything I had. I lost jobs, respect, relationships—spun out of control until life was nothing but debris. And then came the hurricane seasons—years of courtrooms, prison cells, and detox beds, each one washing more of my life away. Every time I tried to rebuild on my own, the storm hit harder. I was out there trying to patch holes in a sinking ship. It wasn't until I stopped blaming the weather and started speaking with authority—that I began dictating my own forecast. I had to stop reacting like a victim and start responding like a victor. God assures me I can outlast the disaster—but only if I open my mouth and command it to move.

Stop letting disasters punk you when God already gave you knockout power through His Son and shelter in His Holy Spirit. You out here choking in deep waters while the lifeboat named Jesus floats right next to you—untouched, unused. Mark 4:39 ain't just a Bible verse—it's a battle cry: *"He arose, and rebuked the wind, and said unto the sea, Peace, be still."* Jesus didn't negotiate with the storm—He shut it down like it owed Him rent money. And that same Spirit? It lives in you. So why you still moving like a victim when you were built to be the voice? You weren't built to cave—you were built to calm. God didn't give you a mouth just to move your lips—He gave it to move your disasters. He gave it to govern. Storms, tornadoes, hurricanes— they all fold when authority walks in the room. But instead of speaking up, you mute yourself. Instead of commanding peace, you cry for it. Speak up. Speak out. The only reason chaos is still talking is 'cause you ain't told it to shut the hell up yet. You're the weatherman—so start forecasting with faith. You set the atmosphere. You shift the pressure. Don't fumble your power before you even speak. When disasters hit, grip that Word, look hell in the face, and say, "Be still!" Then drop the mic.

Spiritual Growth Affirmation: I will **GROW** out of the
carnal mindset that ducks storms instead of speaking to them.
God gave me power to command, not permission to panic.

Take this day to **THINK** about how many times you've begged God for freedom, broken down in tears, promised to never go back—only to crawl right back to the same mess like you forgot how it crushed you. You go back to the same man who beat you. You go back to the same drug that almost killed you. You go back to the same crime that keeps sending you to prison. Strongholds grip you like they own you—they wrap around your throat, drag you through the gutter, then convince you that you need 'em to breathe. And the wild part? You remember the pain. You remember the nights you couldn't sleep, the days you couldn't look in the mirror, the shame that stalked you—and you still go back for more. Like you're volunteering for another beating. Who signs up to suffer again? Only somebody so twisted by trauma they mistake bondage for comfort. You out here cuddling chains like they're blankets, hugging pain like it ever loved you back. For what? Because healing's uncomfortable? Because growth hurts more than failure? You already fought like hell to break loose—so why act like freedom's a revolving door? You say you want better, but you still creeping through sin's back door like you got unfinished business with the devil.

Pills had such a strong hold on me that people no longer recognized who I was. I would have out-of-body experiences—nodding out, grinding my teeth, cursing uncontrollably, and moving in psychotic, involuntary ways. In fact, the time I was caught high on the job, I was in the aisle dancing. And I have no recollection. Addiction turned me into someone unrecognizable, stealing my identity and controlling my actions. Addiction was a ruthless captor who kidnapped me and assaulted me day in and day out. It stripped me of my morals, values, and dignity. And yet I kept signing up for it by relapsing. But after being free for quite some time, and with life treating me very well, I'll be damned if I voluntarily go back and suffer the demoralizing withdrawals of addiction. God shattered that addiction—and He's got the same sledgehammer for you. But it can't be done if you keep satan saved in your contacts. It can't be done if you don't take your keys back and change the locks. You can't fake like you want to break free and text your chains goodnight.

When God rips you out of bondage, don't you dare walk back like you forgot what it cost. What will one more black eye or bloody nose prove? What will one more hit of a drug prove? What will one more drink prove? Going back to a stronghold after God frees you is as twisted as a hostage running back to their kidnapper for one more rape. You think a woman who escapes a monster says, "Let me go back for closure"? No. She runs like hell and never looks back. 2 Corinthians 10:4 says, "*The weapons of our warfare are not carnal, but mighty through God to the pulling down of strongholds.*" That means God gave you spiritual demolition tools—but if you're still holding the wrecking ball like a paperweight, that's on you. Use what He gave you. Tear it down. Stay out. And don't you dare cry when you end up back in chains you never should've been near. The enemy's greatest tactic is convincing you that bondage feels safer than freedom—but that's a lie straight from hell. Freedom's a fight, yes—but it's the only fight worth bleeding for. Fight for your mind. Fight for your bloodline. Fight for your soul. Because you can't rebuke what you keep reaching for.

Spiritual Growth Affirmation: I will **GROW** out of the carnal mindset that keeps texting my chains goodnight. God didn't break my bondage for me to keep who's killing me in my contact list on speed dial.

Take this day to **THINK** about the jealousy that creeps in when you see somebody flashing their so-called "favor." You've heard the line: "Look what God gave me." Let's be real—they lying through their yellow teeth. God didn't bless that lifestyle built on betrayal and blood. That wasn't a trophy from God—that was a trap from the trickster, satan himself. The devil gives gifts too, but they come with strings attached. Just because it shines don't mean it's sacred. The devil's blessings are booby traps—pretty today, poisonous tomorrow. That car? That crib? That clout? If it came through compromise, it ain't from Christ. You out here calling a curse a blessing just because it looks good in pictures. Not all signs of favor are cosigned by God. He don't bless what He can't trust. You think He's about to fund filth with filthy faith? God don't invest in rebellion. God giving blessings to someone knee-deep in sin is like a bank approving a loan for someone with trash credit who's spiritually bankrupt—He's not a payday lender for reckless souls. He knows they're irresponsible. A blessing from God builds— what you chasing is just a ticking time bomb dipped in gold. God won't hang a tree air freshener on dysfunction. He blesses alignment, not ambition that's fueled by deception.

For years, I believed God handed blessings out like party favors to both the wicked and the righteous. In the streets, funerals became so normal I could recite the pastor's script before he opened his mouth: "He's in a better place." And for a while, I believed it. I thought everyone went to heaven, no matter how they lived. I was wrong. That wasn't truth—it was damage control. Comfort speech for the brokenhearted. Meanwhile, I was out there thinking God was cosigning my madness. Turns out it was satan handing me fast money and flash, and my dumb butt was calling it favor. Took me a while to see that God doesn't favor foolishness. All that money ever bought me were coffins, court dates, and prison walls. That wasn't prosperity—that was poison in pretty packaging. And God? He ain't handing out A's for effort. He don't grade on a curve—He grades on obedience.

God don't bankroll fraud—He funds faithfulness. Proverbs 13:22 says, *"And the wealth of the sinner is laid up for the just."* That means everything the wicked stunt with now is on reserve for the righteous. Don't get fooled— what satan hands out comes with chains. You might stunt for a season, but you'll bleed for a lifetime. Stop chasing gain that can't be sustained. Hell's blessings bankrupt your soul. God don't bless shortcuts—He blesses sacrifice. You want to be blessed? Then clean up your life. Because right now, your spiritual credit score is shot. You out here trying to withdraw favor from an account filled with lies, lust, and rebellion. Fornication? Declined. Deceit? Declined. Disobedience? Declined. It's all bad. But the good news? God does credit repair to get you back in good standing—and it doesn't take years to rebuild. If your spiritual credit's shot, stop blaming God for your prayers that get declined. You out here swiping sin like it's interest-free, thinking heaven gon' cosign your charges. God don't approve blessings for accounts in spiritual default. You can't max out on sin and expect God to raise your blessing limit. If you don't get right with Him, you ain't getting in—point-blank. It don't matter what you got. You could bank with Capital One, but heaven ain't asking what's in your wallet—it's asking what's in your heart.

> **Spiritual Growth Affirmation:** I will **GROW** out
> of the carnal mindset that confuses shine with favor. If
> it was built on sin, it's not a blessing—it's bait.

Take this day to **THINK** about why you keep sprinting from the very thing that was sent to level you up. You keep dodging discomfort like it's burdening you, when it's really birthing you. What torments you don't have to trouble you—it can train you. What crushed you can coach you. What drove you crazy can drive you forward. Life ain't just throwing pain at you to watch you suffer—it's offering you a brutal education. Every heartbreak is a textbook. Every failure is a syllabus. Every betrayal is a lesson plan approved by God Himself. But you out here skipping class, flunking tests you were born to pass, wondering why you keep repeating the same grade of pain every year— confused about why life keeps holding you back and why God keeps refusing to promote you. No wonder you're stuck in life. And until you stop loathing the pain, you'll never learn the lesson. Romans 5:3–4 says, "*And not only so, but we glory in tribulations also: knowing that tribulation worketh patience; And patience, experience; and experience, hope.*" The problem ain't the pain— it's you not allowing it to be a trusted advisor, a wise coach, a great mentor, or a dedicated teacher.

Every torment I went through became a mentor I didn't ask for—but one I couldn't ignore. Addiction mentored me when I was throwing up in alleyways, whispering that my one body is all I've got—and I better stop treating it like trash. The drug game mentored me after I buried too many friends and took bullets meant for silence—teaching me that fast money always has a slow death attached. Prison mentored me by stripping me down to nothing, showing me that freedom ain't physical—it's mental—and most people walk free with shackled minds. Cheating on women mentored me when I watched trust die in their eyes, teaching me that using love like a toy only proves how unloved you feel inside. What I once saw as thorns tearing me apart, I now see as tools that sharpened my spirit. Those weren't setbacks—they were sermons. The pain that tried to bury me became the dirt that grew me. That chaos built my calling. That suffering birthed my structure. Every L I took taught me how to lead. You don't need perfect conditions to grow—you need pain that pushes you to pay attention. Your torment ain't just trauma—it's a tutor. So grab a pen. Life's about to test what you've been through.

Your pain wasn't pointless. It's a pillar. Every time you got humiliated, heartbroken, or hit rock bottom—God was laying bricks beneath your brokenness. The same fire that melts wax hardens steel, and the same water that boils an egg softens a potato. It's not the environment that determines the outcome— it's how you respond. Stop crying over what happened to you and start confronting what it's supposed to teach you. The problem ain't the pressure—it's how you process it. Let your pain be your professor and every struggle your study session. Don't drop out of the pain—it's offering you a masterclass to help you graduate from your future problems. The lessons your trials taught you are tools to build the best version of yourself. But here's the thing: You can't just experience pain and expect it to automatically transform you. You have to do the work to turn pain into a lesson plan. God didn't bring you through all that suffering for you to stay how you are. Transformation ain't automatic—it's intentional. God brought you through hell, not so you could sit in the ashes, but so you could rise with authority. What tried to destroy you might be the exact material God's using to rebuild your purpose. Life is the school of hard knocks—pain's the professor. Let it school you.

Spiritual Growth Affirmation: I will **GROW** out of the carnal mindset of resenting my struggles. If pain pulled up a chair, maybe it came to teach—not to torture.

Take this day to **THINK** about the hell that life takes you through and the strength God provides to carry you through it. Life will give you the blues—sadness, isolation, and loneliness. It will have you seeing red—anger, frustration, and resentment. Then there's the black—depression and despair, leaving you numb and disconnected from the world. And don't forget the pink—those humiliating moments when others laugh at your pain, seeing your struggle as entertainment while you're fighting to survive. But through all of it, God is there, giving you what you need to persevere. He's the strength that holds you up when the weight feels unbearable. Isaiah 40:29 says, *"He giveth power to the faint; and to them that have no might he increaseth strength."* God don't leave you to face these trials alone—He equips you with the power to endure.

Addiction took me through every color. The blues were the loneliness of sitting in silence, cut off from my family, sinking deeper into isolation because I thought nobody cared. The reds consumed me with anger—at God for letting me spiral, at myself for being too weak to stop, and at the world for not understanding what I was going through. The blacks came in the form of blackouts, where I wasn't even present in my own life—just high, numb, and completely out of control. And then there were the pinks—those moments of public humiliation, like the time I was escorted out of work, embarrassed as people laughed at my struggles. I thought I was abandoned, but God was always on the line—I just kept hitting decline. But I repeatedly heard Him say, "Can you hear me? Can you hear me now?" God was just waiting on me to accept Him. He didn't take away the pain instantly, but He gave me the strength to survive it.

God is like the only line that never drops when life keeps blowing up your phone with chaos. You get bad reception when nobody shows up for you, weak signals when your spirit feels disconnected, and dropped calls when your cries go unanswered. But God ain't Verizon—He don't lose bars in bad weather. Storms don't weaken His signal—they amplify your reception if you stay connected. His coverage never fails—when you're drowning in blues, blinded by reds, or fading into black, He steps in with strength that don't glitch. And while nothing about pain tickles you pink, God has a way of flipping the script—turning what should've buried you into what built you. With Him, you don't just get by—you get upgraded. God's plan is unlimited, and with His coverage, you pass life's tests in high-resolution 5G—with flying colors. His strength gives you the kind of reception that cuts through noise, distractions, and emotional static. You walk through the darkest valleys with full clarity and a clear signal—because He's your strong tower, the place the righteous run into and are saved.

Spiritual Growth Affirmation: I will **GROW** out of the carnal mindset that lets humiliation define me. Every pink moment they laughed at will be the same ones God uses to lift me.

Take this day to **THINK** about the traits you've spent too much time hiding. The things you call flaws or imperfections aren't mistakes—they're God's stamp of approval. Your birthmark, scar, or unique feature is more than just a physical characteristic; it's a divine patent, proof that you were created intentionally. God don't do accidents, and you're no exception. Psalm 139:14 declares, "*I will praise thee; for I am fearfully and wonderfully made: marvellous are thy works; and that my soul knoweth right well.*" You've been calling God's signature on your life a flaw—like He didn't know what He was doing when He made you. That birthmark? It's your copyright, your spiritual trademark, reminding you that you were made on purpose and for a purpose. If the Creator of the universe took time to mark you, who are you to call it a flaw?

Growing up, I hated my birthmarks. He gave me two. One on my wrist that resembles a cat scratch, and the other the color blue circling my iris. I'm black with blue rings around my eyes. I saw it as a target for ridicule, something that made me stand out in a way I didn't want. I was constantly made aware of it. I went to great lengths to hide it, thinking it was a defect, a reason to feel less than. I never looked people in the face too long for fear that they would notice it. Every time someone noticed it, I felt exposed, insecure, and vulnerable. But as I grew older, I started seeing it differently. My birthmark wasn't just a blemish—it was a mark of identity, a reminder that I was uniquely made. What I used to wish away became something I learned to value. I no longer wanted to erase what God penciled on me. I began to realize that my birthmark wasn't something to be ashamed of, but a symbol of God's personal touch on my life. It was as if He had personally tattooed me with: "You belong to me, and I've set you apart." That shift in perspective changed everything. What the world calls "strange," God calls "signature." What the world sees as weird, God sees as wonder. You're not a mistake—you're a limited edition, stamped with purpose and set apart by design.

That birthmark—or whatever else you've been hiding—ain't just a mark, it's a message. God's way of saying, *"This one ain't mass-produced—this one's custom. One of one."* You are handcrafted, irreplaceable. And that thing you've been trying to erase? That's the very thing God inked in to remind you who you belong to. It's not a blemish—it's branding by the Master Himself. A divine signature written in permanent ink. And here you are, covering it up for likes, validation, and acceptance from people who don't even like, haven't accepted, or validated themselves. You're not flawed—you're featured. Stop letting culture convince you that conformity is confidence. Stop apologizing for the thing God handpicked to make you different. You weren't made to blend—you were made to blaze. Your birthmark is heaven's badge of honor. That scar? That trait? That "flaw"? It's the very proof that you're fearfully and wonderfully made. Your greatness ain't in spite of your marks—it's sealed in them. You ain't a typo—you're a trademark. That scar ain't weird—it's your witness that God handcrafted you. God marked you before you came into the world—now go out there and leave your mark in it.

Spiritual Growth Affirmation: I will **GROW** out of the carnal mindset that calls God's branding a blemish. My birthmark ain't a mistake—it's my spiritual trademark.

Take this day to **THINK** about the way we rationalize our sins. People love to measure their wrongs against someone else's, as if God grades on a curve. We compare, we categorize, and we convince ourselves that our sins aren't "that bad." We say things like, "At least I didn't lie about something major," or, "It's just one drink," or, "I only cheated once." But sin ain't measured on a sliding scale—fail one part, you fail the whole test. Romans 3:23 reminds us, "*For all have sinned, and come short of the glory of God.*" That means every one of us is in the same boat—doesn't matter if it was a canoe or a cruise ship that went down. You can sugarcoat your sin all you want—God still sees it as sour, and it will only leave a bitter taste in your mouth in the end. Justifying sin don't lessen its impact—it only delays the truth that it needs to be addressed. Whether you lied or murdered, you're guilty in God's courtroom—ain't no plea deals. Everyone's guilty.

We were all posted in this busted trap spot—peeling paint, milk crates for chairs, ashtrays made from cut Coca-Cola cans—arguing like drug snobs on a debate team. One guy, rolling a blunt, said, "At least I don't snort coke." The cokehead shot back, "At least I don't do crack." The alcoholic laughed, swigging from his bottle, saying, "Y'all can judge me, but I ain't out here popping pills." I chimed in, like I had any room to talk, saying, "At least I don't shoot heroin." Everybody had a loophole. Everybody had a ladder they swore they were one rung higher on. And I was right there with 'em—counting my vices like discount sins, convincing myself I was "better" because I didn't shoot, smoke glass, or snort. We all nodded like we'd just made valid points—like any of us were better than the next. But the truth? We were all sitting in the same busted house, broke, hollowed out, and slaves to whatever demon had our leash. Doesn't matter if your patron was pills, powder, or Patrón—we were all drowning in the same ocean, just using different anchors. God ain't out here grading on a chemical curve. Rationalization is a trap all its own. Your degrees of damage might sound slick on the block and maybe shave time in court, but in the kingdom, bondage is bondage. Hell don't got VIP sections.

Comparing sins is like comparing different forms of feces. Doo-doo can be runny, solid, or chunky when it comes out, but no matter what form it takes, it's still doo-doo, and it all stinks. That's the raw truth of sin. Whether it's a lie, murder, greed, or adultery, it's all offensive to God. James 2:10 puts it plainly: "*For whosoever shall keep the whole law, and yet offend in one point, he is guilty of all.*" God don't separate sin into black and white—He ain't Jim Crow; He don't believe in segregation, just holy or unholy. Your mess can't be wrapped in religion or rationalization. Sin remains until you repent—you can't Febreze it, hang a car air freshener on it, or stick an incense in it. Stop trying to rank your sins to make yourself feel better—they all carry the same stench before a holy God. Ain't no holy wipes for halfway repentance. The only way out is to stop excusing it and turn your life around. You want to be clean? Let God wipe the mess off your butt that you keep pretending ain't there. After you sin, it's best to wipe yourself clean. 'Cause even a tiny skid mark still proves you filthy. Label your sin "mild" all you want—hell don't got different levels of security. Sin don't come in small, medium, or large— it all fits the same casket.

Spiritual Growth Affirmation: I will **GROW** out of the carnal mindset of comparing sins. I can justify it, dress it up, or downplay it—but God sees one thing: clean or condemned. Period.

Take this day to **THINK** about why your life keeps going off a cliff. It ain't no mystery—you keep trying to play superhero like you can do it all without God. You done bought into these songs and slogans about "doing it on your own" and "being self-made," but now look—your life is a wreck. Kids acting crazy, spouse running around on you, everything falling apart, and you sitting there punch-drunk. That's what happens when you try to run a God-sized life on human-sized power. It's like a lamp that looks good on the outside but ain't plugged in—it can't shine, can't light nuttin', and neither can you without God. The moment you unplug from Him, your light goes out, and now you stumbling through life blind. Psalm 1:3 says, *"And he shall be like a tree planted by the rivers of water, that bringeth forth his fruit in his season; his leaf also shall not wither; and whatsoever he doeth shall prosper."* You want peace? Swim in God's Word. You want progress? Congregate with other fellow believers. It's that simple. 'Cause whatever you're going through, you don't fall off—you let go.

Addiction had me bound, tore up, so they put me on meds to quiet the cravings. I had finally kicked addiction's butt. Damn that medication—I thought I won my life back. The moment I stopped depending on meds, it came back like, "You ain't really think this was over, did you?" Truth is, without someone like my wife by my side 24/7, I couldn't manage it alone. Every time I did, I drifted back into dangerous territory, struggling in the same habits I thought I had escaped. *I didn't need strength—I needed stability.* That relapse beat it into me—without a real anchor, I was always one bad day from drowning for good. I thought I could handle it, but I was wrong. I thought I was strong for standing on my own, but I was just unanchored—floating toward the same destruction I swore I'd never drown in again. The reason I kept finding myself in the same boat was because I kept jumping ship on God.

Your life ain't any different. The moment you let go of God, you start going under. You stopped depending on Him because you thought you had it handled—but now you're gasping for air while pretending you're still floating. Without Him, you ain't anchored—you're just drifting, crashing into every issue that comes your way. And each time you try to fix it without Him, you tear something else down. You're out here slapping duct tape on spiritual sinkholes and calling it progress. God ain't a life preserver for when you're in panic—He's the anchor that keeps your soul steady before the storm even hits. The power you're praying for is impossible to maintain while you're living unplugged. You're not drowning because the waves are too strong—you're drowning because you keep letting go of God. You can't stay afloat when you keep jumping ship on God. If you're tired of sinking, maybe it's time to stop fighting for control and start grabbing hold of the Lifeguard who keeps you from drowning: Jesus.

Spiritual Growth Affirmation: I will **GROW** out of the carnal mindset that confuses independence with strength. Without God, I'm not self-made—I'm self-destructing.

Take this day to **THINK** about how twisted our view of favor has become. You acting like God's got a checklist—waiting for you to be perfect, perform right, or say the magic words before He moves. But His blessings don't need a trigger. He don't bless you because you sneezed—He blesses you because He's sovereign. While you're out here trying to earn what's already been handed to you, God is just waiting on you to receive it. You keep grinding like grace comes with a receipt, like you gotta hustle hard enough to deserve it. But God don't hand out blessings based on your résumé—He gives based on relationship. Actions don't determine blessings—anointing does. That "bless you" after a sneeze? That's ritual. That "bless you" after you do a deed for God? That's reward. God's been blessing your life since before you ever breathed your first breath. You so used to people attaching strings to everything, you keep waiting for God to do the same. But His blessings ain't for sale. They're stamped with mercy, wrapped in grace, and delivered with no strings attached. God's favor runs deep. He don't operate on your effort—He operates on His grace. You don't earn something that's been freely given to you.

During my early Christian walk, it was hard to grasp this truth. Coming from a street mentality, I believed everything came with strings attached. In prison, if a man wanted a "boyfriend," he'd bring food, cover debts, offer protection—but it always came with a price. On the streets, same game. You want to smash a girl? That meant weed, nails, hair, eyelashes, liquor, wings, and lies. Nothing came free—everything had strings. So naturally, I assumed God worked like that too. I thought if I prayed loud, went to church, or posted scripture, maybe He'd finally bless me. But I had it twisted. God ain't a street hustler or a prison manipulator. He don't want performance—He wants posture. He ain't cutting deals—He's offering deliverance. The deeper I got in my faith, the clearer it became: God don't need you to sneeze, shine, or show out to bless you. He already chose you. You grinding like grace is earned, but God's blessings are stamped "Paid in Full." Stop treating Him like the plug—start receiving Him as your Provider. His love ain't transactional—it's relational. The blessing was never about your grind—it's always been about His grace.

We've all heard it—"Nothing in life is free," "What's the catch?" or, "There's no such thing as a free lunch"—because we've been taught to hold suspect anything we don't have to pay or work for. John 1:12 says, *"But as many as received Him, to them He gave the right to become children of God, to those who believe in His name."* Did you catch that? Received—not earned. Not performed. Not bought. We out here breaking our backs trying to impress a Father who just wants us to be obedient. You grinding like favor's on an IOU, forgetting God already paid it off in full with His blood. God already wrote the check—you the one still trying to clock in and earn it. The blessings begin when you stop performing and start receiving. He's not holding your breakthrough hostage until you clean up your act—He's already extended your credit with Him, but you too busy trying to put on a show to receive it. His grace is not up for negotiation—it's already been signed, sealed, and delivered. God don't need a performance to provide. His blessings don't flow through good works—they flow through faith. God ain't Equifax, TransUnion, or Experian—He doesn't run your credit to check your score before He says yes. With Him, your credit can be repaired in one day. After you commit to repenting of your sins, He writes off the debt and signs off on the blessings on the spot.

Spiritual Growth Affirmation: I will **GROW** out of the carnal mindset that ties blessings to behavior instead of belief. Sneezing to receive God's blessing ain't a requirement; I just have to accept Christ, be free from sin, and keep my nose clean.

Take this day to **THINK** about how much authority you've handed over to stress—like it's your god, your boss, your final say. You let your job turn your hair gray, your kids pull your hair out, and your relationship steal your sleep. You act like stress is unavoidable—but most of what you're carrying is stuff you refuse to surrender. Let's get something straight: Holding on to stress ain't strength—it's stupidity dressed up as responsibility. You're not overwhelmed—you're over-attached to things God told you to release. You cry out for peace, but you still go to bed hugging your problems like they your favorite teddy bear. That ain't faith—that's self-sabotage. Jesus was stretched out on that cross so you wouldn't have to be stretched thin. So why you out here gripping every burden like it's part of your identity? You weren't crucified—He was. So why are you still carrying crosses that were never assigned to you? You say you trust God, but you act like He needs your help to carry the load. That's not submission—that's spiritual stupidity.

When I say stress had me stretched, I mean it was pulling me apart at every seam. I had just lost my grandma—the matriarch of the family. My daughter wasn't speaking to me, and that silence hit harder than any scream. I was facing foreclosure on my building, watching everything I built crumble like the lie I'd been living. On top of that, I had two open court cases hovering like vultures, and was still getting high—telling myself I was "managing" it. But I wasn't managing a thing—I was medicating my misery. I cried to God for peace, but reached for pills like they were holy. Instead of relying on the man who carried the cross, I kept relying on the pills I thought could carry mine. I'd pop a pill to escape, nod off to forget, and wake up more broken than before. I cried to God for peace, but I wouldn't let go of the chaos. The stress wasn't just on me—it was in me. Christ had been stretched out on that cross so I wouldn't have to live this stretched-thin, cracked-up life… but I kept rejecting peace like I was allergic to healing. I didn't need more strength—I needed surrender. Back then, I thought holding on was bravery. Turns out, letting go would've spared me years of chaos.

You can't keep hollering, "God got me," while living like you got this. Jesus didn't die for you to stay shackled to anxiety, worry, fear, or depression. He didn't die for you to stress yourself into a casket He already conquered. 1 Peter 5:7 says, "*Cast all your anxiety on Him because He cares for you.*" Not some—*all.* But your problem is you keep casting it like an impatient fisherman—dropping it in His hands, then reeling it back every time something tugs at you. You want peace? Then stop throwing tantrums in prayer and picking your pain right back up after "Amen." What Christ carried to the cross, you keep trying to drag. You weren't designed to carry everything—you were built to trust the One who can. Jesus got nailed to the cross so you wouldn't be so hammered by life. That's not noble—that's nonsense. You're burning out and calling it being "used by God," stressing out and calling it "stewardship." Nah. That's self-inflicted suffering. If you're really too blessed to be stressed, then act like it. Let go, or let it bury you—but don't you dare blame God for a weight you refused to drop. If peace is a promise, then stress is a choice. How you trust God with your salvation but not your Sunday? Make that make sense. What kind of fool are you to think the One who conquered the grave can't handle your grave issues? The moment you give it to Him, don't snatch it back. God can't alter what you won't leave at the altar.

Spiritual Growth Affirmation: I will **GROW** out of the carnal mindset that says, "God got me," while living like I've got to fix it all. Jesus was stretched so I wouldn't have to keep stretching myself past my breaking point.

Take this day to **THINK** about how many times you've begged for a quick fix, crying for God to get you out, when what you really needed was to grow up. You want Him to be your genie, your emergency exit, your Magic Eraser—but what if the pain is the point? God's not in the business of convenience—He's in the business of construction, taking His time to build something solid. He's not interested in shortcuts that leave you unchanged. He's not trying to save you for a limited time; He's shaping you for a lifetime. This ain't God tryna take you out—it's boot camp for your purpose. His timing ain't just deliberate; it's divine. You want divine DoorDash from God to deliver you from the mess you called in, but you dash off as soon as He shows up, like you forgot you placed the order. You want God to drop everything and cater to you like He's your butler. You're not looking for eternity—you're looking for entitlement. But God ain't pacifying you just to keep you comfortable. If He did that, you'd stay weak, shallow, and unprepared. You want favor on demand, but you hand out delay and denial every time responsibility calls. Quit interferin' with God's mission to save you—His intervention is your intermission to get your act together.

At the time, the county jail was booking people and releasing them. I remember sitting in that jail cell praying hard—"God, please let them call my name for early release." Overcrowding had the place packed shoulder to shoulder, and I was desperate for a way out. Just sixteen days left on my sentence, but I begged like I had sixteen years. And guess what? God did it. They called my name. I walked out that door thinking I was free and favored. But wouldn't you know, three days later I was right back in that same jail, booked on a new charge. Why'd He let me out? I wasn't ready. I didn't want redemption—I wanted relief. God gave me grace, and I flipped it into a relapse. Imprisonment wasn't the problem—it was my impulsive pattern. I wasn't locked up because I got caught—I was locked up because I never got changed. That's when I found out that God will take back grace you didn't earn. God will let you taste sweet freedom—just to show you how sour your taste buds really are. And all I had left was sixteen measly days. I traded those for another cycle, because I didn't see God as merciful—I saw Him as my meal ticket. If God expedited every process just to extradite every problem, you'd leave this life unchanged.

In Ecclesiastes 3:11, it says, *"He has made everything beautiful in its time."* God's timing isn't just about delay—it's about development. He's not in a rush to rescue what He's still refining. If He pulls you too early, you'll relapse too easy. You want God to throw you a life jacket when you're drowning in problems, but He's teaching you how to swim. You're not drowning because the waves are too strong—you're drowning 'cause you never learned how to tread truth. You don't need a rescue plan—you need a resistance plan. How are you going to stay out of chaos? Stop asking for an expedient relief and start trusting in His timing. We want triumph without trials, joy without junk, healing without heartbreak. Our glory ain't just in the finished product—it's in the forging process. The struggles we face, the hardships we endure, and the battles we fight all serve a purpose. He's not just solving your problems—He's solving you. The longer He waits to bring you out of a problem, the deeper He's working. God's pauses aren't permanent—they're divine safeguards, allowing harmful situations to pass by while He keeps us secure. God's not ignoring your problem—He's making sure you don't run back to it for seconds. You want to see an exit plan—God wants to see a growth chart. You want release—He wants results. You want a way out, but He wants you to learn what you need to so that you will never find your way back in.

Spiritual Growth Affirmation: I will **GROW** out of the carnal mindset that begs for exits instead of endurance. Quick escapes don't cure cycles—they just hit snooze on suffering.

Take this day to **THINK** about how you let life toss you all over the place like a rag doll. You let chaos run your mind, stress jack up your emotions, and drama drive you insane. God equipped you with peace, but you refuse to use it. Peace is part of the package—it's built in. But what good is it if you won't activate it? You walking around fully loaded with divine stability but acting like you empty. God didn't forget to install peace—you just keep choosing panic. You out here searching for outside solutions to fix an inside problem. You medicate, distract yourself, overwork, overeat, and overthink—all to avoid tapping into what's already been deposited in you. The peace is there, but you'd rather stay busy than be still. You'd rather react than rest. You keep asking God to remove the storm, but you won't use the stillness He placed inside you to ride it out. Just like an engineer designs a car with cruise control to keep it steady, God wired you with peace to keep you cruisin' steady when life gets outta control.

The only "piece" I trusted back then was the one I carried in my waistband—a cold, heavy reminder that chaos was always just one pull away. I didn't know nothing about inner peace; all I knew was paranoia. I relied heavily on my "piece" to bring me comfort. One time, a girl brought a dude down to my shop trying to check me, and without even thinking, I upped my "piece" and aimed it right at her. She froze. I didn't pull the trigger, but I might as well have—the fear in her eyes told me I'd just crossed a line I couldn't uncross. I wasn't protecting myself—I was proving how far gone I was. She filed a report, and I ended up paying her $800 under the table just to make sure she didn't show up to court. That moment showed me the truth: What I thought was power was just weakness in a metal casing. I was using a gun to quiet storms that God had already given me the power to silence from within. I was wired with peace but kept defaulting to war with my distorted "piece." Looking back, the only "piece" I needed wasn't the one that could take a life—but the One that could save mine.

Peace ain't about life being perfect—it's about how you respond when it ain't. If your life is chaotic, it's because you won't activate the peace God put in you. You keep blaming the storm, but the real issue is your refusal to use your inner peace as shelter that God provided. John 14:27 says, *"Peace I leave with you, my peace I give unto you: not as the world giveth, give I unto you."* There! He gave it to you! Activate it! God didn't say you had to earn peace—you already have it. But instead of using it, you're still letting everything outside of you dictate what happens inside of you. God's peace is like cruise control—it don't stop the road from getting rough, but it keeps you steady when it does. Peace came standard when He built you—to help you cruise through life, despite the potholes and speed bumps that lie ahead on life's long road. But just like cruise control won't turn itself on, peace won't either. You're the one refusing to hit the switch when life tries to drive you crazy.

Spiritual Growth Affirmation: I will **GROW** out of the carnal mindset that keeps choosing panic over peace. If God gave me cruise control, why am I still slamming the brakes every time life swerves?

Take this day to **THINK** about why you're so quick to lose trust when you don't see results. You pray one day and expect God to drop a blessing like Amazon Prime—overnight delivery. You track your prayer like it's a FedEx package. Throwing spiritual tantrums like a spoiled kid who's mad they didn't get what they wanted fast enough. Like a fisherman casting a line, you don't see what's happening beneath the surface—but that don't mean nothing's moving. Quiet don't mean inactive. The fish don't bite when you want—they bite when the time is right. And if you yank too early, you ruin the catch. That's what you do with God—you keep pulling back too soon, snatching your faith off the line before He delivers. You claim you trust Him, but your panic says otherwise. How many times does God have to tell you to sit still before you actually listen? You'll camp out for Jordans, wait on weed men for hours or years on toxic people to change—but you can't hold out five minutes for a move from heaven. And that's exactly why everything in your life goes to hell—because you keep jumping the gun when God wants you to keep the safety on and be still.

One of the times I got out of jail, I prayed for a job. I went to programs and sought out resources to help me find a job, but no one hired me. Instead of trusting God to provide in His time, impatience set in, and I went back to the streets. Wouldn't you know it, I got caught up again, and that landed me back in prison. Even though I had given my life to Christ, I took matters into my own hands when the process didn't move fast enough. Three days in, I was sitting in jail on a phone call when a friend I'd been staying with told me a hiring manager had called to set up an interview. I had been begging God for an open door, and it was sitting there waiting on me the whole time—I just couldn't wait long enough to walk through it. My impatience cost me what my prayers had already prepared. Just like a fisherman who can't see beneath the surface but keeps his line in the water, I should've trusted that God was working even when I couldn't see it.

Trust don't need evidence—just obedience. He's working while you wait. He's not stalling—He's staging. His silence ain't absence—it's alignment. He's aligning things, preparing people, and positioning you for His perfect will. Isaiah 64:4 reminds us, "*Since ancient times no one has heard, no ear has perceived, no eye has seen any God besides you, who acts on behalf of those who wait for him.*" Learn to wait on God. Trust that He is aware of your situation and actively orchestrating everything for your ultimate good. God is always at work, moving in our lives even when we don't see or feel it. Stop quitting just because it's quiet. Waiting ain't weakness—it's warfare. Every second you hold the line in silence, God is securing the victory behind the scenes. You want proof He's working? Look at the earth—it revolves around the sun at a rate of 67,000 mph, and at the same time, it rotates around its axis at about 1,000 mph. Yet, even though the earth is moving at incredible speeds, we can't feel it. That's how God moves: Silent, steady, and strong. So stop tripping just because you can't feel God moving. Just because you can't see the setup don't mean God ain't setting it up.

Spiritual Growth Affirmation: I will **GROW** out of the carnal mindset of thinking heaven ain't in motion just because I can't see God's movement. I will trust that God is working it out in my life, even when nothing in my life is working out.

Take this day to **THINK** about how little say you had over your first breath and how little say you will have over your last. Your birthplace, your family, even the color of your skin were handed to you. You didn't pick the broken streets you grew up on or the scars you inherited. And unless you start driving recklessly or decide today is your day to end it all, you won't pick how you go out. But everything in between those two points? That's your ink on the page. You act like life's the author, conveniently blaming fate for every mess you make. Newsflash: You hold the pen. You didn't script your prologue or your epilogue—that was God's move. But the chapters and paragraphs? That's on you. In a race, the runner can't change the starting line or shift the finish flag, but every stride in between is their choice. Proverbs 16:9 says, "*In their hearts humans plan their course, but the Lord establishes their steps.*" You draw the map; He paves the road beneath your feet. You weren't given a vote on how you entered or how you'll exit—but you cast a ballot every day on how you live.

My life started off dirt-ball bad. Government cheese. Food stamps. No father. Single parent. Later on, I chose to walk into situations that got me shot, addicted, and locked up. My riotous living almost expedited my death multiple times. People like to act like life "happens" to them, but nah—I happened to me. Had I chosen different, my whole story would've been different. And I know now, when they lay me in that box, it won't be the birth date or the death date that tells my story—it'll be that tiny dash in between. That dash is everything. That dash is every choice I made, every time I ignored the voice telling me to do better, and every time I chose destruction over discipline. That little line will speak louder than any word said at my funeral—because it's my real story. If your dash don't speak life, don't expect your eulogy to lie for you. Life gives you your first breath. Life takes your last. Everything in between—you own that.

God might've written your prologue and epilogue, but the middle? That's on you. You out here living your life turnt up in a club and wondering why your life ain't turning out right. You waste your breath on gossip, your energy on fake friendships, and your money on moments that don't mean a thing. You sleep all day, chase nothing, avoid everything, and then complain like you were dealt a bad hand. Nah—*you played it wrong*. You want purpose, but you won't pursue it. You want peace, but you stay around drama. You want change, but you keep doing the same dumb things. You don't lack favor—you lack follow-through. And let's be real—if your life feels meaningless, it's because every day you choose to give it less meaning. God gave you the days—you the one throwing them away. You out here burning time like you got more of it. One day, that clock's gon' stop. And when it does, you'll realize all the time you thought you had—you wasted on nothing. So don't expect tears at your funeral if your obituary don't say nothing worth remembering. You the one who wrote it.

Spiritual Growth Affirmation: I will **GROW** out of the carnal mindset that blames fate for what I freely chose. My dash ain't decoration—it's documentation, and I'm the notary.

Take this day to **THINK** about how many times you've asked God to move into your life, but you keep failing His inspection. You say you want a fresh start, but you won't vacate the mess you've been squatting in. You're living in sin like it's rent-controlled, refusing to break your lease with lust, pride, and addiction. God's offering you prime real estate in His kingdom, but you're still living in spiritual slums. He's got keys waiting—but He's not handing them over if the application of your life to Him don't pass inspection. You want the blessing, but you won't clear out the violations in your life. You still got that nasty attitude. You still getting high. You still committing fornication. You still holding on to that toxic mindset. Your body is supposed to be God's temple, but you treat it like condemned property—boarded up with bitterness, cracked with compromise, and leaking with lust. God's ready to sign the deed over to you and hand you a new lease on life, but you won't let go of your strongholds. You're praying for God to take over the house, but you still got sin on the lease.

I once had a tenant who wanted to upgrade to a better unit—more space, better view, brand-new everything. I was ready to approve her request. But I told her one thing: in the new unit, no loud music—senior tenants next door. She hesitated. A few days later, she backed out. She forfeited the upgrade over a volume knob. And that's what most of us do with God—we want His penthouse favor, but we won't lower the noise of sin in our lives. God ain't handing keys to folks who do nothing but trash the place. You can't expect a luxury suite when you still tracking dirt all over the carpet. You can't cry for an upgrade if you ain't ready to respect the rules of the house. He got our spot ready—but we just don't feel like packing. We can't negotiate with the Landlord of heaven like we got bargaining power. The lease is His, not yours—and His properties don't come with loopholes. His properties don't come with compromise—they come with conditions.

Don't ask God to move in if you're still renting space to satan. You have to let go of the mess. Trying to receive God's blessings while clinging to your filth is like expecting to get clean in a tub full of dirty water. In order to take a clean bath, you've got to drain the dirty water. Likewise, to get clean with God, you've got to drain that pride, that pettiness, that perversion. God's got room prepared—custom-built for your calling—but you're still living in faith that's been foreclosed. John 14:2 says, "*In my Father's house are many mansions…*" but you treating grace like a motel—checking in and out whenever it suits you. You can't claim your inheritance while you're still squatting in rebellion. God don't hand out keys to tenants who won't respect the lease on life He gave them. And make no mistake—your lifestyle is either qualifying or disqualifying you for His promises. You're one missed repentance away from being thrown out. But here's the grace—God's still offering you a mansion. All closing costs covered, no down payment, no background check—just surrender. But first, you gotta evict the sin, clean out the property, and let Him move in for good. Stop giving your sins living room. You can't live in heaven until you throw out your sins. Until you surrender the lease to sin, God won't hand you the deed to destiny. He ain't putting you in a mansion while you still letting your sins squat in the basement.

Spiritual Growth Affirmation: I will **GROW** out of the carnal mindset of squatting in sin. Redemption ain't a remodel— it's a relocation. It's time I move into the Master's suite.

Take this day to **THINK** about how fast you tap out when life has you in a chokehold—and how slow you are to tap into God when it matters most. You fold at the first hit—crying over bills, quitting over conflict, spiraling after a setback. You tap into your friends, your followers, your feed, your flesh—but not your Father. You out here tagging in vices, calling on chaos, and depending on dead weight to fight battles they were never built to handle. And meanwhile, God—undefeated, unmatched, and standing in your corner—is watching you get slammed around while you ignore His outstretched hand. It's just like a wrestling tag team match—when one fighter gets worn out, they don't keep getting beat—they tag in their partner. But you? You'd rather tap out than tag God in. You'd rather fold than let the Father fight. That ain't faith—that's foolishness. You're not losing because God ain't near—you're losing because you won't lift your hand. Let God fight what your strength never could.

I'll never forget the freezing night I sat in a busted car, tucked inside my garage, in a building that had already been hit with foreclosure papers. Fog on the glass, numb in the hands, pride on the floor. My stomach growled louder than the engine that wouldn't even turn over, but I was still too ashamed to tell the truth. Instead, I lied—told folks the heat went out or the water line had broken, like I was just crashing there till things got fixed. But the truth? I wasn't house-sitting a problem—I was homeless, hiding in plain sight. I'd rather freeze in silence than admit I'd fallen that far. Truth was, I was homeless and ashamed. I even called the Cat House—an addiction center in my city—begging for a bed. They said they were full. That's when I broke. I looked up and said, "God, I don't wanna live like this. If you can get me out of this—I'm yours." And after that, I reached for the Bible. Not out of devotion—out of desperation. I was out of options. And when I cracked it open, out dropped $220 in cash. I must've tucked it in there when I was high and forgot. Not remembering things or losing them were common for me when I was pilled out the night before. But that money felt like God's whisper: "I see you." I used it to get a cheap room for a few nights, just to get warm and rest. I sat in that room, finally quiet, telling God I hated my life. I wish I could say that was the moment I turned my whole life around. But I didn't— I slipped again. Still, that was the first night I reached—not just out—but up.

Instead of tapping out of whatever situation you're going through, it's time to tap in—and tag in the only One who never loses. You weren't designed to fight every round by yourself. You weren't made to survive slam after slam on your own. Psalm 73:26 says, *"My flesh and my heart faileth: but God is the strength of my heart, and my portion forever."* That means when your fight fails and your faith feels like it's hanging by a thread, His strength steps in where yours stops. Don't get it twisted—He's not kicking the ropes down for you to escape the ring. He's calling you to tag Him in to give you a chance to catch your breath. But how can He step in when you keep reaching for everything but Him? You keep tagging trauma, tagging toxic people, tagging temporary highs—but won't tag in truth. God wants you to reach out to Him. But He won't force His way into the fight. You've got to want Him in the ring. Lift your hand. Open your mouth. Tag in the King. Instead of calling on everyone else, call on God. He's not out of reach—He's just waiting for you to reach out.

Spiritual Growth Affirmation: I will **GROW** out of the carnal mindset that runs to distractions instead of my Deliverer. God ain't my last resort—He's my first Source.

Take this day to **THINK** about how many more signs you're gon' ignore before life wrecks you beyond repair. How many wrong turns, missed exits, and blocked roads does it take before you admit you're lost? Just because you're still moving don't mean you're on the right road. You could be sprinting straight into destruction with your eyes wide shut. God's been flashing warning lights—dead ends, flat tires, spiritual speed bumps—but you too arrogant, flexing behind the wheel to admit you need direction. He's your GPS, not your passenger. He's dropping detours, shouting, "U-turn!" and offering exits—but He won't hijack the car. You gotta choose to follow. That wide lane you're cruising in? It ends in a cell, a casket, or a lifetime of could've beens. You've heard God whisper in the night telling you to turn around— don't go buy that drug, don't go to the hotel with that married man or woman, don't go to the bar and buy that drink—but pride got you hitting the gas like you'll figure it out later. Later might never show up. Let Him reroute you before you total your life. God ain't chasing you—He's waiting at the exit you keep missing.

Lying in that hospital bed with bullets in my body and machines beeping beside me, I should've seen it as the call to action it was. But instead of surrendering, I doubled down. I was still making phone calls, still directing drug runs, still acting like I was untouchable—as if the blood on my sheets wasn't a billboard from God saying, "Turn around." Even when they wheeled me out and took me straight to the police station, I wasn't listening. I had been ignoring detours for years—every close call, every overdose around me, every whisper in my spirit telling me to slow down. God wasn't trying to crash my life—He was trying to reroute it. But I kept treating Him like a backseat driver instead of the GPS. Prison became the only pit stop that forced me to shut up and listen. It wasn't until my last prison stint that I realized God had been flashing "Wrong Way" signs my whole life—I was just too prideful to take the exit.

You think the road you're on is working just because you're still breathing? Wake up! The road that feels smooth might be leading you straight to hell. Matthew 7:13–14 says it plain: "*The wide road is the easy one, and it ends in destruction. That narrow road? That's the one that saves your life—but it's hard, and few find it because few are looking.*" You got the pedal floored on foolishness, thinking you'll turn around when things "get serious." But how many times has God tried to reroute you already? How many close calls, heartbreaks, court dates, breakdowns, and rock bottoms does it take before you realize you're out of range? He's been calling—but the signal is weak. You don't have to go out like that. Let God be your GPS—Guiding Personal Savior—because the turns you've been taking are leading you straight into ongoing traffic. His voice is that one saying, "Slow down before sin spins you outta control." That warning in your gut telling you to yield? That's Him. The urge to take a U-turn? That's Him too. Don't wait for life to teach you what obedience could've saved you from.

Spiritual Growth Affirmation: I will **GROW** out of the carnal mindset that waits for rock bottom to check the map. I'd rather follow God's GPS than crash on cruise control.

Take this day to **THINK** about why your life keeps breaking like a cheap Family Dollar toy. It ain't just life coming at you—it's the fact that you ain't attached to nothing solid. You want to blame the enemy, but for real—it's you. Someone says something to you, and you catch an attitude. Somebody looks at you sideways, and you snap like they just called your mama a slut to your face. Someone gives you advice, and you take it like an insult. You can never seem to keep it together—not because the world is against you, but because you won't let God hold you steady. It ain't always spiritual warfare— sometimes it's just your mouth, your pride, your ego, and your refusal to deal with what's really broken inside. Bitterness, resentment, and zero self-control have had their way with you. You've been glued to drama, stuck to dysfunction, and loyal to your triggers. And you wonder why you keep coming unglued. You can't hold peace because you ain't rooted in it. You ain't always falling apart because of satan—you falling apart because you refuse to stick with God. Simple as that.

I was a walking time bomb, wired with rage and no fuse. The littlest spark could set me off—a slick comment, a stare that lasted too long, someone trying to "check" me in front of others. I'd black out and come to in cuffs. It got to the point where I wasn't just losing jobs—I was losing people. Relationships? Burned. Opportunities? Blown. Courtrooms knew my face better than my own reflection. I wasn't catching charges—I was collecting them like trophies for my temper. Aggravated menacing, domestic violence, felonious assault—I wasn't just reacting, I was wrecking everything. The crazy part? I'd blame the devil, the drugs, even the system. But the truth? I was just unglued—emotionally, mentally, spiritually. I had no anchor. No real connection to anything that could hold me together. I'd stick to pills, pride, or pain, but not to God. If I wanted to stop coming apart, I had to stop sticking to everything but the One who could hold me together.

Let's cut the act—you ain't strong, you ain't stable, and you sure ain't secure. You keep spazzin' out over side-comments, traffic, or somebody looking at you too long. Everything but God's been holding your heart. Every time you turn around, you're saying, "I'm sorry," duct-taping your dignity back together, and calling rage "passion" when it's really just pain with no place to heal. Truth is, you ain't glued to God—you stuck to your pride, and now you brittle. You come apart over the littlest thing, then act like the devil made you do it. Stop it! No, the hell he didn't—you falling apart because you let that anger snap you. And the reason that anger keeps owning you is because you don't stick with God—you've drifted too far from the only One who can hold you together. James 4:8 says, "*Draw near to God, and He will draw near to you.*" But you're doing the opposite, and it shows in how unglued you become when things don't go your way. You've tried life your way—it left you angry, empty, and broken, and it shows… every outburst, every busted relationship, every bridge you've torched just to feel in control. With God as your right-hand man, He won't let you break when you're about to snap. God didn't wire you to be ruled by rage—He built you for self-control through Him. But you gotta be real enough to admit you're not okay and humble enough to be rebuilt. Stick with God, 'cause if you can't stay connected, don't expect to stay composed.

Spiritual Growth Affirmation: I will **GROW** out of the carnal mindset that calls rage "passion" and bitterness "personality." I'm not glued to God until I stop sticking to my ego.

Take this day to **THINK** about why you keep trying to beat satan with weak weapons that never work. You wonder why you stay struggling? Because you walk into war with no ammo. You out here bringing knives to a gunfight—thinking you're tough enough to take satan down with your mouth, your money, your mindset, or your little motivational quotes. You think your ego's enough to shake him? That your street smarts or "good energy" are gon' make him back down? You sound silly—satan ain't flinching at your pride, your presence, or your personality. The only thing he fears is what he can't fight—God's Word. That's it. You keep catching spiritual beatdowns because you keep swinging with empty fists and shooting spitballs at a real assassin. He's walking in with army tanks—you're showing up with all talk. You better start standing on something that actually strikes back. If you don't stay strapped with scripture, satan will keep folding you like a lawn chair and laughing while you bleed. You can't fight a supernatural war with carnal weapons. You can't punch your way out of a spiritual trap. You better load up verses like bullets in a clip—ready to shoot back every time satan tries to trigger you to sin, tempting you to take your life off safety.

One night, I pulled up to my spot, and out of nowhere a shadow stepped outta the dark with a gun pointed at me. Instinct kicked in. I ducked behind my car, upped my piece, and started firing. For two minutes straight it was chaos—bullets flying, heart racing, praying I didn't take one to the head. As fate would have it, neither of us got hit, but that night stuck with me. Now imagine if I hadn't been strapped when that assailant came to kill me. Strong chance, I'd be dead. But since I had my gun, I survived. Yeah, that was a physical standoff—but it was nothing compared to the spiritual ones. Those are much worse. In the drug game, shootouts were part of life, but satan wasn't coming for my money or my product—he was coming for my soul. And I couldn't shoot my way out of that. No pistol, no hustle, no street game could win that war. The only thing that could've saved me then—and the only thing that'll save you now—is God's Word.

Hear this: satan ain't out here playin'! You better start cutting lies with truth and stop walking into battle against an enemy armed with weapons of mass destruction. He'll use drugs, the opposite sex, alcohol, money, fame, and even people close to you to take you out. And you out here playin' like he somethin' to be played wit. When satan comes, he comes hard, and he comes for everything—your mind, your peace, your purpose. He knows exactly what to use to trip you up. The devil don't need new tricks—just the same old ones you still ain't learned from. Jesus already showed us how to defeat him. When satan tempted Him in the wilderness, Jesus didn't panic— He clapped back with scripture. Matthew 4:4 says, *"Man shall not live by bread alone, but by every word that proceedeth out of the mouth of God."* Jesus didn't argue—He hit satan with truth, and satan had to retreat. Now, imagine if Jesus didn't have the Word to defend Himself. Where would we be? If Jesus—with all power—used scripture to shut satan down, what makes you think you can fight without it? Stop trying to fight a spiritual war with street smarts and strength. Every fight ain't about fists—the toughest battles are won with scripture. If you're tired of losing, stop playing and start loading up on the Word. Fire back when satan shows up. Here's some advice: Stand on God's Word to win those standoffs with satan. If Jesus strapped up with scripture, what makes you think you can win a showdown packing nothing but a water gun and wishful thinking?

Spiritual Growth Affirmation: I will **GROW** out of the mindset that tries to play peacemaker with a hitman. It's not about how loud I talk—it's about what truth I stand on when all hell breaks loose.

YOU REALLY JUST GON' READ ALL THAT AND STILL STAY THE SAME?

You just read a book that didn't whisper. It didn't give you comfort food—it gave you a mirror and a match. This wasn't built to entertain you. It was built to expose you. This wasn't a plot twist—it was a pivot point. If you made it to the end and still feel inspired but unchanged, you missed the whole damn message. This wasn't written for your claps. It was written for your comeback. And not the cute kind—the kind that costs you your comfort, your coping, your pride, and your past.

After reading this, you should've been ready to put the bottle down. Ready to flush the pills. Ready to walk out of that toxic relationship. Ready to unfollow those imaginary friends. Ready to break up with your excuses, quit, and confront your cowardice. Ready to stop being manipulated, stop playing victim, stop negotiating with demons, and stop dragging around the dead weight of who you used to be. Ready to stop hiding behind hustle, trauma, or religious routines. Ready to finally forgive yourself.

If this didn't cut you deep enough—then in truth, I don't know what will. Let's get this straight: Reading ain't transformation. Highlighting ain't healing. And feeling seen don't mean you're free. If you walked through these pages and didn't drop the dead weight, cut off that counterfeit love, silence that self-hate, or challenge the chains that have been choking you—then this was just a performance. You wore the words like a costume. You nodded at the pain but never made it pay you back. That ain't growth—it's dress-up for the delusional. You want to evolve? Then prove it. Bleed for it. Sweat through it. Let it offend your ego before it frees your soul.

These pages weren't written to be safe. They were meant to confront the parts of you that you keep defending. You showed up numb. You showed up with a stitched smile over your scar. But if this didn't cut deep enough, maybe you like prison. Maybe you like breathing the same air as a bunch of broken men, comparing war stories and your kids calling another man "Daddy." Maybe you like being the side chick to a man who will never leave his "main" girl. How twisted are you to keep waiting and living in the shadows while another woman lives in the spotlight? If nothing in this book shook you, maybe pain got you punch-drunk—and you just ain't ready to divorce it yet.

Every chapter had a job. The clichés got exposed to break the lies you've been told and the lies you've been living. The morals weren't just stories—they were soul mirrors. They painted the pain in real colors so you could finally see what's been poisoning your peace. The unfiltered quotes? Those weren't phrases—they were pressure points. They weren't written to inspire—they were written to interrupt your cycle. The spiritual pages weren't for Sunday morning—they were to stop you from playing games with God like He ain't watching your excuses.

So now what? Read it again—this time with no armor. Let it mess with your mind and shake your soul. Then hand it off to somebody still drowning in the pain you crawled out of. This wasn't just a book. It was the battlefield for your breakthrough. The death certificate for the version of you that should've been gone. And the birth certificate for the version this world ain't ready for.

P.S. Thank you for purchasing this book. But if you read every page and still have no intention of evolving, I wish you would've left it on the fucken shelf for someone who actually wanted to. Truth can't heal people who still prefer lies. This was never about making a sale—it was about mending a soul. And if yours ain't ready, I kindly ask that you pass it on to someone who is. Because saving you may be a lost cause.

RESOURCES FOR RECOVERY, SUPPORT, & GROWTH

'm committed to more than just writing words—I'm committed to seeing people actually heal. I would be a straight-up hypocrite if I didn't give you something practical to go with the raw truth I've given you. This is bigger than me, bigger than my story, bigger than this book. I'm putting these resources here because too many people stay bound simply because they don't know where to go or who to call. Information changes situations. And I don't want you finishing this book with excuses. So here's a list of agencies and programs you can reach out to—places that can help you rebuild, recover, and rise up—one day at a time.

DOMESTIC ABUSE & HUMAN TRAFFICKING

- National Domestic Violence Hotline—Call 1-800-799-SAFE (7233) or visit thehotline.org for 24/7 confidential help.

- National Human Trafficking Hotline—Call 1-888-373-7888 or text BEFREE (233733), or visit humantraffickinghotline.org.

HOMELESSNESS & EMERGENCY HOUSINGS

- Dial 211—Connect with local food, housing, and crisis services, available anytime nationwide.

- The Salvation Army—Visit salvationarmyusa.org to locate your nearest service center for meals, shelters, and emergency assistance.

- Goodwill Industries—Find job training and community support via goodwill.org.

CHILD & FAMILY SERVICES

- Childhelp National Child Abuse Hotline—Call or text 1-800-4-A-CHILD (1-800-422-4453), or visit childhelp.org.

- National Parent & Youth Helpline—Call or text 855-427-2736, or live chat via nationalparentyouthhelpline.org.

BROTHERHOOD & SINGLE-PARENT SUPPORT

- National Fatherhood Initiative—fatherhood.org | Phone: 301-948-0599.

- Parents Without Partners, Inc.—parentswithoutpartners.org | Phone: 1-800-637-7974.

REENTRY, JOB TRAINING, & LIFE STABILITY

- Starts Within Organization (Carlos Christian)—startswithin.com for reentry and recovery support.

- Goodwill Industries—Job training and support via goodwill.org.

- United Way—Dial 211 or visit unitedway.org for connections to local housing, financial, and job resources.

- Job Corps—A nationwide job training and education program for young people ages 16–24. Learn more at JobCorps.gov.

- National Urban League & SOAR Program—Visit nul.org for workforce readiness, financial empowerment, and community programs available nationwide.

YOUTH & MENTORSHIP

- Boys & Girls Clubs of America—bgca.org

- Big Brothers Big Sisters of America—bbbs.org

- Communities In Schools—communitiesinschools.org

- All Pro Dad—allprodad.com

- Boy Scouts of America—scouting.org

- Girl Scouts of the USA—girlscouts.org

ADDICTION, GAMBLING, PORNOGRAPHY, & RECOVERY

- SMART Recovery—Tools for recovery at smartrecovery.org.

- SAMHSA National Helpline—Call 1-800-662-HELP (4357).

- 12-Step Programs—Alcoholics Anonymous (aa.org), Narcotics Anonymous (na.org), Sex Addicts Anonymous.

- National Council on Sexual Addiction & Compulsivity (NCSAC)—Helpline: 1-800-837-9041.

MENTAL HEALTH & EMOTIONAL CRISIS

- 988 Suicide & Crisis Lifeline—Call or text 988.

- NAMI (National Alliance on Mental Illness)—nami.org | Helpline: 1-800-950-6264.

CIVIL RIGHTS & COMMUNITY ADVOCACY

- NAACP (National Association for the Advancement of Colored People)—naacp.org | General number: 410-580-5777.
- United Negro College Fund—uncf.org.

LOCAL BUSINESS & COMMUNITY SUPPORT

- Local Chamber of Commerce—Business networking and support.

- Small Business Development Center (SBDC)—Free counseling and startup guidance at sba.gov/sbdc.

- SCORE (Service Corps of Retired Executives)—Free mentoring, workshops, and business tools at score.org.

RECOMMENDED READING

ook—I ain't the only voice you need to hear. I can spark some shit in you, but you gon' need other voices to keep that fire lit. These books cracked me open, checked me, stretched me, and gave me perspective I couldn't get just from running the same tired cycles. Growth ain't just about what you've been through—it's about what you expose yourself to. Don't get cocky thinking you already know it all or that this book was enough. It's not. Deep down, we're underdeveloped, nursing wounds that only outside wisdom can rip the bandages off and teach us to treat. Feed your mind with these pages and let these voices help cut the chains you swore were fine jewelry.

Rich Dad, Poor Dad by Robert Kiyosaki

Two fathers, two mindsets: Scarcity vs. abundance. Freedom starts with rewiring how you think about money.

You Owe You by Eric Thomas

Stop blaming everybody else. Own your pain, your purpose, your future. Period.

Unfuck Yourself by Gary John Bishop

A no-BS slap that kills excuses and flips your inner voice from weak to warrior.

Relentless by Tim S. Grover

The killer mentality explained—why the best don't just train harder, they *think* different.

The Four Agreements by Don Miguel Ruiz

Break the mental chains. Live by integrity, not illusions.

The Purpose-Driven Life by Rick Warren

Find meaning beyond the grind. God gave you purpose—live on it.

They Stole It, but You Must Return It by Richard Williams

Reclaim your identity, your vision, your power—nobody else gon' hand it back.

Shook One by Charlamagne Tha God

Raw truth on anxiety, trauma, and surviving as a Black man in a world built to break you.

How to Win Friends and Influence People by Dale Carnegie

Old school, still undefeated—relationships make or break your future.

Secrets of the Vine by Bruce Wilkinson

God prunes you because He's preparing you. Pain is proof you're growing.

The Secret by Rhonda Byrne

Your thoughts shape your world. Keep thinking trash, keep living trashy.

Can't Hurt Me by David Goggins

Pain ain't the enemy—it's the gym where toughness is built.

Think and Grow Rich by Napoleon Hill

Rewire your brain for wealth, success, and purpose—no shortcuts.

Less Than One Percent by Imamu Tomlinson

Testimony of surviving when the odds say you won't—proof that one man can rewrite the stats.

ACKNOWLEDGMENTS

First, I gotta thank my Lord and Savior, Jesus Christ. I used to thank You for the blessings, but now I thank You for the burdens. Every trial, trauma, and tear that felt like it was meant to break me turned into the very thing that built me. Had it not been for the storms, but more importantly, what I chose to do in them, I wouldn't have found the strength. Thank You for trusting me with the pain that carved out the purpose behind these pages.

To my children—Tianna, my oldest, holding it down and raising your son while making your own way; Rah'ara, hustling with your gift in hair and turning it into business; Tyler, moving like a professional in real estate and carving out your lane; and Dionne, pushing through in college on your way to nursing—y'all are my legacy. Every page I wrote, I thought about you.

To my grandsons—DJ, who I lost too soon. Your spirit lives in me. I pray you're looking down, proud of what your granddad did. And Daniel, my little ball of energy, my G-Dad shadow—your joy fuels me.

To my sisters—Tisha, who overcame addiction and showed me what survival looks like, and Kim, who held down six kids with strength most people can't imagine.

To J'voni and Diontay —Though life took its own turns, the time we shared still matters. I'm proud of the role I played and the growth I witnessed. Keep building, keep pushing, and keep becoming.

To my cousin Brandon "Doober" Parker—you never stopped believing, kept pushing me toward books and podcasts, and reminding me my words had weight.

To my church family at From the Heart—you gave me the spiritual foundation I needed to finally grow in Christ.

To Carlos Christian and the Starts Within Organization—you planted seeds in me during incarceration that still grow.

To Ronnie "Heavy" Burden—thank you for speaking up and lobbying for me to come back into London Correctional to pour into those men's lives. You opened a door that let me turn my pain into purpose, and I'll never forget that.

To Fonz, my barber and my brother—thank you for the wisdom in the chair and for sparking my fitness fire the day you asked me to hit the gym.

To Clean Recovery—Thank you for helping me break free from addiction and rebuild my life with clarity and discipline. You didn't give me my life back. You helped me remember I still had one worth fighting for.

To London Correctional Prison—you finally got me serious about transformation.

To The Exercise Coach, EOS, and Planet Fitness—thanks for giving me the chance to showcase my gift and prove my calling.

To my editor—Daniel, I gotta thank you heavily. You didn't just touch this manuscript, you sharpened it. You pulled the rawest parts of me onto these pages and made sure my voice never got lost in the process. You didn't just edit words—you respected the weight behind them. For that, I'll always be grateful.

To Steve—Thank you for taking my words and giving them a home that looks like it belongs on a Barnes & Noble shelf. You brought this whole project to life with skill, patience, and a level of detail that pushed my vision higher. I appreciate everything you put into this.

To my clients—thank you for trusting me with your bodies, your goals, and your growth. You could've chosen anyone, but you chose me, and that means something. Y'all keep me sharp, keep me hungry, and remind me this gift ain't just about me—it's about pouring into people who want to evolve. Watching your transformations fuels mine.

And to every family member, friend, enemy, hater, helper, or passerby—good, bad, or indifferent—thank you. Every single one of you shaped this. It would be impossible to list everyone, but just know I couldn't have done this without all the pieces of the story you played a role in.

Dion Parker didn't grow up with a blueprint—he grew up in survival mode. Born in Avondale and raised on the west side of Cincinnati, he came off the porch early. By the time he hit the English Woods projects, the sidewalk couldn't hold him. He stopped walking straight and started running wild—into the streets, into the system, into a life that tried to bury him alive. Raised by a single mother holding down three kids, Dion never knew his father—not really. His sperm donor vanished before he could teach Dion anything about manhood. But absence doesn't erase influence. Even without knowing him, Dion followed in the same footsteps—straight into prison and addiction. He's been shot a total of seven times on two separate occasions. Stabbed. Overdosed. Suffered a major health scare. Flashed on the news. Booked in jail more than twenty times. Sentenced to prison three times. Wanted by U.S. Marshals. Betrayed. Broken. Twice divorced. He's suffered heartbreak, grief, and loss—including people he never had a chance to fully know, like his first grandson. He's walked through spiritual confusion, battled with addiction, and carried pain most folks can't even name. He's lived a life that would've left most people paralyzed with PTSD—but he keeps moving, even while bleeding. He knows what it's like to beg for freedom, then walk right back into the same hell. He's not just survived—he's become living evidence of what endurance looks like.

Dion is a certified expert in pain—not by classroom hours, but by years in the trenches of trauma. His credentials weren't earned through textbooks, but through the books that were thrown at him by judges. They were earned through blood, betrayal, and battles. Agony became his professor. And every scar turned into a tutor. Today, Dion lives in Florida with his wife, Tayoun, and is a respected certified personal trainer whose clients include doctors, lawyers, teachers, business owners, teenagers, people with special needs, former government personnel from the Pentagon, the White House, the FBI, and the DEA, as well as individuals just trying to get their life back on track—ranging in age from 14 to 88. He's a street-bred life coach and an inspiration to anybody born in hell's delivery room, raised in satan's trap house, and left to rot in this hellhole.

He's gone from pushing dope in the projects to taking on the project of pushing hope into people. He's spoken in the same prison that once held him. He's gone into youth facilities to reach wayward teens. He's filmed messages for the incarcerated. And he's become an accountability partner for others still struggling with addiction—because he knows the weight of the war firsthand. He's a momma's boy. He's a loving father to four beautiful girls. He's a loyal husband—proof that grace can still grow out of broken ground. He has one grandson—who calls him G-Dad. His unfaithfulness and broken choices created consequences—but his growth created a legacy. He didn't have a dad. He didn't have a mentor. But he's become both. He's taken every scar and flipped it into strategy, every setback into a story worth reading. His life ain't polished—but it's purpose-built. And purpose never needed to be perfect to be powerful. This ain't a redemption story—it's a resurrection. Dion Parker is proof the grave ain't final—unless you keep living like you belong in it.